PLATE 1

THE LORD OF THE MANOR
(Early 16th Century)

Life and Work in Medieval Europe

P. Boissonnade

Translated, with a Foreword, by
Eileen Power

DOVER PUBLICATIONS, INC.
Mineola, New York

Published in Canada by General Publishing Company, Ltd., 895 Don Mills
Road, 400-2 Park Centre, Toronto, Ontario M3C 1W3.

Bibliographical Note

This Dover edition, first published in 2002, is an unabridged republication of
the work published by Kegan Paul, Trench, Trubner & Co., Ltd., London, 1927.

Library of Congress Cataloging-in-Publication Data

Boissonnade, P. (Prosper), 1862–1935.
    [Travail dans l'Europe chrétienne au moyen âge. English]
    Life and work in Medieval Europe : fifth to fifteenth centuries / by P.
Boissonnade ; translated, with an introduction by Eileen Power.
      p. cm.
    Originally published: London : K. Paul, Trench, Trubner & Co., 1927.
    Includes index.
    ISBN 0-486-41987-8 (pbk.)
    1. Working class—History. 2. Europe—Social conditions. 3. Industries—
History. I. Title.

HD4847 .B63 2002
330.94'01—dc21

20010142346

Manufactured in the United States of America
Dover Publications, Inc., 31 East 2nd Street, Mineola, N.Y. 11501

CONTENTS

v

CONTENTS

CONTENTS

CONTENTS

Influence of the new feudal governments and centralised monarchies upon labour. Influence of the Western Church upon labour.

Unimportant part played by a money economy in the early feudal period. The renaissance of commerce and its causes; forms of commercial organisation; large-scale international commerce and great mercantile associations. The restoration of means of transport; increase in the use of money and credit; development of markets and fairs. Rise of maritime commerce; predominance and prosperity of Mediterranean trade; progress of trade in Western and Central Europe; the commercial powers. Effects of the commercial revolution.

Industry during the early feudal period. Causes and characteristics of the industrial renaissance in the West. Chief forms of industry in the golden age of the medieval period. Small-scale industry. First manifestations of the great industry. Wide scope of industrial development in the West from the eleventh century; mineral, metallurgical and textile industries; wood, earthenware and glass industries; art industries. Results of this renaissance.

The renaissance of towns from the eleventh to the fourteenth century; formation and early progress of the commercial and industrial classes (tenth to eleventh centuries). Movement of the emancipation of these classes (eleventh to thirteenth centuries). Character, extent and limits of this movement. Civil and economic liberties of the urban classes. Diversity of their political rights. Predominance of economic preoccupations and interests in the urban state. Economic powers of the urban community. Results of emancipation and influence of urban economy.

Formation, composition and power of the patriciate and the gild merchant; their work in the towns. Economic and social tyranny of the burgess patriciate, its ostentation and arrogance. Origins, formation and development of the free crafts and sworn corporations. Organisation of free and sworn crafts; masters and

CONTENTS

journeymen; apprenticeship; administration of the crafts, their privileges, monopolies and regulations; characteristics and effects of this régime. The conquest of power by the urban masses and the democratic and syndicalist revolution in the West (thirteenth century to first half of fourteenth century). Material condition of the commercial and industrial classes; work and wages; material existence and moral state of these classes. Results of this transformation.

The great work of colonisation, its promoters, authors and methods. Defensive works against water and works of drainage and irrigation. The work of clearance in the West. Development of agricultural production, forests, fisheries and silviculture; progress of stock raising. Advance in methods of cultivation: cereals, horticulture, arboriculture, vine-growing, industrial crops. Results of colonisation; agricultural prosperity and the progress of rural population.

The rise in the value of property, landed revenue and agricultural produce. Renewed decline of collective property. Crisis in the history of seigneurial property. Reconstitution of state domains. Accession of the communes and the urban bourgeoisie to rural landed property. Movement towards the emancipation of the rural classes, its causes, character and variety. The liberties or franchises of the emancipated rural classes. Results of their emancipation.

Formation of a rural third estate and a class of small peasant properties. *Censitaires* and copyholders, their condition in the West from the twelfth century. Characteristics of peasant property, its small size and constant subdivision. The new classes of farmers, *fermiers* and *métayers;* formation of a class of agricultural wage-earners, day labourers and servants in husbandry. Survivals of serfdom and slavery. Improvement in the material condition of the peasantry; income from land and wages. The increase in comfort; conditions of material and moral life in the country side.

Decline of the Byzantine Empire; progress of feudalism and of large properties. Decline of small free owner-

CONTENTS

CONTENTS

LIST OF ILLUSTRATIONS

FOREWORD

SINCE the appearance of Cunningham's short sketch of
Western Civilisation in its Economic Aspects (Cambridge,
1908) no study of European economic development as a
whole during the Middle Ages has appeared in the English
language, although an increasing amount of work, both
learned and popular, dealing with English economic history
is published every year. Yet it is perhaps even more unsuitable thus to isolate English economic history in the
Middle Ages than it is to isolate it in the modern period,
for during the greater part of the ten centuries which lay
between the Barbarian Invasions and the Renaissance
national divisions were but faintly marked, and Western
Europe was in some degree an economic unity. Moreover,
to study the history of England alone gives a very imperfect
picture of the main lines of development, for England
throughout the medieval and, indeed, well into the modern
period was on an economic backwater. Just as the centre
of religion was Rome and the centre of civilisation France, so
the commercial centres of Christendom were first Byzantium,
and then Italy, Germany, and the towns of Central France
and the Netherlands. Italy monopolised the rich trade with
the Levant, and Germany the great south European trade
routes and the Baltic and North Seas. The clearing houses
for these two streams of commerce were the Champagne fairs
and the cities of the Netherlands, especially Bruges, where
land and sea routes met. England lay rather off the main
stream, though in a good position to swim into it; she awoke
but slowly to a sense of her own future upon the waters, and
in the early Middle Ages no one would have foreseen
in her the future sea power *par excellence*, although in the
last two centuries of the period she was rapidly advancing,
and in the fifteenth century was a dangerous rival to the
Hansards in the Baltic. Similarly, in the Middle Ages no
one would have foreseen in England a leading industrial
power, for again Italy, the Netherlands, and certain parts of
Germany were the industrial centres of the West, and Eng-

land was important only as an exporter of raw materials, and in particular of wool. Here, too, she made rapid strides in the later Middle Ages, and by the end of the fourteenth century was beginning to oust the cloth cities of the Netherlands from their leadership. But for the greater part of the period she was a client nation and not a leading commercial or industrial power, and no true appreciation of medieval economic progress is to be gained by studying England alone.

There are innumerable other considerations which lend a peculiar interest to the study of European economic history in the Middle Ages. Some of its greatest achievements have too often been swamped by the more spectacular events of political and cultural history, by crusades, chivalry, cathedrals, and the development of the art of government. Of these achievements the greatest was that stupendous work of the colonisation and population of Europe in which kings, landlords, capitalists, and pioneer peasants all played their part. Hardly less important was the rise of vast labouring classes from conditions of dependence to comparative freedom. It serves also to demonstrate (what the study of English history conceals) the early development of certain phenomena which are sometimes described as modern, such as the capitalist entrepreneur and the strikes, unions, and other manifestations of a fierce struggle between labour and capital. The Netherlands was the Black Country of the Middle Ages, and although not very black, it displays on a small scale all the characteristics of the modern " great industry." Similarly, a study of medieval history shows the early evolution of a banking and credit system, in particular by the merchant-financiers of Italy, which the man-in-the-street is apt to attribute to a much later period.

Professor Boissonnade's book is one of those excellent *œuvres de vulgarisation* of which the French alone appear to have the secret. The present translation is offered the public in the hope that it may provide a useful textbook for students, both in England and in America, who are studying the subject as part of a University course, and give to the general reader with an interest in social history, an *aperçu* of European development during the Middle Ages, such as he cannot easily obtain in his own language elsewhere. The period is sown with difficulties and problems upon which

FOREWORD

scholars still hold divergent views. Some might, for instance, contend, in view of the brilliant researches of Professor Dopsch, that Professor Boissonnade attaches too much importance to the destructive effects of the Barbarian Invasions. But where matters are still in controversy every scholar must have the right to his own opinion, and upon the main lines of European economic development there is small doubt. The reader will find here traced the great work of colonisation and clearance, the development of landholding from the evolution of the great feudal estate cultivated by dependent labour to its gradual *morcellement* into the small properties of peasant proprietors, *censitaires*, and tenant farmers with various leases. Professor Boissonnade sets forth the rise and efflorescence of urban civilisation, the development of industry under the regulation of small crafts or of great capitalist entrepreneurs, and the emergence of a " capital and labour problem." He traces the evolution of a large body of wage labourers in both town and country, the development of technical skill and invention in industry and agriculture, and the rise and increasing elaboration of international commerce and finance. He makes clear the economic function of Byzantium, as well as the work of the new nations of the West, and in fine covers the whole of the crucial period between the break-up of the Roman Empire in the West and the advent of the modern world, a period which is, as he justly points out, one of capital importance in the history of civilisation and of labour.

EILEEN POWER.

AUTHOR'S PREFACE

IN this essay, founded upon long years of research, and upon direct acquaintanceship with a large number of documents, monographs, and special and general works, in French and in various other languages, an attempt has been made to construct the first complete, ordered, and precise synthesis of the evolution of labour in Christian Europe during the Middle Ages. It has been sought not only to set out the variations in the legal status of persons and of lands, to which subject alone the majority of historians have usually confined themselves, but above all to set the working classes in the historical framework in which they lived, to trace the reciprocal action of political and social institutions, of exchange, of industrial and agricultural production, of the colonisation of the soil, of the distribution of landed and movable wealth, upon those economic transformations, which brought about the appearance of new forms of labour and which gave to the masses a place in society which they had never hitherto occupied. Thus the Middle Ages will appear in this study in their real aspect, no longer as an empty and gloomy gulf between two epochs full of life and light, antiquity and the modern age, but as one of the most brilliant and fruitful periods of the historic past, a period wherein labour took one of its most decisive steps forward in the direction of well-being, justice, and liberty.

LIFE AND WORK
IN MEDIEVAL EUROPE

BOOK I

CHAPTER I

ROMAN EUROPE AND BARBARIAN EUROPE IN THE EARLY DARK AGES.—THE
SOCIAL AND ECONOMIC ORGANIZATION OF THE INVADERS.

WITH the fifth century there begins a long period of a
thousand years known as the Middle Ages, in the course of
which were accomplished some of the greatest social and
economic changes in the whole history of labour. It begins
with a catastrophe : the collapse of the Roman Empire as a
result of the invasion and settlement of barbarian peoples.
No one could have foreseen this disaster, which was of
capital importance in history, because it very nearly
brought about the complete destruction of civilization.
Happily for the new world which was to spring from the
ruins of the old, the good order established by Rome never
entirely died out, and it was upon the solid foundation
of what remained that the new states of the early Middle
Ages were destined to rear themselves.

Formed of a conglomeration of lands which stretched over
three million square kilometres, the Roman Empire still
occupied at the beginning of this period about a quarter of the
European continent, comprising all the most fertile regions :
to wit, Greece, Macedonia, Thrace, and the Balkan and
Danube lands, which formed the prefectures of the East
and of Illyria ; and in the west, Italy and its islands,
Spain, the Gallic provinces, and Great Britain, which constituted two more prefectures. The whole was divided into
nine dioceses, seventy-one provinces, and over two hundred
territories or " cities." The empire was bounded in the
north by the Danube and the Rhine, and in the British Isles
by the line of the Forth and Clyde. Beyond it barbarism

still reigned over three-quarters of the European continent. In the domain of civilization this empire, which had lately embraced Christianity, and with it the call to a higher morality, had realized a progress as great as any ever accomplished by the human race. It had for the first time set up a government which curbed the will of the individual beneath the rule of law, and brought about the triumph of political unity and authority over the anarchy of the ancient city state. It had created the first great political association, formed of several millions of freemen, " brothers and cousins of the Roman people," who all, since the second century, had enjoyed equal rights, obeyed the same laws, exercised the same civil liberties, and who were protected by an equitable justice against any superior power other than the state. It had even, under the influence of the generous ideas of Stoicism and of Christianity, risen to a conception of the brotherhood of man and of a human society formed of all civilized peoples. It had brought with it everywhere the reign of order and of peace, and assured the safety of the peoples over whom it ruled. Thus it had accomplished a marvellous work of social and economic progress, the effects of which had hardly disappeared at all in the period of the later empire.

Everywhere social life had flourished and was still flourishing in the fourth century, more especially in urban surroundings. Hundreds of towns were living an easy and pleasant existence, adorned with palaces, with public squares, circuses, theatres, temples, hot springs, money markets or basilicas, with their public baths and their aqueducts. From the third century they had been protected by fortified walls, crowned with towers. Amid the unexampled magnificence of the capitals, Byzantium, Rome, Milan, Thessalonica, Treier, and Arles, all the splendours of luxury and of civilization were displayed. The countryside was covered with townships (*vici*) of little free proprietors and with the elegant dwellings, half pleasure-houses and half strongholds, in which the great proprietors lived in the summer season, in the midst of their vast domains (*villae*). In spite of the slow depopulation, which for the last century and a half had been draining away its life-blood, the empire in Europe had a population of over thirty millions, and was the envy of the barbarians who surrounded it. Although the structure of Roman society had remained aristocratic, the upper classes did not form closed castes; any citizen might rise to the front rank through merit, fortune, or the exercise of public functions. The existence of a still numerous middle class of small landed proprietors, merchants, and artisans, who were known as *mediocres* or *honorati*, served to maintain a sort of social equilibrium, which the central power was at pains to preserve at the expense of the nobility, the large owners, and the high officials. In town and country the free labour of artisans, tenant-farmers in perpetuity and day labourers, maintained itself side by side with the semi-dependent labour of the workers in the state workshops and the *coloni* on the great estates. The class of independent artisans and its corporations (*collegia*) were recognized and respected; they figured in the official hierarchy, together with the commercial class of merchants (*mercatores*), which was organized on the same model. Although the empire suffered from the existence of a lazy and wretched urban proletariat, from the growth of pauperism, and from the harshness of the *régime* imposed upon the poor and the lower classes, progress of capital importance had been accomplished in two directions. Under the influence of Stoic and Christian conceptions, and still more under the pressure of economic needs, slavery, that degrading and unproductive form of labour, had almost entirely disappeared in favour of free artisans in the towns and *coloni* in the country districts. A great mass of men had attained, if not complete freedom, at least a semi-freedom. The colonate had become the normal condition of the rural population, preparing the way for medieval villeinage. Its numbers were increased in the fourth century by a crowd of new elements from the towns, and it gave to the cultivators of the soil the rights of Roman citizens, personal liberty, the usufruct of the land, and a secure and stable existence.

In spite of the economic crisis brought about by the invasions of the third century and the excessive imperial taxation, Roman Europe was none the less, at the beginning of the fifth century, in possession of a greater degree of material prosperity than any other part of the world. If certain countries, such as Greece and peninsular Italy, had been sorely assailed by depopulation, war, and economic changes, many other regions provided a picture of fertility, comfort, and well-being which was unmatched; such was notably the case in Macedonia, Thrace, Dalmatia, Northern Italy, Spain, Gaul, and Britain. Ammianus Marcellinus observes that in whole provinces, such as Aquitania, poverty was almost unknown. In four centuries Rome had succeeded in transforming the part of Europe which lay beneath her law into a hive of productive activity. She had transformed even its outward aspect; forests had been cleared, marshes drained, the land cultivated. The plough and the spade triumphed over wild nature; cattle-breeding, corn-growing, the cultivation of industrial plants, fruit-trees, vines, and olives were developed to an extraordinary extent, while the field of Roman colonization grew ever wider. Industrial production outgrew all the results hitherto obtained, as well in the domain of minerals and metallurgy as in those of weaving, leather, earthenware, and glass. Division of labour had begun. The small urban industry of the workshops had grown up and prospered, side by side with the old domestic industry, which it outshone, and the new capitalistic industry, which was just beginning to emerge. Finally, the activity of trade maintained itself on the very eve of the invasions, and was promoted by the appearance of more elaborate commercial institutions, the development of instruments of credit and of river transport, the construction of a magnificent network of over 90,000 miles of roads, and the building of great ports. "Every day the world grows more cultivated and more wealthy," wrote an enemy of Roman society. "Everywhere there is commerce, everywhere towns."

What did the empire, then, lack to enable it to resist the new attack of the barbarians? Only a government less hidebound by the rigid forms of a slow bureaucracy; only a ruling class more conscious of its duty and of its social mission; only military institutions less permeated by the use of mercenary troops; only a public spirit less inert, less vitiated by political indifference and by personal degradation. Other societies have experienced similar miseries, and have escaped death by fundamental reforms. The empire could not, or would not, make them, and it yielded place to the barbarians. But the civilization which it had created left sufficient trace behind to enable Europe to escape from a permanent barbarism.

Among the varied elements of which the barbarian world was composed, the most irreducible belonged to Ural-Altaic races. One variety of these races, that of the Finns of the north and east, consisting of tribes, some nomad and others settled, which inhabited the zone of forests and marshes between the Arctic Ocean and the Upper Volga, covering half of modern Russia, took no part in the invasions. The other variety consisted of peoples of Eastern and Central Asia, Huns, Avars, Bulgars, Khazars, Petcheneges (Patzinaks), Magyars, Mongols, who were for the most part mere destroyers. Fierce and cruel races, knowing only a nomad life and owning no wealth save their herds, they obtained their chief means of existence from war and rapine. They were grouped into hordes or federations of tribes, each of which could place in the field 2,000 warriors, and which were themselves composed of hundreds of patriarchal families; and they recognized the authority of an aristocracy of chiefs or kings (khans, khagans, or judges), who directed their migrations. These peoples of prey were animated by the rage for destruction, and their members considered it a shameful thing not to have slain an enemy and gloried in drinking from the skulls of the vanquished, and in hanging strips of human skin as trophies round their horses' necks. They were, in the words attributed to Attila, " the scourges of God "; they spread nothing but ruin wherever they went, and nothing remained of their invasions but the memory of a savage and stupid work of destruction.

The influence of the Slav races was destined to be far more profound and less negative. Of Indo-European origin, they had lived obscurely up till then in the wide plain of Eastern Europe, for the most part as settled tribes, until the great Hun invasions hurled them on to the wooded bastions of the Carpathian Mountains. Thence, between the fifth and the seventh centuries, they spread over the lands left empty by the migrations of the Germans and Finns, over modern Russia (about a fifth of which they occupied, from the Dwina to the Dnieper and the great lakes), over the plains of the Vistula, which now form Poland, and even all along the Southern Baltic and the Sudetes into Northern Germany, which from Germania became Slavia, and into Bohemia and Moravia. In the south they peopled the Danube lands, Slovakia, Slovenia (Carinthia and Carniola), Croatia, as far as the shores of the Adriatic, and even crossing beyond the Save, sent tribes of Serbs to swarm over Moesia and Macedonia. They drove back, into the lands between their territories and the eastern shores of the Baltic, other tribes, also of Indo-European origin, the Borussi, Livonians and Lithuanians, whose rôle remained henceforth inactive.

These varied races had not risen to the conception of the state. They were grouped in communities of families (*zadrugas, dvorichés, vervs*), each of which contained from thirty to forty members, above which, notably among the Yugo Slavs, there sometimes appeared larger groups, the *brastvos*, which were analogous to the Roman *gentes* and the Greek *phratries*. The Slavs, who were nearer to the patriarchal stage than the Germans, lived in each family under the authority of a chief or elder. Property belonged to the whole family community, and was indivisible and inalienable. Work was performed in common. The rights of bequest and of private property were unknown; everything was held in common, even furniture and goods which were the fruit of individual labour. "Wherever the cow be led," ran the old Slav proverb, "she always calves at home." All the members of a family had an equal right to enjoy the proceeds of the labour of each. Every group cared for the sick, the aged, and the households which were formed by detaching themselves from the parent stem. There was no village community, such as the Germans knew, but only federations of *zadrugas*, tribes (*volosts, rods, jupas*), innumerable little clans, each with its name or surname. At the head of each tribe were its religious, civil, and military chiefs, assisted by the advice of elders and by assemblies of freemen. They had property, forests and pastures, which their members used in common, and arable land, which was periodically divided between the members of the tribal group. The great mass of the population consisted of freemen, jealous of their independence and enjoying equal rights. They recognized no superiors, save a nobility without privilege, consisting of elected chiefs. They set to work for them the Roman *coloni*, whom they found attached to the soil, and the slaves, whom they procured by war, piracy, or trade.

Although they had already reached the stage of settled life, they had no towns, but only places of refuge (*gorods*), circular in shape, surrounded by wooden or earthen enclosures, trenches, or stockades, with a single entrance, round which farms and gardens were spread out in the form of a fan. They usually lived apart in scattered homesteads (*derevnias*), but occasionally they settled together in large hamlets or villages of oblong shape, in which the separate dwellings were built along the line of roads or paths. They were acquainted only with a natural and domestic economy; each family and each tribe was obliged to be self-sufficient. A great part of the soil, especially in the plains of north, east, and south, was covered with marsh and water, whence the Slavs and Letts derived abundant fish. An immense forest, much of it virgin, composed of beech, birch, maple and pine, covered four-fifths of the vast regions where they dwelt. In their clearings these tribes hunted wild beasts, stags, deer, aurochs, and bears, and caught furred animals. They gathered honey from the wild bees, and in the open spaces, the mountain pastures, and the grassy meadows on the banks of rivers, they grazed great herds of pigs, sheep, horned cattle, and horses. The Slavs had a high reputation as cattle-breeders, and even for agriculture they showed more aptitude than the Germans, who borrowed the ploughshare from them. Although acquainted only with the methods of extensive cultivation, they were already producing cereals in the rich soil of these regions, and usually obtained a threefold return on the seed sown. They were familiar with industrial plants, such as flax and hemp, but their industry was still quite rudimentary, except as regards iron work and textiles, and nowhere was it carried on for a market outside the circle of the family and the tribe.

Trade was carried on on the backs of men or of sumpter beasts, along primitive tracks, or by means of boats which followed the course of the rivers, but it was active only in the neighbourhood of the Byzantine Empire. They did not know the use of money, and otter and ermine skins frequently took its place; usually they simply bartered goods. Nevertheless, they admitted strangers (*gosts*) to dwell in special enclosures (*gostinny dvor*) for purposes of trade, and from the seventh century they had a number of big markets, such as those of Julin or Wineta in the Isle of Wollin in Pomerania, Novgorod, Smolensk, Leczyka, and Kiev. But they made no distinction between commerce and brigandage. To them merchant and robber were synonymous terms, and the commercial entrepôt was often the brigand's den (*tovary*). In the Baltic they subsisted by piracy, among the Russians by razzias or tributes levied by force upon the population and kept for their own profit by the chiefs. These Slavs had not yet emerged from the rude customs of primitive peoples; they lived in caves, or in mud huts, and were content with the coarsest of food. Careless and wasteful, they were a constant prey to famine; brutal, quarrelsome, and without pity for the weak, they were so far from being the peaceful folk legend has painted them that a state of war was chronic among them, and was maintained perpetually by family and tribal rivalries, for the mere love of it and the need for pillage. The Russian chronicler Nestor and the Byzantine historians bear witness that these herdsmen, woodmen, and labourers excelled in a warfare of cunning ambush and piracy, lurking in the woods and swimming across great rivers, shooting marvellously with the bow and hurling poisoned darts. It was only under the influence of Christianity that they were destined to rise to a civilized existence.

Their neighbours and kinsmen, the Germans, were no more advanced in civilization than they. A mixture of various elements, brachycephalous, dark and short, as well as dolichocephalous, tall and fair, far from that purity of type which is often ascribed to them, they had been established for a thousand years or so on the misty shores of the Northern European seas. One of their branches, the Goths, had subjugated the indigenous populations of the Bronze Age, such as the Finns of Southern Scandinavia, and had then followed the road of the Varangians, the Dnieper, until they reached the great plains of Eastern Europe, where the Visigoths and Ostrogoths settled. They left behind them

8

on the shores of the Baltic, the Scandinavians, Angles, and Jutes, as well as the Vandals. To the second branch, the Teutons, belonged a number of peoples extending from the North Sea to the Rhine and the Upper Danube, Saxons, Frisians, Lombards, Burgundians, Bavarians, Thuringians, Franks, and Alemanni. There were in the whole of this wide district only about two or three millions of these barbarians in the second century, and probably about four million at the end of the fourth. The most numerous, the Ostrogoths, numbered not more than 300,000 souls, the Visigoths about 200,000, the Franks, Burgundians, and Lombards fewer still. Incessant warfare, famine, the difficulty of material existence, the exposure of children, infanticide, and a high death rate prevented the growth of a race which was by nature prolific. In general, the Germans, ignorant of the conception of the nation or the state, formed only temporary groups or warlike confederations. The only stable elements which they knew were the tribes, which contained from ten to twenty thousand members, and were themselves composed of an aggregate of village communities, families, and classes (*genealogiæ, propinquitates*), the latter possibly of military origin, grouped in several thousands of cantons (*pagi, gauen*). Beyond the illusory authority of the kings, the sole effective power was that of the military chiefs, elected war lords, and the leaders of warlike bands, round whom there gathered a voluntary train of clients (*comitatus*), who followed their fortunes. There was no hereditary nobility, but a mass of freemen who met in assembly to deliberate upon common affairs and to choose kings, military leaders, and village chiefs (*principes*).

In this tumultuous democracy, in the midst of which a military aristocracy was growing up, the principle of greatest vitality lay in the patriarchal family founded upon the tie of blood relationship. All its members shared in its solidarity; they lived indivisibly, and possessed in common an inalienable patrimony. Ranging from 50 to 500 persons, these families recognized the absolute authority (*mundium*) of the father, who exercised full dominion over the women, children, and kinsmen on the paternal or maternal side. In this milieu inequality had grown up, as a result of the social division of labour. There was no priestly class, but a nobility which was distinguished from the mass of freemen only by the prestige of its wealth or by a special talent for warfare. The common occupations of nobles and freemen were the chase, a share in the affairs of the village community or the tribe, and, above all, war. In the eyes of all labour was a subordinate occupation, which they left, as they left domestic cares, either to servile women (*ancillæ*), or to a small number of slaves (*mancipia*), whose price was the equivalent of a horse or of several oxen, or in the case of the arable land to serfs, *lites* or *aldions*, whose numbers were as small as was the extent of the cultivated land itself.

Although they had already attained to a settled existence, the Germans had for the most part remained faithful to the primitive forms of patriarchal organization. Among them the collective property of tribe, canton or village predominated, under the names of *mark* or *allmend*. It comprised not only wastes, marshes, pasture lands, and forests, but also meadows and arable land. A German scholar has found traces of tribal property in the 190 cantons (*pagi*) of ancient Germania, but the property of the village community was of much greater importance. The land belonged to the community of freemen. They were its coproprietors, and possessed equal rights of usage and of temporary occupation in it. They alone had the right to dispose of it, after the group had taken counsel together, and they exercised collective rights of administration and of police over it. In the forest, the heath, the marsh, and the pasture land, each could cut firewood, hunt the wild beasts, gather honey from the bees, and pasture his cattle under the care of the common herdsman. Each could have his cows or mares covered by the common bull or stallion, and make use of the common pond, well, and path. The meadows, which were enclosed in springtime and divided into as many lots as there were families, were thrown open for the cattle of all the members of the mark to graze over after the hay harvest was gathered.

The best lands reserved for cultivation were divided into longitudinal strips (*gewanne*) of equal value, grouped into three great fields of winter seed, spring seed, and fallow. They were allotted annually or periodically among the families. A scholar who has made a profound study of this question considers that each village community comprised from ten to forty of these family holdings, to each of which was allotted by lot an average of about thirty acres, so that the total extent of land under cultivation by each village community was as much as 1,000 acres, each lot containing strips in all three fields. Sometimes above the village communities there existed wider groups, federations or hundreds, which extended over a territory of some 75 to 300 square miles, and grouped together 16 to 120 families for the common use of unallotted common lands.

The family property consisted in the right which each possessed over the common lands and in the lots of arable land thus assigned, in which each member had an equal right. The whole formed the patrimony (*hufe, manse*), which might comprise 30 to 100 acres, and of which the greater part was under cultivation, the remainder being left fallow. This was the Salic land (*terra aviatica*) of the Franks, the *ethel* of the Anglo-Saxons. Not only the land, but also the cattle and the plough belonged to this co-operative family, whose members lived in community and enjoyed in common the produce of their possessions. There were no divisions or dowries, only parts of a whole, divided out among the male children and the households. Private property was restricted to the ownership of arms, of heads of cattle, of food and furniture, and of a wooden house with its little toft.

The economic régime which corresponded to this social system was simply that of natural economy. The Germans knew only how to gather such produce as they obtained without labour, and how to cultivate the soil according to the most rudimentary methods of extensive cultivation. Under a heavy sky, struggling with a damp and cold climate, they lived for the most part the simple life of fishers, hunters, and herdsmen. On the shores of their inhospitable seas, in the midst of bogs and marshes, on sterile mud-flats, inundated by overflowing rivers or drowned in furious floods, under perpetual rains, and in impenetrable fog, the tribes of Jutes, Angles, Frisians, and Saxons derived their existence from fishing and hunting, and, braving the spray in their sealskin garments, launched their coracles of hide or their long pinewood boats upon the wide seas. Inland stretched wastes covered with heath or with the huge forest, whose thick mantle of oak, pine, and beech lay spread over four-fifths of the soil. Like the virgin forests of North America, it was traversed by slow rivers, strewn with drifting tree-trunks, and was peopled by wild beasts. Through it moved hunters and seekers after wild honey, and swineherds led their herds of pigs to pasture in its clearings or under the shade of its trees. Cattle-keeping in the pastures and meadows and on the outskirts of the forest was the chief occupation of the Germans, who possessed droves of horses, horned cattle, sheep, and goats. Idleness and ignorance prevented them from obtaining more than wretched harvests of corn, rye, oats, barley, beans, lentils, and flax, when they cultivated the fields with their hoes and wooden ploughshares. The soil rapidly became exhausted and gave very uncertain returns, for they rested it only by a triennial rotation of fallow, without manure; moreover, the custom of periodical reallotment prevented any improvement being made. Except in the neighbourhood of the empire the Germans had neither gardens, orchards, nor vineyards. Their rudimentary industry was confined to the family or to local groups, and was limited to furnishing the elementary necessities of life. It was usually abandoned to women and serfs, who ground the corn at handmills, brewed the beer, span and wove the wool and linen needed by each household; but among a few peoples there were to be found free artisans, such as the Burgundian carpenters. Only a small number of articles, Frisian cloth and the linens and cloaks of Thuringia and Saxony, were fabricated in sufficiently large quantities for external trade. In Germany the salt-pits and iron-mines were also worked in a primitive fashion, but the common manufactured metals were so rare that men still sometimes made use of stone tools and weapons. Only a coarse sort of pottery was known, and it was in bronze and in goldsmith's work alone that some sort of artistic effort was beginning to be attempted by the German workers.

These barbarians traded with the neighbouring nations, above all with the Roman merchants, from whom on the banks of the Rhine and the Danube they purchased wine, stuffs, and arms in return for the produce of the chase and of their cattle-rearing. But they were almost wholly ignorant of credit and of money, and practised the simple system of barter, or exchange in kind. Commerce was surrounded by dangers. The merchant stranger, treated as an enemy or a suspect, had no guarantee for his life or goods in a land in which piracy and constant raids were considered legitimate methods of supplementing insufficient production.

The Germans had remained beasts of prey. Squatting amid forests and marshes, they lived there in family groups, barricaded in their villages, hamlets, farms, their huts or cabins, which were surrounded by ditches, hedges, and palisades, guarded by fierce dogs, and concealed under a curtain of trees in the thick woods, or perched upon hillocks and islands. They had a horror of towns, and possessed no more than a hundred fortified strongholds, to which they could flee in extremity. They wore breeches and tunics of wool or linen, and cloaks of the skins of wild beasts, went barefoot, and adorned themselves with rough ornaments; some of them, such as the Heruli, tattooed their faces. Their food, consisting of milk, cheese, bacon, and meat, washed down on occasion with ale, was dependent upon the uncertainties of the chase, of their cattle-rearing, and of the harvest. Famines decimated these peoples, or drove them forth upon the warpath. Though boastful and proud, they were capable on occasion of discipline and of devotion, brave and careless of danger, but they led a miserable, uncertain, and perilous existence, which had developed in them instincts of covetousness, grossness, and brutality, a contempt for the weak and the vanquished, and a lust for blood and for the infliction of suffering. Hatreds which nothing could expiate divided each from each. They were superstitious and ignorant, quarrelsome and violent, like wild beasts driven by misery and hunger; and beneath the spur of an imperative necessity, their envy was aroused by the spectacle of the civilization of the empire, in which life seemed so full of charm, so soft and easy, in comparison with the precarious existence led by their race for thousands of years. It was at the very time when the desires of the barbarians were becoming irresistible that the Roman world was sinking into a sort of torpor of indifference, an easeful repose, from which the formidable shock of the invasions was rudely to awake it.

THE INVASIONS AND THE ESTABLISHMENT OF BARBARIAN KINGDOMS IN CHRISTIAN EUROPE.—RUIN OF THE SOCIAL AND ECONOMIC RÉGIME OF ROME (FIFTH TO SEVENTH CENTURIES).

Up to this moment the Roman Empire had for nearly six centuries held back the ceaselessly menacing pressure of the barbarians, by the help of her admirable network of fortresses and fortified camps, in which the 400,000 legionaries of her permanent armies mounted guard. In the end, Rome had come to believe herself invincible and immortal. In the third century she had resisted the gravest attack which had been made upon her since the invasions of the Gauls, Teutons, and Cimbri, and after fifty years of struggle Aurelius, Claudius, and Diocletian had succeeded in restoring the military strength of the empire. But already a policy, which believed itself adroit and was in fact merely short-sighted, had allowed a gradual interpenetration of the Roman edifice, which was fatal to its solidity. Many barbarian elements had been introduced into the provinces; and barbarians of all races had been enrolled in the legions, under the title of auxiliaries (*læti*, *fœderati*), both individually and in groups. A large number of prisoners of war had been distributed among the great estates, which they cultivated as *coloni*. "The barbarians," said Probus, "work for us, sow for us and fight for us." It was a dangerous expedient, for it preserved an illusion of strength and security in a weakened state, increased the general lack of patriotism, relaxed social discipline, and diminished the sentiments of vigilance and energy.

The thousands of barbarians who were now established in the empire could not but be ineffective defenders of a civilization which they certainly did not hate, but to which they were bound only by the most superficial ties. For it was not the hate of the barbarian against civilization which determined those new invasions of the fifth century, which were crowned by success. The invaders were only once more seeking a refuge in the empire, and they asked at first but a humble place therein. In the history of their settlements violent invasions were exceptional, determined, when they occurred, by necessity or by conflicts with other peoples. In general, the future heirs of the empire presented themselves as armed suppliants, who held themselves happy if they received lands and *coloni* in exchange for their services as soldiers of Rome. But the disorder provoked by these invasions, both peaceful and violent, and prolonged throughout two centuries, did in the end destroy, if not the East, which withstood them, at least the West, which did not show the same power of resistance.

The great migrations began from about the end of the fourth and continued until the end of the sixth century, sometimes even longer. First of all came the influx of Western Huns, driven from the banks of Lake Aral, who flung themselves upon the Gothic Empire on the shores of the Black Sea, destroyed it, and, carrying with them a remnant of Germanic and Slav peoples, obliged the Goths to take refuge in Dacia and Mœsia, in the territory of the Eastern Empire, where they were received under the title of *fœderati*. Soon these inconvenient allies sought to extend their settlements into Italy, whence Theodosius had thrown them back by the victory of Aquileia (394). Then the empire, weak and dismembered beneath the feeble successors of that great emperor, underwent the successive shocks of two great invasions: that of 200,000 Suevi, Vandals, and Burgundians, which Stilicho held back at Fæsulæ (406); and that of the Visigoths, which he broke at Pollentia.

The Gallic provinces and Spain, left defenceless, were submerged beneath the flood of other German tribes. For a moment the West breathed again, after the death of Alaric, who sacked Rome and Italy (410). Constantius and Aëtius, following the traditional policy, allowed the Visigoths to establish themselves in Aquitaine and the Narbonne district, and then in Spain (315-346), while the Burgundians were permitted to settle in the Palatinate and then in Savoy, and the Riparian Franks on the left bank of the Rhine (400-436), beside their kinsmen, the Salian Franks, who were already established in Roman territory on the banks of the Yssel. The East seemed now in greater danger than the West, for at this moment there arose also the great Hun empire, stretching from the Caspian to the Danube and the Alps, and forcing the emperors to pay it tribute (434-435). But the fortune of the Huns was broken in Gaul at the Battle of the Seine or Marne (351), thanks to the combination of the Romans and the German *fœderati*, under the leadership of Aetius. The death of Attila (454) delivered Europe from the Hunnish peril, without preserving it from new invasions by Ostrogoths, Alans, Lombards, Slavs, Bulgars, and Avars (fifth to seventh centuries), who ravaged, step by step, the Danube lands, Illyria, Mœsia, Greece, and even Thrace. But the strong military organization of the Eastern Empire enabled it to hold out until the time of Justinian and Heraclius, welcoming some of the invaders as *fœderati* and hurling the others back upon the Middle Danube. The Western Empire, on the other hand, became the prey of the barbarians. In the northwest the pirate bands of Angles, Jutes, and Saxons subjugated the Romanized Celts and Britons, and founded their "heptarchy" of seven kingdoms in Britain. In Eastern Gaul the Burgundians created an ephemeral state in Switzerland and in the Saône and Rhône Valleys (434-531). In the south Visigoths occupied the country as far as the Loire, together with Provence and the whole of Spain (462-80). In the north the Franks spread over Belgium, and then, with the help of the Orthodox Roman Church, founded the first great barbarian empire of the West (486-521). Italy, which remained outside their influence, had now, after the irruption of 406 and 410, to submit to four new invasions—by the Vandals under Genseric (430-55), the Huns under Attila (452), the Heruli under Odoacer (457-476), and the Ostrogoths under Theodoric (475-488); and then, after a brief restoration of the imperial Byzantine rule, became the prey of the Lombards (568-590).

Meanwhile the Western Empire had ceased to exist for over a century, and since 476, by an absurd convention, the Byzantine Emperor had proclaimed the restoration of Roman unity, with the assent of the barbarians, the heirs of the Roman power in Western Europe.

Almost all the bands of invaders and allies at first thought only to live within the empire, under the tutelage and in the shadow of the honoured name of Rome. Almost all of them proclaimed themselves its allies (*fœderati*), its soldiers, and its defenders. In order to secure the obedience of the Roman peoples, they presented themselves in the guise of high Roman functionaries, *magistri militum*, consuls, and patricians, whose insignia they wore above their own robes as barbarian chiefs. These kings and princes ruled with the aid of the framework of the old bureaucracy, and with the support of the old Roman aristocracy and Church. But after a century or more they recognized the futility of a fiction which they began to find irksome. Strong in the servility of the Romanized peoples, and sure of retaining power so long as they kept the monopoly of that military supremacy which Rome had abandoned to the barbarians, they delayed no longer to reveal themselves in their true colours. The civilized world then experienced the fatal effect of a change of rule from which it had been unable to protect itself, and the destructive results of the barbarian conquests began to be felt.

The first of these results was the disruption of the idea of the state. The barbarian monarchies, strange mixtures of Roman despotism and of the Germanic principate, struggled for three centuries in the grip of the leaders of their war bands, who had become the heads of turbulent aristocracies; they allowed the solid armour of the Roman administration to fall to pieces, and showed themselves powerless to prevent a fearful anarchy, in which Western society almost disintegrated. If the world gained thus by the disappearance of Roman absolutism and the Roman fiscal system, it lost for long centuries the blessings of order and internal peace.

Happily for the future of civilization the numerical and social superiority of the Romanized populations was still so great that in the larger part of Europe the barbarian colonization was little more than a thin layer over the deep furrows left by the domination of Rome. The ancient peoples, Latins, Celts, Iberians, Thracians, Illyrians, and Hellenes, whose culture had become unified under the empire, rapidly assimilated, absorbed, or modified the Slav and Germanic and even the Asiatic peoples who were now established among them. If in the contact they lost a great deal of the character of civilized societies, they at least remained, above all in the domain of religion, the repository of Roman institutions. Among the barbarians, some, such as the Heruli, the Rugii, the Ostrogoths, the Suevi, and the Vandals, disappeared without leaving a trace behind. The Germans, Bulgars, and Slavs, who penetrated the Eastern Empire, were almost immediately Hellenized. In the southwest the Lombards and Visigoths remained as conquering aristocracies, but the Germanic colonization left only slight traces, limited to the North of Spain, the duchies of Benevento and Spoleto, Tuscany, and Northern Italy. Similarly Gaul south of the Loire preserved hardly any trace of the Germanic domination which it had temporarily suffered. A few Saxon and Burgundian elements persisted; the one in the Cotentin and Maine regions, the other in the two Burgundies and Western Switzerland. Only in the north and north-east of ancient Gaul and in the Roman lands of the Danube did German colonization leave a deeper mark, and even here it was very unequal. If in the Low Countries Franks, Saxons, and Frisians settled in the Netherlands, Flanders, the Boulogne district, and Artois, the Walloons, descendants of the Romans, still maintained themselves in the valleys of the Sambre and the Meuse. Similarly, the Romano-Celtic peoples of Alsace and the Palatinate preserved the old Latin and Gallic foundations, despite the invasion of the Alamanni; and in England the Britons did the same beneath the Anglo-Saxon deluge. It was only in the lands on the right bank of the Rhine and in those of the Main, Danube, and Central Alps that Germanic colonization, represented in particular by Alamanni and Bavarians, installed itself as mistress and that Teutonic barbarism triumphed, leaving only a few scattered remnants of the old Romanized populations.

But if the invasions had little effect upon the ethnic foundations of the ancient Roman Empire in East and West alike, they had nevertheless disastrous results upon society and upon economic conditions. Humanity has rarely experienced misery as great as that of this period. The masses lost heavily by the change of masters. The upper and middle classes of the old Roman society were swept away in the storm or despoiled by the barbarians, and the surviving members were fused with the conquerors. Property changed hands, wholly or partially. In the Danube and Rhine lands the Germans, not content with having occupied the state lands and the abandoned domain lands, seized upon all private properties. It was the same in Britain, where the Anglo-Saxons completely despoiled the Britons. In Belgic Gaul, from the Rhine to the North Sea, the Franks, ancient *hospites* of the empire, appropriated the state domains, of which they enjoyed only the usufruct, and installed themselves upon the deserted or unoccupied lands, without proceeding to a useless partition by force with the Gallo-Romans. In the whole of this vast zone of the ancient empire, the Roman estate, the *villa*, gave way to the Germanic village community, the *tun, weiller, dorf*. Elsewhere the Burgundians, Visigoths, Heruli, Ostrogoths, in Gaul and in Aquitaine, in Spain and in Italy, invoked and altered in their own favour the rights which the Roman state recognized to its military defenders. They demanded as *hospites*, in virtue of the official custom of *hospitalitas*, not only lodging and dwelling-place, but also a share in all properties and their fruits. The Visigoths and Burgundians demanded and occupied by legal means two-thirds of the great domains of the imperial state and of the aristocracy, leaving the last third in full ownership to the large Roman proprietors. Similarly, they forced the cession of two-thirds of the gardens, vineyards, cattle, slaves, *coloni*, and houses. Old and new landowners, the latter under the title of *hospites* or *consortes*, dwelt side by side on the same domains and shared the revenues, according to the legal proportion. They used forests and pastures in common. Since the Germans were not very numerous, this measure of spoliation was accomplished without difficulty, left few traces, and affected only a minority of landowners. More moderate still in Italy, the spoliation extended only to a third of the lands and landed revenues of the Romans, but the Heruli made odious by their brutality a decision which the more intelligent Ostrogoths of Theodoric were able to render acceptable. The latter confined themselves to taking, as *hospites* through the Treasury, one-third of the revenues in money or in kind of the public domains and the great private estates, which had been allotted to them. But all was changed with the advent of the Lombards; these brutal

conquerors were not content with settling themselves and
their families on the lands of the great Roman landowners,
whom they massacred *en masse*, and of the churches, which
they despoiled, but, in addition, obliged the surviving Latin
populations to pay to the new Germanic *hospites* a third
of the produce of the lands, whose usufruct they retained.
Thus there came about a great transference of property in
the West. It worked in favour of the growth of a landed
aristocracy formed of predominant Germanic elements,
mingled with assimilated Roman elements, to the detriment
of the class of small free proprietors, whose number and
influence naturally diminished very quickly. The large
aristocratic estate, which since the end of the empire had
been tending to absorb the soil, received an impetus in
vitality and expansion from the invasions. At the same
time the primitive forms of landownership, the collective
property of the village and of the family, reappeared in the
civilized West, where the Roman genius had brought about
the prevalence of individual private property.

Far from bearing with them into the empire democratic
principles of liberty and equality, the Germans only spread
therein the oppression of poor by rich and of weak by strong,
and subjected the masses to an oligarchy of chiefs of war-
bands, who were the masters of men and lands alike. Rome
had fused within herself all classes and all races, and had
brought them into an equality beneath her laws. The
Germanic customs established profound inequalities between
the divers peoples of the barbarian states. In Gaul there
were as many as seven different codes of law, according to
the origin of the inhabitants, Romans, Salian, Riparian, and
Chamavian Franks, Burgundians, Visigoths, and Alamanni.
High barriers separated the different social ranks, to each of
which a different penal legislation was applied, shamefully
indulgent towards the upper classes and barbarously harsh
towards the lower, for whom were reserved the punishments
of mutilation and torture. The aristocracy, alone in its
pride, was at pains to prevent any rise in the social scale
by forbidding marriages between its members and those of
other classes, on pain of a loss of rank. The barbarians dared
not openly attack the liberty of freemen of Germanic origin,
who were established side by side with the chiefs upon the

lands of the empire. In the profoundly Romanized districts of Southern Gaul, Spain, and Italy, they allowed the continuance of a number of small free proprietors of Roman origin. But everywhere by means of a steady underground process, made easier by the disappearance of all authority and by the reign of force, the new aristocracies set to work to rob freemen of their landed property and of their personal liberty. In all regions wherein German settlements predominated, the ancient class of Roman landowners disappeared, either decimated or enslaved. In Britain the Anglo-Saxons reduced those Britons whom they spared to the condition of *coloni* or rural slaves. Throughout Belgic Gaul, in the lands watered by the Rhine and the Danube, the free Gallo-Roman populations who succeeded in escaping massacre, and who did not emigrate, were driven to cultivate as semi-serfs (*tributarii*) the domains and farms of the Germanic conquerors, and went to swell the ranks of the ancient *coloni*. Thus the barbarians solved the problem of agricultural labour and were able to live in idleness upon the work of the old Roman landowners and cultivators. A similar fate overtook a smaller proportion of the old free classes of Celtic Gaul, Spain, and Italy; it became general in proportion as the rule of the barbarians grew firmer. Thus in the Italian peninsula the Lombards reduced all the free population, even the priests, to the condition of the Roman or Germanic *coloni*.

The colonate itself, which under the laws of the Christian empire had marked a stage in social progress, in the barbarian period took on the aspect of a retrogressive institution, whereby men became more, rather than less, dependent. While Roman law had assured to the *colonus* his personal liberty and stability on the soil which he cultivated, the customs and laws of the barbarians assimilated the *colonus* to the serf—*i.e.*, to the unfree, and to the urban or domestic slave, who could be separated from his family and transplanted from one domain to another. On the other hand, the serfs ceased to be distinguished from slaves, and their position became equally precarious. At the close of the Roman Empire slavery was on the point of becoming extinct; but during the three centuries which followed the first barbarian invasions, it was reconstituted and spread with extreme rapidity. Constant wars and raids, veritable man-hunts, analogous to those which still continue in Central Africa, threw thousands of men and women upon the market at miserable prices. The penal legislation of the barbarians multiplied the number of these unhappy wretches, decreeing the punishment of loss of liberty for the most inconsiderable misdemeanours, and, on the other hand, so great was the prevalent misery that for numbers of despairing creatures slavery was a sort of refuge. The greater part of the Roman populations, spared by the victors in Britain, in the Danube and Rhine districts, even in Gaul, Belgium, and Italy (during the Lombard period), were thus reduced to servitude. The domestic servants of the aristocracy were similarly recruited, and the cultivation of the land and the care of herds and flocks was confided in part to bands of slaves (*servi rustici, mancipia*). These men, once more reduced to the level of beasts and things, were tied to their terrible condition by the law, which made enfranchisements rarer and more difficult, and forbade marriages between free and servile persons. It once more put the power of life and death into the hands of the masters and delivered over the slaves, almost without defence, to the atrocious and bestial fury of their owners. The enumeration of the cruel punishments to which men of servile condition were subjected—the loss of ears, nose, eyes, tongue, hands, and genital organs—and the various tortures to which they were submitted fills whole columns of the barbarian codes, until the reader cannot restrain a shudder. Mankind had passed far away from that great humanitarian movement which from the second to the fourth century had left its trace on Roman legislation upon slavery.

All the guarantees with which the expiring civilization of the ancient world had surrounded the life and possessions of the individual disappeared in the anarchy let loose by the barbarians. Even among the Visigoths, Ostrogoths, and Franks, who were already half Romanized by a long sojourn within the empire, the sudden awakening of ancestral ferocity transformed these " guests " into unchained murderers. Alaric and his followers in Bœotia, Attica, Thessaly, and Macedonia slew the inhabitants and carried off the women and cattle. " For us," says Salvian, Archbishop of Marseilles, himself the apologist of the barbarians, " there is neither peace nor security." Another contemporary, Prosper of Aquitaine, cries, towards 416: "It is ten years since we fell beneath the sword of the Vandals and Goths; the people has perished, even children and young maids they slew." In Auvergne and Aquitaine in the sixth century the Austrasians were guilty of similar crimes. Fiercer still were those Germans who were untouched by Roman civilization. Angles, Jutes, and Saxons were wild beasts, who must have blood at all costs, and before setting sail they usually put to the sword a tenth of their prisoners. In Britain they committed such atrocities that the Romano-Celtic aristocracy fled to Armorica to escape death, while a large number of the Britons were slain. The cruelty of the Alamanni left upon the memory of Western Europe almost as profound an impression as that of the Huns. The war bands which took part in the great invasion of 406 in Italy and Gaul spread terror far and wide by their atrocious exploits; they transformed the town of Treier into a charnel-house, in which the naked bodies of men and women were devoured by dogs and birds of prey. In Aquitaine and in Spain the faithful and the clergy were beaten, thrown into chains, and burned alive. Everywhere, at the sack of cities and towns, women suffered the supreme outrage. After the capture of Rome Alaric's Visigoths, reclining in the shade, forced the sons and daughters of the senators, captives of their harems, to serve them with Falernian wine in golden cups. With each expedition the women's quarters of the conquerors grew. Throughout the second half of the fifth century a contemporary witnesses that "the forest of swords mowed down the Italian nobility like corn." Later, in the sixth century, the savagery of the Lombards passed all bounds. "Murder is nothing to them," writes the annalist Paul Deacon. "Even as a sword leaping from the scabbard so did this fierce horde ravage, and men fell even as the ears of wheat beneath the sickle." In the East the same terrible sights were everywhere to be seen; men were massacred, women and children carried away, by the invading bands of Turanians, Germans, and Slavs in Macedonia, Thessaly, Greece, Illyria, Epirus, and the Danubian provinces. Ostrogoths hacked off the arms of labourers in Pannonia, and impaled the *coloni* of Illyria; Slavs crucified the peasants and artisans, whom they made prisoners, head downwards, or shot them full of arrows. Throughout the peninsula heaps of whitening bones marked the place where once stood villages, whose inhabitants had been massacred or had died of hunger.

The barbarians took the same delight in destruction and pillage that they took in killing and violence. They carried everything away as they passed, leaving behind them only the glare of fire and dreary heaps of ruins. From 406 to 416, according to St. Jerome's testimony, the barbarians destroyed every sign of civilization from the Alps to the Pyrenees, and from the ocean to the Rhine. "All Gaul burned upon the same bonfire," writes a Bishop of Auch. Prosper of Aquitaine expresses himself in the same terms in his poem. "The temples of God were delivered to the flames and monasteries were sacked. If the waves of the ocean had overflowed the fields of Gaul they would have done less damage." He shows the Visigoths themselves engaged in pillaging Roman villas, carrying off silver, furniture, and cattle, dividing up the jewels and drinking the wine. They bore away the sacred vessels of the churches, and to crown their work set fire to the houses. When they passed through Auvergne, in the time of Sidonius Apollinarius (471-5), their escort, says that poet, was "flame and sword and famine." St. Jerome, travelling through the Italian provinces after the invasions of the first third of the fifth century, could hardly find a house standing or a field under cultivation. When the half-civilized gave themselves over to such excesses, it may be imagined what was the behaviour of the completely barbarous Vandals, Huns, Alamanni, Anglo-Saxons, and Lombards. The Alamanni, in the Romanized districts of the Rhine and Danube, heaped their chariots with furniture, garments, the very stones of the villas, and set fire to what they could not carry away. The Huns destroyed everything and left a desert behind them. The Vandals sacked with a thoroughness which has made their name a synonym for furious destruction, and the Anglo-Saxons merited a like renown. The Heruli reduced North Italy to misery by their raids, and Paul Deacon calls the Lombards a "race of thieves," as prompt to murder as to rob. At the very period when the barbarians had succeeded in making stable settlements, the wars of kings and peoples, tribes and families, perpetuated these customs, which were so destructive of a regular and productive social and economic life. In expeditions such as that of the Austrasians into Auvergne and Aquitaine in the sixth century, all that was left of the prosperity of the country disappeared beneath the brutal hand of the barbarians, who set fire to the harvest, cut down the fruit-trees, tore up the vines, pillaged barns and cellars, drove away before them troops of captives and domestic animals, and sowed desolation and death all around them. Sometimes the very excess of despair drove the peasants to take arms against them; the Bagaudæ of Spain thus resisted the Suevi and Visigoths in the fifth century. But in general there was no resistance, because the masses knew that it was useless.

In such a society, delivered over without mercy to all the abuses of brutal force and of unchecked barbarism, economic life waned, and sometimes seemed about to cease altogether. Agricultural labour became scarce, owing to the great slaughter of men, the slave raids, the famines and epidemics, which had become almost chronic. The growing insecurity discouraged all production, and everywhere in West and East alike stretched vast wastes, unpopulated and uncultivated. All the documents speak of these deserted lands, *eremi, vastinæ, solitudines, loca invia.* Of fifth-century Spain there remained, according to the annalist Idacius, "only a name." Round about Narbonne the site of the vineyards and olive groves could no longer be distinguished beside the ruined farm buildings. Armorica and a large part of Helvetia had relapsed into a state of waste, and Northern Gaul, as the Salic Law witnesses, was full of abandoned lands. The Gothic chronicler Jordanes describes the desolation of the Danube regions, where "not a labourer is to be seen," and Procopius that of the fields of the Balkan peninsula, "which seem," he says, "like the Scythian Desert." Kent, to-day one of the most animated ant-heaps of the world, was, after the Anglo-Saxon invasions, no more than a narrow borderland on the edge of vast forests and waste lands. The forest once more reigned supreme, and covered a large part of Gaul, Britain, the Rhineland, the Danube district, Northern Spain, and Central Italy.

Flanders, which was later to become "one continuous town," was then a marshy woodland. Everywhere fens stretched over the lowlands of the Netherlands, the eastern counties of England, oceanic and Mediterranean Gaul, the valleys of the Po, the Arno, and the Tiber, and, indeed, the majority of river valleys. The barbarians knew neither how to care for nor how to breed the cattle, which were decimated by continual murrains. The land, ill cultivated, according to primitive methods by these new masters, who knew nothing of the agricultural science of the Romans, now gave but uncertain harvests. The Germanic system of common cultivation with periodical divisions of the soil, which was introduced into part of the ancient imperial territory, only aggravated the evil. Rich crops, such as orchards, vineyards, and industrial plants, were partially abandoned in those lands where the Romans had introduced them. Nevertheless, the miserable populations which survived took refuge in the fields and the great domains, which were protected by ditches and palisades, or by embankments of earth and stones, or else in the shadow of the old Roman townships (*vici*), which could serve as a refuge for the small cultivators. Natural economy once more predominated, and life became concentrated and localized in the country districts, where the barbarians preferred to dwell.

Industrial economy, indeed, received its death-blow with that of the towns, which had been the home of the Græco-Roman civilization. The barbarians showed a peculiar savagery in destroying those cities, in which the most flourishing varieties of industry and corporations of artisans had developed and still survived. Everywhere the conquerors dispersed the townsfolk and destroyed everything which might preserve the memory of civilized life—temples, churches, basilicas, theatres, circuses. Buildings and monuments alike were delivered to the flames, and throughout both West and East numbers of still flourishing towns disappeared, never to rise again. The Huns alone destroyed seventy in the Eastern and Illyrian dioceses. The Slavs ruined and emptied the Illyrian, Dacian, and Dardanian towns. In the Danube lands there disappeared Margus in Mæsia, Ratiaria in Dacia, Siscia, Sirmium in Savia,

THE INVASIONS

Aquencum (Bude) in Valeria, Carnuntum and Vindobona (Vienna) in Pannonia, Emona, Virunum (Laibach), Juvavum (Salzburg), Laureacum (Lorch) in Noricum, Curia (Coire), Augusta Vindelicorum (Augsburg), Regina Castra (Regensburg). In the Rhenish provinces Aurelia Aquensis (Aix-la-Chapelle), Xanten, Cologne, Utrecht, Mainz, Worms, Strasburg, Treier, Augusta Rauracorum (Augst), and Speier were destroyed in the course of the fifth century. Tongres, Tournai, Reims, and Metz in Belgic Gaul were similarly destroyed. In Britain the prosperous little towns which the Romans had created—Londinium (London), Eboracum (York), Camelodunum (Colchester), Dorovernum (Canterbury), Venta Icenorum (Norwich), Aqua Solis (Bath)—were transformed into heaps of ruins. In Celtic Gaul the Helvetian town of Aventicum (Avenches) was razed to the ground, and so also was Lillebonne, the metropolis of the Seine estuary. The Austrasians burned Thiers and Brioude, the Alans Valentia, the Visigoths Bordeaux. In Spain the Suevi destroyed Mérida, the Vandals Hispalis (Seville) and Carthagena, the Visigoths Astorga, Palencia and Braga; Tarragona was left half standing. In Italy the Vandals subjected the towns of Sicily, Palermo, Syracuse, Catania, and Termini to such treatment that they had not revived at the end of the sixth century. In North and Central Italy the successive invasions of Visigoths, Huns, Heruli, Ostrogoths, Austrasians, and Lombards brought about the total or partial ruin of Aquileia, Concordia, Odero, Este, Treviso, Viacenza, Padua, Mantua, Cremona, Populonium, Fermo, Osimo, Spoleto, and a number of Cisalpine, Ligurian, and Tuscan towns and others in the Marches and in Campania. The population fled in terror into the islands and forests and mountains. "He may call himself a rich man now who has bread," wrote a contemporary, and the relics of the old population, which crept back to dwell among the ruins, had wild beasts for company. Rome itself, thrice sacked in the fifth century and five times taken by assault in the sixth, was only the shadow of the superb imperial city, and in the time of Gregory the Great (600) numbered only 50,000 inhabitants, a bare twentieth of her former population. Within the crumbling walls of these ghostly towns and in their half-deserted streets a few miserable artisans still vegetated, all that was left of the flourishing crafts of the past. Ploughed fields and gardens occupied the greater part of the open spaces, destitute of houses and of inhabitants. Industrial activity disappeared, and the very traditions of the ancient industry were lost. The West fell back again into the elementary economic life of primitive peoples.

In the midst of the universal disorganization trade was reduced to a simple traffic in foodstuffs or in manufactures of primary necessity, and its range of circulation was very narrow. The great home and foreign commerce, which had developed so brilliantly under the empire, was no longer possible. Everything which was necessary to promote and to facilitate business was lacking. Land was now once more the sole capital, and natural products served as a medium of exchange. Trade by barter, the primitive method in use among the Germans, reappeared in the ancient Roman Empire, where money became rare and credit disappeared. The fine Roman roads, no longer kept in repair, deteriorated, the bridges fell down, the imperial post ceased, there were no more relays. All rapid movement became impossible. Everywhere insecurity reigned; brigands fell upon travellers and merchants on the edge of the woods and at the fords across rivers and marshes. Armed bands prowled about the country, and journeys became perilous expeditions, undertaken only in caravans and with armed escorts. The ports declined, the seas were infested with pirates, maritime trade became as uncertain as land commerce. The great transport companies had for the most part broken up, and the shipbuilders were ruined. "He who once fitted out six great vessels," says a writer of the fifth century, "is happy now if he owns but one little boat."

There was misery and want everywhere in town and country alike. Bands of beggars whined for alms at the doors of the churches, the castles on the great estates, and the royal palaces. It was among these miserable beings that the bands of criminals who swarmed everywhere were recruited. At Rome in 410 no less than 14,000 had to be supported by alms. "Wretched, wretched that we are," wrote Salvian in the fifth, and Gregory the Great in the sixth, century. A long cry of anguish echoes through the acts of

THE INVASIONS

councils and the correspondence of statesmen at this time; "the world seems near its end," lamented Gregory I. Death indeed mowed down in great swathes those who survived the invasions. Many who escaped sword and fire died of privation and hunger, or were carried off by the natural disorders which were now let loose upon mankind. Famine accompanied the invasions in Noricum, Gaul, Spain, and Italy. Even in times of peace the West and the East alike went in fear of dearth. "Anything rather than starvation" ("cuncta fame leviora mihi"), was the saying on all lips. But famine reappeared periodically after droughts, floods, and the ravages of warlike bands, and sometimes in a form so terrible that there were sporadic scenes of cannibalism. In the sixth century, particularly, it was to all intents and purposes permanent, and on one occasion alone (536) 50,000 peasants died of starvation in a single province of Central Italy. In 556 the East itself, in the midst of Justinian's triumphant reign, knew the horrors of famine. Epidemics, dysentery, typhus, and the Asiatic plague completed the deadly work. They flourished in the fifth century, and still more in the second half of the sixth and in the seventh, notably in Britain and Italy. In Ireland and Wales and in the Anglo-Saxon kingdoms from a third to a half of the population perished. In Auvergne (571) one Sunday 300 persons fell dead in a single church. At Rome Gregory I saw in one hour eighty persons lying in the throes of death in the street. From 552 to 570 the Eastern Empire was decimated by the bubonic plague, which reappeared there and spread to Sicily and Calabria in 746 and 747. The Black Death of the fourteenth century alone can be compared to it in destructiveness. The wretched physique of the people caused nervous maladies, leprosy, and St. Anthony's Fire to multiply. The general exhaustion diminished fertility and reduced the birth-rate. The result of all this was that the population of West and East fell in this period to one of the lowest levels reached during the whole of the Christian era. The Danubian, Rhenish, Breton, and Gallic lands, which had at one time in the second century numbered over thirty million persons, lost in all probability a half or two-thirds of their population. Pannonia, Noricum, Rhætia, Helvetia, Gaul, Belgium, Britain, Spain, and North

29

LIFE AND WORK IN MEDIEVAL EUROPE

and Central Italy suffered particularly severely, and the Balkan Peninsula perhaps even more than they. Contemporaries are unanimous in describing the desolation of the world, in West and East alike, the impression of solitude and of desert which it left upon their minds; and some believed that they had reached that end of the world predicted by the Scriptures.

The material and moral disaster was, indeed, immense, and seemed irreparable. Civilized life, especially in the East, had been thrust back into barbarism. Neither labour nor intelligence was honoured. Force reigned supreme, and the warrior band exploited Western society without pity. A minority of chiefs and fighters lived upon war and pillage, oppressed the wretched population of *coloni* and slaves on its domains, heaped up the fruits of its rapine, filled its harems with girls, its stables with horses, and its kennels with hounds, divided its leisure between banqueting and the chase, dog fights, and violent exercise. The nobility and freemen, shunning the ruined towns, lived in their *villæ*, their family dwelling-places, or their hamlets on the edge of the great common forests, like the idle, rude, and brutal conquerors they were. The working classes, who laboured for them, were exposed to all the risks of an unregulated and anarchical society, whose only rule was violence. The idleness, stupidity, coarseness, ignorance, credulity, and cruelty of the barbarians took the place of the well-regulated activity, the polish, culture, and relative humanity of the Romans. There was no longer any respect for the weak, for peasants and women and children. There was no discipline, no moral code to restrain these invaders, who merely added the vices of civilization to the depravity of barbarism. Far from regenerating the world, they very nearly wiped out civilization for ever. They destroyed the ordered societies of the West, only to replace them by anarchy. Far from bringing freedom in their train, they reestablished slavery. Far from diminishing class distinctions, they reared new barriers between the classes. Far from ameliorating the condition of the lower classes, they made it harder. Far from assisting economic development, they ruined all activity by sowing everywhere pillage, disorder, and destruction. They created nothing, but they destroyed much, and they put a stop to all progress for several centuries. In society and in labour the barbarian settlements produced one of the greatest retrogressions which the world has ever known. Their one useful result was that they gave finer spirits an impetus to energy and to action, and thus, out of sheer reaction, brought about a series of attempts to return to the traditions of Roman government, and roused the Church from its mystic dream, in order that it might save the remnants of civilization from shipwreck. In the East the Roman edifice had weathered the storm, and could serve as a model and framework for the restoration of society and of labour. In the West the spirit and institutions of Rome, adapted to new conditions of environment, were destined to inspire those attempts at economic and social restoration which took place towards the end of the Dark Ages.

CHAPTER III

THE EAST ROMAN EMPIRE AND THE ECONOMIC AND SOCIAL RECONSTRUC-
TION OF EASTERN EUROPE FROM THE FIFTH TO THE TENTH CENTURY.
—COLONIZATION AND AGRICULTURAL PRODUCTION.—THE DIVISION
OF PROPERTY AND RURAL CLASSES IN EASTERN EUROPE.

THE Eastern Empire was, during the first six centuries of this period, a harbour of refuge for civilization, where the organization of labour could attain more stability and power than anywhere else. Better protected by its geographical position and by the military system, which it inherited almost intact from the Roman state and itself perfected, this empire braved all the attacks of barbarism for a thousand years. With a marvellous vitality it was able to recover from its defeats; now that its African, Syrian, Danubian, and Western dependencies had been amputated, it fell back upon itself, and found in the concentration of its forces a new element of solidity. For 600 years, with intervals of decadence followed by brilliant returns to prosperity, the most remarkable of which lasted for over three centuries—the eighth to the eleventh—it defended itself against darkness and ruin. Its elegant and refined civilization enabled it to introduce some sort of culture among the barbarian populations of the East and to educate those of the West, as well as to escape the continual anarchy with which the latter had to struggle. It was the first to build up once more a real Hellenic nationality, which, if not founded upon unity of race and language, did at least rest upon a community of political and religious institutions, and was at least animated by an ardent patriotism, zealous for the glory and grandeur of the state. Under the care of a powerful and enlightened government, served by an ordered administration, and protected by a strong religious and military organization, the Eastern Empire facilitated the restoration and development of economic activity in all its forms.

"Two things," said a Byzantine emperor of the tenth century, "are necessary for the preservation of the state—agriculture and the military art." For this reason the repopulation of the countryside and the promotion of agricultural colonization were among the first preoccupations of the Byzantines, who, like the Romans, saw in land the essential source of wealth and power. It was the great honour of the Eastern Empire that it succeeded in solving this problem long before the West. It succeeded thanks to methods of colonization which it had received in large part from Rome, and which it proceeded to follow with methodical perseverance. Numerous military colonies were established in the themes (provinces), and there soldiers cultivated the lands given over to them as a form of military service. The empire was also colonized by means of heretical Christian sects—Manicheans, Jacobites, Paulicians—who were transported from Armenia and Asia Minor into Thrace and Greece. In the seventh century 12,000 Syrian adventurers from Lebanon—the Mirdites—were settled in Thrace, the Peloponnesus, and Epirus. If necessary, slaves were enfranchised, as was done by one emperor in order to colonize the deserted lands of Southern Italy. During five centuries thousands of *coloni* of barbarian origin were installed in all the European districts of the empire; some were Germans, such as the Goths in Thrace and Illyria, the Gepidi, Heruli, and Lombards in Pannonia between the Drave and Save; some were Semites, Arabs, Egyptians; others, Persians, Armenians, and Circassians, were of Aryan race. If need be, captives of Turanian origin were baptized and became, in their turn, labourers. Thus Avars were established in Messenia near Navarino, Bulgarians in Acarnania in the environs of Actium, 14,000 Turks were settled in Eastern Macedonia, and others round the lake of Ochrida. But the most numerous contingent of agricultural colonists was furnished by the Slavs. On a single occasion Justinian II established 70,000 prisoners of this race in the basin of the Strymon and in Eastern Macedonia.

Part of Thrace was colonized by these barbarians, who gave Byzantium a great emperor, Basil I " the Macedonian." They came during five centuries in such populous tribes that they assimilated the Armenians, Persians, Turks, and Asiatic Greeks, who had been transported like themselves into the country, and at one time in the sixth century Macedonia received the name of Slavenia (Slovenia). Southern Thessaly, the Pindus region, Attica, and, above all, the Peloponnesus, were repopulated, thanks to these Slav colonies, and it was by such means that in the tenth century, by an emperor's admission, the whole of the Morea became a Slav district. It was the same in the south of Italy. The great work of Byzantium was to mould these colonists, who had as yet no national consciousness, and to Hellenize them by converting them to the orthodox religion. Out of this assemblage of so many different races sprang forth a re-rejuvenated Hellenic nationality, while at the same time there arose once more a source of agricultural labour. There are many indications that the Byzantine Empire was, in the tenth century, once again the most highly populated part of the continent.

Thus the cultivation of the soil and the development of agricultural production was facilitated. The extent of deserted lands diminished, and the emperors took energetic measures to combat the abandonment of rural domains. First, they decreed that landowners who left their lands uncultivated should forfeit them. Then in the sixth century there was established the *epibole*, by virtue of which those who held arable land were made responsible for the payment of taxes, which fell upon uncultivated land so heavily as to oblige the taxpayers to bring it under cultivation. The *epibole* lasted until the tenth century and was even re-established later. But the renascence of agricultural activity in the East was due rather to civil and military colonization than to measures of coercion. Very soon cultivation produced such great benefits in the now peaceful empire that the state, the great and the small landowners, all set themselves with equal ardour to reap the fruits thereof. After periods of depression the empire did indeed, especially from the eighth to the eleventh century, reach a remarkable height of prosperity, more particularly in Thrace, Macedonia, Thessaly, Greece, and Southern Italy. The Christian East revived once more the Greek and Roman traditions of agricultural science. Treatises on agriculture and on stock-breeding were written in that tenth century, which was an age of gold in the East, and in the West an age of iron. Many improved methods of cultivation, such as irrigation, the perfected forms of arboriculture, and the cultivation of the vine and of industrial plants, for which we are wont to honour the Arabs, seem in reality to have been of Syrio-Byzantine origin. It was

RECONSTRUCTION IN EASTERN EMPIRE

Byzantium which, under the Isaurian emperors, gave the world the first model of a rural code (*Nomoi georgikoi*), and which laid down the rules of a wise agrarian administration.

Nowhere was agricultural production as far advanced and as well balanced as in the East. The Byzantine provinces, then far less denuded than they are to-day, were full of rich forests, notably in the Dinaric Alps, the Balkans, Pindus, Lucania, and Calabria. Princes and great nobles had magnificent parks, and timber was obtained from the forests for building purposes. Fisheries flourished in the Black Sea, the Archipelago, the Ionian Sea, and the Adriatic. Everywhere pig-breeding and sheep-farming prospered, especially in the forest regions and on the plateaux. Cattle-raising was carried on in the plains of Thrace, Mœsia, Macedonia, Bœotia, Elis, Messenia, and Southern Italy. The emperors and the great landowners made it a point of honour to keep up studs, and to raise race-horses and army chargers : those of Thrace and of the Peloponnesus were famous. Grecian honey had lost none of its renown. Thrace, Macedonia, Thessaly, Messenia, Apulia, Sicily, and Campania were still the richest granaries in Europe. No Christian country could rival the orchards of the Eastern Empire; almonds, lemons, oranges, figs, and raisins, the fruit of the Archipelago, Greece, and Southern Italy, were busily exported. The scented wines of Lesbos, Samos, Greece, and Sicily were world-famous. The Eastern Empire held the first place also in the cultivation of dye plants and medicinal herbs, a monopoly in the cultivation of the sugar cane, cotton, and of mulberries and the rearing of silkworms. It was from agricultural produce that it drew the greater part of that wealth for which it was admired and envied by all men in the Middle Ages.

This economic renaissance strengthened in the East the Roman principle of private property, over which its owner had an absolute right, while at the same time common property belonging to the state and to collective owners grew progressively less. The imperial and fiscal domains, although often very considerable as a result of conquests, confiscation, disinheritances, and the devolution of vacant lands to the state, nevertheless diminished, by reason of the inexhaustible munificence of the emperors towards the

Church, or by dint of the continual concession of " benefices " to officers and soldiers. First the municipalities (cities and *curiæ*), then the innumerable rural communities grouped round townships, which were the centres of a district (*metrocome*) and took the place of the old cities, began to find the utmost difficulty in preserving their land from the enterprises of the treasury and, above all, of the clergy and large owners. Nevertheless, by dint of energy and tenacity the communes succeeded in keeping a portion of those common pastures, woods, fields, and meadows, which the mass of the poorer inhabitants of the countryside found so useful.

In spite of all, the concentration of landed property made great strides. Great estates grew, to the profit of the Church and the aristocracy. Already very rich in the fourth century, the Oriental clergy added immeasurably to their territorial wealth in the course of the early Middle Ages, through the piety of the faithful, of princes, of the nobility, through usurpations at the expense of defenceless communities and individuals, and also through the intelligence of their economic administration. The patriarchates, the fifty-seven metropolitan sees, the forty-nine archbishoprics, the fifty-four bishoprics, the innumerable convents, chapels, oratories, churches—nay, even the simple "lauras" or hermitages— benefited by this immense extension of ecclesiastical possessions, to which were attached exorbitant privileges, and which were exempt from part of the state charges, untransferable and inalienable. The Church was even adroit enough to obtain for itself the right of levying dues (*canons*) in money or in kind from the peasants, and minute registers of these, known as *breviaries* or *polyptycha*, were drawn up. Its fortune grew without remission, and if it was sometimes employed to support the useful work of religious propaganda, charity, or progress in the arts and sciences, it served more often still to favour the luxury and idleness of a caste, which pleaded the rules of its Order to avoid manual labour. Wealth only fortified the fanaticism and lust for power of a body which tended always to form a state within the state, while escaping the fiscal and military obligations of the civil population. The best emperors, the Isaurians and the Macedonians, were so well aware of the danger that they vigorously opposed the extension of great ecclesiastical properties, forbade individuals to transmit their goods to clerks and monks, seized the domains which the clergy had usurped, forbade them to acquire any more immovable property, and tried to submit their estates to the common charges by laicizing a part of them and redistributing them in the form of military benefices. The Byzantine state maintained intact the principle that the Church was only a temporary depository of the landed property which it held, and that the government had the right to dip at will into this great reserve fund for the public need. But in practice, anxious to keep on good terms with a power so redoubtable, the state often left an open field to the enterprises of the Church, with the result that the latter succeeded in getting the greater part of the land into its clutches. Thus great estates were built up, such as those held by the sixty-two convents of Byzantium; by the monastery of Neamoni, which numbered 500 monks and owned a fifth of Chios; by the monastery of Patmos, which owned the whole island of that name, besides lands in Crete; by the three famous monastic communities of Athos, enriched by so many gifts; and by the celebrated Abbey of Monte Cassino, whose possessions stretched all over Southern Italy, and whose abbot was the peer of the Princes of Benevento, Capua, and Spoleto. The domains of the Church were vast centres of cultivation, with a whole personnel of administrators, inspectors (*sacellarii*), receivers, treasurers (*logathetai*), stewards (*œconomoi*), deacons; with walled and fortified central buildings, hospitals, inns, cellars, and industrial workshops, round which dwelt the population of *coloni*.

Side by side with the great ecclesiastical estate there developed, after the crisis of the fifth and sixth centuries was past, the great aristocratic estate. This extension of lay property took place in proportion as the high civil and military functionaries, exarchs and strategoi, soon classed together under the general title of archons, profited by the authority enjoyed by the administrative nobility, and identified their interests and ambitions with those of the heads of the great local families and the rich landed proprietors (*plousioi, potentes, dynatoi*), who exercised considerable social influence over their estates. The former, enriched by their endowments, attributed to themselves not only public authority, but also an hereditary property in the benefices which had been granted to them; they added to their possessions and their dependants by forcing the people under their administration to accept or to solicit their patronage and to become their clients. The latter sought to add the prerogatives of sovereignty to the practical authority which they wielded over those who dwelt on their estates. Little by little in the East, as in the West, there was organized a territorial nobility, whose power was based on the possession of great domains or *massæ*, which were classed apart in the land register from the reign of Leo VI (ninth century). Ceaselessly increased by marriage, by purchase, by the usurpation of public and communal lands or of small holdings, as well as by the generalization of patronage, which transformed free into dependent land, to the detriment of small proprietors who found themselves in debt or in need of protection, the territorial possessions of the aristocracy became almost as great as those of the Church. The emperors, who feared the effect upon their own power and upon society in general of the growth of these great noble properties, displayed, notably under the Isaurian and Macedonian Dynasties, a rare energy in hindering the process. The Isaurians in the eighth century by their Rural Code forbade patronage and annulled usurpations made at the expense of small proprietors. The Macedonians prohibited the alienation of domains by the consent of the poorer class to the profit of the great, annulled contracts made under fraud or violence, and even abolished in this connection the forty years' prescription which covered usurpations. They renewed the prohibition of patronage and annulled all acquisitions made to the prejudice of the state or of military benefices. They vigorously defended the interests of the central power and the middle classes, which were menaced by the revolts of the great lords.

At times in the course of this duel it seemed as though the power of the nobility was about to be cast down. But the aristocracy profited by political crises and by the weakness of certain reigns, in order to restore its authority. Though it did not succeed in organizing an independent feudal power, after the fashion of the West, and though it knew neither the hierarchy nor the characteristic institutions of the feudal contract, suzerainty, vassalage, homage, and remained legally dependent upon the central power, nevertheless it had by the end of the early Middle Ages acquired at least a quasi-plenitude of sovereignty in its domains. The great Byzantine landowner was master on his lands and exercised jurisdiction over the peasantry. The government obtained the execution of its orders through him, and from being the mandatory of the prince he tended continually to become a sort of local sovereign. He had his clients, thanks to patronage and commendation, and even his vassals, thanks to the general practice of granting benefices. He continued his usurpations at the expense of those small proprietors who refused to become his clients, and he even brought about the desertion of the imperial service by a number of soldiers and officers, who in the tenth century formed a new category of knights (*kaballarioi*), to whom the great nobles granted possessions in return for military service.

Thus, while they lacked full political independence, the Byzantine aristocracy possessed all that social and economic power which comes of the possession of the soil and a number of subjects or vassals. Not only in Asia Minor, the chief centre of the aristocratic class, but also in the European provinces, great lords, such as the scions of the Phocas, Sclerus, Botaniates, Ducas, Comnenus, Palæologus, Bryennius, and Cantacuzene families, held immense properties, sometimes scattered, sometimes concentrated in a single holding. From the fifth century a great lady, Paula, was mistress of the territory of Nicopolis in Epirus. Five centuries later a great Byzantine noble had no less than sixty domains, with 600 oxen, 100 plough teams, 880 horses, 18,000 sheep. A woman of high rank, Danielis, owned eighty *massæ* in the Peloponnesus alone; she had immense herds and an army of slaves, 3,000 of whom she was able to enfranchise by a stroke of the pen; when she travelled she took with her 300 porters for her litters; she had vast hoards of coined money, vessels, and jewels; she seemed, indeed, the real queen of the Morea. Personages such as the Eunuch Basil and Simeon Ampelas were as celebrated in that age as are the American millionaires of our own day. In this world of great nobles were to be found proud, ambitious, turbulent lords, learned men, good administrators, excellent generals, sometimes even ardent patriots, animated by religious and monarchical ideals. They formed a veritable élite, vastly superior in culture, intelligence, and political aptitude to the aristocracy of the West. They dwelt by choice, so far as their duties at court or at war allowed them, in the midst of their domains, surrounded by their vassals and soldiers, superintending the work of their population of labourers, and surrounded by a crowd of domestics. Their dwellings, half palaces and half fortresses, were elegantly decorated, spacious, and beautiful, furnished with huge apartments and *gynæcea* reserved for their women, and in them they exercised an open-handed hospitality. There they displayed all their luxury, their embroidered robes, their gold plate, gems, enamels, and precious silks, their table groaning under abundant foods, their stables full of fine horses and carriages. They loved the pleasures of intelligence no less than those of the chase and of travel, than the lust of battle, or the pride of rule. In fine, they formed a highly gifted class, which lacked only an open character, a high standard of morality, and an upright spirit.

The lesser nobility also lived upon their rural estates, which were small or of medium size, and moderately well stocked. They made their lands prosperous by their own efforts and the aid of a few servants, and only by dint of hard work and severe economy. Country gentlemen, such as Cecaumenus, who has left such curious *Memoirs*, were not rare in the East. They had large families, loved the land passionately, and obtained good revenues from it. " Cultivate corn, wine, and cattle," the wise Cecaumenus was wont to say, " and you will be happy." They had little taste for court life, and found their real satisfaction in family life, in the exploitation of their rustic domains, and in the practice of solid virtues of piety and charity. After the Church, it was this aristocratic class, made up of the greater and lesser nobility, which played the most active social part.

Despite the progress made by the territorial power of the Church and the nobility, small free ownership maintained itself far more successfully in the East than in the West, and greatly to the advantage of the equilibrium of Byzantine society. Side by side with the urban bourgeoisie, which possessed more or less extensive properties within the *banlieue* of the towns, there was in effect in the empire a middle class of free rural proprietors, who still held a considerable portion of the land. In the front rank of these were the soldiers (*stratiotai*), whom the state provided with fiefs or benefices out of the public domains, and conquered or confiscated estates, charged with perpetual military service upon themselves and their male descendants. In the Peloponnesus there were nearly 3,000 of these fiefs, and in the tenth century they numbered 58,000. These small domains remained the property of the state, but the military small holders enjoyed the usufruct thereof, either cultivating them themselves or arranging for their cultivation. They never incurred the loss of their estates unless they ceased to fulfil their military obligations, or were condemned for an infamous crime, or had allowed the value of the fief to become disparaged by bad cultivation. They were not allowed to alienate their domains, but they could transmit them to their families, and exercised real proprietary rights over them.

After these soldier-owners came other small free proprietors, who had the full ownership of goods, gardens, fields, vines, and meadows, which they exploited alone or with the help of *coloni*, or in association with *métayers*, who took a third part of the produce of the estate. They were bound to pay the state taxes, the clerical tithe, and sometimes also a few rents to great men. They had rights over the common woods and pastures, and, grouped into agricultural communes, they governed themselves through their assemblies and notables (*primates*), under the control of imperial agents. The state, which valued them as its most docile taxpayers and its best military recruits, protected them against the usurpation and violence of officials and of great lords. It allowed them judicial assistance if they experienced any difficulty in the peaceful enjoyment of their estates, and was at pains to enforce the restitution of possessions unjustly taken from them. It granted them a right of pre-emption (*protimesis*) in the acquisition of goods which had belonged to members of their class, and even secured the succession to their lands, if these fell into disinheritance, to collateral relations (*cognates*). A long struggle was waged, in the course of which the imperial power succeeded several times in saving the two classes of military beneficiaries and small free proprietors from the perennial attacks of the clergy and nobility. The Isaurian and Macedonian emperors in particular succeeded in restoring and partly liberating free ownership, which maintained its existence for four centuries longer than in the West. It was only in the long run, and after innumerable vicissitudes, that the invincible tenacity of the great lay and ecclesiastical proprietors prevailed over the resistance of the small independent landowners, and it was not until the eleventh century that most of the holders of military benefices tended to become the vassals of the great landed nobles. On their side, the free peasants fell into pauperism, bent beneath the weight of public taxes, and living under the constant menace of their powerful neighbours, often in debt, possessing neither capital nor credit, and without the means of tiding over crises in production and increasing the revenue of their lands. They formed thenceforth that class of the *penetes*, or " poor," who were obliged one by one to resign themselves to the loss first of their free properties, then of their free persons. Of the numerous middle class, which had been for 500 years the sinews of the state and the best instrument of agricultural labour, only a remnant remained.

The great majority of the inhabitants of the countryside in the Eastern Empire consisted, at the end of the early Middle Ages, of *coloni* and serfs. Indeed, at the same time that the small free proprietors were growing weaker and finally succumbing, the various forms of free labour were also disappearing one by one. The agricultural wage-earners or day labourers (*misthotai*), who still in the fifth and sixth centuries hired themselves out for the cultivation of the large and even of the small estates, in return for a wage (*misthos*), were soon eliminated in a state of society in which the landowners preferred to have recourse to the services of more stable cultivators, whom they kept upon their land by means of long contracts, and in dependence upon themselves. For similar motives tenant-farmers and free *métayers*, bound to the landowners by temporary leases, stipulating as a rule for the payment of a fixed rent of a half or a third of the landed revenue, were less and less employed. They were obliged, like the day labourers, to emigrate to the towns or to swell the ranks of *coloni* and serfs.

It is true that rural slavery tended at the same time to disappear. Although it was still recruited from time to time by commerce, with the intermittent toleration of the ruling power, it was discredited by the campaign waged against it, in the name of the Christian Church and the dignity of humanity, by bishops, monks, emperors, great men, and thinkers, heirs to the humanitarian or the religious tradition of the fourth century. Moreover, slave labour gave very inferior results. Imperial legislation forbade free men to enter into slavery, and allowed slaves to intermarry with persons of free condition, an act which in itself emancipated them; it liberated those who joined the ranks of the clergy or the army, prohibited the sale of slaves, and recognized their right to personal property; it favoured and multiplied enfranchisements. Slavery was limited to domestic service. Nevertheless, although the law had abolished all distinction between the freedman (*libertus*) and the freeman (*ingenuus*), very few men of slave birth succeeded in attaining full liberty, which would, in point of fact, have conferred upon them no practical means of independence in the economic order. On the contrary, they contributed in great numbers to swell the crowd of *coloni* and serfs of the glebe (*adscriptitii*).

The class of *coloni* and of serfs was, indeed, made up of diverse elements—small free proprietors fallen upon evil days, wage-earning labourers, *métayers*, tenant-farmers, enfranchised slaves—all of them forced to enter into a contract of strict dependence, as a means of making a livelihood by the cultivation of the soil. The colonate, which had already been formed during the last centuries of the Roman Empire, became general under the Byzantine Empire, and grew ever larger as newcomers arrived to swell its ranks—insolvent debtors, vagabonds attached by law to the domains, individuals destitute of resources, strangers (*advenæ*) without possessions venturing into other men's lands, prisoners of war parcelled out among public or private estates. The *coloni* were inscribed upon the capitation registers, so that the state might levy the tax due from them. In the estate books of each domain they were classed with the farm implements. Established upon the soil, they cultivated it without having any rights of property over it, and paid a large part of the landed revenue to the landowner in the form of *cens* or tribute, and payments, called *canons*, in money or in kind. But in return they enjoyed a perpetual usufruct, transmissible and hereditary, in the holding which they cultivated.

Nevertheless, there developed among the *coloni* two classes of cultivators. The most favoured class, whose members continued to bear the name of *coloni* during the first centuries of the Middle Ages, possessed most of the prerogatives of civil liberty, such as freedom to contract marriage without condition as to domicile, full marital and paternal authority, and testamentary capacity. The less favoured class—that of the semi-servile cultivators, who were known as *adscriptitii* or *enapographoi*, and became very soon merged into the class of serfs (*servi rustici* or *paroikoi*)—was already submitted to galling or heavy restrictions as to marriage and the transmission of holdings and personal property, while at the same time its obligations had increased in number and it had become fixed to the soil, without any guarantee against changes of domicile. Little by little, despite the prohibitions of the Rural Code (eighth century) the *coloni* themselves lost the right of leaving the domain. They became approximated to the *adscriptitii*, and the two categories of the colonate were, during the ninth and tenth centuries, merged into a single class of serfs of the glebe. Serfdom, then, appeared with its true characteristics—the obligation of the cultivator to dwell on the land and to farm it, and the obligation of the land-owner not to expel the tenant, nor to increase the payments due from him. Over and above the serfs there still remained in the East, at the end of the early Middle Ages, *coloni*, whose condition was more or less similar to that of the villeins of the West. These were the *mortitai*, who had preserved a number of the prerogatives of freemen, had the right to leave their holdings, could not be dispossessed after having enjoyed possession during thirty years, and paid only a tenth of the harvest to the landowner. But they were an infinitesimal minority in comparison with the great mass of serfs or *paroikoi*, among whom were to be found almost all the inhabitants of the country districts. These, subject to invariable rents and strictly determined services, had, nevertheless, no guarantee against an illegitimate extension of their burdens, or against ill-treatment by their lord. They were, moreover, obliged to punish *corvées* in order to cultivate the lord's demesne, and to perform carting and other services.

In the East the transformation of agricultural labour was accomplished in the same manner, and by reason of the same economic and social necessities, as in the West. But the disappearance of the small free owners was much less rapid and complete there, and the establishment of serfdom was compensated for by the disappearance of slavery. Serfdom itself was counterbalanced by the admission of a right of perpetual usufruct, vested in the cultivator of the soil, and by the stability of rural life. For the rest, we have but little evidence as to the material and moral condition of the agricultural populations of the Byzantine Empire. It seems to have varied greatly from period to period, being very hard in the first two centuries of the early Middle Ages, and easier and more bearable in the last three. It varied also according to the landowners. In general tenants on the estates of the Church and of the state enjoyed a superior protection and were allowed privileges hardly known upon the property of the nobility. The Byzantine peasants lived sometimes grouped into villages (*choria*), sometimes scattered in farms and hamlets (*aroi, argiridia*), sometimes in fortified burgs (*castra*), whence the men and beasts went forth each morning to the fields. They were content with houses of roughly piled stones, of *pisé*, and of thatch. Their food was frugal; milk, cheese, eggs, vegetables, and fruit were the foundation, and to these they added fish and a little meat when they were able. They lived a narrow life without horizon, in which the chief part was played by religion, superstition, the need to gain their daily bread, and the cares of family life; they held themselves satisfied with their lot, if they had not to suffer too severely from war and natural scourges, and from the rapacity of the treasury and the landlords. In Byzantine society it was their disciplined labour, under the direction of a state conscious of its tutelary mission, the guarantor of order and public peace, and the promoter of colonization and production, which gave to the Eastern Empire its chief economic supremacy.

CHAPTER IV

THE INDUSTRIAL AND COMMERCIAL HEGEMONY OF THE EASTERN EMPIRE
DURING THE EARLY MIDDLE AGES.

INDUSTRIAL and commercial activity also contributed to bring about the economic supremacy of Byzantium, as well as to enrich the state. Indeed, urban economy, completely shattered in the countries of the West, remained intact and even developed in the Eastern Empire.

Industry, which was far more advanced in the East than in the West, was centred in the towns. It is true that there were upon the estates of the nobility and the Church rural workshops in which servile men or women laboured. Some of these, such as those on the domain of Danielis at Patras, even produced objects of luxury, purple tissues, fine cloths, and carpets, while those of the great monasteries sometimes specialized in industrial arts, mosaic work, illumination, and painting, under the direction of the monks. Moreover, family industry was very widespread among the rural population, both free and unfree, and it sufficed for the essential needs of daily life. But urban industry, which had fallen so low in the West, survived and prospered in the East. It was carried on either in the small workshops of entrepreneurs and of free artisans, or in the great state factories, where workmen laboured who were forced to follow their profession from father to son. The imperial laws or novels, and the collection of police regulations called the *Book of the Prefect* (of Byzantium), which was drawn up in the tenth century, show how numerous and how active were the industrial corporations (*systemata*) of the great towns of the empire, heirs of the associations (*collegia, artes, scolæ*) of the Roman period. In them were grouped together both industrial workers and traders; notaries were to be found side by side with bankers, money-changers and jewellers, spice merchants side by side with butchers, pork-butchers, and bakers. Inn-keepers, wine-sellers, cattle-dealers, and fishmongers rubbed elbows with horse-dealers and fishermen, perfumers and candle-makers with tanners and soap-makers. The most numerous of these corporations were concerned with the textile industries, sellers of raw silk, silk-spinners, silk, wool, and cloth-dyers, merchants who dealt in Syrian stuffs and all sorts of fine fabrics. Other professions—for instance, locksmiths, millers, painters, marble and mosaic workers—were grouped into unprivileged crafts. The corporative régime was applied, above all, to the luxury trades and to those of primary necessity. Furthermore, there were imperial manufactures, the personnel of which worked solely to furnish the needs of the army and the imperial palaces.

The privileged or official corporations and the free crafts occupied special quarters in the great towns—at Byzantium, for example, the central street and the environs of the Forum. Workroom and shop were combined, as in the *souks* and Levantine bazaars. An incessant movement, a ceaseless hum of activity, prevailed there. The state often accorded special privileges to craftsmen, artisans, and merchants; it exempted sailors, parchment-makers, and dyers of purple from military service, while most of the members of crafts received a partial exemption from taxation. All the corporations had their monopolies, their meetings, heads, dignitaries, and brotherhoods. No one was admitted to mastership until he had paid a high fee, served his apprenticeship, and given proofs of professional skill. But in return for the advantages thus conceded the state exercised the strictest supervision over the corporations. Byzantium was the paradise not only of monopoly and privilege, but also of regulation. Placed under the authority of the prefect of the town, who regulated the admission of candidates, every official corporation had to submit to administrative rules, minutely regulating the methods by which it obtained its provisions, reserving to each corporation the right of purchasing raw materials, regulating its relations with foreign merchants, limiting the quantity of purchases, and fixing prices, days, and places of sale, and the tariff of profits allowed to the masters. The same regulation was also applied to the technique of manufacture, in order to secure the quality of the goods. State agents entered the workrooms and shops and examined merchandise and account books. From time to time the governing power even tried to fix a maximum wage, and also the price of articles of luxury. This disastrous experiment, which was inaugurated in the time of Justinian, was several times renewed. The state, an interfering protector and a suspicious inquisitor, endeavoured to regulate every side of the corporate organization, and left no room for economic freedom. But the members of the corporations were freemen, citizens, furnished with monopolies and privileges which guaranteed them against competition and gave them a stable existence and the respect of their fellows. Submitting meekly, they bowed themselves beneath the exigences of the imperial treasury or the tiresome vagaries of the administration.

In spite of its defects, this régime gave to urban industry a strong protective armour and a high technical standard, although it was almost inaccessible to progress and remained inferior in vitality and energy to that which the emancipation of the twelfth century was destined to bestow upon the West. In addition, besides the official corporations, the East benefited by the development of numerous free crafts, which were grouped into associations in innumerable large towns and small, and which included the mass of men engaged in industry and trade on a small scale. In these groups, which were submitted only to the general economic regulations, individual initiative and free labour had more scope. Both corporations and free crafts, by their activity and their skill, gave to the East a front rank in industrial production.

Technical skill and variety of form won for Byzantine industry during six centuries its unrivalled supremacy in the world. Its workers produced for a foreign as well as for a home market, and furnished the West as well as the East with goods. They excelled, above all, in articles of luxury, wherein they · displayed a rare ingenuity and elegance. Byzantine industry then occupied the place now taken by French industry, without having to meet the same competition. The Byzantine Empire was famous for the number and excellence of its manufactures of precious fabrics, particularly its silks and fine cloths. Out of the imperial factories came those splendid stuffs, dyed purple and violet, yellow and green, often worked with designs and adorned with embroidery, sometimes woven with gold or silver thread, which were used to make vestments and robes used in ceremonies sacred or profane, and which were eagerly sought by princes, prelates, and the wealthy classes all over Europe. Plain silks, marvellous stuffs of the most delicate shades and of highly finished and varied texture, imperial purples and cloth of gold and of silver, orfray work, samites, cendals, baldequins, cyclatons, chrysoclaves, and yet others, striped or mingled with metal thread or goat's hair, went to swell the treasuries of churches and the elegant rooms of the aristocracy. It was to the Byzantine workshops that men came for fine trimmings, ornaments, and *galons*. There was an enormous market for such things, and the export trade in them was so active that manufacturing centres such as Byzantium, Thessalonica, Patras, Corinth, Athens, and Thebes enjoyed a celebrity similar to that which is to-day enjoyed by Paris and Lyons. Beautiful fine woollens, adorned with rich embroidery, were also manufactured, notably at Patras, while in Pontus, Macedonia, and Naples fine linen goods were produced. The Byzantines excelled in the art of tapestry; their hangings, made of brocaded or damasked stuffs, and adorned with designs of rare perfection, their carpets which imitated panther skins, their worked leather, their purple-dyed skins were unrivalled and everywhere in demand.

Past masters in mining and metallurgy, they exploited the seams of iron, copper, and lead in Asia Minor and Eastern Europe. They sent forth to the Mediterranean countries their marbles from Proconnesus, Attica, Thessaly, Laconia, and the Archipelago, their salt from the salt-marshes of Southern Italy and Mœsia. They had factories of arms at Thessalonica, at Nicopolis in Epirus, in Eubea, at Athens and Thebes, in the Peloponnese, where they manufactured bows and arrows, lances, and cuirasses, sometimes beautifully engraved and decorated. From their workshops in Byzantium and Thessalonica came also marvellous shrines and reliquaries, altars and crosses, sacred vases, censers, dalmatics, jewelled ornaments glittering with rubies and pearls, precious vessels and silverwork of every kind. From the sixth century they brought the art of enamelling to a triumphant height, and their beautiful *cloisonné* and *champlevé* enamel soon spread far and wide. Their engravers and founders worked in bronze, which they inlaid with silver, executing those ornamented plaques, fountains, and monumental gates of which admirable specimens remain in St. Sophia and at Pavia and Rome. Their ivory-workers made charming carved coffers, diptyches, and covers for the gospels, all in the most exquisite taste. They raised to an unexampled degree of perfection all the decorative arts, stained and filigreed and enamelled glasswork, mosaics, and porcelain; and veritable masterpieces issued from their workshops in Byzantium, Salonica, Ravenna, and Southern Italy. These masters of elegance finally furnished the world with every sort of article of luxury, perfumes, papyrus, manuscripts, psalters, decorated and illuminated gospels, which their laboratories and workrooms alone knew how to make or to adorn. It was due to this superiority in industry, no less than to the wealth which they drew from agriculture, that the Byzantines kept their commercial supremacy for so long.

Indeed, in the early Middle Ages the Byzantine Empire enjoyed a monopoly of the international commerce of Christendom, which continued to be centred in the Mediterranean Sea. Byzantium lay at the meeting-place of all the great trade routes, both maritime and territorial, of Western Asia and Europe, and possessed, moreover, a regular system of land and sea transport and highly perfected methods of exchange, which the West lacked. The empire was thus able to carry on both an export and a carrying trade, and her commerce could attain a width of scope which was impossible for the Western states. For 600 years it continued to flourish incomparably, and the market and Customs dues alone at Constantinople brought into the imperial treasury in the eleventh century an annual revenue of 7,300,000 bezants of gold.

Nevertheless, the commercial policy of the state, inspired by old-fashioned traditions or by fiscal motives, was a great hindrance to trade. The government retained the monopoly of certain articles of commerce, notably of the corn and silk trades. It prohibited the export of various goods, such as luxury textiles and precious metals, as well as of numerous foreign manufactures. Other articles—for instance, the soaps of Marseilles—were merely burdened with import duties. There were further duties on export. In the interior taxes were laid upon purchases and sales; they were fiscal rather than economic in character, but they were infinitely troublesome by reason of their multiplicity, which was aggravated by the behaviour of the tax-collectors. But the gravest mistake made by the Byzantine Empire was to leave to foreigners the virtual monopoly of the import and export trade, instead of stimulating the efforts of its own subjects, who became increasingly idle and passive. The emperors had thought thus to inspire these foreigners, whom commercial necessity had drawn to the shores of the Bosphorus, with a respect for the greatness and wealth of Byzantium; but they were unwittingly preparing the way for the commercial development of the Western barbarians, whom they both despised and feared. In the long run they paralyzed national commerce and reduced it to the rôle of a passive broker, while they made the fortune of the young commercial nations who served them as intermediaries. Byzantine policy both needed and mistrusted foreigners. Thus it welcomed them with exemptions and privileges, but forced them into rivalry one with another by the unequal treatment which it accorded to them. It multiplied inquisitorial measures, formalities, confiscations, perquisites, fines, and vexatious regulations directed against them; but it could not wear out their patience, which was rooted in the love of gain.

In spite, however, of this shortsighted economic policy and this rigid regulation, applied by a swarm of Customs officials and judges, the Byzantine Empire possessed in some ways a superior commercial organization, well fitted for the development of trade. From the beginning of the Middle Ages it inaugurated a régime of international money, a gold standard. This was the bezant, or Byzantine gold piece, the type of good money, usually of invariable value, the standard coin in all the markets of the world. Although credit was hampered by restrictive and complicated legislation, and money-lending at interest (under the influence of the Church) was hardly distinguished from usury, Byzantine commerce, thanks to the abundance of movable wealth, could raise money at the moderate rate of 8 to 12 per cent., and lower still in the tenth century, a thing unknown in the rest of Europe. The law limited the rate of interest, but there was no permanent restriction upon money loans. The number and social importance of the money-changers and bankers at Byzantium, where they had a powerful corporation, are sufficient indication of the development of a money market there. The Byzantines forestalled the Italians in the use of the bill of exchange, or the credit notes which were its equivalent. Traffic was active on the land routes; the old Roman roads of the Balkan Peninsula and Southern Italy were repaired or completed, innumerable bridges were built or rebuilt over the rivers; wells, cisterns, and shelters were made on the caravan routes, and although Justinian was so ill-advised as to suppress the public postal service, the Byzantines usually favoured transport. They attracted merchants from all nations to the great fairs of Byzantium and Thessalonica, which enjoyed valuable exemptions and privileges. Though they established a tiresome system of regulation over markets, they did ensure the security and regularity of business transactions. Though merchant strangers were obliged to reside in special quarters and submitted to administrative surveillance, and though some of them, such as the Russians, were allowed to stay only for a limited period, the majority were permitted to reside permanently within the empire, to form privileged communities, and to have their own consuls. The Bulgarians themselves benefited by this favour. To the Italian men of business, subjects of the empire who came from Amalfi, Naples, Gæta, Venice, or Genoa, Byzantium extended a still warmer welcome and permitted them to establish counting-houses in the ports. The Venetians henceforth had their quarter near the Golden Horn, and the Genoese at Galata. Important exemptions and privileges facilitated their operations.

An intelligent and active policy sought to open foreign markets, if not to the native traders, who, with the exception of the Syrians, were unwilling to expatriate themselves, at least to Byzantine trade, by means of numerous treaties with foreign states. The empire knew how to keep up and fit out its ports, to organize labour services and corporations of dockers. It favoured sea commerce, practised insurance and loans on bottomry, and its code of commercial law assisted the organization of shipping companies, which divided profits and losses among themselves. The Byzantine *Nautical Code*, the work of Leo III, and an adaptation of the ancient laws of Rhodes, was the first body of commercial regulations which prevailed in medieval Christendom. It was under the inspiration of Byzantium that the Customs of the Italian republics of Trani and Amalfi were drawn up in the eleventh century. The Byzantine mercantile marine, easily recruited among the coastal populations of the Archipelago, who were long inured to maritime traffic, was the mistress of the Mediterranean, where its flag was everywhere to be seen. A vigilant police made war upon piracy and kept the sea safe against Dalmatians, Varangians, and Moslems.

An immense movement of exchange, the most active in the civilized world, was thus centred in the Byzantine Empire. Thence, at first through the medium of colonies of Syrian merchants, ancestors of the Levantines, then through that of the men of Amalfi, the Venetians, the Genoese, and the Armenians, there spread throughout both East and West the products of the Byzantine soil and manufactures—beautiful silks, fine cloths, pieces of goldsmiths' work, carved ivories, delicate glass, onyx cups, chased and enamelled vases, mosaics, fruits, delicate wines, and other choice and luxurious articles. By means of Byzantine commerce, fed by caravans which came from the ends of Asia and Africa, and also through the Arab and Turkish merchants established by imperial permission at Constantinople, Europe received the precious merchandise of Asia Minor, Chaldea, Assyria and Persia, of India and the Far East, and of Egypt and the African lands; spices, scents, precious stones, rare metals, sandal-wood, musk and camphor, raw silk and cotton, silken and fine woollen fabrics, muslins, and carpets. From an early date treaties of commerce were concluded with the Moslem powers to facilitate these trades. From the barbarous regions round the Caspian Sea, Turkestan, and the lands of the Volga and Dnieper, by the medium of the Greek republic of Kherson, or even directly by the hands of Varangian, Bulgar, Turkish, and Khazar merchants whom she attracted to the shores of the Bosphorus, Constantinople obtained a mass of natural products—corn, salt fish, wax, skins, furs, salt, honey, caviare, the skins of animals, amber, and slaves. From the eighth century Slav and Bulgar and Magyar traders swarmed to Thessalonica and Byzantium along the rivers and the great trade routes, to retail their flax, honey, salt fish, cattle, skins, leather, furs, and half-worked iron and steel. From Italy, Germany, Spain, and Gaul there came to the Byzantine ports and entrepôts metals raw and worked, raw wool, hempen or linen cloths, coarse woollen goods, and rough carpets. Like innumerable tributaries, all these streams of commerce converged upon the vast empire to swell the great movement of commerce which was concentrated within its walls.

The ports offered a spectacle of extraordinary activity. It was commerce which, together with industry, maintained that town life, which was a privilege preserved by the East alone. The Byzantine Empire was covered with great industrial and mercantile cities, the animation of which astounded visitors from the West. Greatest of all was Constantinople, the finest city in the world, " sovereign over all others," as Villehardouin hailed her; " the richest city in the world, which holdeth two-thirds of all the wealth of the universe," as Robert de Clari said. Constantinople was the entrepôt of world commerce; ships and caravans made their way towards her roadsteads, and in the bazaars of her main streets the products of the whole world were to be seen heaped up; her quays and her docks overflowed with merchandise. A forest of ships lay alongside her quays, and a crepitating mass of people filled her quarters. In this home of wealth and luxury, adorned with all the gifts of civilization, lived a million men, the greatest agglomeration of inhabitants to be found anywhere in the Middle Ages. As many as 70,000 barbarians were to be found there. It was a cosmopolitan city, and underneath it was a Levantine city; but these facts did not affect its air of elegance and luxury, wherein business went side by side with the cult of intelligence and art. The empire possessed other cities, which surpassed all those in the rest of Christendom—Heracleia, Selymbria, Rodosto on the Thracian coast; Thessalonica, the second metropolis and port of the empire, " one of the strongest and richest towns in Christendom," as the Crusaders witnessed, where dwelt 500,000 souls; Negrepont, Athens, Patras, Nauplia, and Corinth in Greece; Corfu, Durazzo, Avlona, Nicopolis at the mouth of the Ionian or Adriatic Seas; not to speak of the Crimean republic of

Kherson and the Dalmatian cities, such as Ragusa and Spoleto, which were under the protectorate of Byzantium. Inland in the Balkan Peninsula Adrianople and Chrysopolis were prosperous. The Byzantine domination made the fortunes of the cities of Southern Italy, Bari and Reggio, Tarentum and Salerno, Brindisi and Naples, which rivalled each other in wealth and prosperity; above all, of Amalfi, which from the ninth to the eleventh century dominated the Western Mediterranean. Finally, it was under the auspices of Byzantium that Venice, a humble settlement of fishermen, became in 600 years the queen of the Adriatic and of Mediterranean commerce and heir to the splendour of Ravenna.

Everywhere in the cities, below the aristocracy of senators, high dignitaries, and great landowners, who displayed all the luxury of an elegant and refined existence, lived an active and intelligent bourgeoisie of bankers, industrialists, and merchants. These, together with the master craftsmen and the small tradesmen, able men and greedy for gain, formed a middle class which was one of the chief forces of Byzantine society and enriched it by its labour. This class grew without ceasing. It took the place of the *curiales* of the Roman period, who had disappeared in the troubles of the sixth century; and in the tenth and eleventh centuries, associating its interests with those of the landed nobility, who were very willing to live in the towns, it won a share in municipal government, elected its representatives (*judices, boni homines*) to assist in urban administration, and obtained economic and financial privileges. This class, which had the faults inherent in a constant struggle for gain, could also display powerful social virtues such as the love of work, economy, a simple and regular life, and the practice of charity. The lower rank of artisans, grouped in their corporations and fraternities, formed, together with the middle class, the vital element of the Byzantine cities. It was to them that the fame of Eastern industry was due; they were intelligent and hard-working, and they knew their own worth. At Byzantium men had seen a workman, Leo the Isaurian, bind the diadem upon his brow and found a dynasty. Corporative life gave them a certain taste for independence and a sense of solidarity.

LIFE AND WORK IN MEDIEVAL EUROPE

Writers who described the life of these small folk of the workshops depicted them full of life and vivacity and sallies, fond of pleasure, content with little, devoted to their family life, and alternately turbulent and docile, sceptical and mocking, devout and fanatical, mobile and exuberant, always easy to lead, if those in authority were able to manage them without brutality and to ensure them plenty of cheap food and amusements. It was only at Constantinople and at Thessalonica that this lower class, at bottom honest and hard-working, and sometimes even showing a certain refinement, intelligence, and sentiment, suffered from contact with the proletariat of idlers and adventurers, who swarmed in the underworld of these great cities. It was these troublesome elements—parasites—who were, turn by turn, cowardly, seditious, bloodthirsty, and fierce, who gave the Byzantine townsfolk the bad reputation from which they suffered for so long. In reality the prosperity of industry and commerce in Eastern society was as much the work of the free urban artisans as it was of the intelligent bourgeosie and of the state, which was the protector of labour. Great landowners and princes who promoted colonization, free peasants and *coloni* wearing themselves out to bring the land into cultivation, merchants labouring to develop trade, master craftsmen and artisans proud of the good name and the activity of the workshops—all of these helped to make the Byzantine Empire the richest state in the world, a state whose public revenue reached the sum of 600 million francs, an equivalent of six milliards to-day, while the imperial treasury was able to heap up a reserve of two to four milliards, a state whose prestige dazzled for so long the nations of the West.

CHAPTER V

ECONOMIC AND SOCIAL INFLUENCE OF BYZANTINE CIVILIZATION IN EAST
AND WEST.

THE Eastern Empire before its decline rendered eminent services to civilization. It restored a new life to Italy, ruined by invasions; the Romagna, the Pentapolis (Ancona and Rimini), Istria, Venetia, Sicily, and, above all, Græcia Magna became once more, thanks to the empire, oases of wealth in a peninsula ravaged by the barbarians. By its diplomacy and its military superiority, and still more by the activity of its missionaries and the prestige of its culture, Byzantium accomplished in the barbarian world of the East the same work of civilization which Rome had once performed in the Western world. She taught them the advantages of ordered and fruitful labour when she civilized them and led them to Christianity. She Hellenized and Slavized the old Roman colonies, the Vlachs of Epirus, Southern Albania, Acarnania, Thessaly, and Pindus, although she never succeeded in weaning them from their habit of brigandage and from a pastoral to an agricultural life. But if she left the Albanians to return to their wild and primitive tribal life, she did at least succeed in elevating to a civilized existence the tribes of the great Slav race, of which she was the true educator. She spread her civilization among the Slavs of Dacia, who had intermingled with Latin *coloni*, the Roumanians of the future, as well as among the Slavs of the Moravian Empire, who were converted to the Greek faith in the ninth century by the Byzantine Apostles Cyril and Methodius, and among the Slovenes of Pannonia and Norica. The influence of the West later displaced that of Byzantium among Moravians and Slovenes, but Byzantine civilization persisted among the Slavized Roumanians of Transylvania.

It was Byzantine culture which triumphed over the barbarism of the Serbs established on the banks of the Danube and Save, and in the mountains of Montenegro, Dalmatia, Bosnia, and Rascia (Novibazar), on the edge of the Vardar

57

basin, and in the Morava district between the seventh and tenth centuries. It was Byzantium which converted them to the Orthodox faith, and under her influence the Serbian and Croatian tribes, grouped into confederations (*plemes*) and tribes (*volosts*), under small chiefs (*jupans*), succeeded after becoming the vassals of Basileus, in organizing themselves into states under a Grand Jupan, to whom in the tenth century the emperor granted the title of prince, or duke, or consul, or king. They formed a court modelled upon that of Byzantium, with a nobility of archons or counts and barons, and a rich and respected body of ecclesiastics. At the same time the family community (*zadruga*) became modified, and grants of individual property on the Roman or Byzantine model began to be found side by side with the primitive tribal or family estates. The more or less homogeneous mass of immigrants split up on contact with the ancient cultivators of the soil, the majority of whom sank from the position of *coloni* to that of serfs under their new masters. A settled existence and the neighbourhood of the empire wrought a partial transformation in the economic institutions of the South Slavs, some of whom followed a pastoral life in the mountains or piracy on the coast, while the others became excellent cattle-raisers, farmers, and vine-growers. Now that their state had become more stable and more peaceful, this agricultural population, which was unacquainted with town life, grew so quickly that Serbo-Croatia in the tenth century had a population of about two millions.

Other peoples also owed their introduction to civilized life to Byzantium. In Mœsia dwelt the Bulgars, rude and fierce Turanians, who had come from the Russo-Asiatic plains to settle on both shores of the Danube in the course of the seventh century (659), and who were converted by Byzantium (864-5) and Slavized with extreme rapidity, and so completely that they adopted the Serbian language. These terrible raiders became like the Slavs, transformed beneath the action of the Byzantines. They renounced their turbans, their horse-tail standards, and their little war-chiefs, in order to adopt the Byzantine dress and institutions. They founded a despotic monarchy, and their prince (*Khagan*) proclaimed himself *tsar*, and at the beginning of the tenth century founded in the Balkans and beyond the Danube an empire, where he posed as the rival of Basileus so successfully that the latter was obliged to destroy him after a desperate struggle. At Preslav, on the great river, he had a capital, wherein he aped clumsily enough the luxury of the Byzantine court. His aristocracy of *boliads* and *boyárs*, a nobility of officials, and great landowners as at Byzantium, married into Byzantine families, and received a Greek education, and his clergy similarly formed an independent church following the Greek rite, which came to own a large part of the landed property of the country. The Roman *coloni* were for the most part reduced to serfdom. Under this pseudo-Greek government agricultural prosperity was very great. A tenth century chronicle bears witness that this Hellenized Bulgaria " abounded in all good things," especially in corn, cattle, and salt, and that the population had grown immensely ("multitudo magna et populus multus "), although there were no towns. The Bulgars, whose rustic airs were mocked by Byzantium, grew rich by trading with Hungary and the Greek Empire, whence they obtained wines, fruits and gold, embroidered robes, pearls, and diadems. In their fortified villages, such as Ochrida, the Byzantines more than once found what great wealth had been amassed by these semi-barbarians, with their veneer of Greek civilization. Indeed the Magyars themselves in the tenth century very nearly succumbed to the attraction of Byzantium, with which they were in commercial relations, and it was not until the eleventh century that Western influence attached them to Latin civilization.

Finally, beyond the Danube, in the great Sarmatic plain, the pagan Slavs, conquered by the Scandinavians, a Slav form of whose name they adopted (Varangians, Rus), determined in the course of the tenth century to turn towards Byzantium, which they had tried in vain to destroy in their expeditions of 907 and 945. The Varangians had founded the first Russian states at Novgorod, Smolensk, and Kiev. They had grouped the Slav population under their war-chiefs, and transformed the old patriarchal nobility into a new military aristocracy of boïards, and the *comitatus* of the chief, which was known as the *druzhína*. But they had been incapable of civilizing Russia, where they had merely built up a business of brigandage on a large scale, which exploited the indigenous populations by means of tributes in kind, and strangers by means of piracy. Byzantium drew them little by little towards a civilized existence. She enrolled them as mercenaries, and lured them with the bait of regular commercial relations by opening her markets to them. From the reign of the Emperor Leo VI in the ninth century she began to send them missionaries, and they were finally converted at the end of the tenth century (989). Thenceforward Russia was half civilized, a strange mixture of Germanic and Byzantine institutions. The first state in which the tribes were merged appeared under Yaroslav the Great (1015-1054), who dignified himself with Greek titles. His power still maintained a half-Scandinavian aspect, and his aristocratic entourage of *gridi* and *boyars* sometimes recalls the comitatus of the German kings, and sometimes the Byzantine nobility. A Church was organized with the liturgy, traditions, and territorial wealth of the Church in the Greek Empire. The patriarchal régime grew weaker, and the class of freemen diminished, while the moujiks ("men of naught") became more and more dependent, after the model of the Byzantine *coloni*. Society became stable; communal property became individual property; culture advanced, and the Russian state grew rich on its active commerce with Byzantium, to which it was united by agreements, which abolished the old barbarian usages. For two centuries more Byzantine civilization impregnated the young Christian Russia so deeply that it left an ineffaceable mark.

The East Roman Empire thus accomplished, during the early Middle Ages, a task of supreme importance. It had received undiminished the heritage of Rome and added to it. It left a profound mark upon every kind of work. It succeeded in colonizing the Christian lands of Eastern Europe, and it civilized the barbarians, calling them to the fruitful labours of peace. It gave a powerful impulse to every form of economic activity, and carried the production of wealth to the highest point. If in the social order it only half succeeded in protecting free labour and free property against the exploitation and usurpations of the aristocratic classes, it yet suppressed slavery, and strove with all its strength to maintain the middle class, both urban and rural. Thus it placed itself in the van of civilization, whose great traditions it carried on, and it was partly to Byzantium that the West in its turn went to school to be prepared for its own civilizing mission.

CHAPTER VI

THE WORK OF CHURCH AND STATE IN THE REORGANIZATION OF LABOUR
AND IN THE ECONOMIC AND SOCIAL RESTORATION OF WESTERN
CHRISTENDOM DURING THE DARK AGES.

DURING the centuries which followed the barbarian invasions and settlements, the Christian West laboured painfully and obscurely at the work of social and economic reconstruction. It was a long business, beset by innumerable difficulties, and only partially successful, but it prepared the way for the great flowering of Western civilization which took place at the height of the Middle Ages.

The attempts at reconstruction were due, in part, to the new governments, but mainly to the action of the Church and of the various classes of Western society. The idea of the state, which had been almost lost at the time of the invasions, came to light once again in the countries of the West. The Germanic kingdoms, after having unwittingly allowed the organization of the Roman Empire to perish, set themselves to study the imperial tradition, which was preserved by the Church and by a fraction of the aristocracy, in order to establish a stable framework in which, step by step, the new society might be reconstituted. The invincible tendency of the peoples of the early Middle Ages to division and localism was thus corrected by a minimum of authority and of unity. The Western states amalgamated as best they could Germanic institutions with the Roman principles of hierarchy and administration, in order to bestow upon their subjects the kind of organization necessary to reconstitute the forces of production. The effort was incoherent and intermittent, and interrupted by periods of anarchy, but it was sufficiently efficacious to bring about a partial reorganization of Western Christendom between the seventh and the middle of the ninth century. This work, which the most intelligent of the barbarian kings sought to accomplish, and which has saved their names from oblivion, was begun by the Visigoth Euric in Aquitaine, by Gundobad in Burgundy in the fifth century, by Clovis, Brunhild, and

RECONSTRUCTION OF THE WEST

Dagobert in the sixth and seventh centuries, and, above all, by Theodoric the Great and the Ostrogoths in Italy at the beginning of the sixth century. The newly converted Lombard kings, Authari, Rothari, and Luitprand, took it up again with greater success in the seventh and eighth centuries, and the Visigothic kings of Spain essayed it after their conversion at the end of the sixth century. It was the chief claim to glory of the Carolingian dynasty, and, above all, of Charlemagne, who spread its effects throughout the West. Finally, in England, it won for some of the successors of the first Christian kings, such as Egbert, and, above all, Alfred the Great (ninth century), a well-deserved renown. Alone among the Christian lands of the West, Ireland was powerless to advance from the political régime of clans and tribal federations to the conception of the state, a weakness of organization which contributed to bring about the eclipse of her brilliant civilization. Everywhere else hereditary monarchies were being organized, with centralizing tendencies which attempted to restore that peaceful and ordered state of society, in which alone work could be effectively carried on. This need for authority led in the year 800 to the restoration of the Western Empire, to the profit of Charlemagne and the Carolingians, the leading promoters of the idea of the state. It was, in a sense, the consecration of the work accomplished during two centuries by the princes of the West on behalf of public stability.

The governments of the West, although obliged to allow full scope to aristocratic influences and to survivals of Germanic institutions, were yet inspired by Roman and Christian principles in the amelioration of their justice, the unification and improvement of their legislation, and the reorganization of their police, and in their attempt to substitute for family or private vengeance the repression of crime by public authority. Everywhere they tried to favour social peace by encouraging the amalgamation of the varied elements out of which the peoples of the West were composed. Everywhere they sought to revive intellectual culture. The barbarian kings, heirs of Rome and servants of the idea of the Roman Church, promoted the conquest of pagan lands and the colonization and repopulation of the West. They stimulated work in their domains with all the forces at their command. They tried to save free landownership, and protected the *coloni* and the serfs; some of them, the Carolingians and the Anglo-Saxon kings, even sketched out a sort of system of poor relief. Their fostering care extended to all sides of economic production. They were at pains to establish public wealth by bringing men back to the land and favouring works of agricultural improvement or the conquest of sterile soil. They made their domains model estates, such as were the *villæ* of Charlemagne. They concerned themselves to prevent the wasteful cutting down of forests. Similarly, they encouraged industrial production and tried, as Charlemagne did, to establish the best workshops on their estates. Above all, they turned their attention towards re-establishing commercial activity, for they saw in it the surest means of enriching their states. Hence the solicitude shown by Theodoric, Rothari, Luitprand, the Visigothic and Anglo-Saxon kings, and the Carolingians, above all, by Charlemagne, in re-establishing and securing the safety of roads, reorganizing means of transport by land and sea, restoring markets, fairs and ports, protecting both merchants and consumers, re-establishing a sound coinage, guaranteeing national commerce against excessive foreign competition, and developing both internal and external trade. Indeed, there was lacking only the spirit of continuity and the power of execution to enable these Western governments to bring about a new triumph of the Roman tradition in the realm of labour. But they could only sketch the outlines of a work, which was destined to be taken up again three centuries later.

The action of the Western Church went deeper, because it was more methodical and more continuous. Heir to the Roman tradition of authority and embodiment of the ancient civilization as transformed by Christianity, the Church offered to the West the only model of an ordered and stable government, in which authority was combined with liberty, the only really living unity, which was founded on a community of beliefs and on the principles of Christian society. Under the continuous, methodical, and clear-sighted direction of the papacy, especially from the time of Gregory the Great, enjoying the support of the Merovingian and Carolingian state and the co-operation of the mystic army of monks and missionaries, Aquitanians, Irish, Anglo-Saxons, and Franks, the Church successively converted the Arian Visigoths and Burgundians, the Celts of Ireland and Wales, the Salian Franks, the Anglo-Saxons, and the pagan Germans, all in the space of four hundred years. She thus founded the provinces of a new Latin and Christian Empire, and gave to Western Europe the form which it kept throughout the Middle Ages. Not only did she carry the frontiers of a restored civilization as far as the Elbe and the Highlands of Scotland, but she also exercised a decisive influence upon the social and economic reconstruction of the West. Clerks and monks occupied an important place among the owners of the soil; they set themselves to attract and to keep there a rural population, either by multiplying the enfranchisements of slaves, or by stabilizing the condition of serfs. The Church laboured on behalf of social peace, introduced the right of sanctuary, and restricted the right of vengeance. She seconded the efforts of the kings to repress anarchy, brigandage, and family feuds. She multiplied works of charity, hospitals, lazar-houses, and alms-houses. She ennobled family life, and elevated the position of women by prohibiting the pagan polygamy, opposing moral disorders, and securing the recognition of the legal right of female heiresses in succession questions. She set herself, finally, to civilize the barbarian society of the West by reorganizing schools and education.

In the economic sphere the rôle of the Church was even more efficacious. From the beginning she never ceased to proclaim the obligation to work as a divine law. Monastic orders inscribed it as a fundamental article of their rule, and imposed it on all their members. Moreover, the requirements of existence and the need to exploit the great domains which she owned forced the Church to take in hand the direction of agricultural colonization, in which she played an important part. Mystical ideal and practical reality alike led her leaders to undertake the reclamation of waste land and the cultivation of the soil, and to take the initiative in improved methods of cultivation. For the same reasons of general and of class interest, bishops and monks supported the renaissance of industrial centres, reorganized production in the monastic workshops, sought to promote and revive trade, and even took a direct share in organizing it. The example of the Church and that of the rulers of the state stimulated the zeal of the lay aristocracy and freemen. A general movement carried the West into new paths and pushed it towards the re-establishment of all that economic activity which the barbarian invasions had destroyed. Under the direction and sometimes with the direct collaboration of these classes, which formed the élite of Western society, the mass of the people became the humble instruments of this work of restoration.

CHAPTER VII

THE work of reconstruction was mainly concerned with the land, which had become almost the sole source of capital in a society in which natural economy prevailed. The whole cycle of production and consumption revolved round the land, which furnished the men of this age with almost all the elements of life. It was the land which provided the material for trade, which was then limited to what could take place between an infinite number of small isolated groups. Upon its development depended the economic progress and the social evolution, which were beginning to manifest themselves. Agricultural colonization was the great concern of those centuries which followed the invasions and settlement of the barbarians. Indeed, if economic events be given the place in history which is their due, it should rank as one of the capital facts in the history of the last four centuries of the Dark Ages, for it had decisive results upon the direction taken by medieval social evolution.

At the end of the seventh century it was necessary to take up again the work of civilization which had been performed by the Romans, and to this work the new states, inspired by the spirit of Rome, applied themselves. This was the policy of Theodoric the Great in Italy, the Lombard kings in the seventh and eighth centuries, the kings of Wessex and Alfred the Great, the Carolingians and Charlemagne. They sought, in the words which Orosius uses of the King of the Ostrogoths, " to turn the barbarians to the ploughshare," and to lead them " to hate the sword." They recalled landowners to their estates, themselves setting an example of solicitude for rural cultivation. They tried to fix the people to the soil. They encouraged the reclamation of waste land by exempting it from taxation and conceding rights of property or of usufruct to the reclaimers. They settled *coloni* on empty lands and transported whole populations to reclaim lands which had been devastated, or the virgin soil of barbarian countries. Thus it was that Septimania (Lower Languedoc) was colonized in the ninth century by Gothic emigrants from Spain, and Catalonia in the tenth by colonists from Gaul. Gallo-Roman and Frankish immigrants began to reclaim the whole of Germany, establishing themselves between the Rhine and the Elbe, and the Alps and the Danube, while colonists of Germanic origin came in thousands to colonize Alamannia, Western Neustria, Austria, and Styria, and Slav colonies were created in Hesse and Thuringia. Military colonization on the frontiers, in the *marches*, aided the development of civil colonization; the soldiers lent their assistance to the colonists who were reclaiming the land. Both were the order of the day, in particular during the Carolingian epoch, and both contributed considerably to transform the aspect of the West.

More effective still was the colonizing activity of the Church and, above all, of the monastic orders. Bishops frequently became the leaders in agricultural improvements: Germain of Paris planted vines, and Eleutherus of Lisieux lived in the midst of his labourers. The Church of Rheims brought its domain under cultivation in the seventh century by means of an appeal for settlers. Western monachism, departing from the contemplative ideal of the monks of the East, and for the most part refraining from settlement in towns, set the cultivation of the soil as an object for the activity of hermits scattered throughout the countryside. This impulse became decisive when the two great reformers of monasticism, the Italian Benedict of Nursia (sixth century) and the Irishman Columban (seventh century), grouped their monks into powerful associations, concentrated them in vast monasteries, and imposed upon them the rule of limited or unlimited manual labour, as an obligation imposed by God Himself, and as a means of subduing the flesh. In order to banish idleness, " the enemy of the soul," Benedict of Nursia assigned six or seven hours of manual labour daily to his monks, whom Europe thenceforth knew by the name of " workers " *par excellence* (*monachi laborantes*). Columban demanded that his monks should labour until they were exhausted; " let them go to their repose broken with weariness, and sleep upon their feet." Moreover, the ascetic ideal fitted in well with economic necessities. Established in forests and wastelands, the monks, in order to live in their communities, were forced to break up the soil. Thus the Benedictines, in virtue of their rule, wore a pruning-hook in their girdles as a sign of their habitual occupation. Columban always moved with an escort of woodcutters. The monk Theodulf, near Rheims, ceased not for twenty-two years to drive the plough, which after his death was kept as an object of veneration at the Church of Saint-Thierry. The famous monastic reformer of the ninth century, Benedict of Aniane, laboured, dug, and reaped, in the midst of his monks. The wide acres of heath and waste and woodland which the great and the pious granted to the Church were immediately attacked by these holy pioneers, assisted by bands of peasants, who knew that beneath the shadow of the cloister walls they would find an easier and more certain existence. In clearings in the woods, on islands in the fens, and round about springs, the monks raised their huts of branches, followed by buildings of wood or of stone; they drained, cleared, cut down trees, rooted out stumps, made meadows and fields, sometimes even vineyards and orchards. During 300 years they constituted themselves the persevering and methodical promoters of the first agricultural colonization of the West.

Even allowing for the exaggerations of hagiographical narratives, it is undeniable that monasticism played a rôle of the greatest importance. Inconsiderable in Spain, where the Arab invasion prevented it from developing, monastic colonization had the happiest results in the other Christian states of the West. In Italy, now in the deserted and marshy plains, now in the mountains, the Abbeys of Monte Cassino, Subiaco, Farfa, Saint-Vincent of Volterno, Polirone, Novalese, Leno, Pomposa, and, above all, Bobbio, rose like so many little centres of culture. Ireland, the isle of saints, which organized the last-named of these Italian monasteries, Gallo-Roman Aquitaine, and England, which was full of ardent neophytes, strove with each other to sow the lands of the West with their laborious monastic colonies, and rendered a service to civilization which should never be forgotten. Ireland, the islands of Scotland, the coasts of Wales, became peopled with great monasteries, such as Bangor and Iona.

LIFE AND WORK IN MEDIEVAL EUROPE

The Anglo-Saxon kingdoms owed the first great enterprises of clearance and cultivation to their monasteries at Jarrow, Crowland, Ramsay, Evesham, and Glastonbury. In Gaul from the sixth century eighty establishments were created by monks in the Valleys of the Sâone and Rhône, ninety-four between the Pyrenees and the Loire, and fifty-four between the Loire and the Vosges. From 228 at the beginning of the seventh century the number rose to 1,108 in the 400 years which followed up to the end of the tenth century. Everywhere to these monasteries there cling memories of lands cleared and villages founded, the names of which still bear witness to their origin. Agricultural centres were organized by hundreds and thousands round great abbeys such as Monte Maggiore and Aniane, Saint-Guilhem du Désert and Moissac, Solignac and Charroux, Saint-Maixent and Anison, Saint-Benôit-sur-Loire and Saint-Mesmin, Saint-Wandrille and Jumièges, Saint-Riquier and Corbie, Luxeuil and Remiremont. Northern Gaul and Burgundy, Alamannia, Franconia, and Swabia were colonized under the direction of pious missionaries—Amandus, Eligius, Columban, Gall, Emmeran. The monasteries of Saint-Omer, Saint-Bertin, Saint-Pierre de Gand, Elnone, Saint-Trond, Stavelot, Malmédy, Prüm, Echternach, Saint-Hubert, Murbach, Wissenburg, Hagenau, Reichenau, Saint-Gall, Kempten, Ebersberg, Friessen, St. Peter of Salzbourg, and many others, were the first centres of widespread agricultural colonization in their districts. In the old pagan Germany, converted by Winfrith (St. Boniface) and his disciples, the monks played a yet more active part. It was there, round Fulda, Fritzlar, Hameln, Erfurt, Marburg, Corvey, and other monasteries, that the work of reclaiming the soil of Germany was really organized. Monastic colonization, in conjunction with official colonization, both civil and military, carried the boundaries of cultivation as far as the Elbe, the Danube, and the North Sea.

The work also received vigorous support from the great landowners, who, more especially during the Carolingian era, sought in the reclamation of the soil an increase in the value and revenue of their domains. More fruitful still was the obscure but determined part played in the work by legions of small free proprietors and peasant pioneers, whose rôle has been too long misunderstood and has only recently been brought to light. Under the protection of kings, bishops, and great landowners, often even on their own initiative, these humble labourers set forth in search of waste and uncultivated lands or tracts of forest, which were given over to their activity. More often still they profited by the recognized right of every pioneer to appropriate, by the act of putting them under cultivation (*aprisio, bifang*), lands belonging to rural communes and other collective owners. They made clearings (*roden, assarts*) with their axes in the forests, and brought the heaths under cultivation. They fertilized the lands thus won by piling up stumps, tree trunks, thorns, and brambles in enormous heaps and setting fire to them. With plough and spade they extirpated new shoots and roots. They built causeways over the marshes and drained them by means of dykes. They undertook, sometimes, as in the time of Charlemagne, with the assistance of the state, to embank rivers such as the Loire, and thus in Italy, Gaul, and Flanders the wild waters were, in part, conquered. A humble work, perhaps, but the intensity with which it was carried on is witnessed by the multitudes of place names in the West, dating from this period, which preserve the memory of these clearings, drainages, embankments by which kings, monks, large and small landowners, free, half-free, and servile pioneers sought, for the first time in the Middle Ages, to reclaim good fertile land from sterile wilderness.

The results were, it is true, inferior to the effort, and agricultural production was far from increasing in the same proportion as the ardour of colonization. The invasions of the ninth and tenth centuries helped to reduce the effects of all this effort. But the principal cause of its relative ineffectiveness must be sought in the predominance of the system of natural economy itself, which was then an insufficient stimulus to activity, content with rudimentary methods of cultivation, and incapable of promoting a greater productivity, by reason of the narrowness of the markets of consumption.

The traditions of a primitive agrarian economy still remained powerful in Western society; men still expected to gather the natural products of the earth without labour, to exploit the woods and the forests, to follow the unchanging methods of pastoral economy. A large part of the soil of Europe, in Ireland, the east of England, the Low Countries and Low Germany, and along the coasts of Picardy, Lower Poitou and Lombardy, was covered with marsh. The plains were full of bogs, and there were still immense tracts of moorland, deserts overgrown with brushwood, furze, and heath, *commons, velds, boschen, houten, loos, hermes, gastinnes, ronceraies, épinaies*, as they were called in different countries. This wasteland covered a large part of Ireland, Wales, and Scotland, a third of England (together with the fens), vast tracts of the Low Countries, North and South Germany, part of Switzerland, the central plateau of France, Armorica, Southern Aquitaine, and Central Italy. Charters constantly contain references to these uncultivated lands, which made up a considerable part of the great domains.

All the Christian peoples of the West obtained an important means of livelihood from river and coast fisheries. They knew the use of weirs and dams for catching fish, and in the Carolingian period monastic and seigniorial landowners made fishponds and stews on their estates; kings and great lords were able to sell the fish from their *villæ*. The coastal populations of the English Channel, the North Sea, and the Atlantic, fished for herring, salmon, lobster, and eel-pout, and even risked themselves in hunting seals, porpoises, and whales. The fishermen of the Mediterranean continued to catch the tunny fish and other species peculiar to that sea. Everywhere fish was an important element in the food supply.

In spite of clearings, forests spread their cloak over a great part of the soil of the West. Ireland, Wales, Cornwall, and the Scottish Highlands, which are to-day bare, were then covered with vast oak and beech and fir and pine woods, the trunks of which are still to be found in bogs. Celtic poetry is full of the enchantment of this old primitive forest. Almost all Armorica was a huge wood, the memory of which is immortalized in the venerable thickets of Broceliande. A third of England was covered with great forests, stretching as far as Sussex and Dorset and even into the lower valley of the Thames, which they completely encircled. Out of their brakes came bands of wolves, which, as late as the ninth century, attacked the villages. The plains of Flanders and the Netherlands, now so bare, were, before the eleventh century, for a great part forest regions—*houtlands*—which stretched until they joined the immense forests of the Ardennes and of Eifel, the famous Charcoal-burners' Forest (*forêt Charbonnière*) of legend. The Vosges, Haardt, and Central Germany were also forest-lands, in which colonization had levelled only small clearings, and the great Hercynian Forest rolled even beyond the borders of Bohemia, hardly reduced at all by assarts. In Gaul everything conduces to the belief that two-thirds of the soil was still covered with forest in the time of Charlemagne, and even in the cultivated districts the proportion seems to have varied from a third to a half. From the Argonne to the Alps and the Pyrenees, from the ocean to the Juras, all was forest, interspersed with open plains which had been brought under cultivation. Forest had recovered its sway in Northern and Eastern Spain and in a large part of Northern, Central, and Southern Italy. Already protective laws defended it against fire and devastation by those who used it. Charlemagne had tried to introduce rational principles of forestry, by regulating the felling of trees and giving instructions for pruning. Indeed, the forest played a rôle of the first importance in the economy of these times. It gave men building timber and firewood, pitch and resin, most of the elements necessary for lighting, and the fruit of its wild trees. Under its shade great herds of pigs rooted for acorns. The chase, which was at first the right of all freemen, but which the nobles usually succeeded in reserving for themselves, provided large and small game in abundance. There were quantities of bears, boars, deer and stags, and animals which have disappeared to-day, such as bison, aurochs, and beavers were still to be met with under the cover of the woods. Part of the food supply of the great domains was drawn in those days from venison.

Cattle-raising was another great resource, and the majority of the Celts, Anglo-Saxons, and Germans remained, even after their adoption of civilized life, first and foremost, herdsmen. The typical Englishman of the ninth century was a herdsman rather than a sailor, for in one district on the Devonshire coast we find 1,168 swineherds as against seventeen fishermen. In Ireland cattle were more valuable than land, and wealth depended on the number of cows which a man possessed. In Central Germany cattle were still a means of exchange in the seventh century. Save in the maritime and Alpine districts, in which grasslands flourished, well-irrigated meadows (*prata*) were rare, and pastures (*pascua*) predominated, together with the common lands. Thus large cattle and horses were most abundant in regions favoured by Nature or in the reserved demesne land of great estates. War-horses, stallions, and bulls were eagerly raised. The horse, rarer than the ass, was very expensive, and was worth a third or a half of the price of a slave in Gaul. Smaller live-stock, which demand less capital and are better suited to primitive agriculture, abounded. Pigs were raised for food, sheep for wool, goats for their meat and skins, poultry for the food of the lord's household, bees for their honey, which then took the place of sugar, and for the wax out of which candles were made—the most luxurious method of lighting. One great community, Saint-Germain-des-Prés, possessed 7,720 pigs; another, Bobbio, 5,000. An imperial *villa* in the ninth century contained 200 lambs, 120 sheep, 150 ewes, 160 piglings and 5 boars, 17 beehives, 30 geese, 80 chickens, and 22 peacocks. Another had a herd of 100 goats. In England the proportion of large as compared with small live-stock was 8 per cent., rising only occasionally as high as 50 per cent. In Spain certain improvements in irrigation had been introduced. The monks and the royal bailiffs had developed meadows, increased stock, and even introduced improvements in the choice of farmyard animals and large and small stock; but these were exceptions. For lack of capital, fat pasture, easy transport, and wide markets, the West did not as yet possess the more progressive forms of exploitation of the soil.

Marl was, nevertheless, known as a method of enriching the soil as early as the time of Charlemagne, but farm manure was, like large cattle, scarce. In general a threefold rotation of crops was practised, which reserved only one year in three for fallow, instead of one in two. It was a mark of real progress, but insufficient seriously to threaten the predominance of extensive cultivation, which continued to exhaust the soil rapidly, and give only small returns. In the Celtic, Anglo-Saxon, and Germanic lands cultivation was often carried out in common, by means of heavy collective plough-teams. But agricultural tools were, in general, confined to the hoe, the harrow, and the primitive wooden plough. Rural transport was often performed on the backs of men, asses, and horses, when the two-wheeled cart could not be used. In the Germanic and Celtic West there still persisted the system of compulsory common cultivation, according to a fixed rotation. The Roman methods of scientific agriculture were unknown, save on a few great domains and on monastic estates. Nevertheless, the cultivation of cereals gained ground in the Celtic and Germanic lands. The West cultivated in particular rye, which furnished the poor man's bread, spelt, and corn, the latter being less widespread than the other two; also oats and barley, for the beasts and the brewhouse. Sudden variations in harvest, combined with inadequate sowings and difficulties of transport, often led to dearths. Moreover, save in the old centres of cultivation, cultivated fields, as well as orchards, gardens, and vineyards, occupied a very inferior place compared with pastures, forests, and heaths.

Nevertheless, during the last four centuries of the Middle Ages there was begun a marked extension of horticulture and floriculture, arboriculture and vine-growing, principally under the influence of the monasteries and the stewards of the great princely domains. In the Celtic regions apple and pear-trees were cultivated. In the Germanic countries of the south gardens and orchards were introduced, and from them were obtained, as in the old Roman times, peas, beans, a few common flowers, a few medicinal plants, and the ordinary fruit-trees. In the Mediterranean lands, Spain and Italy, a great deal of fruit was still gathered, and the produce of the olive-groves was exported far beyond local markets. The vine, propagated by kings, great men, and monks, recovered part of the empire which it had lost; it ventured even into Ireland, and it was planted from the eighth century on the banks of the Moselle, the Rhine, and the Danube; the wines of Spier, Worms, and Mainz had a wide clientèle throughout these regions in the ninth century. In France the requirements of local consumption led to plantations as far afield as Neustria; Burgundy was already celebrated in the seventh century for its wines from the Côte d'Or, and

Saintonge, the Bordeaux and Narbonne districts, Spain, and Italy recovered their old fame. The cultivation of certain industrial plants became general, in order to meet the needs of each domain. Flax was the most widely cultivated of all in the West; the dye plants, madder and, above all, woad, were widespread in those great domains where workshops existed. Aquitaine and Northern Spain furnished them in abundance, but the crop was far from being specialized. In the West at this period agricultural production, although it had been stimulated by colonization, was always kept on a small scale to fit the dimensions of the small local societies, by which it was almost exclusively carried on. But already, before the invasions of the Northmen, the rise of agricultural produce shows that it was making slow progress. Witnesses worthy of belief speak of the agricultural prosperity of Ireland as late as the ninth century, of the Rhineland, Gaul, and Italy during the Carolingian period, and of Spain itself during part of the Visigothic domination.

Another proof of this relative and short-lived renaissance is to be found in the partial reconstitution of the populations of the Christian West between the seventh and tenth centuries. Little by little the races had become fused; Celts and Anglo-Saxons, Germans, Gallo-Romans, Visigoths and Ibero-Latins, Lombards and Italians, had intermingled. The Germanic element had, indeed, easily been absorbed in most of the West, notably in Gaul, Spain, and Italy. Streams of emigration and transferences of peoples had transformed certain regions, such as Armorica and the Rhenish and Saxon districts. In spite of various scourges which still raged at rather less frequent intervals, in spite of epidemics and dearths, in spite of a low birth-rate and a mediocre marriage-rate, the population of Western Europe was, little by little, built up again. In Ireland it was sufficiently numerous to assist by emigration in populating Scotland and Western Brittany. If in England the population was still, in the eleventh century (not counting the four northern counties), only 1,500,000 souls, in Germany the country had become so populous that the number of villages between the Rhine and the Meuse trebled itself in the tenth century. The population of Gaul in the time of Charlemagne has been estimated at between eight and nine million souls.

AGRARIAN COLONIZATION OF THE WEST

In Lombard Italy in the eighth century, peace, in the words of Paul Deacon, "made the people multiply like ears of corn." It was this which made possible this first agricultural colonization of the West, which is, in a sense, the forerunner of the magnificent movement of the twelfth and thirteenth centuries.

CHAPTER VIII

EVOLUTION OF THE RÉGIME OF PROPERTY IN THE WEST FROM THE
SEVENTH TO THE TENTH CENTURY.—THE DECLINE OF THE OLD
FORMS OF LAND OWNERSHIP.—THE PROGRESS OF THE GREAT
DOMAINS.—THE ATTACK ON SMALL PROPERTIES AND THE CLASS
OF FREEMEN.

COLONIZATION and the relative progress of agricultural production turned primarily to the advantages of the upper
ranks of Western society. On the other hand, the free
communities, which owned the soil in common in certain
parts of Christendom, were little by little eliminated either
wholly or partially from this ancient possession.

From the seventh to the tenth centuries the collective
property of tribes and village communities, even more than
that of family communities, was subjected to a series of
severe shocks. Tribal property, the primitive form of
agrarian collectivism, survived only in the Celtic countries,
Ireland, Wales, and Scotland. The soil of Ireland still belonged in the seventh century to 184 tribes or clans, each
of which possessed enough territory to pasture 3,000 to 9,000
cows, and which were subdivided into 552 districts called
carrows of about 525 to 1,050 acres each, each carrow being
in turn subdivided into four quarters, and each quarter containing four family estates. As in Scotland and Wales the
clan held the land in common, and was one in peace as in
war. It had its petty kings, its chiefs and nobles and
clients, but no man possessed any individual property save
his household goods, and each held only a right of usufruct
over his strip of the tribal domain. Heaths, forests, and
pasturelands were kept for common use, and ploughlands
were redivided periodically for a term among the family
groups. There even persisted traces of the ancient co-ownership of cattle to the profit of the clan, although by the
seventh century herds had become private property. In
each district of Ireland the free population lived com-
munistically in immense wooden buildings, protected by
earthworks and divided into three galleries. The people

lived and fed there in common, seated upon benches, and all the free families of the district slept there upon beds of reeds. But even in these regions, where isolation had caused the perpetuation of primitive forms of civilization, tribal property was soon shaken by the formation of great domains by the tribal chieftains (*pencenedl*), and nobles (*uchelwrs* or *machtiern*), as well as by the building up of the wide lands of the Celtic Church and the organization of family property.

Everywhere else in the Christianized Germanic West, the decline of the collective property of the tribe was infinitely more rapid. In England, as Vinogradoff has shown, there is no trace of property owned collectively by the Anglo-Saxon tribes, now formed into states, or of the collective property of the shire or district. At most there are a few vestiges of common lands in the little division of the hundred, and a few survivals of a tribal régime in regions influenced by the Celts. But everywhere the old Germanic institution of the common property of the township survived. Forests, pasturelands, heaths, and bogs remained undivided among the members of the village community, who possessed equal rights of property and usage over them. Meadows and ploughlands were divided into lots, the former enclosed for part of the year, the latter lying in open fields. Each free member of the village community had the right to a certain number of long strips or "furlongs" of about an acre, separated from the others by bands of turf known as balks, so that each family enjoyed an equal share in the cultivated lands and those under fallow. After the corn had been harvested and the hay cut, these fields were thrown open to the cattle of all the family groups, as the common pastures were all the year round. The land was cultivated by the same methods and in common by the members of the rural community, who yoked teams of eight or twelve oxen to plough the soil. The collective property of the Anglo-Saxon village grew rapidly less in proportion as there were organized royal and seigniorial manors, which claimed forests and common lands for themselves, and left the village community with nothing but its old methods of co-operative cultivation and its periodical distributions of the fields.

Germany, breaking away more completely still from the régime of agrarian collectivism, knew tribal property no more, and was little by little giving up the system of collective village property called the mark. Diminished, on the one hand, by legal appropriations resulting on the breaking up of waste lands, and, on the other, by voluntary alienations agreed to by the village communities, and by the usurpations of princes and great landowners, the mark broke up in all the Germanic lands from the Elbe to the Rhine and the Scheldt. It maintained itself henceforth only in the form of numerous commons (*allmends*), over which, moreover, the village community often preserved only rights of usage. In the regions of Gaul, Spain, and Italy, where the mark system had succeeded in establishing itself, it was unable to survive, and left no trace save in the commons, in certain rights of usage such as common of shack over the open fields, and sometimes in the system of co-operative ploughing. The Roman peasants continued to be acquainted only with the public property of the state, which passed to the kings, and the communal property of the townships of freemen, the *vici*, which became less and less important as time went on.

Without suffering the same profound decay, family property in its primitive forms was obliged to undergo a modification under the action of the individualistic conceptions of Roman Law, and the influence of economic necessities, working in favour of individual private property. But at the same time family ownership regained at the expense of the collective ownership of tribe and village a part of the ground which it lost to individual ownership, so that its power was less severely shaken. Family property, at first limited to the possession of household goods, cattle, garden and house, and to a temporary usufruct in the arable holdings (Celtic *tate*, Anglo-Saxon *hide*, and Germanic *hufe*) of about 40 to 120 acres redivided at more or less regular intervals, was in the end extended to these holdings, which began to be held in permanent occupation. Family property was also increased by lands recovered from the waste by the family community, which thereupon became private property. At the same time, however, the old family property (the Anglo-Saxon *ethel*, the *terra aviatica*, *salica*), indivisible, inalienable, belonging to the whole group of relatives, reserved for male members only to the exclusion of women, cultivated and enjoyed in common, this ancient property which still existed in the Celtic and Germanic countries in the sixth century, suffered a series of shocks under the influence of the individualistic tendencies of Roman civilization. Between the seventh and ninth centuries, in these regions, the father received the right to name an heir, to divide up the land, and to make grants thereof. Wills became general. Women and girls were admitted to a share in the inheritance even of land. Alienations of the family domain were allowed within certain limits.

Thus the principle of private and individual property was built up and spread among the new races. Rising out of partition or succession, it was increased by the fruit of personal labour, of what were known as " aquisitions," and especially of assarts, or land recovered from the waste by the labour of pioneers. It received barbarian names, *bookland* in England, *alod* in Germany and Gaul, but it was fundamentally the same as the old Roman property, the *possessio* or *sors*, over which the individual has full rights, which was now triumphing over the primitive conception long surviving among the Celts and Germans.

This movement, which tended to transfer the ownership of the soil, almost the sole source of wealth, from collective groups, whether tribe, hundred, village, or family, to individuals, worked chiefly in favour of the classes which were then in possession of political and social power. It was not the small but the large property which benefited by the disappearance of communal ownership. The possession of the soil became the appanage of those who, in the division of social labour, had seized upon the functions of government and upon material and spiritual power. First of all the new rulers of states, kings and kinglets of diverse origin, built up great domains for themselves. In the Celtic countries they accumulated them in the shape of disinherited lands, the third share in all booty, and tribal lands. Elsewhere in the Germanic countries they acquired a large part of the soil by conquest, by judicial sentences, by the partial appropriation of the lands of village communities and marks, by seizure of the public lands of the Roman Treasury. Much the same thing happened on the territories of the old Roman Empire. Often the new powers thus got into their possession a third of the land, and in Lombard Italy, for a short time, they appropriated as much as a half. Everywhere, it is true, they squandered this treasure, but magnificent vestiges still remained in the ninth century. In the Italian peninsula a ninth part of the soil then formed part of the royal domain, and the Carolingian princes owned at this period 100 domains in Lombardy, 205 in Piedmont, and 320 in Alamannia, Bavaria, Thuringia, and Ostmark. Hundreds of thousands of square miles were in royal hands in the West. They were mainly composed of forests and waste lands, but there was also a good deal of cultivated land among them.

Side by side with this great princely property, the great Church property likewise extended from century to century, slowly built up, a piece here and a piece there, out of the munificence of kings and of the upper classes, even of humbler folk, and by dint also of reclamation and agricultural colonization. There are plain indications that about a third of the soil of Western Christendom belonged to the Church in the ninth century, although it suffered from the policy of secularization pursued by the first Carolingians, and from the frequent usurpations of powerful laymen. In England men saw kings endow forty abbeys at a stroke, and bestow upon them the tenth of their royal domains. In Christian Germany abbeys and bishoprics were overwhelmed with gifts. Prüm had 2,000 "manses," 119 villages, and two great forests; Fulda, 15,000 carucates of land; Tegernsee, 12,000; St. Gall, 160,000 arpents. To the Abbey of Lorsch belonged 2,000 " manses " and two large forests; to Gandersheim, 11,000 carucates of land. Hersfeld had 1,702 domains. Many monasteries had no less than 1,000 to 2,000 carucates of property, and the bishoprics of Augsberg, Salzburg, and Freisingen owned from 1,000 to 1,600 "manses." In the words of a Merovingian king: "All wealth has been handed over to the churches." There have come down 72 grants by Charlemagne in favour of the churches of Germany; Louis the Pious made 600 grants to them, and the two first Ottos, 1,541. The churches and monasteries in the old imperial lands were no less favoured. One Bishop of Langres owned a whole county. The Abbey of Saint-Remi of Rheims held 693 domains, and Saint-Germain-des-Prés had 1,727, covering an area of 150,000 hectares. Saint-Wandrille, near Rouen, had 1,727 " manses " and 10,000 subjects at the end of the seventh century, and 4,824 domains in the ninth. Luxeuil numbered 15,000. The Abbey of Saint-Martin of Tours ruled over 20,000 serfs. In Italy 2,000 " manses " were in the hands of the Bishopric of Bologna and the patrimony of the Papacy was a sort of vast state, the possessions of which were sown all over a part of the West.

The territorial power of the lay aristocracy was due to a combination of usurpation committed at the expense of communal property, violence employed against small proprietors, pressure exercised on the rulers of the states, and colonization. Already growing under the Roman Empire, it overran all bounds during the Dark Ages. It triumphed everywhere in the West from the Celtic lands, in which the *uchelwers* and *machtiern* created vast domains for themselves out of tribal and family lands, to the Roman countries, where the old and new nobility amalgamated and grew rich by despoiling short-sighted kings and the enfeebled ranks of the small proprietors. In England the nobles, earls, thanes, and ealdormen built up opulent manors with such success that in the eleventh century a few great families had succeeded in gaining possession of two-thirds of the soil of England. In Germany a Duke of Bavaria, in the eighth century, possessed 276 " manses " in one district and 100 in another. In the same country the head of the great Welf family, in the tenth century, owned 4,000. It has been calculated that instead of 900 hectares, which was the average extent of a great Roman estate in Gaul, the great Merovingian estate was as large as 1,800 to 2,600. Moreover, the same person usually possessed several such estates. In the Carolingian period the lands of the aristocracy were often scattered in different regions. Nobles of the first or second rank, Gallo-Roman, Visigothic, and Lombard, thus succeeded in completing to their own advantage the process of concentration of landed property, which had been begun in the preceding period.

The possession of land assured to the bodies, families, and individuals who managed thus to monopolize it so great a power that it led to the formation of a new nobility, distinct both from that of Germanic and that of Roman society, but built up of elements borrowed from both and combined with more recent institutions.

Almost everywhere in the West, from the Celtic to the Germanic and Roman lands, the nobility of race or birth grew less, but a landed aristocracy grew greater under a variety of names, and began to coalesce with the aristocracy of service, formed of persons, sometimes of quite humble rank, who were attached to the king's service and with the aristocracy of high officials, to whom was delegated the exercise of public authority, and who gradually transformed their revocable function into a hereditary office. Thus the Irish, Welsh, and Armorican *uchelwrs, pencenedls, cinnidls, machtiern, baires* (cow-owners), the Anglo-Saxon thanes, earls, and ealdormen, the Frankish and Gallo-Roman *edelings, antrustions, nobiles, proceres, optimates,* dukes and counts, the Visigothic and Romano-Spanish *nobiliores, gardings, judices,* dukes and counts, the Lombard and Italian *gasindes, gastaldes,* dukes and counts—all these went to form a single class of lords or great men (*seniores, optimates, proceres, potentes*), which replaced that of the Roman senators and the ancient Germanic and Celtic nobility. Below them and in their service were grouped their agents, familiars, and men-at-arms (*familia, maisnie, comitatus, truste*), whom their patronage ennobled to such a point, indeed, that in Germany, the Low Countries, and Italy, and even for a short time in Gaul, simple serving men, the *ministeriales,* often of servile condition, were promoted to the rank of nobles. Sometimes freely, sometimes by force, sometimes in spite of the kings, and sometimes with their concurrence, the aristocracy, assuming to itself the protective rôle which, in civilized society, the state claims to exercise over individuals, subordinated landowners of small or medium estate by granting them their patronage, by spreading the custom of commendation among them and by enrolling them as vassals. Thus was created a whole hierarchy of domains and of free dependants, under the protection of the great landowners, on condition of a mutual exchange of services and the concession to the vassals of estates known as *beneficia* or *precaria,* which, although granted at first on revocable or temporary titles, very soon became hereditary. Finally, a new stage was reached in a part of the West when the state despoiled itself of the attributes of public power (administration, police, justice, the right to levy taxes and raise troops) by the concession of immunities, and the great landowner became not only a high official, but also a sort of sovereign in his own domain. Then it was that on the top of the seigniorial régime, which placed men in economic and social dependence upon the landed aristocracy, there was superimposed the feudal régime, which, in the ninth, and especially in the tenth, century, finally conferred political sovereignty upon the aristocratic class, at least in France and Northern Spain, if not in Germany, Italy, and England.

Already masters of the greater part of the land, the landed aristocracy thus became, in the course of 400 years, masters of the men who dwelt thereon. The great domain was indeed the solid basis upon which their power was founded. Preserving its fundamental integrity, despite the partitions which detached fragments from it, and bearing in its very name the memory of its chief owner, the *villa*, or *massa*, or *curtis*, or *saltus*, or *sala*, or *fundus*, or *manor*, as it was called, was a little kingdom, almost a little world, governed by a master, the lord, who was invested with absolute authority, and had in his possession all the elements necessary to economic existence. In it an organization, founded on a hierarchy of functions and divisions of labour, secured the satisfaction of all the needs of masters and subjects alike. At its centre rose the seigniorial dwelling-place (*palatium*, *fronhof*, *salhof*, *castellum*, hall), half castle and half farmhouse, often surrounded by a wall or palisade, rough enough in the Celtic and Germanic countries, but already more elegant and comfortable in the Romance lands. Everything was arranged for the sojourn of the master and his household. Farm buildings, stables, storehouses, cellars, barns, workshops, were all grouped round the hall. Everything was there, even a chapel for the life of the spirit, which was no more forgotten than the life of the body.

Economic organization reached the highest pitch of perfection on the great monastic domains, and then on the great imperial or royal domains. In the former, wherein a sort of communistic ideal prevailed, where the rule restrained individualism, and where all the monks were equals in the distribution of labour and of its produce, there reigned an inflexible discipline, which assigned to each his task and his reward, according to the principles of a sort of co-operative society for both production and consumption. The administration of each of the economic services was presided over by a cellarer, or else by a provost or dean. Each monk had his function, just as each subject of the monastery had his; gardeners, labourers, fishermen, foresters, swineherds, oxherds, or shepherds worked under the order of the foremen of each occupation. A strict economy ruled in the distribution and preservation of produce. Everything—harvests, instruments of tillage, and iron tools, even old habits and old shoes—was looked after with the greatest care. In the great royal domains, such as those of Aquitaine, to which Charlemagne's famous capitulary *De Villis* applied, the same organization was applied with less rigidity. Agents (*judices, majores*) or stewards there governed one domain or several, having under their orders special agents at the head of each service, and the whole population of subjects. The Lombard household, with its *gastald*, its *massarius*, its *domesticus*, and the Germanic *hof* with its *meier* or *vogt* present the same spectacle. Everywhere in the West identity of needs gave rise to similar organs in the great domain.

The lands of the great domain were divided into a collection of holdings worked by tenants, to whom their cultivation was confided (*terra indominicata*), and a section reserved by the lord to be farmed directly by himself. The latter was called the lord's demesne (*dominicum, terra dominicata*). It comprised not only the central nucleus of lands, on which stood the lord's dwelling-place, but also other lands scattered about over more or less distant parts of the estate. It was cultivated by the labour of serfs grouped round the central hall, or else by that of *coloni* and serfs, who were provided with separate holdings. The Abbey of Saint-Germain-des-Prés, for example, which reserved 6,471 hectares as its own demesne, and divided up 17,112 hectares among its *coloni* and serfs, farmed the former by means of three days of labour exacted weekly from the tenants settled on the latter. The demesne usually comprised arable lands, meadows, and forests. That of Verrières contained 300 hectares of ploughland, 95 arpents of vines, and 60 of meadows, besides a large wood, and the demesne of Vitry-en-Auxerrois was on the same scale. It was in this way that the great landowner secured the very considerable quantity of the necessities of life which he needed. At Bobbio the demesne of the abbey provided the monks in the ninth century with 2,100 hogsheads of corn, 2,800 pounds of oil, 1,600 cartloads of hay, and a quantity of cheese, salt, chestnuts, and fish. It maintained a large number of cattle, especially swine. All the food products—cereals, meat, oil, milk, wine—all the raw materials necessary to life—wool, flax, wood—and the greater part of the necessary manufactures came from the demesne, and from the rents imposed upon the tenants of land allotted by the lord. The latter and his household got food and clothing and everything which they needed from the demesne. Charlemagne himself lived with his folk in this fashion.

Finally, it was the great domain which was the centre of the social life of the upper classes. Great men dwelt there, sometimes in wooden habitations, rough and devoid of art, as in England and Ireland, sometimes, as in the Roman lands, in stone houses, where the old traditions of luxury lived again, more or less remodelled by Germanic barbarism. These great men there led a life of violent physical exercise, of hunting, and of great meals, mingled with more or less refined amusements, the characteristic life of all aristocracies at half-civilized epochs. Only an élite rose during the Carolingian period to the conception of intellectual pleasures. For the other members of the aristocratic classes, the sensual life of pure materialism, in its different aspects, remained the sole ideal to which they were capable of rising.

This violent, fierce, and ambitious rural aristocracy, which disciplined labour and reduced it to serfdom in the great domain, pursued with tenacity the destruction of the small free properties, which hindered its expansion, just as the independence of the small owners gave umbrage to its authority. Small free proprietors remained for a long time sufficiently numerous in the West to represent a social power, with which kings and great men had to count. Gallic *cymrys* and Irish *fines*, Armorican *boni viri*, Anglo-Saxon *ceorls*, Germanic *frilingen*, Burgundian *minofledes*, Gallo-Roman *ingenui* (free owners), Visigothic *allodiales*, Lombard *ahrimanns,* Italian *primi homines, bozadores,* they all had many traits in common. First of all there was the moderate size of their domains, no more than 120 acres (the *hide* or *hufe*) in England and Germany, and often less in the Gallo-Roman manor. But the small owner was absolute master therein, as absolute as the great man in his *villa* or his *curtis.* He had the right to enjoy all the possessions of the Germanic village community or the commons of the Roman townships. His property and his person were inviolable, and under the special protection of custom and law. He had the right to bear arms; he sat on the judgment seat with his peers; he was summoned to assemblies. He administered the affairs of his village or township, forming with his neighbours the common council, which is even found in Roman lands. But he was a butt for the galling jealousy of the great landowner, because his lands were intermingled with those of the latter and prevented him from rounding off his estate. In a single canton of the district of Salzburg, in the eighth century, 237 small estates were thus entangled among 21 ecclesiastical domains, 17 lands of vassals, and 12 great ducal properties. When all things else bent before the great territorial lord, the freeman with his independent nature, living proudly with his family in his little village, on his isolated holding, or in his Roman township, dared to raise his head and look his powerful neighbour in the face. Therefore, a duel to the death was waged throughout the West between the small proprietor and the great. Decimated by the wars in which it was obliged to take part, submitted to absorbing and onerous public charges, ill-defended by the royal power, which ought in self-interest to have leant upon it, and which only intermittently recognized that this was so, this middle class defended itself vigorously. Already in decay in Italy and Gaul, in the fifth and sixth centuries, it succeeded in building itself up again in the eighth, and became numerous and influential in the Carolingian Empire. The abdication of the central power during the following period; the weakness of Charlemagne's successors, which obliged freemen to commend themselves to the great lords by the Edict of Mersen (847), together with the shock of the last invasions, brought an almost complete victory to the landed capitalism of the time, represented by the great proprietors. It was not obtained without a struggle. We read of freemen grouping themselves together in associations or unions for mutual defence (gilds), organizing revolts at various points, rising in insurrection against the landed aristocracy, and outlawed by princes, who imagined themselves to be defending the social order. The small free properties, usurped by the aristocracy or alienated in its favour, were at last absorbed in the great domains, or else transformed either into benefices or into *precaria* and placed in dependence upon them. Nevertheless, little islands of free landowners managed to maintain themselves everywhere where physical nature and the power of tradition stayed the movement for the concentration of land, which was going on in favour of the aristocratic classes. In Lower Saxony, Frisia, the German Marches, maritime Flanders, in the regions of the Alps and Pyrenees, in Aquitaine and Southern Gaul, in the northern and eastern counties of England, in the high March of Spain, and in a few parts of Italy the population of small owners remained free and proud, a powerless minority in the midst of thousands of men who remained in subjection, or had been cast back into it.

CHAPTER IX

THE DEPENDENT RURAL CLASSES IN THE WEST.—THEIR ECONOMIC AND
SOCIAL ORGANIZATION AND GENERAL CONDITION (SEVENTH TO TENTH
CENTURY).

THE mass of the population of Western Christendom lived
(from the seventh to the tenth century) by the cultivation
of land, which they did not own, but to which they were
bound by more or less close ties. In the highest rank of this
class of non-landowning cultivators in dependence on the
aristocracy were to be found men who retained their personal
liberty and could dispose of a more or less considerable part
of the produce of their labour. Here and there, notably in
Gaul, there still remained a few free labourers or agricultural
wage-earners, the last survivors of a vanished age. More
often, but still not in large numbers, we meet with tenant-
farmers, or *métayers*, holding on more or less long leases,
and bound to the landowners by voluntary contracts, or,
again, with pioneers engaged in bringing wasteland under
cultivation (*hôtes*), whose condition was superior to that of
the mass of the inhabitants of the countryside. Such were
the small cattle-farmers of the Celtic countries—dairy-
farmers, as Seebohm calls them—who entered into stock
leases with rich landowners, or the tenant-farmers (in
særath), who took land-leases for a term of seven years, or
the tenant *métayers* (in *dærath*), who were less independent
and hired out their services as *coloni* paying a produce rent.

Such also were the independent cultivators of tenth-
century Germany—the *hörigen*—who were, in a sense, the
ancestors of the villeins of the next period, and who formed
at this time about half the rural population. Recruited
partly among the pioneer colonists and partly among the old
coloni, they acquired, if not the ownership of the soil, at
least the use of a part of the land which belonged to their
lords, paying in return fixed and moderate dues and limited
labour services, with guarantees set down in their contracts
or consecrated by tradition and custom. In the north of
Gaul free tenant-farmers were tending to disappear, so that
on the domains of Saint-Germain-des-Prés barely eight house-

holds of free cultivators (*ingenui*) are to be found, as against 2,851 households of *coloni* or semi-serfs (*lides*); nevertheless, elsewhere—in Touraine, Anjou, Maine, and Provence—they persisted for some time longer, until the moment when the great landowners found it more advantageous to rely exclusively upon the labour of *coloni* or serfs. For the purpose of colonization, it was found necessary all over Western Christendom to offer special advantages to men who would undertake the reclamation of the soil and who were known as *hospites* or *hôtes*. These are even to be found on the great domains, where colonization was already far advanced. At Saint-Germain-des-Prés we meet with seventy-one, at Neuville-Saint-Vaast thirty-seven, as against twenty-eight *coloni*. The holding of the *hospes* was doubtless often revocable at will and subject to the same payments as that of the *colonus*, but in general he enjoyed special advantages. Nor is it rare in the ninth and tenth centuries to find in Gaul free peasants (*liberi*, *ingenui*, *rustici*), who cultivated lands on leases which stipulated the payment of a *cens* or very small quit-rent, varying from a third to a bare twelfth of the produce. There were also tenants on Church lands, whose contract (*precarium*) laid down a kind of perpetual leasehold, which was advantageous to them. In England there existed similarly in the tenth century a class of dependent cultivators, who were placed under the jurisdiction (*soc*) of a great landowner, but who owed only limited dues and preserved their personal liberty and the right to quit the seigniorial domain. They were known as *socmanni liberi*, *allodiarii*, and *villani*; and this last term was to persist as the designation of this class in the West during the feudal age. In Italy, where free cultivators (*conductores*) were still to be met with in parts of the country at the beginning of the seventh century, there finally prevailed a form analogous to the Gallo-Roman, Anglo-Saxon, and Germanic villeinage. From the Lombard period onwards the class of *massari liberi*, or *livellarii* (free cultivators and tenants), grew, now by means of long leases (*fitto* or *emphyteusis*), now by leases limited to five years in the case of what were called *precaria*, and twenty years in the contract known as *livello*. They had the right, like the *ahrimanns*, to be present at the assemblies; they could leave the estate when their lease was up, and they paid a fixed annual rent (*canon*), in kind or in money, usually equivalent to a third of the produce, together with two or three weeks of *corvées* each year, and a few small boon payments. Bobbio had as many as 300 of these free *manentes*, some of whom, being old serfs or freedmen, were bound to remain on the domain. In proportion as the need of colonization made itself felt, this class of *manentes* or villeins grew steadily throughout the West.

Beneath it the mass of *coloni* maintained their position for some time, the more fortunate of them destined to rise into villeinage, the less fortunate to fall into serfdom. This class existed in the Celtic countries, where the *colonus* was called a *tæog*, as well as in the Anglo-Saxon and Germanic lands, where he was called *cotter, bordar, tributarius, lidus, aldion;* while in the Romance lands he kept the name of *colonus*. Sometimes, like the bordar or cotter, he held only a cottage and a few parcels of land; sometimes, like the majority of tenants in the same position, he cultivated a more extensive holding. In principle he possessed personal liberty; he was a freeman (*ingenuus*), and the holdings which he worked were characterized as *manses ingenuiles*. In the ninth century the *lides, tributarii,* or *coloni,* still formed a considerable part of the population of the countryside. In Germany, on the domains of the bishopric of Augsburg, there were 1,041 *manses ingenuiles,* as against 466 servile manses, and on one estate of the Abbey of Lorsch there were twenty of these free manses out of a total of thirty-eight. At Saint-Germain-des-Prés there were 2,000 households of *coloni* and only 851 of serfs.

The condition of this class of society grew worse. Its liberty was purely theoretical, since the *colonus* was deprived of all political rights. In general, save among the Celts, although the *colonus* theoretically possessed the right to bear arms and to plead in a court of law, even against his master, these prerogatives were in practice nullified by the fact that he was in direct dependence on the landowner, having none of the privileges of citizenship as against him, and holding him as master or lord. To this lord he was bound to pay heavy dues, a poll tax, or chevage, paid on the head of the *colonus,* and a land tax (*agrier, champart, terrage*), which was a payment in kind or in money, varying from a third to a tenth or twelfth of the revenue of the soil. He owed customary dues for the right to use lands, woods, or pastures on the lord's demesne, and that demesne was cultivated by means of his labour services. At Bobbio, for example, the *coloni* (*massarii*) together owed the abbey 5,000 workdays a year. Doubtless the *colonus* had some advantages. He could found a family, contract a legal marriage, and dispose of his " hoard " of personal belongings. He lived an independent life upon his separate holding (*colonia, manse*), and was not bound to submit to the superintendence of a bailiff. His family had full right of inheritance over his holding (*sors, hereditas*). His rent was fixed, and was, above all, payable in kind, a mode of payment which the peasant prefers. It seems sometimes to have been moderate in amount, and it has been shown that at Saint-Germain-des-Prés in the ninth century it was not more than seventeen francs the hectare. As to the *corvées*, they were fixed, and were sometimes as few as twelve or fourteen days in the year. But if the *colonus* was not always downtrodden, he was in subjection, bound to perpetual obedience, and without redress against the possible tyranny of his lord. In actual fact, he became subject to tallage and *corvée* at will, and more often than not his condition became so much like that of the rural slave as to be indistinguishable from it. In the ninth and tenth centuries the fusion of these two classes was to give rise to the class of serfs.

Slavery, indeed, which had revived into new life during the two centuries of the invasions, was tending to become transformed and to disappear during the last four centuries of the Dark Ages. Just as the lack of labour and the needs of agrarian colonization forced the landowners to bind down the *colonus* to the soil, so also it became necessary to keep the slave on the land and to encourage his labour by raising his status. Moreover, Christianity, which proclaims the dignity and equality of all human beings, sapped the foundations of the institution of slavery. It is true that war, misery, criminal justice, and civil law continued to augment the ranks of those who were slaves by birth, and there were slave-markets and slave-traders. Human cattle abounded still, and the price of slaves fell even lower, so low that in 725 it was between twelve and fifteen gold pieces for children and women. In Ireland an adult female slave was worth three milch cows. All the social classes which had access to landownership—kings, nobles, bishops, clerks, monks, freemen—possessed slaves. It was even advantageous to be a slave of the royal domain (*fiscelanus*) or on an ecclesiastical estate (*servus ecclesiasticus*), because a certain status and a few privileges attached to these. The position of the slave was still at first a very hard one; he had no civil personality and no legal family; he was master neither of his wife, nor of his children, nor of his possessions; he was classed with the beasts, and in a barbarous age was subjected to treatment at which humanity shudders. But little by little, under the influence of economic necessity, which caused a greater and greater value to be attached to his life and labour, and under the action of those Gospel maxims of charity which the leaders of religion professed, slavery grew milder. The sale of slaves was regulated or prohibited, their life was guaranteed by religious or civil law, their spiritual personality was recognized, since they were admitted to the priesthood, and their moral value was elevated, since they were proclaimed to be sons of the same God as their master, and, like him, destined for the rewards and punishments of the future life. The marriage of a slave and certain of his family rights were recognized. He acquired the beginnings of a civil status. His right to movable property was recognized, since he was allowed to own his " hoard " of possessions. The Sabbath rest was assured to him, and his masters were taught that they had certain charitable duties towards him.

The greater number of slaves became, during this period, cultivators (*servi rustici, mancipia, ancillæ, operarii, massarii*) or agricultural labourers. Some, grouped in gangs, laboured on the lord's demesne, or looked after his cattle. These were the *servi non casati*. The greater number in the ninth and tenth centuries, known as *servi casati, curtisani, mansionarii, hobarii*, were scattered on holdings on the great domains, living on the piece of land and in the hut assigned to them by their master, who wished to interest them in the work of cultivation and to rid himself of the trouble of feeding them. To both, but above all to the latter, enfranchisement brought, as its first benefit, personal liberty.

RURAL CLASSES IN THE WEST

The Christian Church, to its honour, helped forward the liberation of slaves with all its might, and made their emancipation the "good work" *par excellence.* Popes, bishops, and monks sought to put an end to slavery, and their example inspired kings and nobles. Moreover, in the great work of colonization which was going on, capital itself was not slow to recognize what a powerful stimulus the grant of freedom was to labour. This is the reason why throughout the West enfranchisements multiplied in all sorts of forms—by a formal act before the king, or in church, or by will, or by simple letter of enfranchisement. Nothing distinguished the freedmen from one another save their Roman or Germanic names—on the one hand *libertus, romanus,* on the other *lides.* This emancipation did not produce a new class of landowners or freemen, since the freedmen remained under the patronage of their master, tied to the soil and bound to the payment of various services, but it had the result of raising millions of men and their families to a sort of semi-freedom and, above all, of hastening the formation of a new social class—that of serfs of the glebe—into which were finally merged the fallen *coloni,* the freedmen, and the rural slaves.

An old name—that of serfs (*servi* or slaves)—came, in fact, to denote a huge new class, which grew up above slavery. The greater number of cultivators and stock-raisers were grouped in this category, so that throughout Western Christendom serf and peasant, *servus* and *rusticus,* became in general synonymous. The colonial, lidile, or servile holdings or manses, which were at first distinct from one another, became in the end the same, because they were subject to the same payments, rents, services, and *corvées,* and because their holders were under the same obligations and the same authority—that of the landowner, lord, and master. Apart from all law, by the mere force of custom, the mere stimulus of self-interest, which forced the owners of the soil to cut up their domains into holdings, in order the better to exploit them by the help of small cultivators, serfdom became the predominant condition of the inhabitants of the countryside. Each serf received a holding, known under different names in different countries—here *hoba, hufe, hide,* there *manse, mas, meix*—which varied in size, but in Gaul and

Germany was as large as ten to thirty hectares, the size necessary for the support of a family. The great domain was progressively divided up into peasant holdings. The Abbey of Saint-Germain-de-Prés possessed 1,646 of these in the ninth century, and the great estate of Marengo in Italy 1,300; those of Bobbio numbered from 30 to 3,000. According to the district, the number of cultivators on an Italian *curtis* varied from 20 to 6,500. Each peasant family averaged four or five persons. The manse itself grew smaller as the number of small holdings increased.

The cultivator lived with his family in his cottage or hut, in the midst of ploughlands, vines, and meadows which he cultivated, and within easy reach of woods and pastures, which he was allowed to use. An association was thus formed between capital and labour, between the owner and the cultivator, which each found to his advantage. The owner guaranteed to the cultivator the enjoyment of enough land to allow him to maintain himself and his family. He granted to the men on his estate rights of use over his woods and pastures. He ground their grain at his mill, and pressed their apples, olives, and grapes in his press; he repaired or made their tools at his forge, and brewed their barley in his brewhouse. He thus placed at their disposal costly establishments, which the peasants would have been unable to create for themselves. He was bound to feed them in time of famine, he provided them with spiritual help by organizing a chapel and providing a priest to serve the rural parish, he safeguarded them against outside attack by assuring them of the protection of his strong arm and his justice. The serf, on his side, was not master of his land, but he enjoyed a perpetual usufruct over it, he could not be expelled, and his family inherited it, even when the father had incurred sentence of death. He found upon this land, which sometimes even took the name of free domain (*sors, hereditas, alodium*), stability and security of existence, since the unattached individual was then a mere outlaw, a vagabond without hearth or home, the destined prey of slavery or hunger. If it was to the interest of the lord to keep the servile family in order to cultivate the small holding, which would have remained sterile without it, the servile family found it no less to its own advantage to remain on this soil, where it was born, which its labour had made fertile, and whence it drew the elements of existence. There the serf founded a home blessed by religion, inviolable and sacred as that of the freeman, since it was based on the indissolubility of Christian marriage. The serf was the equal of his master before God, and, once emancipated, he might even become his superior, since he was eligible to be a priest or a monk. The son of a goatherd sat in the episcopal chair at Rheims, the first bishopric of Gaul, in the time of Louis the Pious. The wife of the servile peasant became the Christian mother, protected during her years of motherhood, and free of almost all *corvées*, for which she was allowed to substitute some domestic work or money payment. The serf could now live in the midst of a wife and children, who worked at his side and were his before they were the lord's. In return for a strict obedience, a complete subordination, and an exact payment of his dues, he could live on his holding in relative security. Elevated henceforward to a higher moral and material position, owner of a home, and quasi-owner of land of which he had the use and retained a part of the fruits, he learned for the first time the virtue and the value of labour. Serfdom was a great economic and social advance upon slavery. But it was still only a transitory state, precarious and imperfect, which delivered over the peasant classes to an often arbitrary exploitation by the lords of the soil.

In truth, the servile masses were still held within tight bonds, to the great advantage of the landed proprietors. The serf, who lacked all civil personality, was still only an object of property, a *homo in potestate*, as he was called. He had no legal status; the law knew him not. Like the live-stock on the demesne, he could be sold, exchanged, handed over together with the land and the cattle. The members of his family, like the " brood " of animals, had no guarantee against separation. He needed his lord's consent to marry, and could possess only his stock of movables, a few heads of cattle, and personal gains or " winnings," nor could he transmit these to his children, save by the authorization of his lord. That lord was his sole representative in justice and exercised an unlimited authority over him; there was no redress against the violence of the seigniorial power. In fact, the self-interest of the landowner was the sole rule which limited his demands upon the peasant. It was upon this peasant that the lord lived. At Prüm, for instance, the abbey maintained itself by the aid of the 6,000 bushels of corn, the 4,000 hogsheads of wine, the 20,000 eggs, the payments of flax (600 pounds a year) and poultry (600 fowls) furnished to it by the tenants. It was their labour alone which permitted the demesne to be cultivated. At Prüm they furnished as many as 70,000 days of labour and 4,090 carting services. It has been noted, it is true, that on certain monastic estates the servile labourer paid no more than ten to twenty-three francs rent per hectare. But such conditions seem to have been obtained but rarely by the peasants. In practice the lord was free to pile up at will rents, *corvées*, customary payments for the use of woods or pastures, rights of feorm or hospitality, works, *suffrages* or petty obligations, poll taxes and succession taxes. The arbitrary character of the lords' rule, aggravated still more by that of their agents, too often caused serfdom to degenerate into a state not unlike that of the old slavery.

The life of the rural classes during this period of the Middle Ages remained full of uncertainty. Rough and coarse, it differed little from the conditions of existence in the barbarian ages. In the Celtic lands the peasant lived in huts made of branches, or in veritable burrows, rarely in hamlets (*trefs*). The Anglo-Saxon cultivators preferred to group themselves into villages (*tuns*), where each had his wooden house (*ham*), cut off from neighbours by sacred boundaries, by ancestral oaks adorned with figures of animals, or by poles set up in the midst of marshes. There the peasant lived a half-barbarous existence in his muddy hut, with its few sticks of furniture and floor of beaten earth, side by side with his animals and not unlike them. In the Germanic lands of the Continent the peasants were sometimes grouped into more or less considerable villages (*dorfen*), lying along the roads, with the lands of the rural commune round them, or sometimes scattered in hamlets (*weiller, villaria*) on the great domains. In a certain number of regions—Frisia, the Low Countries, the lands of the Salian Franks, the Alamanni, and the Bajuvarii—they preferred the isolated farm (*hof, heim, huis*), protected by solid doors and a stockade of strong planks and guarded at night by dogs, standing in the shade

of great trees close to some spring. The house was sometimes of wood and sometimes of rubble, square, rudely furnished with wooden seats and benches. The stables and
barns stood next to the common room in which the whole
family lived round the hearth. A hole in the roof sufficed
to let the light in and the smoke out.

Even in Gaul the townships (*vici*) and agglomerations of
people formed in the centre of the great estate (*villa*) gave
place, from the eighth and ninth centuries onward, to a
multitude of villages and hamlets, where only fifty to sixty-
five had been known two centuries before. They took the
name of a saint, in memory of their monastic origin, or of
their lord, to which they added characteristic suffixes (*court,
ville, inge, ingen, villier, villard*). Over a large part of the
Gallo-Roman territory the system of separate farms still
prevailed, notably in mountainous regions and in the old
Celtic districts. Everywhere the peasant dwelt in hovels
(*pisilia, tuguria*) made of branches or clay, and occasionally
of stone, roughly and scantily furnished. In Italy, where
malaria raged, and where the length of the coastline favoured
piracy, the old townships (*vici*) had been abandoned, but
innumerable little villages had sprung up on the newly reclaimed lands, and there were many new townships. They
were often grouped in the shadow of fortresses, furnished
with watch-towers, and they were fain to avoid isolation.

Everywhere the rural classes made their garments out of
the flax or wool which they worked, and the skins of beasts
which they reared or hunted. Cloaks, tunics, and breeches
of linen or coarse cloth, and the skins of animals sufficed for
their clothing. The peasants usually wore their hair short
or shaved their heads; certain laws obliged them to do so,
for long hair was the mark of the freeman. They wore woollen
or fur caps, and often went barefoot or shod only in the
roughest of shoes. Their food was simple and frugal. Oat-
meal among the Celts, barley bread, or bread made of a
mixture of rye, barley, and oats, or of beans, among the
Anglo-Saxons, rye, and rarely wheaten bread in the old
Romance countries, was the basis of their food, together with
milk, cheese, and butter, the latter having been introduced
into Germany by the Roman populations. Their only meat
was pork or bacon, and they made little use of beef or

mutton. Fresh and salt fish and, above all, vegetables often furnished their tables. A sort of beer and a variety of cider made from the fruit of wild apple-trees served them for drink in the Celtic and German and even in the Gallo-Roman lands. In the Romance countries they drank water or a kind of light wine made from the dregs of the vintage. Thus generations of men lived, with no care for hygiene, and exposed to all those skin diseases to which the lack of such care gives rise, and to divers epidemics, fevers, small-pox, typhus, plague, dysentery. The problem of daily existence pursued them incessantly; the least failure in the harvest in this small and enclosed world resulted in famine and aggravated the conditions of material life.

The habits of the lower classes were yet more brutal than those of the upper classes. Brawls, murders, family vendettas, attacks on person or property, assaults upon women and children, were as frequent among the former as the latter. The peasant of those days was usually greedy, dissolute, vindictive, sly, and a cheat; he was still showing the effects of slavery, and serfdom itself was not a school of morality. Religion alone, which had spread, thanks to the multiplication of rural parishes, might have raised him above his instincts, were it not that it was too often, among the people and the aristocracy alike, reduced to superstitions or to external practices, and cumbered with a mass of pagan survivals. The ignorance of the peasant classes was profound, although monks and bishops tried to spread instruction among them, and serfs were even at times admitted to the monastic or episcopal schools. The best hope for the future of the moral life of the countryside was to be found in the profound sense of solidarity of the rustic family, that united and disciplined group, that school of devotion and of labour, and in the existence of co-operative associations of families, villages, or domains (*consorteria, vicinia, condoma*). Throughout the West these associations lent each other a mutual assistance in the labour of the fields, in the reclamation of new land, and in the defence of the peasantry and of rural interests. It was in these little united societies that the lower classes of the country districts served their apprenticeship in the responsibility, laborious effort, and energetic and intense life which were to prepare them for liberty.

RURAL CLASSES IN THE WEST

During the last centuries of the Dark Ages the horizon seemed so closed to them in that direction that a profound unrest, despite the progress which had been realized, agitated the rural world of the West. Among the restless and violent elements in the population, this life fixed to the soil, this existence without any doors open to a more independent condition, this perpetual subjection which so often degenerated into tyranny, provoked a sullen discontent. Thence came the passive resistance and ill-will (*pravus excessus*) with which the serfs sometimes opposed their masters, and thence, too, that epidemic of desertions which bore away some of their number. Charters not infrequently mention lands abandoned by their cultivators (*servi absarii*), who took to the roads, grouped in bands of beggars and vagabonds, although harsh laws were laid down for bringing back the fugitives in chains and inflicting severe punishments upon them. Hence also those sly revenges, the vengeance of the weak against the oppressor, those poisonings and murders of individuals, which the law sought in vain to prevent. Hence, finally, those secret associations, brotherhoods, gilds, *stellungen*, prohibited by the authorities, wherein were organized seditious movements, and those peasant revolts which broke out on all sides in Italy, Gaul, Frisia, Flanders, Saxony, at irregular intervals during the eighth and ninth centuries. Then bands of serfs and their womenfolk, who were more cruel even than the men, attacked the seigniorial domains, pillaged, burned, tortured, massacred without discernment or pity, until a cruel repression brought them back for a while to obedience. A sort of dumb ferment, broken by sudden accesses of rage, and followed by long periods of prostration, was at work in this rural world, for which serfdom was only a provisional stage on the way to liberty and a greater well-being, those eternal aspirations of the people, which are so slowly realized.

CHAPTER X

In this Western society, where a natural economy prevailed,
or where agricultural production was the foundation of
existence, industrial production and exchange outside the
limits of the domain held only a small, strictly limited place.

Industry confined itself to meeting immediate needs, and,
not having for its object the furnishing of external or distant
markets, it was, above all, exercised upon the great domains.
It was no more now than an annex of agriculture. In every
family, to begin with, each member of the family community,
according to sex, age, and aptitude, sought to produce the
manufactured goods necessary for the elementary necessities
of existence. The peasant built his house, made his furniture,
repaired his ploughshares; his wife and daughters made
bread, span wool or flax, and wove garments. He needed
to seek hardly anything from the workshops of the domain.
Raw materials were worked up in the same domestic circle
which produced them, and each shared as consumer in the
fruits of his labour as producer. There was no need in such
a régime for specialization, complicated tools, or capital.

Above this form of industrial production there was that
of the great domain, where there could be division and
specialization of labour, but where the sole object was still
to provide for a larger group than the family, without seeking to feed outside markets. The economic needs of the
domain were so simple that its industrial activity was somewhat restricted. Moreover, its workmen were slaves or serfs,
who had no other stimulus to effort but the fear of punishment, and no personal interest to spur them to work. They
received from other slaves the raw materials, which were
grown on the domain, so that in this system there were
neither entrepreneurs nor capitalists to be remunerated, nor
wages to be paid, nor cost and sale prices to be considered.
Sometimes the workman worked by himself, in which case he

had to pay servile dues (*cens*) to his master, in the form of manufactured articles. Sometimes he was grouped with other workmen in the seigniorial workshops. The degree of skill required for his trade was the criterion by which his personal value was determined in the eyes of his master and of the law, and it was for this reason that the goldsmith, the smith, the miller, the weaver, or the embroideress were placed in the highest rank of the hierarchy of servile labour.

Every great domain had a personnel of workmen, who are enumerated in Charlemagne's famous capitulary *De Villis*, and in the charters and regulations of monasteries. These artisans were distributed in male workshops (*cameræ*) and female workshops (*gynæcia, sereonæ*), grouped into gangs under the disciplinary authority of an hierarchy of foremen—*ministeriales* and *magistri*—who were of servile birth like themselves. They might number several hundreds in an imperial *villa*, in which all the industrial services were gathered—milling, baking, butchers' work, brewing, fishing, fowling, carpentry, woodwork, ironwork, weaving, spinning, rope-making, saddlery, laundry work, and soap-making, up to the workshops of the goldsmiths and painters of coats-of-arms. The women were specially occupied in spinning and weaving flax and wool, which they dyed madder blue or vermilion, and in making and embroidering stuffs and garments. Every domain, however small, usually possessed its oven-keepers, bakers, butchers, brewers, weavers, fullers and dyers, a few goldsmiths, and, above all, smiths—indispensable in these rural surroundings—as well as shoemakers and needlewomen. This organization reached its highest point on monastic domains, where monks at the head of each service directed the different classes of workers, who had to provide the necessities of life. Episcopal domains were furnished with the same personnel.

On the monastic domains, moreover, the monks were able to organize true schools of arts and crafts for difficult specialities; and artists (*artifices*), as distinct from artisans, were trained there. The reputation of the Limousine Abbey of Solignac in this respect is well known; it was there that the goldsmith Eligius worked. Furthermore, certain abbeys became industrial centres, in which there was a still further specialization of labour. Thus, whereas Corbie had only four chief workshops with a personnel of twenty-eight workmen, most of whom practised the indispensable trades, Saint-Riquier in the ninth century had already gathered round itself a real industrial town, in which the armourers, saddlers, binders of manuscripts, shoemakers, butchers, and fullers were grouped in separate streets according to their professions, and bound to the payment of dues suitable to their trades. The same advanced organization is found at Sithieu (Saint-Omer), which depended upon the Abbey of Saint-Bertin. For the encouragement of servile craftsmen their dues were fixed, like those of their brethren of the soil; they were sometimes freed from paying the succession tax, called *mainmorte*, on their little stock of possessions. Already, with this degree of industrial organization on the domain, the workshops were able to produce enough to offer a small surplus for sale.

In face of the competition of family industry and domain industry, the town workshop, which had, moreover, lost its markets, languished and disappeared, surviving only in certain occupations and certain regions, where the vestiges of Roman civilization still lingered on. It underwent a timid renaissance during the Carolingian period, without making any great advance. The old imperial manufactures had disappeared, and the manufacturing class which existed before the invasions existed no more. The *collegia opificum*, or Roman corporations, had been dissolved almost everywhere, the artisans had been reduced to a servile condition when they remained in the precincts of the towns, and now paid dues to the bishop or lord. Nevertheless, the labour of free artisans still maintained a sporadic existence in certain districts, in Gaul, in Spain, and, above all, in Italy. At Naples at the beginning of the seventh century there were still craft gilds (*arti*), such as that of the soap-makers; and a fishermen's gild has been found at Ravenna in the eighth century. The artisans of Comacchio were free to go from one town to another to work, and could acquire and sell land. In the last two centuries of the Dark Ages there also appeared artisans, living in industrial towns (*vici*), as at Saint-Riquier or Corbie, which had grown up on the domain, or else in villages (*castra*) outside the domains. These seigniorial workmen, some entirely free, some half free, were often migratory, called in to exercise their craft where it was needed, and bound only to the payment of certain dues in money or in kind. Such were the men whom we meet with at Soissons, Saint-Omer, Corbie, Saint-Riquier, Comacchio, Nonantola, and Brescia. They exercised the most diverse trades, and among them were to be found moneyers, tailors, shoemakers, coppersmiths, goldsmiths, blacksmiths, masons, weavers, and armourers. Sometimes it happened that they formed, either with or without authorization, societies for mutual assistance, or fraternities of a religious type (*confratriæ*, *geldoniæ*, gilds) similar to the co-operative associations (*conserteriæ*) of cultivators; these were forbidden by those in authority when they took the form of unions organized under an oath.

In these various shapes—family, domain, free, or half free—industrial production remained inactive and with little variety. It served only to satisfy the simple needs of agricultural or pastoral societies, and produced only objects of primary necessity. It was not until the Carolingian age, under the influence of the renaissance of Roman tradition brought about by the monasteries, and of the example of the Byzantine and Arab civilizations, that the industry of the West awoke for a moment from its torpor.

The already perfected methods of Græco-Roman technique had, in general, been lost. In parts of the West—for instance, in England—only the handmill was now known. Elsewhere, among the Visigoths of Spain, the use of water-power for mills had been preserved. The sole form of mineral industry which remained fairly active, because it was a primary necessity, was that of salt, which was collected by evaporation from the shores of the North Sea to the Mediterranean, especially at Batz and Guérande in Lower Poitou, and round Narbonne in the marshes of the Lower Po, or else by treating the waters of salt springs in Central Germany and in the districts of Salzburg, Lorraine, and Burgundy, or else from the saltpans of Cardona in Catalonia. But most of the iron, lead, and tin mines of the West were abandoned, because the skilled mining practised in the Roman period had been forgotten. It was only during the period of the Carolings and the Ottos that a feeble beginning was once more made in working those of Central Europe. A few mineral springs were used, notably in Sardinia and the Meuse country; those of Aix-la-Chapelle were patronized by Charlemagne. Very little was known about the working up of minerals and metals in the primitive little foundries which alone existed, and no technical progress was made in iron-working until the twelfth century. This useful metal was so rare that on one of Charlemagne's domains there were to be found only two axes, two spades, two gimlets, a hatchet, and a plane. A hundredweight of iron was then worth fifty times as much as it fetched at the end of the nineteenth century, and the smith was the most honoured of technicians. Side by side with him, the armourer was considered a workman of the front rank; the Burgundians had acquired a certain reputation in this direction. A breastplate was worth six oxen or twelve cows, a swordbelt three, a helmet six, a sword seven, and a bit cost more than a horse.

In the domain or monastic workshops, and in each family, only the more or less coarse linen or woollen fabrics were made to serve for clothes. Vestments were embroidered in the gynæcea and the nunneries, but all the fine or luxurious materials came from the Byzantine East. At the most in the Carolingian period there grew up among the free peasants of Frisia, who utilized the wool from their sheep, a specialized cloth industry, which for three centuries fed the commercial markets of the West. Some artisans introduced this industry into Mainz towards the ninth century. There were still a few urban workshops producing linens, notably at Metz, Treier, and Rheims.

It was mainly the luxury trades which emerged above the other varieties of industrial activity. Their artisans worked for a restricted clientèle, but one which had the monopoly of wealth—the princes, great lords, prelates, and monasteries. It was to meet their demands that there were organized—above all, in the abbeys and sometimes in the towns—workshops of architects or masons, of sculptors, mosaic workers, painters, glaziers, goldsmiths, enamellers, who built or decorated churches, palaces, and seigniorial *villæ*. Luxury, which was at first, in the Merovingian age, coarse and half barbarous, became refined under Byzantine influence in the Carolingian period, more especially in Gaul and in Italy. Architects set up buildings inspired by those of Byzantium, out of which Romanesque architecture developed. Italian and Gallo-Roman artists went to Germany and England, bearing with them the tradition of stone-building, which was, for this reason, known as "Italian work" (*opus italicum*) in those countries. Sculptors renewed the degenerate art of ornamentation, and decorated baptisteries and sarcophagi. Mosaic workers and painters of frescoes appeared in ever-increasing numbers to adorn palaces, monasteries, and churches. Italian and Gallo-Roman glaziers spread their art from cloister to cloister. There still remained in the towns a few makers of porcelain. The most prosperous of all the industrial arts of the West was that of goldsmith work and enamelling, which provided churches with shrines and reliquaries, and individuals with gold and silver vessels and jewels. This art flourished at once in Ireland, England, Gaul, Spain, and Italy. It was carried on in the towns, on the great domains, and, above all, in the monastic workshops, notably in those of Solignac in Limousin and Saint-Denis, near Paris, the latter having been founded by the celebrated Eligius (Saint Éloi). There craftsmen worked, not only in precious materials, but also in glass and garnet, which they set in gold (*verroterie cloisonnée*), or in enamel, with which they inlaid metals. Engravers on delicate stones, bronze workers, ivory workers, and a few moneyers also sought to imitate the methods of Byzantine art in the West. Finally, a large number of artists, collected in the Irish, English, French, German, and Italian cloisters, particularly at Iona, Armagh, Jarrow, Lindisfarne, Saint-Martin de Tours, Rheims, Saint-Denis, Fulda, Saint-Gall, and Bobbio, copied manuscripts, decorating them with miniatures or adorning them with golden letters on a purple ground, for the collections of princes, bishops, or monasteries. But all these different manifestations of the arts were not enough to bring about the rise of a real industry, working for large markets and capable of supplying a wide trade.

Commerce, severely shaken by the barbarian invasions, recovered a certain activity between the seventh and ninth centuries, but it was a limited activity. Business enjoyed small consideration, as in all backward eras in civilization, when the value of commercial relations in the hands of middlemen is ill-understood. The merchant in the Carolingian period passed often enough for a parasite or a trickster. Most of the fruits of production were consumed on the spot, and in many cases the intervention of the trader was unnecessary. Traffic was often reduced to the mere barter of natural products, the exchange value of which was often determined by law, as though they were money. The merchant was not distinguished from the cultivator, and trade was carried on directly between producers. It has been pointed out, for instance, that the Anglo-Saxon laws do not mention the trader as such. In that state of civilization the intervention of commerce was necessary only to secure goods which the economy of the family or domain was unable to supply; that is to say, rare natural or manufactured articles, which were luxuries too expensive for the mass of the poor consumers of the West. It was only in the Lombard or Carolingian age that this situation was modified by the opening of easier relations with the Byzantine and Arab Empires, and, in addition, by the activity displayed in the workshops of the great domains, which could put into commerce their small surplus produce. Sovereigns and ecclesiastical bodies gave a certain protection to trade and tried to improve and regulate its circulation by punishing forestallers, speculators, and usurers, by publishing laws restricting the export of certain commodities, such as cereals, and by fixing the price of others. But their casual and sometimes clumsy intervention had only a slight effect, and sometimes had a harmful influence on the ephemeral commercial renaissance of this period.

Nevertheless, a commercial class was timidly being formed. Migratory commerce, peddling, developed side by side with the sedentary local or regional commerce. The germs of international trade appeared with the traffic in articles of luxury, which was set on foot between the West on the one hand and Byzantium and the Arabs on the other, and in which the immensity of the gains compensated for the greatness of the risks. Indeed, we find in the Carolingian era not merely retailers and pedlars, but also wholesale merchants (*negotiatores*), such as those traders in the produce of the Levant (*negotiatores transmarini*) mentioned in the law of the Visigoths, or those merchants selling costly articles of luxury (*mercemanni cariorum rerum mercatores*), referred to in other texts. Already they have their depôt (*domus*) at Paris, and elsewhere their street, as at Saint-Riquier or Verdun, besides their shops (*stationes*) and their tables in the markets. They are grouped into gilds or associations for mutual defence against violence, and for reciprocal insurance against the risks of war, spoliation, or fire. They set out in caravans with their ships or carts and their cargoes, stopping at fairs or at their entrepôts (*emporia*) in the chief ports or halting-places. They take with them their agents or slaves, even travellers and passengers. The clergy, to whom trade is forbidden, readily give them commissions, and princes, notably beyond the Rhine, furnish them with armed escorts. Moreover, the merchants carry lance and sword. Not infrequently they have obtained fiscal or judicial privileges, which authorize their sojourn and their operations, guarantee their safety, and fix their tolls, especially among the Visigoths and Franks. A large number of these merchants were Orientals, Byzantines, or Syrians, who had veritable colonies in Italy, Spain, and Gaul, notably at Ravenna, Marseilles, Narbonne, Bordeaux, Tours, and Paris. Others were Jews who penetrated into the farthest ends of the Celtic lands, selling spices and buying slaves; they swarmed most of all in the cities of Spain, Languedoc, and Provence, and were even to be found at Paris, Clermont, and Orleans. The Westerners, in their turn, began to take part in large-scale commerce. From the sixth century onwards Lombard merchants appeared at the fairs of Saint-Denis, and in the ninth the Venetians obtained from Charles the Fat their privilege of 883. On their side, too, the Gallo-Roman traders began to risk themselves in the trade with Ireland, Germany, and the Slav countries, while the Frisians became masters of the traffic of the Rhineland and Low Countries.

This large-scale commerce brought with it a beginning in the organization of credit. In spite of ecclesiastical prohibitions, Jews and even clerics practised loans at interest, by virtue of an intermittent toleration. In Spain loans on bottomry were known. The currency, at first very rare and often reduced to the stock of old Roman moneys, increased slightly, when kings all over the West reorganized workshops and began to strike money, the gold or silver *sou*, and then from the Carolingian period the latter only, which became the standard coin. Its intrinsic value was equivalent to four francs thirty, and its relative value to between twenty-eight francs thirty and forty-three francs fifty. But since precious metals were rare, the coinage in circulation remained insufficient, and recourse often had to be had to the system of barter. In spite of the adoption of the Roman weights and measures by the barbarians, there was such disorder in the Western states that the Carolingian *muid* or hogshead came to represent twice the capacity of the ancient *modius,* and the pound weight varied between 327 and 400 grammes, so that there was ample opportunity for fraud.

The Roman methods of transport no longer existed. The imperial posts, restored for a short time by Theodoric in Italy, disappeared in Gaul from the sixth century. The Carolingians tried to restore and keep up the Roman roads, fallen into disrepair, by means of forced labour. Both they and the Visigothic kings regulated the width of roads and put them, together with navigable rivers, under the protection of public law. But these regulations were not observed for long, and roads and tracks of all kinds were left alone. Transport was slow and difficult—upon the backs of men or of sumpter beasts, or by means of heavy carts drawn by oxen and horses. As in primitive times, river was often preferred to road transport. Monks and merchants were very ready to make use of it, and regular fleets, which had their stopping-places (*portus*), circulated on the great rivers of Gaul and Southern Germany. But no active movement was possible on account of the degradation of the roads, the insufficient upkeep of the rivers, the multiplicity of tolls, and the persistent menace of brigandage.

Nevertheless, in a few regions of the West commerce woke to a feeble life again. Along the valleys of the Rhône, Rhine, Danube, Main, Scheldt, and Meuse merchandise came from east and south. By the same routes and across the passes of the Alps the raw materials of Central and Northern Europe—amber, skins, furs, and slaves—reached Upper Italy. Merchants met at the fairs, which often coincided with pilgrimages. The fair of Troyes was in existence from the fifth century, that of Saint-Denis, or Lendit, was founded in the seventh (629), and drew an enormous gathering of traders during four months of the year. In the Low Countries there appeared the fairs of Thourout and Messines. In the neighbourhood of abbeys and important towns weekly markets were organized. Sea-borne trade became more animated, and in order to reap its benefits merchants risked the continual dangers of piracy. It awoke even as far as the Atlantic Ocean and the Channel, and pressed into the North Sea. In return for the salt, wines, oil, linens, and cloth which they received from Gaul at the hands of Gallo-Roman traders, the Celts of Ireland and Wales were bold enough to brave the seas in their leather coracles, and carried their skins and salt meat to the Continent. But this traffic was infinitesimal, as was that of the Anglo-Saxons, who had become confirmed landlubbers, and, turning their backs to the sea, left the Frisians and the Gallo-Romans to monopolize commerce between their island and the Continent, to which they sent skins and unworked metals, lead, tin, and copper. The Frisians, on the contrary, foreshadowing the future fortune of the Netherlands, invented the type of large-decked ship (*hogge*) which was best suited to the northern seas, and made their ports of Dursteede and Sluys into active commercial centres, trading from the Baltic as far as the estuary of the Seine. In the Channel and the Atlantic the Gallic ports, Boulogne (whose lighthouse was restored by Charlemagne), Quentovic at the mouth of the Canche in Ponthieu, and, above all, Rouen, Bordeaux, and Nantes, maintained increasingly active relations with the Low Countries, the British Isles, and Spain.

But the Mediterranean remained the real centre of this large-scale commerce. It was the true intermediary between the half-barbarous West and the East, the home of civilization; it was the natural road for that luxury traffic which then overtopped all the others. By the Mediterranean the ports of Eastern Spain and Southern Gaul, especially Narbonne, Marseilles, and Arles, as well as those of Lombard Italy, received the silken and cotton tissues and worked leathers of the Byzantine Empire and the Arab caliphates, the cloths and carpets of Antioch and Laodicea, the flax and papyrus of Egypt, the wines of Syria and Cyprus, the perfumes of Arabia, the spices, pearls, and precious stones of the Far East and India, and the ivory of Africa, in exchange for the raw materials of the West. The restored relations with the Levant were never to cease again, and it was their persistence which brought about the great renaissance of movable wealth two centuries later.

The first result of this revival of industrial and commercial activity was the partial renaissance of urban life. In the old Roman lands a large number of cities (*oppida, civitates*) rose again in the midst of their ruins. The majority were pale shadows of their past, but some owed a partial return of their ancient prosperity to their geographical situation at the intersection of natural routes. In addition, in many parts of the West new towns were born in the shadow of episcopal power, so that the names of city and bishopric became synonymous. In the fortified enclosures (*castra*), which multiplied and served also to denote urban groups, a crowd of little centres of population were likewise formed. By analogy a number of centres of seigniorial domains (*villæ*), protected by fortified stockades, received agglomerations of subjects, and thus became nuclei of urban life, and gave to the towns of the future their name of *villes* or *vills*. But it was, above all, industry and commerce which gave rise, especially in the West European plain, or on the edge of highways and rivers, to the birth of industrial boroughs, entrepôts, markets, halting-places (*portus*), which attracted population and gave rise to more important urban groups. These had as yet no fixed name and were known variously, in different countries, as *urbes, curtes, oppida, castra, burgs, burchs*, so indefinite as yet was their character.

The unevenness with which this renaissance of urban life developed exactly reflects the profound differences which separated the Western countries, from the point of view of the revival of industry and commerce. The Celtic districts, where a pastoral régime and a primitive economy reigned, had no towns; and, indeed, trade played so small a part there that market-right does not appear in Wales before the Anglo-Norman conquest. Anglo-Saxon England possessed only numerous fortified villages (burghs), and a very few places of commerce (ports). The most populous of the English towns, London or Winchester, numbered no more than 8,000 inhabitants, and the total number of town dwellers in 1060 was a bare 166,000, of whom 11,000 to 25,000 were free burgesses, out of a total population of 1,500,000. Similarly, in Central and Northern Germany the numerous strongholds (*burgs*) and royal towns (*urbes regiæ*) founded in the ninth and tenth centuries were little more than fortified enclosures, inhabited by peasant-soldiers (*milites agrarii*). The agglomerations of people round episcopal sees and monasteries, such as Bremen, Hamburg, and Magdeburg, were as yet of very little importance. Urban life developed principally in the same region, crossed by the Scheldt, the Meuse, the Moselle, and the Rhine, in which it had formerly taken root in Roman times; here in the ninth and tenth centuries there grew up Ghent, Cambrai, Liège, Maestricht, Aix-la-Chapelle, Treier, Metz, the capital of Austrasia, Cologne, Mainz, Worms, Speier, Bâle, and the " populous " Strasburg. This zone was the richest and most active part of the Carolingian Empire. The urban renaissance there, as in the Main and Danube lands, was linked with that of commerce.

On the rivers which met the roads from the Alps, the East, and Central Europe there grew up Wurzburg, Augsburg, Passau, and Ratisbon, " the meeting-places of merchants and of manufacturers," if we may believe a writer who visited them in 887. In Gaul it was similarly on the main trade routes that towns were reorganized, such as Toul, Verdun, Arras, Soissons, Paris, Rheims, Lyons, Vienne, Orleans, Tours, Poitiers, and Toulouse, while in Visigothic Spain there flourished Saragossa, Carthagena, Valencia, Cadiz, Seville, and, above all, Toledo, the splendour of which struck the Arab conquerors. But it was chiefly in Italy, that animated home of the urban life of antiquity, that towns were reconstituted most rapidly, near fortresses or the places where fairs (*mercata*) or weekly markets (*fora*) were held, on the outskirts (*suburbia*) of monasteries, and on the sites of Roman cities. Milan was the queen of these restored cities, among which were also Verona, Padua, Modena, Bologna, and Pisa, and beside which there rose new centres such as Ferrara and Pavia.

But in spite of all, town life still languished, even in Italy, because the true political, social, and economic activity of the time was concentrated in the great rural domains. This is why only a minute portion of the population gathered in the towns, the average size of which was from 1,000 to 1,500 persons in the tenth century, and the most populous of which in France and Germany barely reached 7,000 or 8,000 inhabitants. The town, which of old had been closely united with the country in a single district (*civitas*), was now isolated. It vegetated and took on the aspect of a large village, which, in the case of an old Roman town, seemed like a dwarf in the armour of a giant. It had become rural, and in its empty spaces were gardens, vineyards, and ploughed fields. The only thing which distinguished it was that it possessed fortified walls, furnished with gates and towers (Milan had 310 of these), and that within it there were to be found palace-fortresses or old Roman buildings, converted into strongholds, and numerous churches, side by side with the ruins of ancient monuments, which were strewn over the ground. The winding roads, stony or muddy or dusty, were flanked by houses made of wood or clay, covered with thatch, dark and smoky, possessed of neither chimneys nor windows. In the suburbs there lived a wretched population of artisans and small traders. Life there was monotonous and gloomy.

These towns had no political or judicial unity. Administrative and judicial authority and the functions of economic regulation were quarrelled over by rival powers, high officials, counts or dukes or judges, who held sway from the fortress (*castrum*), or bishops, who were masters of the city, the centre of religious life, even castellans and other feudal lords, who possessed fortified palaces or towers. The autonomous Roman organizations, courts, and councils had disappeared. Alone in a few centres, under the control of agents of the crown, there were organized assemblies of notables, landed proprietors, or freemen (*vicini, ahrimanns*), who took part in the administration of the town. But the greater number of the inhabitants of the town—artisans, merchants, gardeners, cultivators—were indistinguishable in their general condition from the countryfolk round them. They were reduced like these to villeinage and serfdom, and subjected to the same obligations. The agrarian economy weakened the urban economy to the point of stifling it, or else forced it to vegetate beneath its law.

Just at the moment when a renaissance of economic life

was beginning in the West a fresh crisis suddenly arrested its evolution and almost ruined the new civilization, which was being thus painfully elaborated. In the ninth and tenth centuries new invasions covered the West with ruins. The Scandinavian pirates, or Northmen, renewed for almost a century (830-911) the sinister exploits of the Germans, massacred the people and reduced them to slavery, burned the towns, and pillaged or ruined Christian Germany, the Low Countries, Western France, Scotland, Ireland, and England. In the East the Magyars, kinsmen of the Huns and the Avars, spread desolation in the Danube lands and in Central Europe, Northern Italy, and the east of France. In the south the Saracens, pirates of Berber or Arab race, carried their ravages into the islands and coasts of Italy, and into Provence and Dauphiné. But this time resistance was organized; the new military class of feudalism opposed a solid wall to the last of the invasions. In the tenth century the Scandinavians were converted to Christianity and founded stable settlements in Frisia, the north of Scotland and England, the Low Countries, and Neustria (911), where they became the champions of Christian civilization. The Magyars, stayed in their course by the Ottos (935-955), founded a Christian kingdom in Hungary. The Saracens were thrown back upon the islands. By 950 the new danger had been exorcised. Almost everywhere, with the exception of Ireland and Scotland, which fell back into barbarism, the new civilization which had been born in the West was saved, and the feudal age began.

An immense effort lasting for six centuries had been necessary to elaborate the new society. The fall of the Roman Empire seemed to have resulted in irreparable disaster, which dragged humanity back to the worst ages of its history, ruined every kind of production, restored slavery, substituted anarchy for order and poverty for wealth, and delivered the world over to the brutal force of barbarism. But by good fortune the Byzantine Empire had been able to put a stop to this work of retrogression and destruction in the East. It had shown that but for the invasions a normal evolution would have been possible, and that from Roman institutions there might have issued a new order of things, born of the ancient culture itself. It had been the first to hold up and stay the movement of the invasions, and it maintained intact for eight centuries a powerful state, in which was preserved the brilliant civilization which it had received, and of which it had become the sole repository. It had brought lands back to cultivation and restored agricultural production. If it had not succeeded in preventing the growth of an aristocracy and of great landed properties, it had at least safeguarded the prerogatives of the central power and protected small ownership. It had been able partially to maintain the middle class of small landed proprietors and the free artisans of the towns, as well as the great mercantile or industrial associations. If it had not prevented the formation of serfdom, it had worked for the disappearance of slavery. It had given a prodigious development to industry and commerce, and had made the Christian Europe of the East the incomparable centre of the world's wealth and civilization.

The work of the Christian West had been less brilliant, more toilsome, and slower. There only a few men of genius were able imperfectly and momentarily to re-establish the power of the state, and their range of action was limited. The Church, a corporation with vaster and more continuous designs, had more success. Popes and monks took up the work of Rome and laboured at the diffusion of Christian civilization, the heir to a large part of the civilization of Rome. It was thanks to them, and to the more intelligent elements among the aristocratic and popular classes, that the West was able to rise from among the ruins heaped up by Asiatic, Slav, or Germanic barbarism. A first attempt at colonization had brought about the reconquest of part of the soil, which had fallen back into a wilderness, and had revived agricultural production. To the primitive forms of ownership, tribal property, property of the village community, property of the undivided family, there were substituted, in an increasingly large proportion, forms more suited to stimulate economic activity, such as private property, vested either in the individual or in the family. But in Western Christendom this progress had been partially annihilated by the extension of the great domains. The aristocracy had seized the land, to the detriment of the small free proprietors. The absence of a strong central authority had allowed powerful bodies, such as the Church and the military class, to seize upon dominion as well as property, and to make general those systems of patronage, commendation, and benefice, out of which the feudal system was evolved. Millions of men had thus found themselves subjected to the domination of a few thousands. For the old free landowners and the *coloni* this transformation had been a fall. For the majority of other inhabitants of the West it must be conceded that it had been an improvement. Slavery had been almost wiped out, and the multitudes, who had no means of livelihood other than the cultivation of the land, had found in serfdom a far more tolerable refuge than the ancient slavery, while the great landowners were thus able to secure the means of exploiting the landed capital, of which they held a quasi-monopoly. A first stage had been reached under the influence of forces which were almost entirely economic in character. The mass of the peasantry had escaped from the degrading condition of slaves, and had acquired two inestimable possessions—human personality and the stability of the home. But the hard existence which they still led gave no hint of the era of liberation, which they were to know two centuries later.

In spite of the predominance of the régime of agricultural economy which characterized the early Middle Ages in the West, the economy of movable wealth had made a timid reappearance. Regional markets had been organized, and a beginning had even been made in international commerce. Industrial production was reviving on the domains of princes and monasteries, or in the resuscitated towns. Western Christendom needed now only a framework strong enough to preserve it from another collapse into barbarism, and a new lever, that of liberty, to raise the latent powers of a regenerated world. Hitherto it had been the East Roman Empire which had been in the van in the history of labour; its rôle was now to pass to the West, where a society full of vigour had arisen. The great work of the one had been to preserve the ancient civilization; the other was destined to inaugurate a civilization of its own, superior in greatness to any which had gone before.

BOOK II

CHAPTER I

THE first period of the Middle Ages bequeathed to the West a political, social, and economic régime, which had assumed definite shape by the tenth century, and which reached the height of its power in the three centuries which followed. This régime, which we call feudalism, provided a sort of frame for the activities of labour during some 400 years.

A publicist, Adalbero, Bishop of Laon, has indicated plainly enough its main principle, which was that of a division of social functions. "God's house," he writes, "which men think to be one, is threefold; some pray in it, some fight in it, and some work in it." In order to allow the first two classes, the clerks and the soldiers, to accomplish their superior work, they must enjoy a monopoly of the sole existing capital, the land, which alone ensures them a domination founded upon their natural mission, and guarantees their economic independence. The other classes must hold themselves fortunate if, in exchange for the spiritual and material protection extended to them, they are permitted to enjoy the produce of this capital. Their labour is but the legitimate payment for the patronage thus granted to them.

At the time of the dissolution of the Carolingian Empire and the disorders of the last invasions, this division of social labour did indeed present some show of reason. It was the Church which had safeguarded and still preserved civilization. It was the warriors, the "soldiers" (*milites*), as the Middle Ages called the feudal knights, who, bound to each other by the duties of vassalage, of which the chief was military service, saved the Christian West from complete dissolution. They had introduced some elements of order and organization into the general disorder and disorganization. The feudal contract was then the useful and necessary

119

form of the social contract, and everywhere throughout Western Christendom the feudal régime, born of vassalage, commendation and patronage, institutions which stood for solidarity and protection, had supplied the place of the weak or absent state, whose task of government it had assumed either in virtue of a mandate (or " immunity ") conferred upon it by the sovereign power, or else by usurpation.

The military and ecclesiastical classes had at the same time based their social and political power upon a solid economic foundation. They had succeeded in getting the soil of the West into their hands. The double maxim of French feudal law sets forth this conception in its most logical form : " No lord without land " was the primary declaration, and the corollary " No land without a lord " followed naturally. Lands, offices, money payments, become in the same way possessions reserved to the ruling classes. Functions or offices (" honours ") became assimilated with domains granted for life or for a term of years ("benefices"), and then on a hereditary title ; together they formed a single category of property, the fief, which was the solid basis of the fortune of these classes. The feudal system imposed itself upon the whole West, modified, it is true, by the previous traditions and the particular organization of each country. Its most logical form, French feudalism, conquered England, Northern Spain, the two Sicilies, and the Levant, while a less fully evolved form, German feudalism, adapted itself to the institutions of the Low Countries and the North of Italy.

The feudal régime, in its various aspects, was incompatible with the old forms of ownership, both with the collective property of the village and with free individual ownership, which hindered its expansion and evaded its monopoly. Everywhere common lands which once belonged to tribal or village communities, the *marks* of England and Germany, the *allmends* of the Germanic lands, the *communia* or commons of the Latin countries, were, as a rule, transformed into private or seigniorial possessions. By virtue of the right of appropriation attaching to assarts, the area of the common lands was continually diminished to the profit of lay and ecclesiastical lordships, or of their non-noble tenants, who undertook to bring them under cultivation and to pay to the lord as rent a part of the produce of the appropriated lands. In most cases the lords seized the common lands as their property, while allowing the use thereof to the community of *roturiers* and serfs in exchange for a rent. Nevertheless, a small number of rural communities in Germanic countries, and notably in the Netherlands, Switzerland, and other parts of Germany, succeeded, even in the full tide of feudalism, in preserving certain marks, the last survivals of the collective property of the village, and in maintaining them as late as the fifteenth century.

The small or moderate-sized free properties were also overthrown by the spread of the feudal régime. In the greater part of France, the Rhineland, the Low Countries, England, Italy, and Spain, free holdings, usually known as *allods*, were transformed perforce into fiefs because the lord looked sourly upon these lands, which were exempt from rents and services, and upon which he could exercise no rights of justice or of police. They formed so many inviolable and independent lordships in the midst of the seigniorial estates. By means of intimidation, threats, persuasion, force, the feudal powers set themselves to bring about their disappearance and transformation into fiefs. They were only partially successful in Germany, Spain, and Italy, but they succeeded more effectively in England, the Low Countries, and France. In Germany free properties diminished in number in the Rhineland, but survived in a large measure in Switzerland, the Tyrol, Upper Bavaria, Swabia, Thuringia, Saxony, Frisia, and Holstein, thanks to the power of the village communities and the comparative weakness of feudal organization in these regions between the tenth and the twelfth centuries. Here there continued to subsist peasants who held their property directly from the prince (*schäffenbären, biergelden*), some of whom, the *lehnbauern*, could even acquire fiefs, while others were veritable territorial sovereigns in their lands, which were known as " fiefs of the sun " (*sonnenlehen*). These small free proprietors of the countryside (*freie bauern*), subject only to the royal jurisdiction, had courts formed of their peers, under the presidency of a royal delegate, the *amtmann*, and enjoyed the right to carry arms like nobles. In Northern Spain, in the shelter of their wild valleys, the communities of the Pyrenees, groups of foresters and shepherds owned their own woods and pastures, concluded conventions with each other, made federations and alliances, and acted as sovereign powers. In the Basque provinces of Alava, Guipúzcoa, and Vizcaya, and even in Castile, whole territories, the *behetrias*, were peopled with freemen owning their own lands, who had decided to put themselves under protection, but who had retained the right to choose their lord out of a particular family, or out of all those among which it suited them to make choice, and who changed him when they pleased. Even in other parts of Northern Spain groups of free landowners were to be met with. But in general, they were obliged to resign themselves to accepting seigniorial patronage (*patrocinio*), and to consent to do homage and pay certain services, while still reserving the power to change their patron. Most of these landowners, as in France, entered the ranks of vassals. In Italy free proprietors also survived from place to place, particularly in Lombardy and Tuscany, where they were known as *ahrimanns*, and in the two Sicilies, where the Normans called them *alleutiers*, after the French fashion. The Republic of San Marino is probably one of these ancient allodial estates. Nevertheless, in all these countries, and even in Germany, feudal property gained steadily in importance at the expense of small or moderate-sized properties, and the latter often had to become semi-feudalized, by accepting patronage, in order to survive at all.

In other parts of the West, where feudalism was more strongly organized, or where the struggle was more difficult for the small proprietors, it usually ended to their disadvantage. In France the allod maintained itself sporadically in Normandy, where the legendary kingdom of Yvetot is a survival of it, and where burgage tenure (*tenure en bourgage*) seems to have been a form of free property, as was that of the vavasours. The same thing happened in Nivernais, Brittany, Auvergne, and, above all, in Aquitaine, Guienne, Gascony, Béarn, Bigorre, Dauphiné, and Languedoc, where the allodial owners sometimes formed themselves into defensive associations. In the Low Countries, Zeeland,

Holland, Frisia, maritime Flanders, Campine, and Eastern Brabant, free property persisted by reason of the energy of their population of sailors and pioneers, and of their isolation in the midst of marsh and heath. But everywhere else victory went to feudal property, such a victory as was won in England after the Norman Conquest, which, indeed, only completed the work of the Anglo-Saxon period. In 1086, the Norman terrier, Domesday Book, recorded only 44,531 free landowners out of a total of 1,500,000 inhabitants in the Anglo-Norman kingdom. Only a quarter of these were bound to military service, the usual charge which lay upon free land. The rest were bound to pay light services and even a few labour works in return for their holdings, although they shared with the nobility the obligation of investiture and the oath of fidelity. As the thirteenth century approached the absolute freedom of these small properties tended to disappear throughout the West, and the allodial estate tended to approximate either to noble land or to peasant land (*terre roturière*), to some of the obligations upon which it was already bound.

The grip of the military and ecclesiastical class upon landed property and upon most of the fruits of labour is thus a characteristic of the feudal régime. The Church, in the first place, was able to play a large part in the seizure of landed property and of the wealth represented thereby. By usurping royal domains and sovereign rights, still more by gifts due to the piety of the faithful and by acquisitions due to the clearance of waste lands, it acquired the greater part of the land of Western Europe, and was well able to turn it to the most profitable use. Bishops and abbots took their place in the feudal hierarchy, accepted or submitted to most of its obligations, and exercised sovereign rights over their subjects. They patiently repaired the losses to which the violence of laymen and the intermittent secularizations decreed by rulers subjected their patrimony. One part of the landed property of the Church, it is true, was not assimilated to the fiefs; those lands which were granted, according to the formula, "for the service of God" or in "frankalmoin," were in principle free of rents and services, and held only of God, but in fact they were soon attached to the feudal hierarchy, since the lords exercised therein rights of justice and patronage. Many ecclesiastical domains were, moreover, true fiefs, distinct altogether from lands held in frankalmoin. Their extent was considerable. In England certain bishops had fiefs which furnished as many as sixty knights to the army, and a large part of the soil of England and Ireland was owned by the Anglo-Norman church. In Germany a full half of the soil was in the hands of the Church. " The bishops own everything there," said a King of France in the twelfth century. The Rhineland, in particular, was nothing more or less than " a street of priests," as the famous saying went. In the Low Countries the bishoprics and the twenty-seven Benedictine abbeys stood in the front rank of landed proprietors. In France certain abbeys owned over 100,000 hectares of land, and bishops, such as the Bishop of Langres, held a whole county. In Spain, where gifts multiplied and the kings reserved a third (*tercias reales*) of all conquered lands for the Church, abbeys and bishoprics appropriated vast territories; those of the Archbishop of Santiago had a circuit of not less than twenty-four miles. In Lombardy the Church owned a third of the soil; the Bishop of Asti held 100,000 arpents of land; the Bishop of Florence owned 200 castles; the Abbey of Farfa, 132; and the Bishop of Bologna had 2,000 manses or domains. In the whole of the West the proportion of the soil which passed into the hands of the Church seems to have been between a third and a half of the whole.

The sovereign princes themselves were obliged to enter into the feudal framework, and the domains which they reserved for themselves, and upon which they based a good deal of their social power, took on a feudal character. They were far less adroit than the clerks, and they often, by means of alienations and grants, lost a part of this landed wealth, which suffered incessant changes. Sometimes, as in Anglo-Norman England, their power was great enough to enable them to build up a vast territorial reserve, made up in 1085 of some 1,422 great estates, to which, in the twelfth century, they added the major part of the soil of Ireland, over and above forests, waste lands, disinherited lands, and the confiscated possessions of rebellious vassals. Thus it was that in 1188 they commanded the highest annual revenue of all the sovereigns of the West, £750,000 sterling, whereas the royal domain of the kings of France at the same period, although economically managed, only produced an annual income of six million pounds *tournois*.[1] Elsewhere, in the two Sicilies, the Norman kings were at one period able to gather together territorial resource sufficient to raise them to the second rank among the richest princes of the West. It was easy for the Spanish sovereigns to build up similar domains by conquest under the name of *realengos*. But the possessions of princes, like those of the feudal lords, were most frequently diminished by incessant grants of fiefs, or by the careless administration of those who held them. This was particularly marked in the case of the royal domains (*königshufen, reichsgüter*), once so numerous, which the German dynasties had at their disposal and squandered with such complete lack of foresight.

The rest of the soil of the West was occupied by the possessions of the nobility. They formed the totality of fiefs, and a fief consisted primarily in land, though functions or offices, pensions or perpetual revenues, were also granted in fief. Noble land was in principle a conditional and revocable property, over which the grantor reserved a superior right (the *dominium*), but it very quickly became a form of transmissible and even alienable property, under certain conditions designed to guarantee the execution of those pecuniary and military obligations which were binding upon the vassal. The latter became the grantee by means of the symbolical ceremony of investiture and in return for the payment of a nominal rent. After the eleventh century a special deed of concession (*aveu*) was drawn up, and an inventory of the possessions granted was executed. In France and in countries where the French feudal régime prevailed—to wit, in England, the two Sicilies, and the Spanish March—all land was presumed to fall within this system of fiefs. Elsewhere—for example, in Italy—a title-deed was necessary in order that land should be recognized as of this quality. Similarly, the principle of the heredity of fiefs established itself in the north and centre of Italy later than in France, by virtue of the imperial constitution of Pavia. In the kingdom of Castile one part only of the

---

[1] A pound *tournois* was worth about a quarter of a pound sterling.

feudal estates (*honores*, *tierras de señorio*) resembled the French fief; many of the other lands (*tenencias*, *encomiendas*, *mandaciones*) were given in the form of temporary and revocable grants for a life term by the kings during the period of reconquest. In Germany, where the Carolingian rule had left deep traces behind it, the transmission of the fief (*lehn*) remained subject to numerous restrictions; it remained inalienable and indivisible, and the right of succession lay in the direct masculine line alone. It was not assimilated to noble land unless it was granted to a soldier or to an official, and the French adage (*nulle terre sans seigneur*) remained unknown to Germanic as to Italian law. Finally, there existed in Germany a form of tenure or benefice which was inferior to the fief, the *eigen*, or *dienstgut*, which was charged with duties to which the fief was not submitted, analogous in some ways with those appertaining to servile tenure in France.

Noble property was subdivided among a multitude of co-sharers. The feudal system was founded upon a more or less complicated hierarchy of suzerains and vassals, united by ties of homage and fidelity, by a sworn oath and by certain obligations which were defined in the contract. The lord needed soldiers, and obtained them only by granting them a part of his domain. In return for the right to demand military service, attendance at his court, the *aids* which he might need at important crises in his existence, lodging, and entertainment for himself and his followers when on a journey, he was obliged to hand over to his vassal a sufficient portion of his property to enable the latter to support and arm himself and to maintain his family. The great estate was the one essential economic force for the noble, but it was always breaking into pieces, because the suzerain was continually obliged to build up his military resources, and could do so only by the grant of fiefs. Every time he gained a vassal he lost a part of his lands. The inconsiderable money payments which he drew from the latter on transmission or sale, or in similar circumstances, were in practice far from compensating for the loss of landed revenue, which he suffered every time that he created a new fief.

Thus the number of noble landowners grew unceasingly as a result of this propagation of the feudal system. In

France there existed, over and above some forty great fiefs (duchies and counties), an enormous mass of seigniorial domains held by castellans, viscounts, *avoués*, and knights. At the beginning of the twelfth century a Duke of Aquitaine led 12,000 of these upon a crusade. Only the poorest of the nobles, the esquires, were landless. In the Low Countries a great feudatory, the Duke of Brabant, had no less than 3,000 vassals; below the great lords (*potentes*) was a very numerous military class (*ordo militaris*) of barons, viscounts, castellans, and knights, not to mention the multitude of squireens (*ministeriales*) living the life of country gentlemen in their rustic forts of stone. In Germany below the eight dukes and the nobility of the first rank, which included counts, landgraves, margraves, burgraves, and *landvogten*, there flourished the order of free knights (*freie ritter*). In 1180 Frederick Barbarossa was able to assemble as many as 40,000 of these knights, as well as 75 princes, at the Diet of Mainz. The German imperial army, in the twelfth century, usually contained 30,000 knights and 100,000 nobles, including esquires and varlets. The Germanic nobility, moreover, comprised also a numerous class, unknown in France, known as *ministeriales*, semi-servile nobles, who could be alienated and transmitted together with their land, and paid the *mortuarium*, but whose service and office raised them to the rank of those permitted to acquire free lands and even serfs. In two countries only, England and the Two Sicilies, was there a clearly defined class of noble landowners. In the former there were only 1,400 barons of the first rank, the tenants-in-chief beneath the king, and of these nine held between 100 and 793 manors apiece. Then came the knights, whose numbers fell from 7,871 in 1088 to about 5,000 at the end of the twelfth century. In the lowest ranks are the tenants in serjeanty, who served as foot soldiers in the army. In Southern Italy, under the Norman dynasty, an official list, the *Catalogue of Barons*, reveals the existence of 4,233 nobles, mostly vassals of the second rank (*milites, barones, minores*). In Central and Northern Italy the great feudal houses, such as those of Verona, Montferrat, and Este, towered above a crowd of vassals and vavasours, beneath whom again was a nobility of service, officials of the Carolingian type, known as *masnadores*, who at one time owned as much as a third of the land of Tuscany. As to the Iberian kingdoms, the very conditions of their development, combined with the incessant conquests at the expense of the Moslems, brought about a multiplication of noble landowners, ranging from those of the first rank, who were called "the rich men" (*ricos hombres, magnates, optimates*), and were almost as powerful as the kings in Aragon, to those of the second order, known sometimes as *infanzones*, vavasours (*valvassores, vasallos*), knights (*caballeros*), sometimes, as in Italy, as *masnaderos*. Thus it was that some hundreds of thousands of men, both soldiers and officials, had taken possession of the land of the West, or had received more or less extensive portions of it in the form of fiefs.

The property of the nobility sometimes took the form of great domains, but more often, in the case of fiefs belonging to the second rank of nobles, who were far more numerous, it took the form of medium-sized or small properties. The royal domains and those of the Church, on the contrary, can almost all be classed as great properties, though they were rarely concentrated, being usually scattered about. Nobles of the first rank might possess a considerable number of manors or domains. Thus in England the estates of one great baron comprised 793 farms or holdings spread over twenty counties. In Italy certain of the great lords had as many as 11,000 manses, and one is recorded to have held 90,000 hectares in the eleventh century. Others held 500 to 600 manses, and the Papacy itself had in one district a group of domains covering 78,541 hectares. But if a minority was thus fortified with vast possessions, the majority had to be content with less considerable domains, though even these, given the fact that the value of the land was less, were proportionately larger than are small or medium-sized estates to-day. In Dauphiné, for instance, a fief was composed of from three to twelve manses. In England there existed fiefs formed of three or four manors, or the territory of three or four villages. While large domains were gradually broken up by the grant of fiefs and by all sorts of alienations, small or medium fiefs were subdivided by dint of changes of ownership or partitions. The medium or small property tended to crumble into innumerable little holdings, some of which in Poitou and in Saintonge comprised only the fifth part of a manse. In the two Sicilies a quarter, or a fifth, or a seventh of a knight's fee was not infrequently to be met with. In the Low Countries it was by no means rare to see the country squires driving their own ploughs and living the life of peasants, from whom they were distinguished only by their turbulence and ferocity.

Nevertheless, a certain number of domains still preserved the characteristics of the great properties of the preceding period. They may best be compared with the *plantations* formed in new lands or in colonies in the eighteenth and nineteenth centuries, or with the vast possessions of the Russian aristocracy before the abolition of serfdom. In the central period of the Middle Ages the holders of these great domains—princes, bishops, monasteries, and the upper rank of the nobility—divided them into groups, which were variously named in the different countries. Such were the German *fronhof*, the English *manor*, the Alsatian *colonge*, the French *prædium* or *terra fiscalis*, preserving the memory of the Carolingian *fisc*, which was a collection of several manors, and the Italian *curtis*, which corresponded to the French fisc or *massa*. The ancient *villa* no longer subsisted, save as a more or less extensive territorial framework. Each group had its economic centre in one of the lord's residences, the castle. This was often little more than a rough structure of unworked stone with a turfed enclosure, like a fortified farm, but in great seigniorial domains it was an imposing collection of buildings grouped round a donjon, where the lord dwelt, together with his family and his civil and military followers. The castle, which now replaced the villa as the lord's dwelling-place, was built first of wood, then of stone, and fortified with greater and greater skill as time went on. It was at once a fortress, and the heart of the economic life of the estate. There his provisions and reserve stores were garnered in cellars and barns, and his live-stock in stables. There also were sometimes to be found gardens and orchards clustering under the walls of the enclosure, or even within it, and buildings such as wine-presses and ovens, the adjuncts of the farm. Such was likewise the appearance of the great abbeys, which were fortified and turreted in the same way, but which often enclosed huge granaries, barns, and stables.

LIFE AND WORK IN MEDIEVAL EUROPE

Here the old system of economic administration was kept up, with its specialized offices (*ministeria*), under the control of the lord or the abbot. The great lay feudatories entrusted the organization of these offices to high officials—the marshal, the constable, the chamberlain, and the butler. Sometimes, as in the Low Countries, they even had a whole bureaucracy of notaries to transmit their orders. Usually each great centre of cultivation had its more humble agents called stewards, mayors, *écoutêtes*, bailiffs, *gastaldes*, provosts, or judges, who supervised the work, sometimes with the assistance of a specialized staff of foresters, huntsmen, master swineherds, master grooms, and and other foremen in the various rural occupations. They supervised the cultivation of the domain, collected its produce in the central buildings, and undertook the economic organization of the whole estate.

The property of each great domain, excluding the fiefs of vassals which had been detached from it, was made up of two unequal parts, the lord's demesne and the holdings of peasants, both free *roturiers* and serfs. The former was made up of all the land directly farmed by the lord himself. In some Western countries it was usually a third of the cultivated land. Some of these demesnes were as large as 130 to 140 hectares, and were ploughed by great teams of eight oxen. The lord cultivated them by means of *corvées*, free labour services, which his tenants, both *roturiers* and serfs, were bound to do for him. This reserved demesne might also include private vineyards, meadows, fishponds, and forests, but, as a rule, uncultivated lands, pastures, heaths, and woods, over which the lord usually possessed proprietory rights, remained undivided, and the use thereof was allowed within certain limits to his subjects.

The medieval lord was a bad administrator, seldom fitted to farm his land himself, and at the same time a wasteful and improvident spendthrift. Thus in order to increase his revenues and to obtain the utmost from a soil which threatened to remain unproductive, he had a perfectly natural tendency to multiply tenants from whom he drew rents in money and in kind, more abundant than those which he could obtain himself from his demesne. Thus great domains tended more and more to break up into little farms granted to tenants. In France and in the North of

Spain they were called *manses, bordes, condamines, cabanes, quintanes, meix, colonges, casaux;* in Germany, *hufen* and *colonicæ;* in Italy, *massæ, massarizie, casalini* or *corticelli;* in England, *holdings.* Instead of the four to eight manses received by the vassal, a tenant usually obtained but one, but the services and payment which he rendered were a more important return from an economic point of view. This is why, notably in England and in Italy, two-thirds of the manor was usually cultivated in the form of *roturier* or servile holdings.

Thus each great domain, which formed a self-contained and isolated organism, was able to suffice for the needs of the feudal landowner. He led the life of a soldier and leader of the state. The "hereditary *gendarmerie*," which was his social function, and which allowed him to lead a largely parasitical existence, remained possible only by dint of his seizure of the land, and distribution of that land into fiefs and holdings. From the first he drew his military, from the second his economic, power. The feudal system in the last resort rested upon an organization which, in return for a protection, which was often illusory, placed the working classes at the mercy of the idle classes, and gave the land not to those who cultivated it, but to those who had been able to seize it.

CHAPTER II

ECONOMIC AND SOCIAL ORGANIZATION OF THE RURAL DISTRICTS OF THE
WEST DURING THE EARLY FEUDAL PERIOD.

SIDE by side with the minority who owned the soil, millions
of men were, indeed, deprived of all rights of property, and
it was the immense mass of the rural populations of the
West who found themselves in this condition. An almost
impassable gulf separated them from the landowning class.
The peasants were all more or less dependent (*hörigen*, as
was said in Germany); all were considered merely as instruments for the exploitation of the domain (*villa*), whence their
name of villeins; all were regarded as socially valueless and
esteemed solely for the economic value which they represented.

They were not all, however, classed in the same category.
There were among them free and half-free peasants, distinct
from the serfs and the last slaves. On the one hand were
the free villeins (*vilains francs*), on the other the servile
villeins (*vilains serfs*), to use the French terms. This distinction was found with divers variations all over the West,
except in England, where since the Norman Conquest
villeinage had become unified in the form of serfdom. But
in Germany free villeinage was represented by free cultivators
called *freien landsassen, freie hintersassen*, and by half-free
peasants, the descendants, probably, of the freedmen or
lites of the preceding age (*halb freien, meier*). In Alsace
these *censitaires*, holding their land by payment of a *cens*,
or quit-rent, occur again under the name of *coloni* (*landsie-
deln*). They have some analogy with the *læten* of the Low
Countries, with the *villanos, pecheros*, and *juniores* of Spain,
and with the *coloni sedentes, manentes*, and *fictaiuoli* of
Italy. In France they formed the great class of peasant
" labourers," or *roturiers* (*ruptuarii*), which was commonly
amalgamated with that of the serfs under the general name
of villeins (*villani rustici, pagesii, nativi*) or subjects (*homines
de potestate, hommes de pœste*), but which was distinguished
therefrom by the title of *franc* or free. The distinctive

characteristics of free villeinage were, on the one hand, the recognition of a man's personal liberty, and, on the other, the contractual nature of his tenure. In principle he was a freeman like the noble, but in practice his liberty was apt to be remarkably attenuated. If some villeins, like the *juniores* of Castile, preserved the right to change their domicile, the majority were unable to leave their holdings without the permission of the lord. They had none of those political rights which distinguished and elevated the noble class. It was only quite exceptionally that a few among them were called to the possession of fiefs or admitted to knighthood. The opinion of the upper classes would admit no point of contact between the tenant, even when free, and the noble landowner; free and serf were regarded with the same disdain. In practice the free villein was almost as closely tied down as was the serf to the social rank in which Fate had placed him.

But the free villein's land was, nevertheless, a degree higher than that of the servile villein. The former enjoyed the benefit of a contract, which the latter never knew. Tenure in villeinage was sharply distinguished from the fief, but it was distinguished no less sharply from servile tenure. As in the case of the fief, tenure in villeinage presupposed the retention of the actual ownership of the land by the lord, while at the same time the use thereof was granted to the free villein. Some lands—for instance, in Germany—were even granted with full rights of property, but without the obligation of military service. Usually the free villeins cultivated their holdings in virtue of real or fictitious leases with various names, such as *baux à cens*, *précaires*, *mainfermes*, *champarts*, and *complants*, the conditions of which differed greatly. Some granted the land for a term of years or for life, others on hereditary leases. Some conferred almost plenary possession upon the villein, as did the perpetual lease or *locatairie perpétuelle* of Languedoc, the *métairie perpetuelle* of the Limousine March, the *albergement* of Bugey, Savoy, and Dauphiné, the *mainferme* of the North of France and Belgium, the *bordelage* of Nivernais and Auvergne, and the fee farm (*fiefferme*) of Normandy. Lastly, there were leases which associated the owner and the farmer more intimately, assuring to the former, instead of a fixed *cens* or rent, a varying share (*champart*) in the annual produce of the villein's farming. When the lord welcomes assarters on to his estate, he makes a sort of treaty with them, and the lease is called *hostise;* he stipulates, as in the case of the *champart,* for the payment of a variable rent (*cens*) upon the land or house granted. Taking them altogether, tenures in villeinage fall into two great categories. Some—*précaires, emphytéoses, fieffermes, censives, complants*—guarantee to the landowner a fixed rent and the actual ownership of the land. Others—tenures or *champarts* and *hostises*—provide him with a certain proportion of revenue, analogous to the modern system of *métayage.*

The free peasants who cultivated these lands did not owe homage or guard-service for them, but they were obliged to pay a part of the revenue in the form of a fixed or variable rent, usually called a *cens* (German *zins,* Spanish *pecho,* Italian *fitto*) in the first, and a *champart* in the second case. They were not landowners in the strict sense of the term, but for the most part they enjoyed the perpetual usufruct of the land; they had, in medieval terminology, property in use, in default of full or direct property. In certain countries—for instance, in Alsace—the peasant benefited by improvements (*jus palæ,* or spade-right), which were held to belong to him. In France the *complanteur* shared the soil which had been planted with the landowner. Originally the villein held his land only by an inalienable life tenure, but contracts and customs soon transformed this peasant holding into a patrimonial possession like the fief. The villein was the true owner of the land, despite the services with which it was burdened. The majority of the free villeins of the West were able to hand on their holding to their children, like a real inheritance, by simply paying a succession due, called in France a *double cens, relief, rachat, mortaille,* in Spain *luctuosa,* in the Low Countries and in Germany *mortuarium, besthaupt* or *vinicopium.* This due was payable when the heirs entered upon possession. The land of the free villein could also be alienated, on the payment of other taxes (*lods et ventes*). The villein had the right of dividing it up as much as he desired and of cultivating it as he chose, unless his cultivation were subject to the *champart.* In most cases he benefited by the fixity of his dues, which could only be levied at stated times, mostly consisted of products of the soil, and had often to be collected by the lord at his own expense. Accessory money payments were low. Once his rents in money (*cens, oublies*) or in kind (*champarts, agriers, terrages*) were acquitted, the villein remained in legitimate possession of the rest of his revenue.

There were even highly privileged tenants to be found in the ranks of villeinage. Such were the *censitaires* of monasteries and churches, who were called *læten, cerocensuales, homines ecclesiastici, hommes de sainteur* in Germany and the Low Countries, and *abadengos* in Spain; and such, too, were the *censitaires* of princes, such as the Spanish *realengos*. They were an object of envy to the rural masses. They paid more moderate rents, among which were numbered payments in wax for church lights, whence they got the name of *cerocensuales;* they performed a limited number of field works; they had only to pay light taxes on marriage; and they were not only free from the exactions of lay lords, but better protected against war and dearth. But the majority of free villeins, despite their rank of freemen and all the stipulations of contract and custom, possessed neither the right to carry arms for their own defence, nor, as a rule, the possibility of changing their domicile or their lord. They were shut out of political society and consequently had no real guarantee against oppression. The lord had not "full enjoyment" over them, as was recognized by the famous jurist Pierre de Fontaines in the thirteenth century; but the sole guarantee which the villein possessed against an abuse of seigniorial power lay in the conscience of his lord. Between lord and villein there was no judge save God. To exact arbitrary payments from a free peasant was only a moral fault, a "larceny" committed at the peril of the lord's soul. But of what avail was such a restriction against the suggestions of selfishness or of cupidity? There was no remedy against arbitrary power. Hence it befell that, in spite of custom, the free villein was often subjected to labour services, payments in kind, monopolies, dues, the whole conglomeration of extortions which the age knew as exactions, *maltôtes*, evil customs, and to a multitude of abuses, which time at length consecrated, and which increased still further the old obligations of the free tenant.

The villein's freedom was only a sort of semi-servitude, but his condition was, nevertheless, much better than that of the serf. It was serfdom which was, in the tenth, eleventh, and even in the twelfth century, the dominant social institution as regards the great mass of the workers. Indeed, into the general class of serfs were confounded all the old categories of *hôtes*, freedmen, *coloni*, *colliberti*, and personal or household slaves. The human capital available for the exploitation of the seigniorial domains of France was composed of these *hommes de corps*—male and female serfs, who could be tallaged and subjected to *mainmorte* at will, and were known sometimes as *questaux*, sometimes as "liege men of their bodies" (*hommes liges du corps*), capitation men (*hommes de capitation*), natives (*nativi*). In Anglo-Norman England the 109,000 villeins entered in Domesday Book, who were labourers owning a pair of oxen and thirty to fifteen acres of land, were classed with the 90,000 cotters and bordars, who had no plough-teams, but only a cottage with a garden and five acres or so of land, and also with the 25,000 agricultural bondsmen, whose condition was that of slaves, to form a single category analogous to that of the French and Norman serfs. These Anglo-Norman villeins, reduced to serfdom, formed more than three-quarters of the population of England from the eleventh to the thirteenth centuries. Germany possessed a large number of peasants of the same condition, called *leibeigenen*, *eigenleute*, unfree (*unfreie*), servants (*knechte*, *servi*, *homines proprii*), because they were the property of others. In the Low Countries they were given the name of tributaries or *hagastalds*, and in Spain they were known under various names—*solariegos* in Castile and Navarre, *collazos* in Navarre, *villanos de parada* in Aragon, *pageses de remensa* (peasants fixed to the soil) in Catalonia. Nine-tenths of the rural population of Italy also was composed of this class of cultivators, who were known as "subjects" (*vassali homines*, *homines*), or else under the ancient appellations of *aldions*, *coloni*, or *censiles*.

Everywhere, whatever the name by which they were called, the ranks of the serfs were recruited in the same way—either by birth, by mixed marriages between free and servile persons, by the mere fact of dwelling upon servile soil, or as the result of a feudal war and the captivity resulting from it, or of a judicial sentence of condemnation. It even happened that men presented serfs, or offered up their children as serfs, to churches and convents. Better still, a man would sometimes offer himself, a rope round his neck and a penny on his head; and there was a whole class of serfs called, for this reason, *oblates*. Force, misery, piety— all increased the number of serfs, and before the twelfth century multitudes of people were often unable to obtain a home, a scrap of land, and their daily bread, save by accepting or begging for the condition of serfdom, even when they had not been born to it.

There were, however, degrees of serfdom and a whole hierarchy of serfs. At the bottom of the ladder were domestic serfs (*vernaculi*) or artisans (*operarii*), called in England villeins in gross, who hardly differed from the old slaves, having no home of their own, but living in the lord's house, where they were brought up and performed the humblest domestic services. A permanent sojourn in the lord's household meant that they were the butt of insult and ill-treatment. Cruelly used, and beaten for the least fault, they formed a sort of proletariat of serfdom, exploited and embittered, aspiring, like the slaves of antiquity, only to escape by flight from the odious prison in which they were held captive. But at the top of the ladder there were, on the other hand, privileged serfs, such as the *colliberts* of the eastern provinces of France and of the Île-de-France and Nivernais, whose families were not allowed to be dispersed, and who were probably freed from rights of *formariage*[1] and *mainmorte*. Happiest of all were the royal and ecclesiastical serfs who dwelt upon the domains of sovereigns and of the secular or monastic Church, and enjoyed full juridical rights. They were less subject to being given away, sold, or exchanged, and they possessed a material security and guarantees of well-being which ordinary serfs lacked.

The great mass of ordinary serfs stood halfway between the rightless men at the bottom and the privileged men at the top. They were under similar obligations, and their condition was the same. The sole characteristic which dis-

---

[1] Payable on the marriage of a serf to a person belonging to another lord's estate. See below, p. 138.

tinguished them from slaves was that they had a legal personality, which was recognized by custom or by law. Also, as soon as they were established upon a holding they could possess a home, a family, even a patrimony of movables; and the majority of them were in this position. But they had in no degree the free disposal of their persons. They were as much a part of the demesne as were the live-stock. They were considered as essential elements of farming capital, as economic securities. The loss of a family of serfs was as prejudicial to a lord as the loss of a number of his cattle—perhaps more prejudicial. Thus these human cattle were forbidden to abandon the land they cultivated, on pain of pursuit; whithersoever they fled, they ran the risk, by virtue of the right of *suite*, or *parée*, of being captured and brought back to their original home. The serf was bequeathed, sold, exchanged, together with the land upon which he lived. He could not appear or give evidence in a court of justice, more especially in causes which concerned freemen. He was shut out of the ranks of the clergy. In England he was not admitted to serve on the jury or in assizes. Only a small number of serfs were able to obtain permission to leave the domain, while continuing to pay personal dues and payments, or else abandoning their servile holding, together with a part of the possessions which they had been able to amass. Another not less serious restriction upon the liberty of the serf was the prohibition against contracting marriage outside the demesne, for fear that the children of such a marriage would escape the ownership of the lord. The serf could not contract a union of this kind without permission and an indemnity known as *formariage*, on pain of punishment and confiscation. In such a case certain fixed conventions ruled the division of the future servile family between the lords concerned. Finally, no serf had the right of property. Servile tenure differed essentially from the tenure granted to the free villein. The latter was derived from an irrevocable contract, whereas the former arose out of a purely voluntary and always revocable concession. The conditions and payments of the one were fixed and invariable; those of the other might be modified at the will of the lord, and aggravated if it so pleased him. The tenement of the free villein became hereditary and alienable, like a true property, but a servile tenement was never considered to be property, even in the sense of usufruct. In principle it could be neither inherited nor alienated, and the serf could not dispose of it by exchange, by sale, or by will. Nevertheless, in the interests of cultivation the lord was led to permit the serf to hand on the holding which he farmed, in order to stimulate the activity of the farmer's labour. But the serf could make such a transmission only to his direct heir, and the latter had to redeem the servitude (*mainmorte*) wherewith the land was burdened by the payment of a tax. This tax was the indelible mark of a servile condition, and for this reason he was described as *mainmortable*.

Finally, the servile farmer was bowed beneath special burdens, from which the free villein was legally exempt. The serf paid a capitation fee or chevage (*capitalis census*), a personal and annual tax of low amount (fourpence in France), but the outward and visible sign of his peculiar subordination, as the *obrok* used to be in Russia. He paid a personal *taille*, another mark of subjection, and the amount of this payment, which was also called *queste, tolte*, exaction, forced loan, was dependent upon the will of the lord, who could thus, according to his own caprice, dispose of the whole movable fortune of the serf; that is to say, of the only property which the serf was able to possess. Originally the payment was marked in primitive fashion by a notch upon a wooden tally, split into two parts, of which tax-collector and taxpayer each retained one. Finally, the lord could call upon the serf for labour whenever he wanted it, in all circumstances and at all times. By virtue of works or *corvées* (*corporis angariæ, operæ*), some ordinary and some extraordinary (*perangariæ*), the serf was bound to cultivate the lord's demesne, to cart his farm produce, to share in all the field work and in all the buildings undertaken by the lord. He was requisitioned for the upkeep of the castle and the escort of criminals, for relays, for the repair of roads and bridges, and for the defence of fortresses. His person, his labour, and the produce of his labour all belonged in theory to his lord. Such were the burdens peculiar to the servile peasant.

But there were many others also, which he had to bear in a heavier degree than had the villeins who were likewise subject to them. These were payments in money and, above all, in kind, called *champarts, complants*, customs, which consisted of corn, wine, cattle, poultry, wax, gifts at certain times of year (*salutes*), and fees for the use of the undivided lands of the lordship. Like the villein, the serf had to submit to seigniorial monopolies, the *banalités* of the oven, the mill, and the winepress. Often he had to recognize the lord's exclusive right of hunting and warren, and of keeping a dovecote, and his privilege of selling his vintage and wine before anyone else (*banvin*). To the lord, as to the head of a sovereign state, the villein and the serf were bound to render military service in person or to pay commutation taxes. They had to contribute to extraordinary taxes called aids, due on the knighting or marriage of the lord's children, to provide his ransom, or to pay the costs of his crusading expeditions. In the same way they had to provide him with lodging, food, and other objects (rights of *prise*), and to entertain and board himself and his followers (*procuration*). They paid him yet more tolls for the right to use the roads, and to frequent markets, fairs, and ports. The seigniorial police and justice served as pretexts for fines and confiscations. With the exception of the clergy and the princes, the propertied classes were ignorant of sane methods of economic administration, and did not understand that the best means of increasing their landed revenue was to protect the peasant who procured it. For them, and still more for their harsh and rapacious agents—mayors, provosts, bailiffs, *ammans*, who often held their offices by heredity—the rural masses, " exploitable at will," were no more than human herds, to be used till they were utterly worn out, solely in the interests of the moment.

No attempt was made to improve the economy of peasant production. The feudal classes were both ignorant of scientific agriculture and contemptuous of the labourer's task; they had no idea of encouraging or assisting his efforts to obtain a better return from the soil. Left to himself, without guide, counsel, or support, possessing no capital, insufficient cattle, and inadequate tools (sometimes no more than shovel, spade, and wooden ploughshare), the villein continued to farm his holding according to the wasteful methods of extensive cultivation. He did not understand the rotation of crops, he was ignorant of the use of root or grass crops to recuperate the soil, he was sparing of manure. He practised to excess the customs of fallowing the land and burning weeds. Agricultural colonization made but slight progress during the first two centuries of this feudal period. The greater part of the soil of the West remained under heath, marsh, and forest; cereals, vines, and industrial crops occupied only a small area. The smaller live-stock still predominated in the byres, and pasturage still prevailed over meadows. Confined within the narrow limits of the manor, in which there were no sufficiently vigorous stimulants to excite him to increased production, the villein supplied only what was strictly necessary for his master and indispensable for the subsistence of his own family.

His holding was as a rule fairly large, though it varied in size with the fertility of the soil. In Alsace it contained on an average 30 acres, in Germany 20 to 180 acres, in England 15 to 30 acres, and in exceptional cases 50 acres, which was the usual size in France and elsewhere. It must be added that the peasant had a share in the use of the heaths, pasture-grounds, and woods belonging to the village community and the lord. But in certain countries, such as England, Germany, and the east of France, the arable lands were scattered in narrow strips, cultivated according to a common routine; and this, together with the extreme *morcellement* of the manse or holding in other parts, due to the introduction of the principle of equal shares, rendered labour difficult and was a bar to agricultural improvements. Moreover, there was nothing to encourage the villein to increase the value of his landed capital, since he was not its master, and it was not easy for him either to transmit it, or to sell it, or to alienate it at will, or even to gather in security the fruits of his labour. He had no encouragement to attempt an intensive cultivation, since he would not have had any opportunity to dispose of the supplementary produce which he would have drawn from it. Far from being the co-partner of the farmer, the landowner under the feudal régime was, as far as the peasant was concerned, a mere parasite, always harsh and always capricious, for whom any improvement in the soil was but the pretext for some new exaction. He discouraged initiative and dried up all energy at its source, by taking from the villein an exorbitant part of the fruits of his work, so that labour was half sterile. Indeed, the initial error of the feudal lords was that they exploited the peasant, instead of assisting him to exploit the land.

Nevertheless, unintelligent as was agrarian economy during the first period of Western feudalism, it did at least secure for the peasants some of the elementary necessities of existence. In a society in which human life was dependent almost exclusively upon the enjoyment of land, the only thing which made it possible for millions of men to live at all was the occupation of parcels of that soil, which was the monopoly of the feudal classes. Bound to the land which enabled him to live, the villein was no longer what the slave had always been—a stray, a rootless being, a piece of furniture tossed about from estate to estate. He had his home, his cottage, his family. He knew nothing of the anguish of unemployment, the search for work, the anxiety which are the lot of the wage-earner. There was plenty of land, and every cultivator could be sure of obtaining a part of it, on a grant of free or servile tenure. If he could not own the landed capital, the villein was at least certain, by dint of his labour, of participating in the income therefrom. On the other hand, the master's interests coincided with that of the peasant in securing him, if not the possession, at any rate the indefinite enjoyment, of the land. If the landowner jealously retained the actual property in the land for himself, together with the major part of the revenues accruing from it, the villein, who alone by his labour made the continued existence of such revenues certain, found himself invested by means of a formal or tacit contract with a perpetual usufruct, hardly less valuable than complete property. He could hand on his holding to his heirs, despite many obstacles; he even succeeded in obtaining permission to sell or exchange it. This type of possession is a step in the direction of the formation of peasant property, which was later on to appear. Meanwhile the villein with his usufruct enjoyed a certain independence in his holding, and could cultivate it as he liked. All that was asked of him was the exact fulfilment of his obligations. Finally, under the system of natural economy which then prevailed, the cultivator profited directly by the produce of his toil, since he consumed or himself retained the nett total which remained after his dues and payments had been acquitted.

Although the villeins had no definite legal status, they did at least live under the protection of the contract or custom, which fixed, or tended to fix, their duties, and which recognized their rights. This stability was not established without effort, and it was subject to a number of restrictions. But as the necessity of bringing the land under cultivation became more urgent this concession almost imposed itself upon all lords, who were solicitous of their own interests, which were bound up in the improvement of the soil. Thus the villeins were able to obtain a steadily increasing fixity of payments, which in the end sensibly improved their position, but to which only a few of them had attained by the eleventh century. If direct accession to landed capital was still withheld from them, they could already, by economy and ingenuity, obtain possession of movable capital—money, cattle, and reserve products of the soil. Thenceforth there existed, even among the serfs, certain classes of workers who had reached a condition of comparative comfort. In spite of customs and prejudices, the villein was not absolutely bound to his state. Sometimes an act of valour might raise him to the ranks of the nobility; more often still his intelligence enabled him to become a clerk. The free villein could improve his state by changing his lord, and even the serf, despite all the rules of seigniorial farming, could with difficulty be kept upon the land against his will. So great was the need for labour that from this time onward attempts were made to attract the most hard-working and energetic individuals by special advantages and better treatment. Enfranchisement enabled a number of villeins to raise themselves a step in the social hierarchy of the lower classes. The most adroit members of those classes even insinuated themselves into the ranks of the administrative nobility.

The villein might be defenceless against the arbitrary will of his lord, but he was usually sheltered from the attack of tyrannous neighbours. Seigniorial government here gave him a relative protection. There was as yet no analogy with the continuous security enjoyed by labour in modern society, but in feudal society a minimum of security was nevertheless obtained. The feudal régime was, in effect, born of a social necessity, of a contract of safety, the protection accorded by the soldier in exchange for the useful services of the peasant. The lord took charge of the military defence, policing, and administration of his tenants. It may be that he often showed himself a brutal and capricious protector, but at least, out of self-interest, he sought to perform these functions in such a way as not to diminish the number and value of his human capital. It is true that he did not admit his subjects to a share in the exercise of political rights and sedulously maintained them in a condition of dependence in this matter. But customs became established—the expression of wisdom, experience, tradition, according to the German term (*weisthümer*)—and commanded a respect which guaranteed to the peasants a certain minimum of privileges, which even the lord dared not violate. Thus in England the peasant could appeal to the royal court if he suffered violence from his master; in Germany he was allowed to interrupt his labour services in order to go and assist his wife in childbed; in many parts he had to be fed and sometimes given a small payment when he worked upon the lord's demesne. Throughout the West he was permitted to group himself with his fellows in associations for common cultivation and police; he was called upon in his village assemblies to decide rules for pasture and the use of woods and waters, and, finally, was eligible to sit in the manor court which judged his peers. The seigniorial régime was not a hell, in which the villein must abandon all hope; and, hard as it was for the peasant, it left him several openings in the direction of a better future.

Nevertheless, during the first two centuries in which it prevailed, this régime was exceedingly hard. Although good and charitable lords were to be found, like Count Gérard d'Aurillac, who was canonized by the Church, and also intelligent administrators, such as the Dukes of Normandy and the Counts of Flanders and Anjou, the majority of the feudal lords were exacting and capricious masters, incapable of controlling their violent passions. They liked to boast that they were responsible to God alone in their relations with their subjects, and the feudal conscience was a fragile protection, nor was it even invariably guided by an enlightened selfishness. The feudatory did not realize the advantages of a more liberal régime than that which was ordinarily in use upon the domain. In every possible way he hindered the activity of his subjects; he would never moderate his dues; he burdened the cultivator with innumerable taxes, which were prejudicial to good farming. The peasant was unable to dispose of his own time or of the produce of his holding, and he could not even enjoy the common lands without coming up against abusive restrictions. He was subjected to heavy monopolies, in exchange for services, in assessing the remuneration for which he had not been consulted. At every step he was met by seigniorial regulations or *bans*, which cramped his initiative. He had to see his fields devastated by rabbits and pigeons bred in the lord's warrens and dovecotes, or by wild animals which were preserved for the lord's hunting. At any moment he could be forced to give up his carts, or cattle, or provisions, by virtue of the *droit de prise*, and to ruin himself in order to lodge and feed the lord and his officials, by virtue of the rights of hospitality (*gîte*) and *procuration*. He was not free either to buy or to sell. The perpetual tutelage of the lord paralyzed his labour.

It was for these reasons that the material and moral existence of the peasants was so uncertain and often so wretched before the twelfth century. Certainly there were regions in which it was tolerable, such as the Rhineland, Aquitaine, Flanders, part of the north of France, and the Mediterranean South, but in general it shows in sombre colours during the first 150 years of the feudal era in the West. Isolated in their farms, or more often grouped into the thousands of villages which had grown up upon the territory of the dismembered villas of antiquity, or often, in the south, collected in little fortified townships, the villeins lived day by day under material conditions not far removed from discomfort and actual want. The mass of cultivators was made up of poor folk, who were bowed beneath the weight of rents and services, and who had no means of improving their daily life. Their dwelling-place was a hovel, with thatched roof and floor of trodden earth, furnished with the utmost scantness. The type remained unchanged for centuries. Their clothes of woollen or linen cloth were rough and coarse, their food was frugal. The villein, says a moralist of the early

twelfth century, never drinks the fruit of his vine nor tastes
a scrap of good food; only too happy is he if he can keep his
black bread and some of his butter and cheese.

> S'il a grasse oie ou la géline,
> Un gastel de blanche farine,
> À son seigneur tot le destine.

> If he have fat goose or hen,
> Cake of white flour in his bin,
> 'Tis his lord who all must win.

He may keep only what is strictly necessary. By the
social law of his time, says Bishop Adalbero, he is bound
before all else to furnish the propertied classes with " money,
food, and clothes "; and another pious publicist, Étienne
de Fougères, agrees that the function of the villein is to
plough the soil and rear live-stock for the profit of his
masters.

> Car chevalier et clerc, sans faille,
> Vivent de ce qui travaille.

> For the knight and eke the clerk
> Live by him who does the work.

Bad methods of cultivation, exactions, brigandage, and
feudal warfare, natural disasters, murrains, floods, droughts,
defective harvests—all seem to have conspired to make the
life of the workers of the West more difficult. Since they did
not know how to husband their reserves, and since each lived,
as it were, isolated within his own lordship, famine was an
almost endemic scourge. Like a sinister handmaid of death,
it moved swiftly, ravaging as it went. In France between
970 and 1100 there were no less than sixty famine years. In
England the tradition is still preserved of the terrible dearths
of 1086 and 1125. The whole of Western Europe experienced
in turn this frightful scourge, which decimated the population
of entire districts and brought in its train a revival of the
practices of primitive bestiality. Privations and the lack
of hygiene also multiplied epidemics of plague and leprosy.
Yet such was the effect of family life and of the facilities for
establishing families upon the soil, that the gaps were filled
and, in spite of misery and want, the population rose, even

to the point of disturbing the equilibrium between the production and consumption of means of subsistence. But this fertility created a new cause of distress in those countries wherein colonization did not open up the prospect of a better material existence for the wretched inhabitants.

Worse still, perhaps, was the moral state of the rural classes. The state of mind of the majority was a gloomy passivity. Left to his own resources, the villein in his isolation found solace only in the bosom of his family, in the village community, and in his participation in the ceremonies and beliefs of a Christian life, which were brought within his reach in the thousands of parishes which had been created in the West. But in him, as in his masters, the old ancestral spirit still maintained itself, unquenched by education, with all its train of ignorance, superstition, brutality, cruelty, coarseness, and violence. The low and abject trickery of the mass of villeins and serfs was the melancholy heritage of centuries of oppression, to which the feudal régime had only added its own. No one sought to raise up these lower classes or to inculcate in their breasts the sentiment of human dignity. Aristocratic society, despising the villein, was not wise enough to improve him by treating him as a man. In spite of evangelical maxims about the equality of Christians before God, which are sometimes to be found in the sermons of preachers or in the writings of theologians, the propertied classes held that villeinage and serfdom were institutions consecrated by divine right, and placed the serf a degree lower than the beast of burden. In the eleventh century a French serf was worth 38 *sous* and a horse 100. The Church itself did no more than counsel the lord to use charity and the serf to show unlimited obedience and respect. But the seigniorial class was devoid of the spirit of kindness and justice, which might have won the peasants' attachment. The lord had only hard treatment and contempt for the villein, by whose labour he lived. His pleasure, as a churchman of the age admits, was to trample, rail, and scoff at the peasant, and, ignorant of the spirit of equity and pity, he reigned by violence and terror.

The propertied classes, unskilful organizers of labour as they were, had sown hatred all about them. They roused the spirit of revolt, which tacitly or openly threatened the powerful social and economic organization upon which the feudal system rested. As in the Carolingian period and for the same motives, now still more violent, the rural populations of the tenth and eleventh centuries were not always content to suffer with resignation the hard conditions which had been imposed upon them. They tried by flight or by emigration to escape their too often intolerable existence. The severity of the regulations dealing with the right of recapture is a manifest proof of this. Sometimes the villeins departed to offer their labour as pioneers on uncultivated lands (*hospites*), to kinder or more sensible masters. Sometimes, concealing their civil status, they managed to slip into some lordship, where they became permanently fixed after the lapse of a year and a day. Sometimes they joined the bands of pious pilgrims travelling to sacred shrines, and under this pretext sought a better fortune elsewhere. Sometimes they went to swell the troops of vagabonds who thronged the roads, men without home or fealty, outlaws, who sought in the shelter of forests and mountain gorges a refuge for their freedom and their rapine. At other times they pondered in the shadows some sly revenge, and often enough years of ill-treatment and cruelty were avenged by isolated acts of violence, murders, ambushes, and poisonings. Advice to beware of the serf is a commonplace in literature designed for the upper classes. He is considered capable of anything. Sometimes excess of misery even drove him to open revolt; sudden outbursts occurred, like the slave wars of antiquity. These tumultuous *jacqueries* of hopeless men seem to have been provoked more especially by abuses of *mainmorte*, by restrictions upon rights of using commons, and by arbitrary payments exacted from villeins. The chroniclers of the age rarely consider it worth while to record them in their annals; they only note the most serious—those of Saxony, Frisia, and Holland, the revolts of 1095 in the Low Countries and France, and of 1008 in Brittany, and the risings in Normandy at the beginning of the eleventh century. The latter were immortalized a hundred years afterwards in the poem of Wace, who, by a literary fiction, has put into the mouth of the rebellious peasants a sort of rustic " Marseillaise," so energetic is its tone and so bold its claims of equality. In reality these peasant revolts, accompanied by burning and massacre, let loose at hazard, without programme or bond of union, always ended in the same way—with a savage and pitiless repression by the upper classes, as soon as these had recovered from their surprise. Thus in particular ended the Norman *jacquerie* at the hands of a sinister butcher, the great lord Raoul de Fougère. But force was powerless to stop this social fermentation, which was still going on at the beginning of the twelfth century, as the most perspicacious of contemporary observers bear witness. It was the forerunner of the great social and economic revolution, which 200 years later was to transform the whole system of labour.

THE primary condition necessary to stimulate the activity and progress of labour was the formation of some tutelary authority able to assure the necessary protection and order to the masses.

For over two centuries feudal government showed itself powerless to realize this condition. A work of circumstance, which imminent dangers had brought to birth, it left too free a hand to the force and greed of thousands of little local sovereigns, who knew neither faith nor law. The feudal system had undoubtedly brought certain principles of progress into medieval society. In France, above all, from whence it spread all over the West, feudal civilization substituted for the ancient Græco-Roman conception of the omnipotent state, with its absolute power over individuals, the new idea of a political association founded upon liberty and upon the reciprocal obligations of men voluntarily bound together by contract. It favoured the revival of the sentiment of human dignity and individual energy, of voluntary devotion and discipline, of faith and loyalty between suzerains and vassals. Under the influence of the Church the military institution of chivalry was transformed, and for an élite it became a moral and educative force which tended to put might at the service of right, to guarantee public peace, and to protect the labouring masses against violence and anarchy. In the upper ranks of society were born the chivalrous virtues of humanity and courtesy, which resulted from the softening of manners. But this transformation of feudal society had only a limited effect. It had little influence upon the condition of subject classes, and, in fact, liberty remained for the first two centuries of the feudal age limited to the nobility. The terms freeman (*liber*) and baron or knight (*miles*) remained for a long time synonymous. The sentiment of equality which reigned in feudal society, all the members of which, down to the humblest, looked upon each other as peers, never extended beyond the limits of the aristocratic class. The lower classes, the immense mass of the workers, were still despised, and the institution of chivalry itself barely modified the relations of lords and their villeins.

Feudal government, indeed, never succeeded in fulfilling at all efficaciously the tutelary functions of a regular power, the permanent and enlightened protector of labour. Born out of the fear of the invasions and the need for protection against anarchy, it was for its subjects little more than a prolonged military dictatorship, with all the inconveniences of a despotism established upon brutal force. Instead of order it had only an ill-determined hierarchy, which merely gave rise to confusion, and the freedom of the feudal contract perpetuated this lack of discipline. Several hundreds of thousands of little local sovereigns, as turbulent as they were brutal, served by rapacious agents, who were both unscrupulous and ignorant, crushed the subject classes beneath an irritating tyranny, which was often no better than a kind of regular brigandage. A rough and incoherent fiscal system erected arbitrariness and extortion into a system. "The lords," declares a cleric of this period, "seek to fleece and to devour their subjects." Justice itself fell into their hands, and became, not an institution guaranteeing social peace and equity, but an instrument of extortion, the essential object of which was to *exploit* the person under jurisdiction—that is to say, to overwhelm him with fines and confiscations. The worst of it was that the villeins had no recourse against the abuses of this government, which were aggravated by the total absence of an organized police and by the multiplicity of feudal wars.

In the absence of a real system of regular government, to take up arms was the sole resource left to feudatories, in order to secure respect for their power or their rights. Thus war was perpetual; it died down in one place, only to break out again in another. It was the usual accompaniment of spring and summer, and let loose upon thousands of little states all the horrors of devastation, fire, and murder. Cottages went up in flames, harvests were burned, cattle killed or driven away, vines and fruit-trees cut down or uprooted, mills destroyed, and even churches profaned. When the peasants were unable to take refuge in the heart of the woods they were seized, fleeced, tortured, mutilated, hanged. Sometimes their hands and feet were cut off, or they were flung upon the fire; captives had their eyes put out, women were violated and their breasts were hacked off. After exploits such as these whole provinces became deserts. Not infrequently famine followed in the train of prolonged feudal warfare to complete the work of destruction and death. It was essentially this chronic state of insecurity and robbery which for 200 years caused the stagnation of all cultivation and the poverty of the mass of the people. The feudal warrior, indeed, easily became a brigand, and war degenerated into an enterprise of pillage. " Honour," says a troubadour at the beginning of the twelfth century, " is (for a gentleman) to steal and to plunder."

Thus as long as the feudal régime was all powerful, order, the elementary necessity of every society, was lacking to stimulate the progress of labour. Strangers to any idea of a real economic administration, the feudatories deprived labour of any possibility of improvement or of a lasting emancipation. It was only when great centralized feudal states were formed, side by side with reviving monarchies, that the Middle Ages began to move towards a happier future. From the eleventh century, in Normandy, Aquitaine, Anjou, and Flanders, then in the county of Barcelona and the marches of Brandenburg and Austria, there sprang from the feudal world itself governments, which took up once again, in concert with the monarchies of France, Germany, England, Navarre, Castile, Aragon, and the two Sicilies, the tradition of the supreme state, the dispenser of justice, the defender of order and public interest. Great politicians and administrators, such as William the Conqueror, Henry II Plantagenet, Philip Augustus, St. Louis, Henry II and Henry III of Germany, Frederick Barbarossa, Frederick II of Swabia, Roger II of Sicily, Alphonso VII and Jaime I of Spain once more established the framework of a strong civil and military administration and set to work to reduce the abusive power of the feudatories, and to substitute the interests of national groups for those of individuals or of local groups. Everywhere they sought first to re-establish order by decreeing what was called in some parts the Duke's

Peace, as in Normandy, in others the Count's Peace, as in Flanders and Catalonia, and in others still the King's Peace, as in France, Germany, Castile, or the two Sicilies. They made repeated efforts to limit and then to forbid feudal and private wars, and to prohibit the bearing of arms, trying to transform the anarchical and warlike society of their time into a peaceful and ordered one. Thus they laid the first foundations of a national economy, and, in the teeth of many obstacles, began to inaugurate a more far-reaching régime than that of the feudal economy, which never looked beyond local considerations.

The princely or monarchical state had henceforth a more or less clear-cut economic policy, the object of which was to protect and favour labour in its various forms, and to encourage production and exchange. Great feudatories and kings were among the most ardent promoters of agricultural colonization. They often protected the rural masses against the abuses of seigniorial government, and even favoured the mitigation or suppression of serfdom, sometimes on their own domains, but, above all, outside them. Everywhere laws began to be put forth to protect agriculture, to prevent the seizure of cattle and farm implements, to encourage reclamations, or to prevent their abuse by forbidding the destruction of forests. Some rulers, such as the counts of Flanders, the dukes of Normandy, and the kings of the two Sicilies, set up model farms and studs, introduced new crops, or legislated, like the kings of Castile, for the development of stock-breeding and the prevention of murrains. They were the enlightened protectors of all manifestations of the industrial renaissance, of urban activity, and of the corporations of artisans, and they promoted the exploitation of mines. Sometimes, as in the two Sicilies, they even anticipated the economic system of modern monarchies by creating veritable state manufactures. Their policy was wider in scope than that of the feudal governments, and they devoted all their efforts to promoting the development of circulation and exchange; merchants were granted not only security, but a whole host of exemptions and privileges, the interests of external trade were protected, and within their realms they created fairs and markets with special franchises, improved the means of communication both by sea and by land, and restricted the multiplicity of weights and measures, which they sometimes, as in England and France, even attempted to unify. They tried at the same time to develop credit, and to repress its abuse. They granted foreign bankers permission to set up banking-houses, and regulated the rate of interest and the exchanges. They restricted the circulation of feudal coinages, and promoted the movement in the direction of monetary unity by bringing about the prevalence of the royal coinage, and sometimes reserving the right to mint it for themselves. For the first time in centuries England, the two Sicilies, Flanders, Hainault, France (in the time of St. Louis) knew a fixed and pure coinage. But more often yet they proved to be still unable to shake off the practices of the feudal governments, and destroyed the effect of their more enlightened economic policy by a fiscal policy which bristled with abuses and was a mass of hampering restrictions and incoherent customs regulations. The national economy of which they were the representatives was painfully seeking its way in the chaos of feudalism, from which it had not yet completely emerged.

In the foreground at this period we must place the action of the Church, which was superior in continuity, power, and scope to that of the secular governments. With the whole of Western Christendom under its eyes, the Church inaugurated therein the first international economy, and sought to give to labour a system of protective regulations designed to increase its efficacy. The Papacy and the French monastic orders took the lead in this work of reconstruction. Under the inspiration of the religious idealism professed by the monks, the great medieval popes from Gregory VII to Innocent III succeeded in partially freeing the Church from the feudal bonds which threatened to stifle it, and set its feet boldly in the path of progress. In concert with the Cluniacs and Cistercians they restored the idea of authority, the conception of the solidarity of interests of Western Christendom, and tried to establish order and public peace in feudal Europe. The Church assisted monarchical government to re-establish itself, playing a tutelary rôle towards it which was useful at the time. Its doctors revived the Christian and Roman tradition of the state as protector of the community of labour and defender of collective interests. It propagated the common basis of Christian civilization throughout the West, proclaimed the necessity and dignity of labour, and was the sole society open to the lower classes, wherein the son of the villein or artisan could rise to the bishop's mitre, nay, even to the papal tiara, as did the erstwhile swineherd Nicholas Breakspear (Adrian IV). Strong in its spiritual and temporal power, recruited by dint of its elective system from the élite, furnished with a centralizing government served by the ever-increasing monastic militia, the Church in this period of the Middle Ages can justly claim the honour of having taken the lead in social and economic progress and in material civilization, as it led in intellectual and moral civilization.

Popes and councils, monks and clerks, sought to regulate feudalism, to soften its manners, and to raise its ideal by the institution of chivalry. They tried to reform the abuses of feudal government and to prevent the exploitation of its subjects. In 1179 the Lateran Council was bold enough to condemn arbitrary tallages, and in the thirteenth century the Franciscans are found encouraging the movement against the payment of seigniorial dues, and supporting the emancipation of peasants and burgesses. Themselves victims of feudal brutality, clerks and monks often made common cause with the people against the feudatories. The ideal of the Church was a well-ordered society, in which work should be able to go on in security, and of this society it constituted itself the guardian. Likewise from the eleventh century onwards it began a missionary campaign, in part fruitless, and yet a true source for pride, to limit, regulate, and even to suppress war. With the support of popes and princes, the French Church, promoter of so many generous ideas, spread the Peace and the Truce of God throughout the West. By virtue of these two institutions, feudal expeditions were entirely forbidden for part of the year—Advent, Lent, religious festivals, and were prohibited every week from Wednesday to Monday morning. Non-combatants, clerks, merchants, peasants, and their goods were placed under the safeguard of religion so as to protect them from the brutality and devastation of the soldiery. Armed associations (*paixades*, " fraternities of peace " or " fraternities of the cowl ") were founded under oath to maintain these salutary regulations. Ecclesiastical censure, the withholding of the sacrament, and excommunication fell upon those who disturbed public order or work. The Church lacked the power to bring an effective force to bear in support of its generous conceptions, but it had at least the merit of showing the way to the monarchical state, which was later to carry out the great social work thus planned by churchmen.

At the same time the Church gave to the masses the powerful, moral, and idealistic armour of its Faith. It multiplied schools and universities for the people as well as for the chosen few, and spread abroad the teaching of which it had the monopoly. It was the Church which founded higher education, and in the professorial chairs of its doctors political economy was born and problems were discussed relating to the organization of labour, the origin and limits of property, individual or communal ownership, wages and the just price, the rôle of commerce and of money. All these high questions were there studied with the utmost boldness, and the audacity of speculative thought on this point knew no bounds among theologians and canonists, though practical reason tempered the boldness of theoretical reason, as the mendicant orders found at the end of the thirteenth century, when they were minded to take up communism and an anarchical equalitarianism.

In the social order the Church had been at pains to organize the relief of the labouring classes, the poor, the sick, and the captive, multiplying, with the help of the laity, alms-houses, hospitals, *maisons Dieu*, lazar-houses, and organizations for the ransoming of prisoners. Charity, a Christian form of social solidarity, was made a formal obligation, and a corrective of the right of property. In the economic sphere the Church then played a part of the first importance, for it united organizing ability with the breadth of mind and idealism of the most talented body of men to be found anywhere in that age. Its domains became centres of attraction, by reason of the superiority of the agricultural methods employed there and the favourable condition of the peasantry. It was " good to live beneath the cross," provided that one gave up all spirit of independence. It was in the Church that there appeared the first signs of pity for the working classes; theologians and preachers, Yves de Chartres, Geoffrey de Troyes, Raoul Ardent, Maurice de Sully and their like, proclaimed the social value of the work of the poor and humble and the original equality of serf and freeman before God and His sacraments, even while they preached obedience to the villeins. They castigated the oppressors of the poor, and some even raised a voice against the institution of serfdom.

The clergy, a tradition-loving class and conservers of the feudal order, showed scant favour to the political and social emancipation of the peasants, but they set an example in the amelioration of their lot in the economic sphere. They showed immense activity in pushing on the agricultural colonization of the West, in which the great French monasteries were the leaders, and deserve the eternal homage of history. The ecclesiastical domains were centres in which agricultural science was developed, forestry and scientific breeding improved, model farms created, new crops tried, and agricultural production regenerated and stimulated. It was on the lands of the Church, and in towns in which episcopal authority ruled, that there appeared the professional division of labour, the first perfected industrial technique, the first schools of arts and crafts; and there, too, the working classes first organized themselves. Above all, the monasteries, during this period of three centuries, taught to one generation after another the various higher forms of industry, the production of luxury fabrics, tapestry, embroidery, enamel work, goldsmith's work, porcelain, glasswork, architecture, sculpture, painting. From the schools of Moissac, Saint-Savin, Saint-Denis, Fossanova, Chiaravalle, Saint-Gall, and many another abbey there went forth craftsmen who taught the men of their day the skilled practice of industrial arts. Finally, the Church began early to assist the development of a new form of wealth based upon movables. It favoured the formation of groups of merchants round the centres of its dominion, both urban and rural; it sought to secure the safety and to provide the means of transport, organizing under its ægis the first associations for the repair of roads and bridges and creating the first long distance transport services by road or river;

it stimulated the creation of markets and fairs; and it tried to repress or abolish barbarous customs, such as piracy and wreckage, which hindered maritime commerce. Although the Church tended to consider mercantile activity as sterile and the trade in money as usurious, it was nevertheless the first to create reserves of capital, to inaugurate the system of deposits, credit, and banking, to proclaim the wise doctrine of a stable coinage, and to take part in large commercial enterprises. In short, by establishing between the states of Western Christendom the bonds of a true international solidarity, the Church prepared the way for the renaissance and development of a money economy which was destined to give to labour an expansion and a freedom hitherto unknown to it.

CHAPTER IV

THE APPEARANCE OF A MONEY ECONOMY AND THE DEVELOPMENT OF
WESTERN COMMERCE FROM THE MIDDLE OF THE TENTH TO THE
MIDDLE OF THE FOURTEENTH CENTURY.

EVER since the brief economic renaissance of the Carolingian
age had proved abortive, the predominance of natural or
domanial economy had grown steadily firmer. During the
first two centuries of the feudal age, a movable or money
economy, which has its source in commerce, possessed only
an infinitesimal importance. The rôle of money was very
small, and it was the land and its produce which constituted
wealth. Economic life had become, as it were, stationary in
this purely agricultural society, enclosed in the rigid framework of the landed aristocracy. Feudal government was
designed rather to hamper than to assist commercial activity.
Moreover, the public opinion of all classes misunderstood the
rôle of trade, and continued to look upon the trader as a
parasite, a speculator, a usurer, and movable wealth as the
fruit of fraud and rapine, but not of labour. Moreover, the
conditions of economy on the great domain left only a limited
field of action to commerce. Each group produced almost
everything necessary for life, and trade took place only in a
small number of natural or manufactured commodities, which
arose from an excess of production, and were exchanged on
the spot, usually for ready money, and often by the primitive
method of barter. A man would trade a horse for a sack of
corn, a piece of cloth for a measure of salt, a pound of pepper
for a pair of boots. The only markets known were local, held
in the gateway of a castle or monastery, or on the outskirts
of a neighbouring town. Insecurity, anarchy, the multiplicity of seigniorial monopolies and tolls, the scarcity and
difficulty of means of transport, the chaotic diversity of
weights and measures and moneys, the scarcity of the
currency, and the imperfection of instruments of credit were
all obstacles to the circulation of merchandise.

The consumption of foreign goods was so feeble and the
means of purchasing them so inadequate that, with the
exception of certain regions, such as Italy, Southern and

LIFE AND WORK IN MEDIEVAL EUROPE

Northern France, Flanders, the Rhineland, and a few of the Danube lands, there did not yet exist in the West a special class of native merchants (*mercatores*)—that is to say, of middlemen between the producer and the consumer. This class was, to begin with, composed almost exclusively of adventurers and strangers, even of non-Christians, Jews who existed on the edge of feudal society, and traded more especially in articles of luxury and the precious metals, or practised moneylending, in order to satisfy the needs of the aristocracy. They were not, as a rule, sedentary; they took the road as what we should call pedlars, on a large scale, or travelled in caravans from country to country to the fairs, which the lords organized during the fine weather on the occasion of some religious festival. But in spite of the privileges which were granted to these commercial assizes, the merchant, like all strangers, was treated as an intruder, a "foreigner." His goods, his ships, his person, were exposed to seizure 'and confiscation by virtue of rights of escheat, waif, or wreck. Upon him by virtue of the right of reprisal fell the revenges and retaliations which the feudal lord considered it his right to exact from the enemy lord to whom the merchant was subject. Neither by sea nor by land was there any security for a profession, whose members were of necessity true adventure hunters, whom only the love of gain emboldened to persevere in their dangerous career.

Commerce was rescued from this hostile atmosphere at the end of the eleventh century by a combination of favourable circumstances. A great movement of expansion, roused by the Church to defend Christendom against the Moslems and to spread the Christian faith among the pagans, snatched the West for two and a half centuries from its primitive isolation. In the north and east of Europe there were now opened to trade the new provinces of this universal Christian Empire, the organization of which was being carried out by the Papacy, Scandinavia, Hungary, Bohemia, Poland, and the Baltic lands. In the south and south-east Christian states sprang up in the Moslem lands, in Spain, Portugal, Sicily, and Syria, and commerce followed the arms of the Crusaders. Great pilgrimages in France, Spain, Italy, and the East carried along a crowd of the faithful, and the merchants went with them. Not only were new fields of activity opened in the Western lands on the shores of the northern seas, but the Mediterranean once more became the great trade route between the new lands of Western Europe and the old countries, the homes of wealth and civilization, which lay within Arab and Byzantine Empires. The feudal world, with the ardent sap of youth afire in its veins, sprang forward from all sides to seek new settlements, where all—nobles, clerks, peasants, and merchants—hoped to make their fortunes. The development of trade now received a great stimulus, for everything was in its favour, the protection of feudal and monarchical states, interested in increasing their resources, the formation of urban republics, the prosperity of which was bound up with the progress of trade, the development of agricultural and industrial production, which furnished it with increasing elements of activity, the creation of new markets and great fairs, even the transformation of social life, which gave rise to the need for new comforts or luxuries. Commercial life blossomed into an activity hitherto unknown, surpassing even that of the best periods of antiquity, when trade had a much narrower field of action.

The new economy now had its special organs. It brought to birth distinct classes and varied forms of organization. Above the small peasant producer and the local artisan, who continued to sell directly to the consumer, there appeared the professional trader (*negotiator*, *mercator*), the middleman, whose essential function was the purchase and resale of commodities. Originally, great merchants and transport organizers were merged in this class with pedlars and small retailers. It was formed of diverse and often of disturbed elements, traders dwelling by preference on the outskirts of towns, and at crossways, where roads or rivers met, where a special right, the *jus mercatorum*, protected them. Before long they were reinforced by the capitalists and money-dealers of the towns.

Distinctions began to appear in this class born of inequality of wealth or division of labour. The majority of the merchants became settled. A small urban commerce developed and became distinct from the great national or international commerce, which was reserved for an élite, and from the pedlar's traffic, exercised by nomads. This urban commerce centred in the town, the banlieue and the district, and its home was the daily or weekly market. There the merchant offered for sale, either in the open square or closed market-hall, or more often still in his shop or stall, those local commodities which were necessary for the elementary requirements of existence, and sometimes also imported goods, especially corn, wine, fish, cattle and meat, wood, wool, flax, wax, as well as goods prepared or manufactured on the spot. Thus the various forms of local commerce appeared and developed with rapidity, especially the food and clothing trades, which grew up side by side with crafts, in which direct sale was practised, concurrently with sale through middlemen. Above the sedentary traders, who carried on retail commerce, was a minority of notables and rich merchants (*meliores, divites*), who monopolized wholesale commerce. These two classes only just tolerated the wandering traders, pedlars, and "foreigners," and the "regraters" or retailers, submitting them to strict regulation. But urban commerce, limited as it was in range, disposing of only small resources and moderate supplies, and bound by rigid regulations, did not lend itself to operations on a large scale.

It was for this reason that the great merchants—the spicers, mercers, skinners, transport organizers, shipowners, and bankers—organized a new kind of trade with a wider scope, to wit, national and international commerce. This class specialized in the traffic in articles of luxury, spices, fine fabrics, furs, and raw materials necessary to manufactures, as well as in operations of credit and in the management of business which required the employment of a good deal of capital, but, at the same time, brought in large profits. Thus the merchants who engaged in this commerce often pooled their resources and shared risks and profits. Christians began more and more to take the place of Jews in this large scale traffic, in which the Italians quickly took the lead. They organized commercial societies on lines of limited liability, in which capitalists, merchants, and their agents were all associated. From the middle of the twelfth to the middle of the thirteenth centuries they served as intermediaries between the peoples of the Christian West and those of the East. Enterprising, ingenious, sharp, and somewhat unscrupulous, these Lombards, Genoese, Lucchese, Siennese, and Florentines dispatched their caravans of merchants to the fairs, multiplied commercial houses and depôts, and exercised a kind of commercial monarchy over Central Italy, France, Spain, England, and the South of Germany. There were sixteen Italian houses in Paris in 1292. Flourishing merchant colonies of the same nationality were to be found in Naples, Barletta, Nîmes, Montpellier, London, and many other towns. For 200 years the Italian merchant—the Lombard, as he was called—was the real master of international commerce.

Soon the Catalans, the Provençals, and the merchants of Languedoc organized themselves in their turn to share in this trade, while on their side the traders of Northern France, from the district round Paris, Normandy, and Picardy, and those of Flanders and the Rhineland were, from the end of the eleventh century, associated in gilds, or societies for mutual defence and protection similar to the gild of Saint-Omer (1072-1083). They soon began to form themselves into federations called Hanses, which became extremely powerful in the twelfth and thirteenth centuries. Such was the Hanse which comprised seventeen towns, and finally rose to sixty cities of Champagne, Picardy, Hainault, Flanders, France, Normandy, and Brabant, the object of which was to facilitate business at the fairs of Champagne. Such likewise was the Hanse of London, with its capital at Bruges, which included seventeen towns, among which were Ypres and Lille, with the object of regulating trade, more especially the wool trade, with the British Isles. It was on this model, too, that the famous German Hanseatic League was created to monopolize traffic between the northern countries and the West, while in England there arose the Company of Merchants of the Staple (1267), which contained English merchants exporting the butter, cheese, salt meat, wool, and metals with which England supplied the markets or *staples* at Calais, Bruges, Antwerp, and Dordrecht.

Meritorious efforts were made under the impulse of the great feudatories, and particularly of the town governments, the merchant companies, the Church, and the central governments, to re-establish roads and rivers, and the means of transport. In France there appeared the first royal highways, and in the two Sicilies, Germany, and the Low Countries military or national roads (*heerstraten*) were made. The Church organized pious fraternities of bridge-builders, the Pontiff Brothers or *Frères Pontifs*, the most famous of which was founded by a French shepherd of Vivarais, Saint Benézet, who had imitators in Italy. A useful spirit of emulation multiplied wooden and stone bridges during three centuries, and the bridges of Avignon, of Pont Saint-Esprit, of Lyons, Paris, Tours, London, Stratford, Florence, and Valencia in Spain belong to this period. War was waged upon brigands, and an attempt was made to thin out the complicated forest of tolls. The great continental highways between Italy, France, and Central Europe, by Geneva, Mont Cenis, the Saint-Bernard, the Saint-Gothard, the Splügen, and the Brenner Passes were covered with caravans of merchants, as were those of the Rhône, Rhine, Meuse, Scheldt, Seine, Loire, and Garonne Valleys leading to the West of Europe, or the passes of the Western Pyrenees by Roncevaux and of the Eastern Pyrenees by Cerdagne, which led to Spain. River transport developed even more widely than land transport, because of its greater speed and the freight capacity of the boats, which was 500 times greater than that of the sumpter beasts employed on the roads. Navigable rivers were improved by the construction of dams, inclined planes, and sea-gates, in default of chambered locks, which were not yet known. By means of boats of small gauge and very varied type, numerous transport companies, Hanses, like those of the Water Merchants of Paris, the Lower Seine, or Rouen, which were united in 1315, carried all sorts of produce and of merchandise. From the Guadalquiver, the Ebro, and the Po to the rivers of North Germany, the whole network of Western rivers became, especially from the twelfth century, the scene of a prodigious activity. "Staple" towns, river ports, such as Cremona, Arles, Niort, Douai, Malines, Duisburg, Cologne, Frankfort, Regensburg, developed, thanks to all this active navigation. The first more or less regular services of passenger carriages, couriers, and goods waggons were organized by the care of ecclesiastical or urban trading corporations, or even of states. A postal service appeared in Italy in the twelfth century, and in Germany towards

1237. Inns and refuges, like those founded by St. Bernard
of Mentone in the Alps, sprang up in mountain passes.
Journeys became increasingly easier and swifter. Henceforth transport waggons could carry heavy goods from Paris
to Genoa in thirty-five days. The couriers of the banks
covered the distance between Florence and Naples in five or
six days, and the convoys of merchants took ten or twelve.

Commerce found a means of expansion hitherto unknown
in the increased amount of money coined and circulated, as
well as in the new organization of credit. It was thus that
a money economy developed at the expense of the barbarous
economy of barter and exchange in kind. It was born in
Italy and the Netherlands, and spread to the other Western
countries. The supply of metals gradually increased by
means of relations with the East and by the working of
mines of precious metals. Some enlightened governments,
those of the merchant republics of Italy, of the kingdoms of
the two Sicilies and England, of the county of Flanders, and,
for a moment, that of France in the time of St. Louis,
inaugurated the wise policy of a stable coinage, so favourable to the development of commerce and in striking
contrast with the fatal habit of altering and varying the
currency which persisted in most states. The Norman kings
of Southern Italy and the merchant republics of Florence
and Venice, who were taught by the experience of Byzantium, and the counts of Flanders, the kings of England,
France, and Castile, and the Hohenstaufen in Germany, who
learned from Italy, all struck either gold coins—*taris*, sequins,
ducats, *sous, marabotins, maravedis*—or silver coins—*deniers,
dinars, tournois, parisis*—of invariable value and fixed ratios
and proportions of alloy. The gold coins, in particular, to
which must be added the Byzantine bezants, greatly
assisted the progress of international commerce by furnishing the West with a method of payment, hitherto almost
unknown.

Up to the eleventh century credit had existed in
primitive forms, which were only suited to a system of
natural economy, in which there was neither active production for the market nor a widespread trade. Nothing was
then known but loans for use or consumption, made in order
to meet the elementary needs of existence—that is to say,

loans in kind, and loans on the security of a pledge. The Church held that to stipulate for any interest for this kind of credit was usury. But the necessities of commerce and industry led to the development of loans for production, in which the capital advanced served the borrowers for the increase of their business and their profits. Henceforward it became difficult to maintain the rigidity of the old rules. They were eluded in all sorts of ways, the requirement of interest being concealed in the contracts by describing the capital as larger than it really was, or by all sorts of compensatory payments, notably for any delay in repayment.

The Canonists themselves, while continuing to prohibit as usurious all interest upon loans for consumption or for use, which it was becoming difficult to distinguish from other varieties, recognized, with St. Bonaventura and Innocent IV, the legitimacy of payment for capital invested in commercial and industrial enterprises, when risks were run (*damnum emergens*), or when the lender was temporarily deprived of the use of his capital (*lucrum cessans*). In the thirteenth century we find popes taking the Italian bankers under their protection, placing them under the safeguard of the ecclesiastical courts, and forcing their debtors to repay loans by the threat of spiritual censure, while continuing at the same time to hunt down usurers. The time was at hand when the lay jurists of the fourteenth century were to proclaim with Baldus the legitimacy of contracts, and later of all loans at interest.

Meanwhile, in order to avoid the thunders of the Church or the slow procedure of ecclesiastical courts, credit was taking on new forms, better adapted to the necessities of commerce, such as sales with power of redemption or with guarantees, advances on life annuities or redeemable securities, loans on mortgages, and, above all, loans on a limited partnership basis, on security of specie or against a bank deposit, and loans on bottomry, the last being used in the great enterprises of sea commerce. From the thirteenth century interest in the leading commercial countries, such as Italy and South Germany, fell as low as 10, 12, and 17 per cent. for commercial undertakings, while in others, such as England and sometimes even France, it rose to 15, 20, 25, 43, 50, and as high as 80 per cent.

PLATE II

GENOESE BANKERS
(Late 14th Century)

face p. 166

GROWTH OF WESTERN COMMERCE

The circulation of paper, or fiduciary currency, practised by the Byzantines and Arabs, was introduced into the West by means of the Italians, the merchants of the South of France, the Catalans, and the Flemings, in the form of letters of credit and of payment, forerunners of the modern draft notes, or, again, of bills of exchange and "fair bills," which avoided cash payments. The system of payments by clearance and by offset of debts, with power of postponement, subject to commission, was introduced at the great fairs. By these means a far more extensive trade could be carried on.

Exchange and banking became the appanages of a special class of exchangers and bankers. The former, charged with arbitrating between the countless moneys of the day, found their rôle diminishing as fiduciary circulation increased. The latter, on the other hand, grew in importance. Leaving the Jews to meet the demands of the common people and to carry on most of the business of making loans on the security of pledges, which, on account of the risks involved, necessitated rates of interest (sometimes as high as 80 per cent.) which were considered usurious, and which roused the hatred of the people and the cupidity of princes against the lenders, the Christian moneylenders organized themselves everywhere in order to inaugurate new forms of credit. While the Jewish rank and file suffered expulsion, confiscation, and massacre, the Christian aristocracy of banking prospered in abbeys, in thousands of houses of Templars, and, above all, in the innumerable counting-houses of the Lombards and Caorsini.

The Order of Templars, which had relations throughout East and West, was inaugurating great operations of international capital at the same time as the Italian merchants; but they rivalled and surpassed it, and in 1307 took over the greater part of its business. The trading cities of Italy, which, from the twelfth century onwards, became the active middlemen between Levantine and Western trade, organized themselves with the object of putting all the diverse forms of credit at the service of commerce. Everywhere in the centre and north of the peninsula, at Venice, Cremona, Bologna, Piacenza, Parma, Asti, Chiari, Genoa, Lucca, Siena, Pistoja, Rome, Pisa, Florence, companies of merchant bankers multiplied. Originally composed of members of the same families, or of citizens of the same town, they soon began to form unions and cartels to compete with each other for markets or to dominate them. They had at their disposal the powerful capital made available by association, together with a strong and flexible organization, and they spread a network of agencies from Syria and Cyprus to North Africa and Western Europe. For nearly 300 years Christendom was obliged to reckon with the power of these capitalists, Lombards, Tuscans, or Caorsini; for without the Riccardi, the Bardi, the Peruzzi, the Scali and their like, large scale operations had become impossible. From the middle of the thirteenth century the Florentines held the first place among them, with eighty great banking firms, which threw those of Siena and Lucca into the shade.

Swarming in the Levant as well as in the West, they displayed an economic activity as incessant as it was varied; they maintained branches in Acre and Famagusta, in Southern Italy, and in France, in which country they entirely dominated both the Champagne fairs and Paris, where they had sixteen houses; they were masters both of the Flemish market at Bruges and of the English market at London, and penetrated into Central and Northern Europe as well. They carried on both wholesale commerce on their own account and a carrying trade, and dealt alike in commodities of general consumption and in luxuries. They bought and re-sold corn, wine, oil, spices, sugar, raw materials, such as timber, wool, silk, cotton, flax, hemp, metals, dyes, and medicinal drugs, manufactured goods, such as woollens, silks, cottons, linens, worked metals and leather, glass articles, *objets d'art*, and jewels. They organized transport both by land and sea. They practised territorial and maritime insurance. They led or organized great industrial and commercial enterprises. They undertook the collection of bills of exchange and the liquidation of debts. They opened current accounts and regulated mercantile business by means of transfer or clearance. They issued and accepted bills of exchange. Together with the Templars they were the first to create banks of deposit and of discount, and to organize public and private credit. They received precious objects and money on deposit and return on demand, and issued receipts. They not only practised loans against bills of lading, but also against mortgages and on goods at rates varying from 4 per cent. to 175 per cent. Their clientèle comprised all the rich or comfortably-off classes and the corporations. Among their debtors were municipal republics, such as Florence and Genoa, communes, such as Rouen, bishops, and abbots. In the thirteenth century the Archbishop of Cologne owed more than £40,000 to Italian bankers, and the French and English bishops owed them hundreds of pounds. The greatest of lords of the day, counts of Flanders and Champagne, dukes of Burgundy, borrowed from them what were huge sums for that time; the popes, the emperors, the kings of Naples, France, and England were in debt to them. They advanced Charles IV of France almost two million francs in a single year; they lent over £240,000 to Edward I and over £400,000 to Edward III, and in 1340 the latter, who then owed them nearly £1,400,000, " the value of a kingdom," could only escape from his position by declaring himself bankrupt.

Protected by the Papacy and strong in their position as Christians, and in their powerful organization, these bankers extracted privileges and exemptions from princes, and, what was more, made the growing power of money felt in political life. They offered to popes and kings all the resources of their organization in framing fiscal systems, and furnished them with administrators and financial agents. Subtle, adroit, and quite unscrupulous, they made their services appreciated in diplomacy. Their wealth ensured them an eminent, indeed, a preponderating position in social life, especially in the Italian communes and in the upper ranks of European society. Into it they introduced large-handed and sumptuous habits of life and the taste for art and science, while at the same time displaying to the common people all the arrogance of the *nouveau riche*. In fine they initiated the middle classes of the West into the science of commerce and credit, and boldly threw open new paths for trade, and an enormous field of expansion for economic activity. Hated by the people whom, according to a French saying, they " fleeced and flayed," turn by turn hunted, despoiled, and exploited by princes, they nevertheless took their place among the indispensable elements of the new society.

Commercial activity was not only exercised in the daily and weekly markets of the town and country districts, which increased every year in number, and where the exchange of local produce was carried on in market-squares and market-halls, which were everywhere being built; it was also carried on in the fairs, the great activity of which is a characteristic feature of this period of the Middle Ages. Towards these fairs the long caravans of merchants of every nation wound their way, armed with spear and shield, their heavy waggons escorted by men-at-arms. They brought such wealth to the rulers of the state that the latter hastened to bestow upon them special protection, safeguards, and privileges, such as complete freedom to trade and exemption from the most onerous dues. The Church blessed them, extended her protection to them, and opened them with religious ceremonies. A special justice, similar to that which attached to the celebrated fairs of Champagne, was dispensed by Chancellors and Keepers, for the maintenance of good order and equitable transactions. Merchants were assisted to attend them by the grant of safe-conducts, guaranteed by treaties. There they enjoyed the privilege of sanctuary, and were sheltered from rights of escheat and reprisals, and out of reach of all prosecutions. A tariff of charges for food and lodgings was laid down in their favour. The commerce of all the lands of East and West met at the most famous of these gatherings. Each country sought to organize its own fairs—England at Stourbridge; Germany at Aix-la-Chapelle, Frankfort, and Constance; the Low Countries at Lille, Messines, Ypres, and Bruges; Castile at Seville and Medina del Campo; Italy at Bari, Lucca, and Venice.

But they prospered, above all, in France at the crossroads between the great regions of the West, notably at Nîmes, Beaucaire, and Bordeaux, Chalon-sur-Sâone, Caen, Rouen, Corbie, and Amiens. Two great French centres were universally famous in this respect, the Île-de-France and Champagne. Every year from the 11th to the 24th of June (*Lendit*), merchants flocked to the plain of Saint-Denis. They came in still greater numbers to the great fairs of Champagne, which followed one another annually from

January to October, each lasting from sixteen to fifty days, at Lagny, Bar-sur-Aube, and, above all, at Provins and Troyes.

The Champagne fairs were of capital importance from the second half of the twelfth to the first half of the fourteenth century. In these plains of the Upper Seine and the Marne, at the meeting-place of the great European routes which united the Mediterranean countries to the lands bordering the Channel and the North Sea, or watered by the Rhine and the Rhône, these commercial gatherings attracted the wholesale merchants and small travelling traders of all the European nations from the Levantines, Italians, and Spaniards to the Flemings, Germans, English, and Scots, to say nothing of the French themselves. Armed with precious privileges, placed under the special protection of the Church and of the counts of Champagne, they guaranteed safe journeys and transactions to commerce. Guides and escorts were supplied to caravans; spiritual penalties, a sort of commercial interdict, were declared against all who hindered the movements of travellers on their way thither. An official organization, under the direction of a Chancellor or *garde des foires*, assisted by sheriffs, notaries, brokers, measurers, criers, porters, and sergeants, secured the maintenance of privileges and good order. Fairs were the sanctuaries of international trade, entrepôts where merchandise benefited by reduced tariffs and where business of all kinds was carried on in full and entire freedom. The merchants of every nation and even of every religion were there out of reach of abusive rights of escheat and reprisals, of execution for debts or bodily coercion. There they could freely carry on all sorts of traffic, even the traffic in money. The seal of the *garde des foires* guaranteed the authenticity of their contracts, which notaries drew up under the authority of the Chancellor. A special jurisdiction, both prompt and swift, was adapted to their needs.

To the towns of Champagne, therefore, came caravans of merchants, among whom Italians and Flemings were predominant, grouped under the authority of their consuls or captains; they found there immense cellars, several stories high, true subterranean cities, and galleries with massy pillars similar to the *souks* or bazars of the East, to receive the merchandise, piled up in enormous heaps. Unpacking went on for eight days after the opening of the fair. Then the sales began, regulated according to a fixed order, known as *divisions*. For the first period of twelve days woven stuffs of all sorts, woollens, silks, muslins, cottons, carpets, cloths from East and West, were sold or exchanged. Then the sergeants declared the cloth fair closed with cries of " *Hare! Hare!*" (pack up). Then the fair of leathers or cordovans, skins and furs, opened for eight days and closed in the same way. During these two periods innumerable transactions were being carried on over horses, cattle, wines, corn, herrings, salt, tallow, lard, and all kinds of merchandise which were sold by weight (*avoir du poids*), as well as raw materials, wool, flax, hemp, raw silk, and, above all, dye stuffs, medicinal drugs, spices, and sugar. An enormous clientèle, composed of wholesale as well as retail merchants, pedlars, and individuals, from feudal lords and burgesses down to peasants, came to lay in supplies at the fairs.

It was the most original feature of these great gatherings that men could practise openly there not only the great international trade in merchandise, but the trade in money itself. Operations of credit could be carried out there in full freedom. Indeed, on the twentieth day there began the fair of the money-changers and bankers. For four weeks they set out their counters or tables, their money-bags, and their balances, in order to weigh and exchange ingots and coins, and for fifteen days more they proceeded to the liquidation of debts and the auditing of accounts from the opening of the fair. Special couriers (*coureurs de hare*) were engaged in carrying the instructions of commercial and banking-houses, rates of exchanges and currency, orders of payment and drafts. In the last period appeared the " couriers of payment," who made known to the representatives of the banks the amount to be collected or paid out. Quantities of loans were arranged during these days, when loans were authorized and negotiated at rates varying from 6 to 30 per cent., and quantities of payments were made, not only by merchants, but also by noble debtors scattered throughout the West. Regulations authorized proceedings against recalcitrant debtors and the recovery of debts. Bills of exchange or " fair letters " were met or issued, furnished, if necessary, with the official seal. There were practised transfers of debts, transfers by clearance and carry over from one fair to another. It was there that the first great international stock exchange and produce market was opened. During the whole duration of the fairs a cosmopolitan crowd jostled each other in the roads of these Champagne towns, stopping at stalls, pressing into the shows and displays of buffoons and jongleurs, flocking to the taverns, which were crowded with women of light life. By a remarkable piece of toleration games of chance were allowed, and no penalty overtook dabblers in illegitimate pleasures.

In all ways the fairs exercised an incomparable power of attraction, and mark one of the chief stages in the advance of Western commerce. They brought classes and nations together, and made for the pacification of Christian Europe. They opened a way for conceptions of commercial law wider than those of the civil law. They stimulated international and national trade, and with them the spirit of enterprise. They did much to bring to an end the economic isolation in which the West had lived during the early Middle Ages, and they gave irresistible openings to a money economy.

Maritime commerce, so limited during the first five centuries of the medieval period, began to develop from the time of the Crusades, and realized a progress similar to that which the fairs accomplished for land commerce. Seaborne traffic was easier since the West had become a sort of Christian republic, and since the Western peoples had expanded into the Northern and Levantine lands. Navigation became more active and more certain. The odious right of wreck, exercised at the expense of shipwrecked cargoes, was abolished in Italy, Catalonia, France, and England. The use of letters of marque and of reprisals, which allowed shipowners to be attacked as responsible for the individual or collective misdeeds of their compatriots, was restricted and regulated. Maritime law was laid down in collections such as the Statutes of Trani and of Marseilles, the Usages of Tortosa and Barcelona, the Rolls of Oleron and the Ordinances of Wisby, which regulated armaments, pilotage, sea risks, and harbour dues. In order to protect commerce or to regulate the litigation arising from it, special jurisdictions were set up, sea consulates on board ship, ordinary consulates, sea courts, *mercanzie*, admiralty courts in maritime cities. Maritime insurance policies appeared to guarantee the value of ships and cargoes, while the governments engaged in a war against piracy, which, though energetic at times, was fitful and of varying efficacy.

At the same time the construction of lighthouses and the maintenance of ports was receiving attention. Naval dockyards were built, notably at Venice, Genoa, Marseilles, and Barcelona. Side by side with small ships of low tonnage there were launched transport vessels of 500 to 600 tons (*ussiers*), which could carry 1,000 to 1,500 passengers. The Western states organized the first navies in order to protect commerce. Venice, Pisa, and Genoa owned the most powerful of these, and in 1293 the latter had 200 ships manned by 25,000 sailors. The Catalans were creating their navy in the thirteenth century at the same time as the Capetians, and France possessed at one time 118, and later 200 vessels with 20,000 sailors. Sea pilotage began to make strides, thanks to the use of the compass, borrowed from the Arabs and perfected by the Sicilian sailors, who were the first to think of putting the magnetic needle on a movable pivot. The Italians and the Catalans made the first sea charts. Navigation, though limited to the six spring and summer months, attained enormous proportions, in spite of the high cost of freight, and the incoherence and ceaseless variations of fiscal laws and customs.

Commercial interests obliged states to conclude the first commercial treaties with each other, and even forced the Christians themselves to negotiate agreements with the Moslems. The maritime powers obtained the concession of quarters and depôts in foreign towns, and sometimes, as in the Levant, jurisdictional privileges, the maintenance of which was entrusted to consuls and captains, and letters of protection and safe conducts. Already a fierce economic struggle was being waged between the commercial states, and often determined the orientation of their general policy. Commerce, now one of the great sources of wealth, attracted the most energetic and intelligent elements among the Western peoples. The Mediterranean, for a thousand years the cradle of civilization, became once more the most active centre of commerce, to the detriment of the Danube route,

which had served in the Middle Ages as the road of inter-
course between the Westerners and the Byzantine East. The
Crusades had turned this sea into a Latin lake, whereon the
Italian republics and the cities of Provence, Languedoc, and
Catalonia could give free rein to their rivalry. These republics set up counting-houses everywhere in the Levant,
in Egypt, in Cilicia (Lesser Armenia), at Cyprus, at Byzantium. Barcelona, Narbonne, Montpellier, Arles, Saint-Gilles,
Marseilles, and, above all, Genoa, Pisa, and Venice grew rich
by transporting pilgrims and crusaders, or by trading in
Eastern goods. They went to Alexandria, Tyre, Famagusta, Trebizond, and Byzantium to fetch the spices,
sugars, and sweet wines, the medicines and dyes, the pearls
and precious stones, the perfumes and porcelains, the silks
and the cloth of silver and gold, the muslins and cotton stuffs,
the carpets, the glasswork, damascened arms, and goldsmith's work, which came from the East. In the Black and
Caspian Seas they procured the corn, fish, skins, and even
(despite prohibitions) slaves in which they traded. They
carried to the Levant the produce of the West, corn,
woollens, linens, and unworked metals.

The greatness of Venice was founded upon trade. The
city of the lagoons, born in the fifth century, but dating her
rise to fortune from the conquest of the Adriatic (1002) and
the charter of privileges of 1082, which granted her free trade
for a century in the Byzantine states, won for herself in 1204
a vast colonial empire in the Archipelago, seized the keys of
the Dardanelles and the Bosphorus, and tried to get into her
hands not only the commerce of the Levant, but also that
of the Black Sea and the Sea of Azov, where she founded
a counting-house at Tana, and sought to open up fruitful
relations with the Far East by sending out missions of
commercial exploration, the most famous of which was that
of Marco Polo. Genoa, on her side, set up factories from
Corsica to Caffa, at the edge of the great Russian plain;
she established herself at Chio, and in 1261 obtained a leading position at Byzantium, where her allies, the Palæologi,
succeeded in restoring the Greek Empire; she disputed the
Levantine trade with the Venetians and the trade of Northern
Africa and Spain with the Pisans, whom she finally vanquished, launched a fleet on the Caspian, and sought to

monopolize trade with Russia, and to drain a large part of that of Central Asia. Venetians and Genoese heaped up enormous riches by means of this commerce, but they had to give up a share in it, with a very ill grace, to the merchants of Provence, Languedoc, and Catalonia after the middle of the twelfth century.

In the East and centre of Christian Europe, Spain, Western France, the Low Countries, and Germany were carving out for themselves a place of growing importance among the commercial powers. Both land and sea commerce reached an extent hitherto unknown in those regions. The unending flow of merchants followed two great internal trade routes. The road which went by way of the Po, the Alps, and the Danube put Genoa and Venice into connection with Vienna, Augsburg, Nuremburg, and Constance, while the route which followed the Rhône and Sâone united Mediterranean and Levantine Europe with Western Europe by means of the commercial centres of Champagne, the Île-de-France, and Flanders, and even by way of the Meuse and the Moselle with the Rhenish lands. The sea routes of the Atlantic, so little frequented during the early Middle Ages, brought a happy animation to the ports of Galicia and Biscay, which exported salt, wine, oil, lead, tin, and iron to the West, and, above all, the French ports became active. Bordeaux revived in the twelfth century at the same time that Bayonne was developing and Rochelle was founded; Nantes, Rouen, Honfleur, and Dieppe likewise grew rich by trade with the British Isles and the Low Countries. Salt, corn, wine, honey, fruit, wool, hemp, flax, wax, and French linens were actively exchanged against the wool, skins, unworked leather, tallow, salt meat, copper, lead, and tin of England and the manufactures of Flanders. Soon the advantages of this trade drew the attention of the Italians, who opened up relations with the Low Countries at the beginning of the fourteenth century by establishing their annual service of Venetian galleys, with its terminus at Sluys, the port of Bruges.

While England, satisfied with her wealth as a privileged agricultural country, as yet felt no premonition of her future commercial vocation, Germany was trying to develop a maritime power. The trading cities of the North, the most active of which was Lübeck, organized their great association, known as the Hanse, in the thirteenth century (1241). They aimed at monopolizing the two seas recently opened to trade by the Christian peoples, the North Sea and the Baltic, by way of which the West provided itself with fish and, above all, with raw materials—timber, tar, ashes, tallow, skins, leather, and furs—in exchange for the produce of the Levant and the merchandise of the South and West of Europe.

In the space of 250 years commerce, far surpassing the bounds which it had reached in antiquity, transformed Christian Europe and brought about a real revolution in the history of labour.

In truth, by opening a crowd of new markets, it provoked the development of industrial and agricultural production. The old economy of the domain was forced to transform itself and to open its doors to progress. The increase in consumption, the opening of external relations, the development of movable wealth, obliged the owners of landed capital to adapt themselves to the new conditions of economic life, to bring the soil under cultivation, and to seek by means of colonization to increase the value of the income from landed property, so as to avoid the ruin which dogged the footsteps of careless or unenterprising landowners. The industrial workshops, working henceforward not merely for the local market, but also for regional and national, sometimes even for international markets, increased in activity. Industry felt the impulse given to it by commerce, which provided it with capital, raw material, orders, and outlets, and which stimulated both the spirit of enterprise and the division of labour.

A new power was born and grew up, the power of movable capital, which transformed the character of trade and the circulation of goods, substituted a monetary for a natural economy, gave extraordinary flexibility, variety, and width to economic relations, and by the accumulation of commercial benefits allowed the constitution, renewal, and continual increase of forms of wealth, which were easily mobilized and capable of yielding high revenues. It opened the way to forms of economic activity far superior to those of the feudal economy, while at the same time it brought about the rise of mercantile and industrial classes, which were to become the rivals and sometimes the equals of the old feudal classes. It was thanks to this fruitful movement that workmen and peasants, now indispensable instruments of economic progress, were to become aware of their strength and to win their freedom. The economic and social transformation of Western Christendom was largely the result of the commercial revolution, which manifested itself and advanced ever more swiftly from the end of the eleventh century.

DURING the early feudal period (tenth to eleventh centuries) industrial activity was as yet embryonic. In the régime of natural and manorial economy which then prevailed the work of the artisan was seldom differentiated from that of the peasant, and industry was carried on only within the circle of the family or of the domain. The only existing forms of production were domestic industry and manorial industry on the great domains.

In the former each family group sought to produce the necessities of life for itself, without recourse to external sources of supply. By means of the latter the governing classes, lords and men of religion, obtained for themselves goods manufactured by the labour of various groups (*familiæ*) of servile workers, traditionally attached to the work—millers, bakers, brewers, weavers, tailors, tanners, shoemakers, masons, carpenters, smiths, potters, armourers, and even goldsmiths. Thus the bakers on the manors belonging to the Chapter of St. Paul's in London were obliged to furnish the canons with 40,000 loaves a year, and the brewers delivered them 67,800 gallons of beer. Just as the serf of the soil was required to pay rents in kind and labour services, so the artisan serf was bound to perform his own peculiar work or to pay rents in manufactured goods. In such a system industrial production was, perforce, limited to a small number of products, and remained a stranger to the spirit of progress, for there was no individual interest to stimulate it. There existed also the rudiments of a class of urban artisans, distinct from the predominant industry of the domain workshops, notably in Italy and in France; they carried on their work in the suburbs or within the walls of the towns. But here, as in the country, the artisan was unfree and beneath the dominion of the lord, having but a restricted clientèle and field of action.

From the eleventh century onwards a profound and progressive transformation took place under various influences in the organization of industry. The most powerful influence was exercised by the rise of a money economy and of commerce, which provided middlemen and workmen alike with what they had hitherto lacked—capital, sufficient supplies of raw material, and wide markets. Thus at first merchants and artisans were often included under the same name as traders (*mercatores*). It was in those parts of the West where commerce had sprung up again that industry received its first impetus, and just as commercial activity was cradled in the towns, so industrial activity, escaping from the sleepy atmosphere of the domain, grew in urban surroundings. For centuries industry developed in an urban form, henceforward eclipsing both domestic and manorial industry, attracting rural labour to itself and bringing about an enormous expansion in the number of artisans.

At the same time the expansion of the field of consumption and exchange stimulated the productivity of the workshops. In peace as in war, by commerce, by voyages, by crusades, the West was introduced to the industrial methods and the more perfect forms of Byzantine and Moslem industry. She served her apprenticeship and soon equalled and sometimes surpassed her masters. Italy and France became, in their turn, the great initiators and promoters of progress and of the industrial revolution, which was, moreover, favoured by the intelligent efforts of monks (especially those belonging to French Orders), of princes, and of town governments.

Technique itself was transformed. The use of wind power and of hydraulic power began to spread, and in a certain number of industries mechanical methods were introduced side by side with manual labour. The latter reached a high degree of skill in the textile industries and in the art industries, which often attained an incomparable perfection by reason of the careful training of the workers and the finish of execution.

The most active forms of industry exercised within this urban framework were those which may be grouped under the name of the " small industry " of artisans. A special class of men became organized independent of the domain and distinct from the agricultural class. These men had technical knowledge and lived on the produce of their craft, which the Middle Ages called their *art*. Under this régime the workman or *artisan* sometimes worked alone, and sometimes gathered together a few assistants in his workshop. He was the head of the business, and he chose his profession freely, according to his capacity. Above all, he worked for an urban or regional clientèle and market, and not merely for the lord and the domain. By dint of paying certain dues to his erstwhile masters, he won the right to dispose of the work of his hands; he was the owner of his tools and of the produce of his labour.

His professional skill was manifested in various ways. Sometimes the artisan worked at home upon tasks which demanded no advanced specialization, either alone or with the help of his family. This form of domestic industry, adapted to urban conditions, sufficed for the needs of restricted groups of consumers. Side by side with home or domestic industry there also developed *hired* or *wage labour*, which the lords had allowed to grow up in consideration of the payment of dues, and which was organized in a more independent manner. The artisan worked on order, by the piece or by the day, in his own room or at the house of another, upon materials furnished to him, but with his own tools and with no need either of capital or of middlemen. He was paid directly by the employer in money or in kind. If his work was irregular, at least he was entirely free and he took the entire remuneration. Nevertheless, neither domestic work nor hired work lent themselves to that active production for a market which the economic evolution of the Middle Ages was rendering necessary. Thus they both diminished in importance before the development of what is the form *par excellence* of the small urban industry, to wit, the *craft*, or workshop industry.

In this the artisan became essentially a small entrepreneur, whose centre of activity was the workshop in which he worked, assisted by his family or by a few apprentices and journeymen (*compagnons*). He possessed all the means of production; first, capital—that is to say, the raw material and the tools with which he had furnished himself—and, secondly, labour, which he provided himself, with the help of a small number of assistants. Because of its modest size, his business did not require borrowed capital, and so he was able to enjoy the whole produce of his labour. Sometimes he worked at an agreed price for customers who gave him orders; sometimes he worked for the local or regional market, either setting out his merchandise for sale on a stall in front of his shop, or taking it himself to the market-place, or selling it directly to a merchant. He never produced more than the normal amount of his sales, and his gain was therefore limited; but it was at least stable, and he shared it with no one. Thus it was the craft which attracted the mass of artisans, above all, when they had become emancipated. Thanks to it they made for themselves " a golden field," in the words of the picturesque German proverb, and could find vent for their energies beneath the stimulus of personal interest and of liberty.

Within the framework of the free craft labour in the Middle Ages became productive and varied. It lent itself easily to the extensions demanded by the progress of specialization and the requirements of the market. It could subdivide itself into as many distinct professions as technique and demand required. Thus in the woollen industry alone there were twenty-five distinct specialities in the thirteenth century. But the division and specialization of labour, far from leading, as they have in our own day, to the concentration of business enterprises, led in the Middle Ages to the multiplication of small urban industries, without altering their nature or threatening the autonomy of the little workshop. The progress of industry was then accomplished by means of a multitude of individual enterprises, which sprang up on all sides and unceasingly increased production, and which provided the consumer with carefully made and abundant goods at prices which, though still expensive, were within his means. The honour for the magnificent industrial development of this period of the Middle Ages lies with the small industry and the class of urban artisans, which opened the way for the great industry of modern times.

The latter was, however, beginning to announce itself, from the thirteenth century onwards, in a few special industries and in districts such as the Low Countries, Italy, and Northern France, where a great international commerce had developed. It was here that there arose the first enterprises working for a universal market, such as the cloth manufactures of Ghent, Ypres, Lille, Douai, Amiens, and Florence, the silkworks of Venice, and the copperworks of Dinant. Rich entrepreneurs, and even powerful corporations, undertook their direction. Such was the *Arte di Calimala* of Tuscany, which in the twelfth and thirteenth centuries monopolized the purchase of English wool, and of the half-finished cloths coming from Flanders and Northern France, and finished, dyed, and prepared these stuffs, finally sending them out to all the markets of the Mediterranean. Such also was the Florentine association of merchants and manufacturers known as the *Arte della Lana*, which was the rival of the *Calimala*, and established all the different varieties of the woollen manufacture upon the banks of the Arno.

Elsewhere it was great merchants, like the *poorters* or *coomannen* of Flanders and Brabant, who maintained the activity of the individual workshops. At Ypres, 140 merchant drapers kept a whole industrial district at work. Sometimes, as at Amiens or in the Rhenish towns, subsidiary entrepreneurs of the drapery trade (*gewandschneiders*) existed side by side with the great merchants. At Florence the business was so complicated that it was possible to distinguish beside the merchant drapers who acted as entrepreneurs for the manufacture, dealers who bought wool wholesale, washed and then retailed it (*lanivendoli*), and merchant entrepreneurs of worsted (*stamauioli*), who specialized in selling wool which they had previously spun, beaten, and combed.

Whether it was simple or complex, the great industrial business thus emerging was distinguished from the small industry by certain original characteristics. Its organs were not yet the factory and the works. The merchant entrepreneurs contented themselves with setting up offices in their houses, served by a limited number of clerks, serving-men, and messengers, together with a warehouse for raw materials and finished goods. Nevertheless, in this elementary form of the great industry the separation between capital and labour was already manifest. The merchant entrepreneur was the sole owner of the materials, sometimes he provided the tools, always he disposed of the orders. He was the sole buyer and the sole seller of manufactured goods. The work-people—spinners, combers, carders, weavers, fullers, dyers—were no more than instruments of production in the hands of the capitalist, who paid them, directed them, hastened, slowed down, or stopped the work at will. Henceforth the nascent great industry exercised a social influence which was far from happy, but it helped to bring about the vigorous economic expansion of those forms of industry in which it appeared.

The expansion which took place during these three centuries in industry, following in the wake of the expansion of commerce, extended to all branches, from mineral industries to manufactures, and from necessities to articles of luxury. To fulfil the needs of monetary circulation, men taxed their ingenuity to exploit the veins of precious metals once again, reviving old methods or discovering new ones by experiment. Gold-seekers sifted the grains of gold, polished by the waters, from the sands of the rivers of the Alps, Cevennes, and Pyrenees, and especially from the Rhône, the Rhine, and the Po. They attacked the silver, lead, and argentiferous copper-mines of Upper Italy, Tuscany, Sardinia, Calabria, Upper Aragon, Dauphiné, Savoy, Auvergne, Viverais, Alsace, Derbyshire, and, most important of all, those of the Fichtelgebirge, the Erzgebirge, and the Harz district. Now began the fortune of the German mining towns, Freiberg, Annaberg, and Goslar, where the art of mining was perfected. Beds of metallic minerals were sought out and exploited. Iron-mines were worked in the Harz, Westphalia and Styria in Germany, Sussex in England, Namurois in the Low Countries, Haute-Champagne, Normandy, Dauphiné, Berry, Haut-Poitou, Périgord in France, Biscay in Spain, Bergamo, Calabria, and Sicily, and, above all, the Isle of Elba in Italy, where the first mining companies appeared.

The West obtained its chief supplies of lead from Derbyshire, and Cornwall had almost a monopoly of tin, which was, however, disputed by Bohemia from about 1240. England and Germany profited by their copper-mines; Spain by her mercury-mines at Almaden, which were reopened in the thirteenth century; Italy by the beds of sulphur and alum at Volterra, Pozzuoli, and Ischia. Lapidaries sent for rare and beautiful stones from the Pyrenees, from Auvergne, and from the Asturias. From the fine quarries of Italy, the Pyrenees, the Tournai district, Hainault, Brabant, High Burgundy, the Île-de-France, the Caen country, and Westphalia architects obtained stone for the great buildings which were being reared on all sides. Coal-mines were beginning to be appreciated, although the use of vegetable fuel was still general. At Newcastle and Durham, in Hainault, above all in the basin of the Liège, in Bas-Languedoc, and in Forez, coal-mining was found profitable. The exploitation of salt-pans, salt springs, and salt marshes reached an extremely high level; in 600 years those of the Salzburg country yielded 10,000,000 tons of salt. Salt from the salt-pans of Limburg, Swabia, Lorraine, and Franche Comté sufficed for a good part of European consumption, the needs of which were met more especially by the salt marshes of the country round Nantes, of Bas-Poitou, and of Saintonge; and from the end of the thirteenth century the trading fleets of the North and West of Europe came in increasing numbers to this district. In the south the salt of Portugal, Spain, the Lower Po district, and the two Sicilies provided the Mediterranean market.

Although metallurgy had not advanced far in the treatment of minerals and metals, for which it could only make use of vegetable fuel, a primitive furnace, a small hammer, or manual labour, nevertheless, under the stimulus of necessity, production had advanced by leaps and bounds. Little forges multiplied in all districts which combined the three elements necessary to their activity—wood, minerals, and waterfalls. Sometimes these workshops even worked for export. Manufactories of helmets, cuirasses, shields, swords, and other arms prospered in Italy at Milan, Pavia, Venice, Lucca, Florence, and Naples; in Spain at Toledo, Valencia, and Saragossa; in France in Guienne, Périgord, Poitou, Dauphiné, Languedoc, and Lyonnais; in Germany in Franconia, Saxony, Styria, and Carinthia. Barcelona, Vich, Lerida, Gerona, and, above all, Biscay, possessed many ironworks, and so also did the Alpine districts of Italy, France, and Germany, the French provinces of the east and the centre, the Meuse country, and Central Germany. The foundries of Lorraine won a growing renown. Valencia in Spain was noted for skilled workers in brass and copper, but they were surpassed by those of Dinant and Huy, from whose workshops the beautiful brass wares, known by the name of *dinanderies*, spread through Europe. Châtelleran-dais, Auvergne, the Bray country, and Haute-Champagne established the manufacture of cutlery, Paris that of iron and copper articles, Germany, France, and Italy that of wrought iron, hardware, and locksmiths' work. In the thirteenth century a great French artist, Villard de Honne-court, prepared the future progress of clockmaking by the invention of clocks worked by weights and by escapement.

The enormous development of the food industries, and of the majority of manufacturing industries and industries of luxury and art, bears witness to the strength of the move-ment of wealth and trade in the West at this time. In the towns the food manufactures, which belong to the domain of the small workshop, multiplied and subdivided themselves to an infinite extent. Mills abounded in the country, thanks to the general use of water power, and from the twelfth century windmills also came into use. In 1086 Domesday Book records 5,000 water-mills in England alone, and in the thirteenth century there were 120 windmills in the single *banlieue* of Ypres. In the urban centres, corporations of butchers, bakers, pastry-makers, cookshop-keepers, and a crowd of others of the same sort became numerous and powerful associations. Italy was already producing pies and sea biscuits for export; Catalonia, Galicia, England, and the Low Countries exported salted provisions; and Flanders and England beer. The first manufactories of sugar, pre-served fruits, and syrups were set up, in imitation of those of the Arabs, in Provence, Andalusia, and Eastern Spain.

In the weaving of fabrics, furniture, decoration, and art the West became the rival and soon the fortunate conqueror of the East. The conquest of this great industrial domain began with the cloth manufactures. Italy gained the leader-ship here, to the detriment of Byzantium, from which she snatched the monopoly of the production of fine cloths. From the twelfth century Milan was said to employ 60,000 workers in this industry; a celebrated gild—that of the *Umiliati*—fostered the work there, and it spread to Venice, Bologna, Modena, and Verona. In this last town in 1300 as many as 30,000 pieces of cloth were produced annually, irrespective of stockings and caps. Lucca, Siena, Pisa,

THE RENAISSANCE OF INDUSTRY

Palermo, and Naples in their turn organized workshops, which were soon outstripped by those of Florence, where the *Arte di Calimala* had begun, in the twelfth century, to work up cloth imported from the West, and where the powerful corporation of wool (*Arte della Lana*) organized, in the thirteenth century, with the help of capitalist merchants, a great manufacture of fine cloths, which it exported all over Christendom. By 1306 the city on the Arno was manufacturing in her 300 workshops more than 100,000 pieces of woollen cloth, worth 1,000,000 golden florins. In 1336 a third of the Florentine population (30,000 workmen) drew their livelihood from this industry, the annual revenue of which was estimated at 1,200,000 golden florins.

From the twelfth century onwards the Low Countries began to rival Italy. Flanders and Brabant became great manufacturing districts, where woollen cloth was woven, so that the names of Fleming and weaver became synonymous. Saint-Omer, Douai, Lille, Bruges, Cambrai, Valenciennes, Louvain, Saint-Trond, Huy, Maestricht, Ypres, and Ghent sent forth to the great markets of the East and West their fine fabrics, serges, *brunettes*, striped, plain, or mixed cloths, dyed in bright colours, greens, reds, blues, and violets, and eagerly sought for everywhere. At Ypres the manufacture in 1313 had risen to 92,500 pieces. At Ghent 2,300 weavers worked at the cloth-looms. Here France, too, played an eminent part, and her cloth industry became her most important form of industrial activity. It prospered in Picardy at Amiens and Saint-Quentin; in the Île-de-France at Beauvais, Chartres, Senlis, Saint-Denis, and Paris; in Champagne at Provins (which had 3,200 looms at work in the thirteenth century), Rheims, Châlons, and Troyes; in Normandy at Rouen, Elbeuf, Pavilly, Montivilliers, Darnétal, Bernay, Honfleur, Vernon, Aumale, Les Andelys, and Caen; in Central France at Bourges; in Languedoc at Toulouse, Carcassonne, Narbonne, Béziers, and Montpellier, which were beginning to export their manufactures to the Levant. The drapery of Rousillon and Catalonia, of Lower Aragon, and of Valencia, arose to rival that of the South of France. In the Germanic lands the woollen manufactures of Bâle, Strasburg, Cologne, Augsburg, and Magdeburg, and the scarlet cloths of Regensburg and Passau became famous, and the French Cistercians and the Flemings introduced the art into Northern Germany. It even began to spread in England, and Stamford was exporting serges in the thirteenth century.

The manufacture of hemp and flax began to emerge from the little family workshops, and became extraordinarily active, on account of the growing use of body linen and the demands of trade. From the Arabs and Byzantines Southern Italy and Catalonia learned to make fine linen. This industry flourished in France, in Champagne, Normandy, Maine, the Île-de-France, and Burgundy, which exported their linens all over Christendom.

In the Low Countries the manufacture began to pass from the country districts into the towns of Flanders. In Germany, Cologne, St. Gall, Swabia, Franconia, and Thuringia rivalled the French provinces and towns. Navarre, Guipúzcoa, and, above all, Brittany, excelled in the production of sail-cloth. Under the name of muslins and fustians there even appeared the first cotton fabrics, imitated from the Byzantines and Arabs, and manufactured in Italy, in Catalonia at Valencia, in Languedoc at Carcassonne, and in Provence at Arles. From the East, also, the West stole the secret arts of the silk manufacture. It appeared as early as the eleventh century at Lucca, in the twelfth at Palermo, thanks to Roger II, then at Lucera, Reggio, Naples, Venice, and Florence in the thirteenth century, and at Zurich at the beginning of the fourteenth. Christian Spain, on its side, inherited the Arab silk manufactures at Almería, Valencia, Carthagena, Jaen, and Seville. The Western dyers, Italians, French, and Flemings, became the fortunate rivals of the dyers of the East. Tapestry work ceased to be the monopoly of the Arabs and Byzantines. Cuenca and Chinchilla in Spain carried on the Saracen tradition. Florence began to fabricate many-coloured carpets and rugs. Low-warp rugs and tapestries, first woven in the workshops of Poitiers and Limoges, later brought wealth to those of Paris, Rheims, Amiens, Arras, and Lille. "Turkish" carpets of velvet pile, and then, at the beginning of the fourteenth century, high-warp carpets made their appearance side by side with native rugs. Embroidery became a really artistic industry. Byzantium, mistress of fashion, was, in

PLATE III

GLASS MAKING
(15th Century)

the thirteenth century, dethroned by Italy and France and, above all, by Paris.

Work upon skins and leathers, practised in a number of districts where tanning and currying prospered, particularly in Italy, France, and Germany, gave rise to the opening of innumerable workshops, of which the most famous were those for the sale of furs and skins at Paris, for saddlery, harness, and footgear at Paris, Florence, Naples, Valencia, Cordova, Saragossa, and Barcelona, and for gilded leathers at Cordova and Venice, and also in the two Sicilies and France.

The shipbuilding industry gradually became organized in the West. Furniture making, in which the French, Italian, and Flemish carpenters excelled, was inherited from the Byzantines, just as in the thirteenth century the Italian and Spanish mosaic workers and potters supplanted the Greek artists at Palermo, Pesaro, Lucera, Valencia, Toledo, Seville, Calatayud, and Majorca. Glassworks sprang up in France devoted to the manufacture of common glass, while Venice as early as the eleventh century robbed Byzantium of the secret of making mirrors and artistic glasswork, and in 1292 founded the famous workshops of Murano. The Parisian and Italian ivory-workers of the same period surpassed their Byzantine predecessors.

Finally, in the domain of the art industries the West outran the East and took the lead, both in originality of design and in extent of production. Here France held a supremacy recognized by all. She covered Christendom with admirable monuments of Romanesque and Gothic architecture, with her sculptures, her wall-paintings, and her stained glass. Her master craftsmen, bred in hundreds of workshops maintained in the abbeys and towns and country districts, went everywhere, with thousands of workmen, bearing witness by their work to the superiority of the French industry (*opus francigenum*). It was France again which gave to Christendom her masterpieces of goldsmiths' work, her *champlevées* and *cloisonnées* enamels, her richly illuminated manuscripts. Mistress of science as of art, she had innumerable workshops of parchment-makers and copyists, until the paper and cotton manufactures created in imitation of the Arabs at Palermo, Jativa, and Valencia in the thirteenth century, and later in various French provinces, permitted the old costly material, by the aid of which thought was transmitted, to be superseded by an economical substance, which was to facilitate the diffusion of the works of human intelligence.

A teeming activity transformed the Western world. A multitude of artists and artisans created, regenerated, or developed the different varieties of industrial work, and tore the sceptre of industry from the Byzantine and Moslem East in its decadence, endowing the West with new sources of wealth. The commercial and industrial classes made their entry upon the stage of history ; they were now ready to win for themselves a social position which corresponded to the growing importance of their rôle.

THE first effect of the resurrection and development of commerce and industry was to bring about a renaissance of town life. From the middle of the tenth to the fourteenth century this movement became extraordinarily widespread, and it was then that almost all the towns of Christian Europe were created or reborn. The old Roman cities, usually situated upon the great trade routes, rose in numbers from their ruins. In the shelter of monasteries and strong castles, *burgs* grew up almost daily; and about 420 towns out of 500 French towns originated in this way. Many were simple manorial centres (*villæ*) promoted to the dignity of towns, when walls were built up round them; others arose to serve as a refuge for colonization, under the name of *villes neuves* (new towns), *villes franches* (free towns), *bourgs neufs, sauvetés*, and *bastides*. Such was the intensity of this renaissance that, besides those countries in which urban life had always lingered on, such as Italy and the South of France, almost the whole of the West became covered with cities. Germany possessed as many as 3,000, although the majority of them remained no more than fortified villages or *burgs;* England possessed 275. The reappearance and extension of this urban life, which had been so shattered during the early Middle Ages, was closely connected with the formation and progress of the industrial and commercial classes.

At first merchants and artisans lived in a state of subordination in the little town of the feudal era, which often numbered a bare thousand souls and usually had to bow to the authority of several rival masters, bishop, abbot, count, governor, or feudal lord. They were grouped into services (*familiæ*), attached in a servile capacity to the lords of the place and to their officers; they dwelt in the shadow of the church or the palace of the count or lord, side by side with a population of small officials, domestic serfs, and even cultivators and gardeners. But the merchants were more mobile by reason of the exigences of their profession, and more adventurous by temperament, and sometimes, indeed, were of foreign or suspect origin, and preferred to live in the suburb, which lay along road or river, by the side of which they established their shops and houses, surrounded by a palisade or enclosure, adjoining that of the castle. It was these merchants who formed the progressive element, to which is due the emancipation of the towns. As early as the eleventh century they are sometimes found enriching the towns by their active traffic—for example, in Upper Italy, on the Danube, Rhine, Meuse, Scheldt, and on the shores of the Mediterranean. Thus Venice grew, and Milan, Pisa, Amalfi, Genoa, Narbonne, Montpellier, Arles, Amiens, Saint-Quentin, Valenciennes, Cambrai, Ghent, Bruges, Cologne, Worms, Speier, Strasburg, Augsburg, and Regensburg. They often organized water transport, whence their name of *poorters* in the Low Countries, and they carried on banking at the same time as commerce. The richest of them formed an aristocracy of notables (*meliores*), which was sometimes numerous; there were 600 at Cologne. Some of them gave their daughters in marriage to knights. In Italy they even approached so closely to the nobility as sometimes to be reckoned noble; at Venice the patriciate was formed of great merchants, among whom was the Doge himself. Everywhere they sought to win the social rank to which their fortune permitted them to aspire. As in all analogous crises in the history of labour, commercial and industrial activity, in proportion as it bred wealth, engendered at the same time the need for freedom.

Moreover, very soon the servitude in which the merchant and artisan lived became incompatible with the exigences of their economic expansion. The feudal system, which allowed the trader and the manufacturer neither property, nor civil and commercial liberty, nor even personal freedom, strangled labour in such tight bands that its vitality could not develop. The system, by its fiscal regulations, its tyranny, and its anarchy, impeded the development of trade and the activity of the workshops. It did not even maintain order and security, conditions which are indispensable to economic progress. It was for this reason that the merchants, who between 1004 and 1080 were beginning to be called burgesses (*burgenses*) because of their habitual residence in the suburbs and new quarters of the fortified towns (*burgs*), sought in voluntary association the means of defence, which the feudal authorities could not provide for them. The associations which they organized, under the various names of gilds, hanses, fraternities, brotherhoods, charities, banquets, and which had their heads, their secretaries and officials, their assemblies, their subscriptions and their treasuries, were not political in character. But they grouped together under a solemn oath both great and small merchants, in order to give them the benefit of mutual assistance, both in the realm of religion and charity and in the protection of common economic interests. The association kept up the house of the community, or gildhall, in which the members met together; it arranged for markets, docks, ports, ships, organized caravans and armed escorts, guaranteed indemnities in case of theft, damage, or loss, sometimes even negotiated commercial treaties with the feudal governments. The gild merchant was at this time far bolder than the artisans' fraternity, which as yet had only a religious purpose, and bolder also than the nascent industrial craft or corporation, which was being timidly formed in a small number of trades, with the permission of the lord and under the permanent control of his officials. The craftsmen possessed as yet neither the wealth, nor the cohesion, nor the breadth of view of the merchants. It was the latter who conceived the common programme of emancipation and brought it to triumphant success by their co-ordinated, considered, and energetic action, and it was the merchant gild which engaged in the battle, directed it, and won it.

The movement began in the eleventh century in those Western countries in which the renaissance of commerce allowed the merchant classes to realize their power and gave them the will to break their bonds. The merchant patriciate, upheld by the mass of small traders and artisans, leaning now upon the Papacy and clergy, now upon the smaller nobility, profited by the divisions of the feudal classes and played off each against the other. At Venice from 976 they broke the monarchical power of the Doge; at Milan (in four revolutions between 987 and 1067) that of the archbishop;

at Piacenza (1090), at Lodi (1095), at Cremona (1095), at Viacenza, Bologna, Pavia, Lucca, Genoa, that of the feudal nobility. In Provence and Languedoc, knights and merchants led the assault against the seigniorial power. At Marseilles the merchant fraternity of the Holy Spirit roused the sailors' quarter and proclaimed a consulate and municipal autonomy. Le Mans (1069), Noyen (1027), Corbie, Amiens (1030) revolted to gain freedom of trade. At Beauvais (1074-1099) it was the dyers who waged war against the bishop. At Cambrai (1057-1076) and at Cologne the rich merchants engaged in a desperate struggle with the archbishop. In this initial phase the majority of syndicalist revolutions (as we may call them) collapsed, but a few succeeded. Sometimes, as at Saint-Quentin (1080), Douai, Arras, and Saint-Omer, the gild succeeded in winning its first liberties by peaceful means. From the eleventh century in Italy, the South of France, and Béarn the merchant classes obtained in certain places the right to participate in political life through the election of doges, consuls, or bishops, or were associated in a consultative capacity in the administrative life and financial administration of the town. In the majority of Western countries the merchants, in default of civil and political rights, obtained fiscal exemptions, economic privileges, and, above all, a special jurisdiction (*jus mercatorum*), which removed them from the caprices of local justice, and a special peace—the town peace, imposed upon all by oath—which guaranteed the security of their persons and property.

But these concessions were insufficient. Thus in the twelfth and thirteenth centuries merchants and workers joined in vast federations, sometimes public and sometimes secret, called *paix, communes, communia, conjurationes*. In vain the Church tried, by the voice of her canonists and saints, Yves of Chartres and Bernard of Clairvaux, to bar the way to these confederations of workers " of new and execrable name," as the historian Guibert of Nogent describes them. In vain the feudal baronage, and sometimes even the monarchy, tried to stay the revolution by a policy of rigorous and often atrocious repression. Everywhere the movement of emancipation triumphed more or less completely, sometimes by peaceful, sometimes by violent means. The merchant and industrial classes, exploiting the divisions of their adversaries, in one place joining the smaller against the greater nobility, in another the Church or the royal power against feudalism, in yet another feudalism against the Church. They profited by the cupidity of the feudal powers and bought charters of freedom from them. The more intelligent among those in authority even made spontaneous concessions of authority to their subjects, in the hope of increasing their productive power by emancipating them.

But in a large number of places violence was the midwife of liberty and of the new society of communes. In Lombardy and Tuscany the bourgeoisie and the people, with the bold merchants of Milan at their head, won their independence only at the cost of sanguinary struggles with the great nobles and the imperial power. It was by repeated risings that the working people of Languedoc and Provence, the towns of Arles, Marseilles, Nîmes, Carcassonne, Avignon, Béziers, Montpellier, and Toulouse succeeded in shaking off the feudal yoke. On the initiative of French and Italian merchants in Spain, at Compostella (1103-1136), Lugo, Orvieto, Sahagun, the people rose against ecclesiastical authority. In the twelfth century a wind of revolution blew upon almost all the towns of the West. In 1134 Poitiers, at that time an industrial and commercial town, tried to form an urban federation after the Italian model, in conjunction with the cities of Poitou. Cambrai in 1127, Compiègne in 1128, Amiens in 1113 and 1177, Orleans and Mantes in 1137, Vézelay and Sens in 1146, Rheims in 1144, and in the north and east the Flemish and Rhenish towns—Ghent, Tournai, Liège, Speier, Worms, Cologne, Mainz, Treier—sought to safeguard their economic future by rising in insurrection against the arbitrary power of lord or monarch. London itself tried to proclaim a commune in 1141. The revolution sometimes assumed the implacable and tragic aspect of a class war. At Laon burgesses and peasants assassinated their bloodthirsty and debauched bishop. At Vézelay and at Sens the rich Burgundian merchants rid themselves of rapacious and oppressive abbots by murder. The tenacity and energy displayed by these traders and artisans in their fight for freedom was unequalled; at Laon they thrice took up arms, at Vézelay five times, and at Tours twelve. The victory of the communes and their success in winning emancipation was a proof of the new power of the urban associations, united as they were in the firm determination to make good their right to work and to an independent life.

The movement towards emancipation was the outcome of such imperative social and economic necessities that it triumphed throughout the West. But it was far from presenting the same character everywhere, and from conferring the same degree of independence upon all urban populations. In lands where monarchical and feudal governments had preserved or acquired a certain amount of power, the commercial and industrial classes were obliged to content themselves with the grant of civil and economic liberties and a small number of administrative liberties, such as those which are stipulated in the Charters of Lorris, Breteuil, or Beaumont, from which 380 towns in France, the Low Countries, and England benefited. Rather more extensive liberties were conferred upon boroughs with a considerable burgess population, which received charters of the type of the *Établissements* of Rouen, but they were not granted political autonomy. In Germany, under the Hohenstaufen, in France under the Capetians, in England under the Plantagenets, and in the two Sicilies under the Anglo-Norman monarchy, the urban populations were able to win only a minimum of emancipation. Only a small number of towns in Italy, Southern and Northern France, and the Low Countries, where commercial life was most fully developed, reached complete independence, and formed real states, bourgeois republics, on the same footing as the old feudal states. But the general result of the communal movement, which may perhaps be called the first syndicalist revolution, was none the less favourable to the masses who gained a livelihood in the towns by their labour and by the pursuit of commerce and industry. For the first time thousands of men, forming, perhaps, a tenth of the whole population of the West, won equality and civil liberty, benefits which, throughout antiquity and the Dark Ages, had been enjoyed only by infinitesimal minorities. For the first time in the towns the mass of the workers, from the great merchant to the journeyman, found themselves members of a free association, an urban association endowed with a legal right and distinctive privileges.

The urban group—the town—really came during this period into the full enjoyment of a life of which it had hitherto possessed merely the shadow. It became a young and vigorous organism, greedy to enrich itself with fresh blood, and one in which the economic function dominated all the rest. Anxious to enrich itself with human capital or labour power, the urban community, or burgess body, granted the enjoyment of its right and privileges to serfs and villeins, artisans and merchants, who took refuge within its walls. It could exercise a legal right of admission (*droit d'accueil*). In order to be admitted to full burgess privileges, it was sufficient to reside for a year and a day in a town, to contract marriage there, to possess there a freehold of low value, or merely a rent, which could serve as guarantee in a court of justice. The community did not even exclude immigrants without resources, who brought only their strong arms with them. It granted them civil without political rights. In the southern lands it was also open to the class of knights, which did not profess that disdain for the bourgeoisie which was habitual with the higher military castes. In fact, the urban community was justly suspicious only of irreducible elements, whose interests were clearly opposed to its own—to wit, the feudatories and the churchmen, whom it formally excluded from burgess rights. It was an association for mutual defence, and it exacted from its members an absolute devotion, sealed by an oath, in exchange for the precious rights which it assured them, above all, in the domain of practical interests, and in return for the independence which it conferred upon their work.

In principle, indeed, according to the original law of each urban group, all the citizens of the town enjoyed equal rights. This is the fertile germ out of which, far more than out of the equality proclaimed by the feudal group, there sprang medieval democracy, the mother of all modern democracies. No one was admitted among the burgesses in order to claim special privileges. Further, the burgess, artisan, or merchant enjoyed personal liberty. "Town air makes a man free," said the German proverb. If there were still serfs or villeins in towns like Chartres, they were not to be found within the true circle of the urban community, but in that part of the city which had remained beneath seigniorial authority. But the town was so essentially the refuge of liberty that it was called a *franchise*, and the dweller therein was essentially *free*. Consequently he possessed all the rights which derive from civil liberty. He could marry and give his children in marriage at will, could move away at his pleasure, come and go, dispose of his property as of his person, acquire, possess, alienate, exchange, sell, will and bequeath his goods, movable and immovable, without being subjected to seigniorial control. His lands could be transmitted, burdened with rents and mortgages, pledged, in a word, easily realized, so as to facilitate all the operations of commerce. This is why burgess property was often valued at a higher rate than feudal property, which was hampered by a crowd of restrictions in all contracts involving alienation or pledges. The town dweller obtained freedom of trade; he became master of the urban market, where he was no longer hampered by monopolies, tolls, tonnage, rights of *banvin* (or the sale of wine), of hospitality, and of procuration, dues, services, *corvées*, and the seigniorial privilege of buying on credit, which had hitherto so greatly hindered production and trade. By the power of money he was able to overthrow the barriers which feudal power had set in the way of free economic activity. He obtained the grant of privileges, which enabled him to recover his debts speedily, and of guarantees, which put an end to the arbitrary judgments and penalties of seigniorial justice. Sometimes he bought freedom from that justice and substituted for it the court of the commune itself. Almost everywhere he extorted from those whom he found in authority exemptions from and reductions of tolls. He obliged them to reform and simplify procedure and civil and criminal law. In questions of debts, pledges, mortgages, commercial affairs, he obtained the simple and logical legislation and the rapid means of execution which are required by business. Finally, he imposed upon all, and especially upon the feudal class, if need be by force, a respect for the *town peace*, which was necessary for the safety of economic relations. He decreed the abolition of family wars within the city; he safeguarded the quiet of market, fair, and highway by rigorous rules. He succeeded in bringing about the triumph of the principles of equality, liberty, and order, so indispensable to mercantile and industrial societies. He placed them beneath the protection of the sacred symbol of the stone cross, which stood in every village, the visible sign of the new rights of the bourgeoisie.

The urban communities of the West experienced various degrees of political emancipation. The greater number of them, towns with a large burgess class, or centres of colonization, particularly in France, Southern Italy, England, Spain, and Germany, were obliged to recognize the sovereignty of a suzerein, who granted them charters of privileges, on which was based the legal existence of the municipal body. Paris, London, Rouen, Bordeaux, Palermo, Messina lived under this régime, as well as thousands of little urban groups. Under the control of officials appointed by the power which made the concession—bailiffs, provosts, judges, sheriffs, *écoutêtes*, *corregidors* — the burgess body, represented by *pairs*, *jurats*, and aldermen, nevertheless obtained considerable autonomy in administration, the choice of magistrates, finance, and, above all, economic affairs, in conformity with its essential needs.

Elsewhere, in Northern and Central Italy, the South and North of France, and the Low Countries as early as the twelfth century, and in the Rhine and Danube lands of Germany from the thirteenth century, there appeared republics, quasi-sovereign states, communes, *villes de consulat*, free towns which reached a higher degree of power. These urban communities governed themselves through their general assemblies, representative bodies, senates, great and small councils, aldermen's courts, and through their elected magistrates, mayors, *jurats*, consuls, and aldermen. They formed collective lordships, as independent, proud, and jealous of their liberty as the feudal sovereigns themselves.

But alike in the boroughs and centres of colonization and in the consular towns and communes, the commercial and industrial classes succeeded in winning the essential object of their efforts—to wit, the recognition of their right to free and equal association. This association, composed of all the merchants, artisans, and householders, rich and poor, held collectively the complete or partial sovereignty, which was conceded to it. It was the whole body of burgesses which delegated the exercise thereof to its agents, whether an oligarchy aspired to govern in its name, or whether it participated directly in all business. It was in the name of the whole community, the *universitas* of burgesses, that the municipal government was carried on. It was the whole mercantile community which contributed by direct and indirect taxes to the municipal treasury and met the expenses of administration, of the magistracy, and of defence, which formed also the staff and the troops of the communal militia. Upon it rested the political power of the city, and its economic activity was the guarantee of the liberties which it had won.

Thus, beneath the gilding of romance which covers the history of the medieval communes, through the noise of the tumultuous life which was played out within their walls, in their public squares, under the shadow of their belfries and town halls, and amid all the fierce struggles of parties disputing with each other for power, there appears clearly a united, continuous, and realistic policy pursued by the urban states, a policy which has almost always been misunderstood, for lack of a careful study of their organization. That policy was entirely governed by economic interests; its aim was to develop the power of production. The urban community, whether it was ruled by a bourgeois patriciate, by a democracy, or by bodies recruited from among the different classes in the city, was inspired by the same aims that had guided it in its efforts to gain emancipation. It pursued with untiring energy and rigid logic the maintenance and increase of its economic privileges, the enrichment of the community by means of organized work, so as to assure the power and greatness of the municipal state. It was in order to realize these practical ends that it struggled against the established powers—empire, kings, lay and ecclesiastical lords. In order the better to preserve them, it even resigned itself to renounce its exclusiveness and to form fraternities and leagues with other towns, such as those which were organized among the Lombard and Tuscan cities, the sixty-two cities of the Rhineland, the sixty-seven Flemish cities, the thirty-two cities of Leon and Galicia, and the maritime cities of Cantabria, whose action safeguarded the liberties and economic prosperity of vast regions. In general these governments were inspired by a jealous local patriotism, a selfish particularism, born of an unyielding attachment to the commercial and industrial interests of the urban community, upon which was founded the power of the municipal state; they represented the ideas and tendencies of the producing classes, who were now sovereign, or at least invested with partial sovereignty.

It was, however, in economic affairs that these urban communities, boroughs, centres of colonization, and communes possessed the widest powers, powers, indeed, the extent of which astonishes the historian. Everything was done to endow the mercantile and industrial bourgeoisie, in all its elements from the humblest to the greatest, with a body of privileges, monopolies, and regulations destined to stimulate the power of work, the expansion of trade, and the growth of wealth. Careful to attract immigrants, who brought to it the help of their labour, their inventions and their precious capital, and to stimulate a development of agricultural colonization in the surrounding country which would secure the urban food supply, the bourgeois state worked solely for the profit of its members, without any regard for the rights of neighbouring and hostile communities. For this reason it set itself implacably to destroy seigniorial domination in order to substitute its own; it subjected the peasants of the surrounding district to itself, prevented commerce and crafts from being carried on outside its walls, and set narrow limits to the competition of strangers (" foreigners "), whom it suspected of defrauding its members of part of the reward of their activity. These strangers were forbidden to trade retail; they were strictly supervised and obliged to find sureties, and subjected to a variety of regulations and prohibitions and differential payments. Each town made itself a sort of sphere of influence on land or sea, to which it admitted no rivals, and access to which was forbidden if necessary by force of arms, as is seen, for example, in the case of the Venetians, the Pisans, the Genoese, the Florentines, and the Flemings. When it opened or raised its barriers the municipal state obtained for itself treaties or conventions of reciprocity and friendship, in such a way as to risk the alienation of none of its essential prerogatives.

LIFE AND WORK IN MEDIEVAL EUROPE

The constant aim of urban policy was to develop trade and production. To this end the commune was at pains to attract entrepreneurs and workmen by privileges, and afterwards to preserve its trade secrets with the utmost jealousy. In virtue of the right of *staple*, it arrogated to itself the power of stopping foodstuffs and raw materials in transit, or buying them on preferential terms. It obtained monopolies of transport, purchase, and commerce. The urban governments reserved the right of buying and selling for the members of the community, and conferred upon employers and workmen the privilege of exercising crafts and forming corporations. For traders and manufacturers they created ports, market-halls, markets, highways, sometimes canals, and passenger and transport services; they promoted the organization of banks and stabilized the coinage. They defended the interests, persons, and goods of their members in the outside world.

They held that commerce and industry were functions which should be exercised for the common advantage of the community. Thus by a body of rules which fixed wages, prices, the division of purchases of raw material, the technical standards of manufacture, and sales in open market, they sought to prevent monopolies, abusive speculations, frauds, anarchy in production and trade, so as to maintain a sort of economic equality within the city, and to discipline and co-ordinate individual effort, and increase its efficacy for the greater good of the community. Nor did they neglect the interests of the consumer; they gave him rights of pre-emption by the regulation of the market; they sought to guarantee that all transactions should be honest and open, and they were at pains to provide a cheap and regular food supply for the masses.

This dominant preoccupation of urban policy, which always gave the first place to economic interests, had magnificent results. It made the medieval towns living and progressive centres of activity. To most of them it brought wealth, due to the productive capacity of a labour which was emancipated, honoured, and protected. It drew into the towns an ever-increasing population. In those which were enriched by commerce and industry the movement and life of days gone by was born again—for example, in the Two

Sicilies, in Central and Northern Italy, in Eastern Spain, in the South and North of France, in the Rhineland, and in the Low Countries. Great urban populations appeared once more. Palermo numbered about half a million souls in the twelfth century; Florence had 100,000 in the thirteenth, Venice and Milan over 100,000, Asti 60-80,000, Paris 100,000 at the end of the twelfth century, and perhaps 240,000 at the end of the thirteenth; Douai, Lille, Ypres, Ghent, Bruges, each had nearly 80,000, London 40-45,000. Henceforth about a tenth of the population of the West flowed into the towns, which became the homes of a vivid life. The industrial and commercial classes which had created them displayed eminent aptitude for the art of government, far superior to that of the feudal classes. It was among them that the class of administrators, which was to furnish the monarchical governments with their most useful staff, served its apprenticeship. They possessed, above all, a clear insight into those economic interests which are the basis of the fortune of states. But these merchants and artisans recognized also and cared for the greatness of the little municipal fatherland, wherein they had succeeded in acquiring freedom and power. Thanks to them there was born a new urban civilization, which was manifest in all spheres, social, intellectual, and artistic. It gave rise to a magnificent harvest of charitable institutions, centres of learning and even of literature, the inspiration of which was essentially bourgeois. It developed among the towns that spirit of generous emulation to which we owe so many works of public utility or of art, the market-places and halls, ports, bridges, quays, fountains, town halls, belfries, cathedrals, and churches, with which each city sought to adorn itself, and on which it was fain to set its mark.

The emancipation of millions of men belonging to the commercial and industrial classes, to whom this marvellous expansion of urban life was due, is one of the capital events of history. The urban commune, which was the work of the merchant and the artisan, took its place in the political and social hierarchy, side by side with the feudal lordship. Henceforth it was, for the West and for the whole world, one of the most active instruments of progress and liberty. At the same time it gave the commercial and industrial classes a framework in which they could group themselves and give themselves a powerful organization, and thanks to which they were able to improve the conditions of their existence and for the first time to enforce a recognition of the value and the power of work.

THE commercial and industrial classes had united to conquer their freedom; now after the victory they began definitely to organize themselves. While, on the one hand, their associations became legal organisms, on the other, the elements of which they were composed fell into distinct groups, according to their natural affinities. The richest among them formed a veritable aristocracy, a patriciate, while on their side the masses formed a vast democracy of free crafts and sworn corporations.

For about a century and a half, and sometimes longer, the patriciate occupied the leading place. It differed in character in the different countries. In Italy and the South of France the lesser nobility of knights (*milites*), who had taken upon themselves the direction of the work of emancipation, profited thereby in the majority of towns by seizing control of the municipal government. These knights owned rural manors in the country, and possessed, within the city walls, palace-fortresses, built out of enormous blocks of stone, crowned by high square towers, and adorned by platforms and battlements, to which access was gained by narrow posterns kept bolted with iron bars and chains. In Florence, Bologna, Milan, Avignon, and in a number of southern towns these proud towers pricked the sky, and symbolized the domination of a patriciate of nobles; there were 1,500 of them at Florence, 300 at Milan, and legend asserted that Pisa boasted no less than 10,000. Grouped into military associations (*societá d'armi*), these nobles, who cared for nothing but their interests as landed proprietors and their family feuds, disturbed the life of the commune by their street fights, and oppressed the working classes with a heavy tyranny. Sometimes, however, in commercial towns such as Venice and Genoa, the patricians, whose fortune was founded upon trade, governed with moderation and wisdom.

Elsewhere, notably in Castile, the class of gentry allied with the rich bourgeoisie and shared social and political influence with it. In Germany the patriciate of nobles amalgamated with the class of great burgesses. In Northern France and the Low Countries it was absorbed, or more often eliminated, sometimes by intermarriage, sometimes by severe measures against the feudatories. In the greater part of the West, however, the patriciate identified itself with the haute bourgeoisie, an association composed of great men of business, organizers of transport, great industrial capitalists, shipowners, money-changers, and bankers, together with rich urban landholders and *rentiers*. This association, in which the mercantile and industrial aristocracy predominated, received a legal and official existence. It was usually called the *gild*, or *hanse*, sometimes the *fraternity* or *confrérie*. From an early period it was obviously oligarchical in character. In certain English towns it numbered barely 200 members, and at Ghent, in the thirteenth century, it comprised only the heads of thirty-nine families. The members of the burgess patriciate or gild called themselves the greater burgesses (*majores, principes, optimates, proceres*), or else the worthy folk (*bons hommes, prud'hommes, honorés*). They came to form veritable dynasties, such as the *lignaiges* of Northern France and the Low Countries, the *paraiges* of Metz, the *geschlechter* of Germany, the *honrats* of Catalonia. Their ranks could be entered only by right of birth or of fortune, and on condition of exercising no manual profession and paying high admission fees. Gilds, hanses, fraternities kept out small traders and all craftsmen. The patricians formed a close corporation, the members of which were united by a solemn oath and by community of interests. They submitted themselves to a strict discipline, under the authority of their elected administrators, consuls, captains of the merchants, provosts, wardens, or *échevins*. These chiefs, such as the provost of the *marchands de l'eau* at Paris, the count of the hanse at Bruges, or the *schildrag* at Ypres, were assisted by councils of elders or *prud'hommes*, who numbered twenty-four at Paris, and twelve to twenty-four in the English gilds. The gild had its personnel of clerks and treasurers, recorders, sergeants or employés, its meeting-place (the gildhall or burgesses' parlour), its financial resources, made up of the subscriptions of its members or other taxes, its treasury, its budget, which permitted it to make payments warranted by the common interest, its assemblies, in which its affairs were discussed and its rules drawn up, its feasts and banquets, which helped to strengthen its solidarity. It secured recognition for its immunities and economic and jurisdictional privileges. It had its courts, and sometimes its coats-of-arms. Thus the patriciate made the gild an instrument of its power.

These burgesses, who formed so clearly marked a patriciate, profited by their ascendancy, their close union, the aptitude which they had already shown in directing the movement for emancipation, and the wealth which they had acquired, to arrogate to themselves the monopoly of government and economic supremacy in the urban commune. In a large number of cities they reduced the general assemblies or parliaments, which were the organs of the community, to a purely passive rôle, and often they eliminated the smaller burgesses and the artisans from them. They seized control of the councils, the magistracies and the courts, and tended always to transform municipal offices into hereditary fiefs. The patricians proudly named themselves " the lords of the town "; they wished to turn the " lordship " of the urban state into a possession, a " lordship," reserved for their own caste. Sometimes, as at Venice, they managed to associate the fortunes of other classes with that of the patricians. If in most towns they showed little adaptability, at least they had almost everywhere a real sense of the grandeur and general interests of the municipal state. They energetically maintained urban independence against the assaults of princes, feudatories, and the Church. They were animated by an ardent patriotism, and they gave the communes a high place in the feudal world. Their external policy was inspired by the determination to secure the economic preponderance of the town which they represented. It was often they who founded the power of the city. These patricians possessed in innumerable ways a profound grasp of realities. They emancipated the towns from the fetters of feudalism, and organized a remarkable system of administrative, fiscal, and military institutions and magistrates.

They knew how to govern. Their despotic activity multiplied works of public utility, commercial and industrial enterprises, roads, canals, docks, market-halls, ports, works of defence or of adornment, schools, hospitals, orphanages. In England the gilds created as many as 460 charitable institutions. Everywhere they favoured the intellectual and artistic development of the towns. They helped to enrich the urban communes, and prepared the way for the triumph of the lay spirit. But these bourgeois patricians, superior to the feudal lords in the art of government, were their equal in arrogance and tyranny. They displayed a caste spirit which was just as exclusive, as proud, and as jealous as that of the noble class. They oppressed the working classes and dragged the towns into warlike adventures. Too often they pursued a policy of ruinous magnificence, squandering the resources of the community, crushing the people beneath the weight of taxes, driving the towns to bankruptcy, and arousing explosions of revolution by their despotism.

Their tyranny was yet more insupportable in the economic and social sphere. The patricians exacted a heavy payment for the services which they rendered in the development of production and exchange by the monopolies and privileges which they arrogated to themselves. Gilds and hanses seized control of the export trade and of all the most lucrative forms of commerce, and reserved these for their members or for those to whom they were pleased to allow them. In England the gild even laid its hand upon the retail trade in certain articles, such as cloth and fells. In Florence the "art" of the *Calimala* alone possessed the right to import and sell foreign cloth. Every hanse had the monopoly of various means of transport or of trade; in one place it was river transport, in another the wool or cloth trade. Often the gild obtained the farm of weights and measures, sale by auction, tolls, brokerage, pilotage, and advertisement. It built offices, quays, and docks, and levied dues for its own advantage. Rarely did the patricians show sufficient sense to allow the masses to participate in the profits of their enterprises. On the contrary, they deliberately sacrificed the interests of the small trader and the artisan to their own.

Not only did they seek to exclude these lesser folk from public life, but they used the power which they had seized to bring the working classes into subjection. They forbade associations of artisans, and refused them the right of union and strike, under pain of banishment and death. They decreed the obligation of all to work. Patrician oligarchies are to be found making treaties with each other to secure the reciprocal extradition of artisans who were suspect. Masters of the town councils and of the magistracies, the patricians were able to regulate at will the hours of labour, the level of wages, the price of food, to submit trade and the crafts to a rigid discipline, and to promulgate or revise the statutes of the corporations. In those centres, more especially, in which the great industry appeared, great merchants and entrepreneurs made use of their authority to regulate the conditions and administration of labour in such an arbitrary manner that they reduced the workers to complete slavery.

The patrician oligarchs finally succeeded in exasperating the masses by their arrogance and the display of their wealth. In the northern towns the great burgesses were eager to call themselves esquires and *damoiseaux;* everywhere they assumed titles of honour. They sometimes surpassed the old landed aristocracy in pomp. " It is trade which now breeds wealth," said a great tanner of Basle to his guest, the Emperor Rudolph of Habsburg. At the state entries of princes they were noted for their luxury, as was observed at Cologne in 1236, when the 1,800 leading burgesses of the town welcomed the betrothed of Frederick II. They gave their daughters larger dowries than the nobles were wont to give, and built themselves great stone houses, sometimes crowned with towers and battlements. Brunetto Latini admires their dwellings in France, " great and spacious and painted, their fair chambers wherein they have joy and delight," with orchards spreading round them. They live nobly, says a satirist of Champagne, " they wear kings' robes, and keep goshawks and falcons and sparrowhawks." Their wives were like queens in their sumptuous attire, as Jeanne of Navarre, Queen of Philippe le Bel, remarked, not without vexation, at the sight of the 600 bourgeois ladies of Bruges. They kept an abundant table, and their enormous meals were washed down with priceless wines, while their silver plate was displayed on their tables in all its magnificence. They aped the nobility, and were fain to flaunt themselves at tourneys, even as they flaunted at feasts and processions. The spectacle of this luxurious life was a real source of provocation to the masses, on whom the despotism of the patriciate weighed heavily, and was aggravated by their insolent disdain and by their assaults upon the honour and dignity of the common people. Thus they aroused against themselves the hatred of powerful associations, free crafts or corporations, the formation and development of which they were unable to prevent.

The small traders, the small masters, and the workmen had already, with the permission of the Church, formed associations for piety and mutual assistance called fraternities or charities, side by side with which professional or trade groups (*ministeriales*) had been formed by the consent of the seigniorial authority, particularly among the industries which catered for primary necessities. This had been taking place at Paris, Chartres, Étampes, Pontoise, Douai, Saint-Trond, Bâle, Strasburg, and Coblenz from the eleventh century and the first half of the twelfth century. In rare cases the old Roman and Byzantine corporations, such as the *scholæ* of Rome and Ravenna, had survived. But these primitive unions, subjected to a close supervision and enjoying only a few privileges or monopolies, were not very strong. In the communal revolution their rôle was only that of a sort of make-weight.

The general emancipation, of which the masses took advantage to acquire civil and economic liberty, was favourable to the spread of the movement of association among the working classes. Its progress was so rapid that it soon became the normal framework in which work was carried on. It took two forms, that of the free craft, and that of the sworn corporation. The former prevailed in the majority of Western towns, where the old and new authorities resigned themselves to accept organizations which were less dangerous to their predominance than were the corporations. The free craft, enjoying a monopoly of sale and production, and guaranteeing professional obligations which were in conformity with the general interests, grouped together the great mass of the small traders and artisans. It gave its members the love of honest and independent work, but if it secured them the benefit of professional liberty and dignity, it did not set itself up as a privileged body in opposition to the governing classes. The latter preserved rights of police and jurisdiction, and exercised full political authority over the free crafts.

Little by little, in spite of the suspicion and resistance of the sovereign power, whether king, church, feudal lord, or bourgeois patriciate, the mass of the people began to organize other groups, sworn corporations, which were joined by the most powerful or active minorities. These exercised a political, economic, and social activity which was far more profound than that of the free crafts. Their number grew in proportion as the labour of the masses became the preponderant element in the prosperity of the towns. Sometimes in virtue of a decision brought about by the interests of the city or of the governing class, sometimes as a result of the pressing demands of a group of workers, the free crafts and even the dependent crafts became transformed into sworn associations. These corporations—known under various names as *fraternités, confréries, frairies, métiers jurés, scuole, paratica, arti, mestieri, gremios, zünfte,* craft gilds, some made up of single unions, others (*arti, zünfte*) of federations of unions, such as the *Arte della Lana di Calimala,* multiplied throughout the West between the middle of the twelfth and the middle of the fourteenth centuries. At the beginning of this last century Venice possessed 58 of them; Mantua, 21; Genoa, 33; Bologna, 20; Bergamo, 18; Parma, 24; Padua, 36; Pavia, 25; Florence, 21. Paris, which, about 1180, had only a dozen, possessed 100 at the time of St. Louis. Amiens numbered 26 at the beginning of the fourteenth century; Poitiers, 18; Cologne, 26; Treier, 20; Magdeburg, 12; Frankfort-on-Main, 14; Strasburg, 15. The average number in most German towns ranged from 12 to 15. Sworn corporations were organized rather late in those regions in which the patriciate was dominant, for example, in the Low Countries. The trade union succeeded in setting itself up as a privileged body most easily among the food, building, and clothing industries, the trades of primary necessity.

Often also, however, aristocratic professions, in which brain work dominated manual labour, such as those of the notaries, physicians, apothecaries, and goldsmiths, formed themselves into corporations at an early date, and were, indeed, among the most renowned. Such was the case with the *arti maggiori* at Florence. At other times it was the trades whose members had been able to impose themselves upon the consideration of the public by their more rapid acquisition of wealth, such as the bankers, money-changers, and great manufacturers, who took advantage of their plutocratic prestige to organize themselves into similarly privileged associations. Finally, a number of trades, such as baking, when they ceased to be carried on as family and domestic industries, often succeeded in their turn in entering the ranks of corporations.

The free crafts and sworn corporations, unions under common law and privileged unions, into which the commercial and industrial classes were grouped, exercised a powerful influence upon the organization of the labouring masses. They taught them solidarity and discipline, under the direction of freely chosen leaders and beneath the rule of statutes and regulations drawn up by themselves and amended by the urban community. They gave them a powerful hierarchy, founded upon professional capacity, and assured them the independence and dignity of labour. They it was who enabled the worker to enjoy the fruits of his toil by working for the suppression or limitation of ancient seigniorial rights, and by guaranteeing the economic equality of their members. Both in the free craft and in the corporation access to mastership and the right of exercising a trade was permitted to all who were able to offer guarantees of morality and technical skill. In order to set up as a master in this golden era of the Middle Ages, it sufficed to have served an apprenticeship, to undergo an examination (the so-called masterpiece) which was then both simple and practical, or even to furnish a simple attestation of capacity according to public repute, to pay moderate entry fees, and to bear the cost of a not very expensive dinner or feast; often, indeed, the aspirant had to pay no fee and had no expenses.

Between the workman, who was called the journeyman, and the master there was no other difference than that which was brought about by a slight and often temporary inequality

of fortune or position. Both had received the same professional training. The workman could become a master on the
day upon which he married a master's daughter, and at any
time when he had collected the small amount of capital
necessary for him to set up on his own account. The journeyman was free to work as he liked; he was bound only by a
contract of limited duration, furnished with definite guarantees and stipulating reciprocal obligations. Master and
journeyman lived together in daily comradeship. The
journeyman had his place in the trade, he shared in the
choice of officials, and in the fraternity he found moral and
material assistance. His individuality was recognized and
protected by the free or sworn association of which he
formed part. In it he found a support and not an obstacle,
and his personality became freer and more respected, inas-
much as he was a part of it. The craft assured the future
master and workman alike the benefit of a professional
education, an apprenticeship of varying length (two to eight
years) according to the difficulties of each profession, but
serious and effective. The apprentice found in the master a
rough and stern teacher, who gave him a careful and virile
education, and one of such high value that the working
classes have never at any period had a better technical preparation for the fulfilment of their function.

Masters, journeymen, and apprentices formed autonomous
groups, administering themselves freely, and imposing upon
themselves the economic and social discipline necessary to
secure their power and prestige. By the practice of self-
government they accustomed themselves to the habit of
liberty, the sense of responsibility, and the civic virtues.
The sworn corporations, and even sometimes the free crafts,
had their assemblies, parliaments, or chapters, in which the
masters, and sometimes the workmen, deliberated, the latter
having more or less restricted rights therein. They made
statutes concerning common affairs, elected administrators,
and controlled their actions. These administrators—*jurés,
prud'hommes, baillis,* wardens, *rewards, gardes, esgardeurs,
veedores, majorats,* consuls, rectors, *podestats,* vicars, doges,
as they were called in different places—sometimes had at their
head a president—the prior, proconsul, master, *mayeur de
bannière, capmeister;* they made police regulations, managed

the finances and the courts of the association, with the assistance of councillors, syndics, treasurers, auditors of accounts, agents, clerks or secretaries, apparitors or esquires, sergeants and messengers. They visited the workshops and markets, imposed penalties and fines, administered the master's oath, and presided at ceremonies and feasts. They were elected annually, and they exercised their power in the interest of the whole body, of which they were the mandatories.

The association was a juridical personality, which could sue in a court of justice, possess movable and immovable property, rents, meeting-places (halls, mansions, *steuben*, *scuole*, *parloirs*), sometimes even shops and industrial establishments. It had its own recognized and respected place in the urban commune. In the Church it built its own chapel, which it adorned lovingly, and in which, as at Chartres and at Bourges, stained windows displayed the insignia of the craft. It had its title-deeds preserved in its archives, its seal, its armorial bearings, even as the lord and the commune had them. It displayed its standard or banner, whereon might be seen the image of the patron saint of the corporation, together with the attributes of the craft, the carpenter's axe, the shoemaker's awl, the golden cup or cross or crown of the goldsmith, and the *agnus Dei*, with red and yellow halo upon a field of blue, which was the mark of the clothworker. Labour thus by means of association proclaimed and won its title to nobility.

The urban workers, like the other social classes, won privileges for themselves. They succeeded in securing the recognition of their property in their craft. Just as the merchant was sovereign in his gild and the lord in his fief, so the master and the workman were rulers in their craft. They had a monopoly in it. At a time when free labour was organizing itself, it was useful that the sphere of activity of each professional speciality should be delimited in order to prevent any wastage of productive power, and to assure a secure existence to the producers. Moreover, the monopolies were far from being rigorous; if they guaranteed the privileged enjoyment of the local market to the small traders and artisans, they were modified by the co-existence of free and sworn crafts, by the survival of domestic industry, by the permission of foreign competition on certain days, and, finally, by the recognized power of the sovereign authority, royal, seigniorial, or municipal, to proclaim the freedom of labour. This last power was from time to time unhesitatingly used by kings, such as Philippe le Bel, and by communes, such as those of France and Italy.

Monopoly gave rise to interminable lawsuits among the corporations, arising out of the difficulty of determining the sphere of activity of each. It brought to blows shoemakers and cobblers, lorimers and saddlers, bladesmiths and handle-makers, drapers and mercers, and many others. Such difficulties have arisen at all periods of history, and our modern patents give rise to fully as much litigation as grew out of the interpretation of the statutes of medieval corporations. Moreover, monopoly did not check emulation at this period, when the corporation had not yet acquired the rigidity and spirit of routine which were to characterize it later. The rivalry of the towns obliged the crafts of each town to improve and to watch carefully over their work. In the matter of technical skill and finish, the work of the artisans of the Middle Ages can compare advantageously in many ways with that of modern workmen.

Each craft, within the limits allowed it by seigniorial or municipal authority, concerned itself with the task of reconciling the interests of producers and consumers. The rules of the corporation were not inspired merely by selfish preoccupations, but also by a high care for professional probity and for social equality and solidarity. The rules or statutes of the crafts repressed pitilessly all bad workmanship, fraud, scamped or dishonest work. By an elaborate system of inspection, control, and trademarks they guaranteed that manufacture and sale should take place in public, and that transactions should be honest. They did not, it is true, eradicate the spirit of fraud and all abuses, but they limited them. Similarly, they were at pains to safeguard the morals of the craft by keeping out doubtful and undesirable elements, and by imposing the observation of the laws of morality, religion, and humanity upon the working classes. It was their object to maintain a sort of equality among masters by forbidding them to exercise more than one craft, to entice away each other's workmen or customers, or to

engage in the various manœuvres of monopoly and speculation, so that each might obtain the equitable and remunerative fruit of his labours. The regulations thus hindered the
formation of large fortunes, but they made possible a fair
division of profits. The workman himself found his right to
work recognized; the master was obliged to give him a job,
to employ him in preference to strangers or to the other
masters of the town, and not to subject him to the competition of cheap female labour. For the first time professional
union founded voluntary discipline by its action, fixed
the just hierarchy, rights and the duties of the working
classes, and gave them, together with liberty, the consciousness of their dignity and responsibility. The
world was enriched by a new social force of incomparable
power.

The free or sworn union, the craft or the corporation, were
increasingly redoubtable fortresses, from whose shelter the
masses set forth on the conquest of political power. The
urban democracies were not slow to perceive that their civil
liberties and their economic privileges were at the mercy of
the selfishness and caprices of the sovereign power, king or
lord or patriciate, which ruled the town. The wide privileges
which had devolved upon this power permitted it to annihilate,
restrict, or diminish the autonomy of the crafts and to assail
their material interests. On the other hand, the workers also
suffered from the oppressive, adventurous, and rash administration of the group of privileged persons who governed the
city. It was the masses who bore the chief burden of
common obligations, who furnished the police, the watch
and ward, and the medieval equivalent of the fire brigade;
it was they who paid the heaviest taxes and were enrolled
in the militia. With their labour, their money, and their
blood they contributed to the power and vitality of those
urban states, in whose government they were called upon to
take only the smallest share.

Thus from the thirteenth century a democratic movement,
which often assumed a revolutionary character, began to
appear with growing intensity among the crafts. Its object
was to destroy the political monopoly of the patriciate of
nobles or gilds, and its programme was to obtain a share in
or the monopoly of municipal authority. Its weapons were

strikes (*takehans*), workmen's unions, and, finally, armed risings. The movement spread to all the countries of the West. In France, from the second half of the thirteenth century, strikes, fomented by corporations or fraternities, broke out on all sides, especially in the industrial districts. In Beauvais in 1233 the mayor and the money-changers were insulted and ill-treated, and the king was obliged to imprison 1,500 rioters. At Provins and at Rouen (1280-1281) the workmen rose up against the merchant drapers, and the mayor of the Norman capital was murdered. At Paris, in 1295 and 1307, the attitude of the workers' unions was so menacing that Philippe le Bel dissolved the fraternities. In Castile, Aragon and Catalonia, notably at Cordova and at Ubeda (1312-1332), the urban patriciate of nobles (*caballeros*) was faced with the tumultuous demands of the people. In France, as in Spain and in England, the royal power was strong enough to put an end to the abuses of the oligarchies, giving partial satisfaction to democratic aspirations, and re-establishing order beneath its own authority. It granted guarantees to the popular classes, favoured their ambitions by developing the sworn corporations, and (as at Amiens) opened the councils and municipal magistracies to them.

The democratic revolution was far more vigorous in countries where the central power lacked the same means of action. In the Rhenish and Danubian districts of Germany, at Ulm, Frankfort, Nuremburg, Mainz, Cologne, Strasburg, and Basle there were fierce struggles in which the patriciate was finally obliged to abandon the town government to the corporations. In the Low Countries especially the movement assumed an extraordinary intensity. The " *povre peuple,*" the democracy of the crafts, or *klauwaerts*, as they were called, employed all sort of methods, coalitions, strikes or *takehans*, insurrections, alliances with the great feudal nobility, the counts of Flanders and Hainault, in order to break down the despotic power of the gilds or *Leliaerts*, who relied upon the support of the King of France. At Liège (1253) the crafts rose against the power of the provosts and the bishop. At Dinant (1255) the copperworkers, and at Huy (1299) the weavers, were at grips with the gilds of merchant entrepreneurs. At Tournai (1281) and all over Hainault (1292) the weavers and other artisans were struggling against the patricians. From 1275 Flanders was in open revolution; at Ghent, Bruges, and Douai the count was helping the craftsmen to sap the authority of the patriciate. Everywhere the struggle was accompanied by measures of implacable violence on both sides. The great burgesses (*majores*), who loved to call themselves the " worthy folk " (*goden*), as well as the artisans, whom they referred to as " wretched canaille " (*minores, gwaden*), made use of execution and of banishment. For nearly thirty years, between 1297 and 1328, a formidable wave of revolution broke over Flanders. The Flemish crafts, inspired by the spirit of democracy and by municipal patriotism, rose at Ypres, Douai, Ghent, Lille, Bruges, and Oudenarde, massacred the French at the so-called " matins of Bruges " in May, 1302, and won the brilliant victory of Courtrai on July 11, 1302 over all the chivalry of France. The weaver Conink defied the most powerful prince of Christendom, Philippe le Bel, and in spite of the revenge which he took at Mons-en-Pevèle (August 18th, 1304), the king was obliged to treat with the democracy of Flanders (1305). The revolution was successful in winning its legitimate demands. In the Low Countries the monopoly of the patriciate was abolished; the crafts secured the admission of their delegates and leaders into the councils and magistracies. They suppressed the abusive privileges of the gilds and decreed freedom of trade. They obtained full powers of economic administration. They were allowed to exercise rights of jurisdiction over their members, and wage labour was emancipated. They abolished the excessive penalties, such as death and banishment, which the patricians had imposed upon the workmen for professional faults, and which were now replaced by fines. They conferred upon the workers the right to buy raw material freely and to sell the produce of their labour directly to the public. For the workers in the great industry of Flanders, the conquest of political power was the instrument of their economic liberation.

The revolution obtained nowhere else such remarkable results as in the Low Countries. In the South of France and in Italy, indeed, the movement was less successful in bringing about the triumph of the democracies of workers than in breaking the anarchical tyranny of the patriciate of nobles.

There the small folk (*minutus populus, mediocres, minores*) allied with the rich burgesses of the great corporations, sometimes even, as in Provence, with the clergy, against the insolent domination of the feudal lords of the towns. The craft unions (*arti*) and the fraternities had recourse to every possible weapon, to secret agreements, trade strikes, even the general strike (as at Bologna), conspiracies, street fights, everything in order to seize political power. Everywhere the *popolani* formed themselves into militias with their "captains of the people," and united under the direction of chiefs, "priors" and "elders" of the crafts (*arti*) so as to oust the nobles from the government, the councils, and the magistracies. Milan and Brescia (1200-1286), Reggio, Pistoia, Pisa (1254), Genoa (1257-1270), Siena and Arezzo (1283), and, above all, Bologna (1257-1271), and Florence (1250-1293) were the chief scenes of these dramatic struggles, from which the patriciate of nobles emerged beaten, decimated by proscription and massacres, and ruined by confiscations. The victorious coalition of bourgeoisie and democracy closed the councils and offices to them, and made the exercise of a craft the condition of admission to political rights. It handed over executive authority to the captains of the people or gonfaloniers, leaders of the popular militia, and the councils to the priors and rectors of the crafts. Government and assemblies were placed under the influence of the mass of the population, but, in general, the concession of political rights stopped with the *arti minori*. The common people, the wage-earners, remained outside the civic body.

In the South of France the revolution was analogous in character, and was no more profitable to the lowest rank of the democracy. At Marseilles (1213), Avignon (1225), Arles (1225), Nîmes (1272), Carcassonne (1226), and Montpellier (1246), the crafts succeeded—sometimes by risings—in winning a partial entry into the councils and parliaments; sometimes even in forcing their way into the magistracies. Nowhere, except in the Low Countries, did the common people, who were then indeed quite incapable of the duties of public life, benefit by the conquest or partition of municipal power, brought about by the energy of the urban democracies. But for the mass of the working classes that victory was the natural and legitimate complement of the effort which they had made to organize themselves and of the part which they had played in bringing about the prosperity of the urban economy.

The emancipation of the commercial and industrial classes, as well as their growing participation in public life, brought about a great improvement in their condition. Master of his own person and activity, the urban worker, master or journeyman, could exercise his initiative and energy in whatever direction he liked. In the tutelary shelter of the free craft, the sworn corporation, and the municipal regulations, he won at one and the same time freedom and security of labour. Only a minority, made up of wage-earners in the nascent great industry, found itself deprived of the benefits of this organization. In Flanders, Tuscany, and the North of France, and everywhere where great entrepreneurs were becoming the distributors and regulators of work, they submitted the journeymen and the small masters whom they employed to the iron law of the wage slave. They distributed orders and raw materials as they liked, they were the sole buyers and sellers of manufactured goods, and they imposed arbitrary conditions and tyrannical rules on masters and workmen alike. By a cleverly calculated system of advances they led them into debt, the better to keep them in dependence; they paid them only famine wages, and sometimes even paid them in kind according to arbitrary valuations, by what was afterwards known as the truck system.

Fortunately, the wage-earners of the great industry formed a not very numerous proletariat in the West. The great mass of workers found in the conditions of the " small " industry, in the craft and its body of organized artisans, a stronghold of independence, and a guarantee of well-being. Voluntary and disciplined association made them strong enough to be out of reach of the caprices and despotism of the old feudal powers. It preserved them from excessive competition, unemployment, and over-production, from parasitic middlemen, from the manœuvres of speculators and exploiters of labour. Masters and workmen could labour without taking heed for the morrow, sure of finding in the little workshop exercise for their well-regulated activity, and in the urban market a sale for their produce. The statutes of the crafts made mastership accessible to all, and established a happy equilibrium between the rights and duties of everyone. They maintained a certain equality in production and in distribution; they prevented the formation of large fortunes by masters, and favoured ·the wide diffusion of a standard of comfort. The workman was sure to find employment when he betook himself to the market-place to hire out his labour, either by the day or the week, or for a longer term. He had not to fear the overcrowding of the trade by the competition of foreigners and women. It is true that the work was hard, and that the working day varied in some trades—for example, in Paris—from 16 hours to $8\frac{1}{2}$ hours; in others, from 14 to 11 hours. But in practice, deducting intervals for meals, it was usually from 8 to 13 hours; night work was, in general, forbidden, and paid extra when it was allowed; and numerous feast days provided the artisan with intervals of rest, which together amounted to at least a quarter of the year.

Wages were not subject to sudden fluctuations, and corresponded fairly exactly with the cost of living. Those of the journeymen were not sensibly less than the earnings of their masters. In London, for instance, in the fourteenth century, when the master tiler made according to the season $5\frac{1}{2}$d. to $4\frac{1}{2}$d. a day, the journeyman received $3\frac{1}{2}$d. to 3d. In France, at the end of the thirteenth century, the master mason or the master slater received for his day's work about the same sum as his successor at the beginning of the fourteenth century—to wit, 2 fr. a day and his assistant 50 c. At Strasburg the master carpenter earned 2 fr. 60 without board in summer. In general, the wages of apprentices and of women were two-thirds less than those of the masters. These wages sufficed to purchase the material necessities of life. It has been calculated that in the towns of the North of France a year's real wages represented a purchasing power equal to 19 to 30 hectolitres of corn, and that the daily wage would have allowed for the purchase of 1 kg. 9 of beef, or 1 kg. 7 of bacon, or 2˙8 litres to 6 litres of wine. Artisans, in the thirteenth century, could buy 1 hectolitre of peas for 4 fr. 50 to 11 fr. 42, a sheep for 3 fr. to 4 fr. 50, a pig for 6 fr. to 12 fr., a chicken for 32 c. to 50 c., a dozen eggs for 11 c. to 12 c., a kilogramme of butter for 43 c. to 65 c., and a hectolitre of wine for 5 to 15 fr. Moreover, the unmarried workman and apprentice were usually boarded and lodged by their master.

The material life of the working classes during this period of the Middle Ages seems to have been comfortable. It was simple and usually removed from the temptations of luxury. They were ordinarily content with simple food—vegetables, beans, dough-cakes, bread and soup, and a reasonable proportion of meat. They reserved their great carouses and their big bumpers of wine and beer for feast days and meetings. They were not very particular about housing. In France they were crowded together in houses of wood or clay, with pointed gables and slate-covered fronts, the projecting upper stories of which overhung the road and almost met one another across it. On the ground floor the masters had their workshops, serving at the same time as workrooms and shops. Usually they all lived together with other members of their trade in the same quarter, and each road bore the name of a corporation. There, during the hours of work and sale the customers moved, all along the dark and narrow alleys, among the stalls protected by penthouses, above which hung creaking signboards. Pedestrians, horses and carts jostled domestic animals, especially pigs, running about amid heaps of filth. The cries of each trade might then be heard in all their original zest, from that of the taverner or the cook with sauces to sell to that of the basketmender and the old clothes man.

Families lived often in the most primitive simplicity in a few rooms barely furnished with chests, tables, and various utensils. The clothing of the workman and small master was made of strong woollen or linen cloth, and cost him little. Nevertheless, little by little the growing standard of ease aroused a taste for comfort. Inventories belonging to the end of the thirteenth and first half of the fourteenth century, and surviving tax assessments, show that modest fortunes were being made, and that the working classes of the towns were at some pains to obtain substantial food, more elaborate furniture, including pewter vessels, table linen, and garments made of more varied and less coarse stuffs. The use of body linen became general. Hygiene had made great progress, as is shown by the numerous bathing establishments or public stews, and the existence of bath-tubs in private houses.

The moral condition of the working classes had also improved greatly. They were, no doubt, coarse and brutal, moved by a gross and rude sensuality. They loved the tavern, gaming, and carousing. They were reproached with their grumbling temper, and sometimes with insolence, laziness, or dishonesty. They were frequently licentious, and sexual morality was low. But taking everything together an immense progress had been made. Masters and workmen had acquired the virtues of freedom. They were passionately in love with independence, imbued with the spirit of equality and of justice. Their common organization in the crafts, no less than the simplicity of the material conditions of existence, brought them close together. In general, neither capitalists nor proletarians were to be found among them. In those days harmony reigned within the world of labour, which had no other enemies than the feudal powers and the patriciate. Artisans were conscious of their individuality and of their value as workmen; they had the new sentiment of the dignity of labour. At no period have there been so many clever masters of technique, indeed so many real artists. Legions of master-workers, image-makers, or sculptors, painters, miniaturists, ivory-workers, potters, embroiderers, wood-carvers, enamellers, goldsmiths, and armourers raised labour to the level of an art. The statutes of the corporations contributed to the creation and maintenance of a tradition of honesty and loyalty.

Intellectual curiosity awoke among these ignorant masses. The artisan willingly sent his children to the universities and schools, and already there was beginning to be heard the eternal plaint of the upper classes concerning the danger of popular education and the peril of taking people out of their class. A whole literature was created in order to satisfy these intellectual aspirations of the townspeople, epics and romantic tales declaimed by *jongleurs* and street-singers, pious mystery plays and gay comedies or *soties*, the satirical couplets of the *fabliaux*, ballads and sentimental or mocking songs. The townsfolk loved fêtes, state entries, processions, masquerades, and the magnificent shows afforded by jousts and tourneys. Crafts and corporations took their share in the pomp of public ceremonies, with their dignitaries clad in brilliant liveries, their banners and the insignia of their trades. The workers possessed in the highest degree the spirit of brotherhood and of charity, which was enshrined in their fraternities or *amitiés*, their hospitals, and their organization of help for the sick and for widows and orphans. The same solidarity was manifested in the coalitions which they formed to defend their interests and demand their rights. They were animated by a naive and sometimes mystical faith, which led them to regard the Church as the people's house; and so they adorned it with chapels, fair windows, paintings, and sculptures. They had their patron saints there, celebrated their fêtes there, and sometimes performed their plays there. Occasionally their religious sense exalted them and drove them to the bold dreams of heretics—Vaudois, Fraticelli, and Lollards—who advocated a radical transformation of the whole social order, under the guise of a religious revolution.

A few centuries of freedom and prosperity sufficed to bring this new world to birth in the Western towns. For the first time labour took a leading place in society, and made its power recognized. The rehabilitated merchants and artisans, escaping from the prison of serfdom, had become freemen. Better still, they had set themselves up as equals of the landed proprietor, the knight, and the clerk. In the proud and wealthy bourgeoisie, in the independent people grouped in their associations, a new power was manifest, rivalling that of feudalism and the Church. This power was founded upon the high social and economic value of the worker, who, up till then, had been largely despised by the old aristocratic societies of antiquity, as well as by the military and agrarian society of the Dark Ages and the first feudal period. Not only had the working masses succeeded in the conquest of civil and political liberties, but they had also, by the voluntary discipline which they had imposed upon themselves in their associations, created a tradition of the honesty and dignity of labour. They had given an incomparable impetus to all the forces of production and for the greater number of their members they had won stability, security, independence, and comfort. Out of the erstwhile oppressed and despised serf they had made the free, honoured, and

PLATE IV

MAY DAY IN A FLEMISH TOWN
(*Early 16th Century*)

[*face p. 224*

respected artisan of the new world. Urban civilization, born of their efforts, meant, finally, an irresistible ferment of change in the old agrarian civilization, and it was by their example that the rural classes in their turn were to conquer the position which was theirs by right.

CHAPTER VIII

THE ADVANCE OF COLONIZATION AND AGRICULTURAL PRODUCTION AND THE PROGRESS OF RURAL POPULATION IN THE WEST FROM THE ELEVENTH TO THE FOURTEENTH CENTURIES.

BETWEEN the eleventh and the middle of the fourteenth century the agrarian populations of the West had, indeed, accomplished a magnificent work, which justified their emancipation. The great business of colonizing Europe, sketched out in the Carolingian period, was taken up again and achieved by them in a century and a half. Production developed enormously, and the West was repopulated. At no other period of history has so great an enterprise been conceived and brought to so full and successful a realization, save, perhaps, in our own day, in which the conquest of new worlds by European civilization has been begun. It was one of the capital events of history, although historians have commonly passed it by in silence.

At the close of the Dark Ages, by reason of the recent invasions, the constant anarchy and warfare, the insufficiency and inertia of labour, and the predominance of a primitive form of economy, the greater part of the soil of the West was under forest, waste, or marsh. In Italy, save for the two Sicilies, and in Christian Spain, only a very small proportion of the land was under cultivation. Half or more of the territory of France, two-thirds of that of the Low Countries and Germany, and four-fifths of that of England was uncultivated. It needed the social and economic revolution brought about by the rise of commerce and industry to shake the rural world of the West out of its torpor. The needs of consumption and trade gave rise to an impulse of reclamation which imposed itself upon all the landowning classes, who desired to keep up their revenues, as well as upon the agricultural classes, who were stimulated by the hope of ameliorating their lot by labour. All the élite of society placed itself at the head of the movement. The Church, in particular, held colonization to be a work of piety, which increased both her influence and her fortune. She

226

blessed it, she forbade men to disturb it, and she often herself took the initiative in it. The French monastic Orders deserved well of civilization for the success with which they pursued this peaceful crusade. The 2,000 Cluniac priories, the 8,200 Cistercian abbeys, the countless monasteries of Carthusians, Premonstratensians, and Trappists were rallying points for the thousands of pioneers who cleared, reclaimed, and drained the soil of the West. On their side, too, the rulers of feudal and monarchical states, such as the kings of England, Castile, Aragon, and the two Sicilies, the Swabian emperors, the Capetian kings of France, the counts of Flanders, and the German margraves, often stimulated the work of reclamation. The urban communes, in their turn, favoured the work and sometimes even made it obligatory, and rich burgesses sank their capital in it, particularly in the Low Countries. Finally, the rural masses furnished the necessary labour—thousands of pioneers (*hôtes*, *advenæ*, *sartores*), without whom the enterprise which made the fortune of medieval Europe would have been impossible.

An immense programme was thus quietly carried out for the defence of the land from the ravages of the fierce waters, for the conquest of littorals, river valleys, and marshes, and for the clearance of heaths and forests. In England the drainage of the fens on the shores of the North Sea was begun. In the Low Countries the sea had stolen a fifth or a sixth of its soil from the Netherlands, and between the eleventh and the thirteenth century, it had on no less than thirty-five occasions swept over the land, creating the gulfs of the Zuyder Zee, the Dollart, and the Hondt (Western Scheldt), destroying in a single invasion 3,000 square kilometres, and in a hundred years swallowing up more than 100,000 human beings. Now abbeys, princes, burgesses, and peasants formed themselves into associations for dyking and draining the land (*wateringues*), under the direction of dyke-masters (*djik* and *mœrgrafen*). At a cost of seven and a half milliards of francs, and in the course of five centuries, they built out of solid blocks transported from Scandinavia and Central Germany the strong " golden wall," which braved the furious assaults of the sea from maritime Flanders to Frisia, and in the shelter of which the fertile *polders* were reclaimed.

North of the Meuse alone 19,000 hectares of land were thus conquered. Engineers (*zandgrafen*) arrested the advance of the dunes by means of osier plantations. Drainage canals and pumping machines kept up by the *wateringues* drove sea and river from whole districts, and in their place flourished rich farms (*schorren*), in which pasture and harvest, cattle and sheep prospered alike, together with a mass of cornlands (*granges*), formed of rectangular fields, the limits of which were marked by crosses. Half the Netherlands and a third of Belgium thus rose from the bosom of the waters and the marshes.

In Low Germany, Frisians, together with Flemings and Saxons, built up a similar rampart of dykes against the North Sea floods, which had chiselled out the Gulf of Jahde and carried away over 6,000 square kilometres of coastland between the Texel and the Cimbrian Peninsula. They converted into fertile agricultural land (*koge*, *marschen*) the *mooren* or marshy and inundated lands of Schleswig, Holstein, and the Brême country. Between the Elbe and the Oder they transformed the inland marshes into great domains (*königshufen*) lying in parallel bands along the March of Brandenburg. In the thirteenth century, with the help of German settlers, they created in the flooded districts of the Lower Vistula and Prussia those magnificent alluvial ploughlands which are their pride, the *werder* of Marienburg, Elbing, and Dantzig. In France a similar work was accomplished by the monastic Orders, such as the Templars and Cistercians, and also by unions of peasants. Thus were drained and conquered the low-lying and marshy lands of Saint-Omer and of Calaisis, the *molières* (wet lands) of Bas-Champs and of Marquenterre in Picardy, the swamps of the Caux country, the estuary of the Seine, Dive, Bas-Cotentin, the Dol country, part of the Breton littoral and of the Lower Loire, Bas-Poitou, Bas-Languedoc and Basse-Provence, and in the interior those of Basse-Auvergne, Limagne, " wet " Champagne, and Argonne. The Lower Rhône was dyked by associations of *levadiers*, and in the Poitevin marshes were built the long lines of *bots* (dykes), with their network of sluices and canals. In Bas-Roussillon in the thirteenth century a large number of swamps were drained.

In Upper Italy communes, princes, Cistercian abbeys, and

peasants united to build embankments and regulate the course of the Po, the Lambro, the Mincio, the Brenta, to drain the marshes round Mantua, Ferrara, Cremona, Lodigiano, Milan, Montferrat, Bologna, and the country round Ravenna. The peoples of Spain and of the Italian peninsula, taking up again the methods of Roman hydraulic science, and imitating those of the Arabs, profited marvellously by irrigation in Cerdagne, Roussillon, Catalonia, Aragon, Castile, the Balearic Isles, the land of Valencia, the kingdom of Murcia and Andalusia, as well as the Lombard plain, Tuscany, and Sicily. The most remarkable of these works were the dams and reservoirs of Eastern Spain and the famous Lombard Naviglio Grande, built between 1179 and 1257. The latter carried the waters of Lake Maggiore over 35,000 hectares and fertilized the lands on the banks of the Oglio, the Adda, and the Po.

Even more considerable results were obtained by the magnificent and determined work of clearance accomplished throughout the West during three centuries and a half, at the expense of heath and forest. At no period has the conquest of agricultural land been carried on with so much discipline and ardour. Lured on by the bait of freedom and property, thousands of pioneers responded to the appeal of monks, prelates, princes, lords, and communes, and came to prepare the way for the work of plough and hoe, by burning away brushwood, thickets, and parasitic vegetation, clearing forests with the axe, and uprooting trunks with the pick, a process known as *assarting*. The whole face of the West changed. Germany, in particular, was transformed. In its immense forests, through some of which an eleventh-century missionary could ride for five days on end in complete solitude, pioneers made clearings (*roden*) and assarts (*schwenden*), established great farms all along the side of the roads or on the edge of the woods (*waldhufen*), as in Austria, Silesia, and Moravia; or, again, as in the northern plain and on the southern plateaux, they established town and village settlements. From the shores of the Baltic and the North Sea to the Central Alps, from the Vistula to the Rhine and the Vosges, across the forests and wastes of Northern, Central, and Western Germany, Austria, Switzerland, and Alsace, a multitude of new agrarian estates appeared. Geographical terminology, with its *reut, rode, wald, heim, loh, holz, hagen, brand, schwend,* bears witness to their importance and to their wide diffusion. German agriculture dates, indeed, from this fine period.

The same is true of England, where reclamation by monastery, prince, and peasant performed a similar masterpiece between the eleventh and the fourteenth centuries. The woods were attacked with such vigour, especially in the south, the south-east, and the midlands, that nothing was left of the ancient forest which once covered the soil of Britain, save a few rare remnants. From having been one of the most thickly wooded regions of the West, Great Britain became, like the Low Countries, one of the clearest, as a result of the work of the pioneers. The enormous number of names of towns and villages which end with the suffixes *den, holt, word, falt, hurst,* shows how potent was their labour. This work attained the highest degree of efficacy in the Low Countries. The *wastines* or wastes, the *velden* or heaths, the immense forests which still covered more than three-quarters of this region, disappeared in the Netherlands, Brabant, Hainault, and, above all, in Flanders, and were replaced by ploughlands and meadows surrounded by drainage ditches, hedges, and lines of trees. Ninety-five per cent. of Flemish villages date from this time; everywhere the suffixes *sart, rode, kerche* attached to their names indicate the work accomplished long ago, by means of which a plain of marshy forests and heaths became the fairest agricultural country of the West.

In France, Cistercians, Premonstratensians, Carthusians, and Templars, together with the wisest of the feudatories, and supported by a whole multitude of peasants, transformed into hayfields, meadows, and ploughlands provinces hitherto covered with great forests, such as Artois, Picardy, Ponthieu, the Île-de-France, Normandy, " wet " Champagne, Morvan, Upper Burgundy, the Meuse and Vosges districts, Brittany, Poitou, the Loire districts, Aquitaine, and the south-east. An immense work of clearance was carried on for three centuries, and gave the French countryside its present appearance. In Christian Spain, so backward in comparison with Moslem Spain, an intensive colonization, the agents of which were the monks and the princes, assisted by a crowd of immigrants of French origin and of peoples rescued from the Moslem yoke (the Mozarabs), brought to pass the disappearance of a large part of the undergrowth, the wastes (*hermes, yermos*), and the abandoned lands (*despoblados*) of Roussillon, Cerdagne, Catalonia, Lower Aragon, Galicia and the Castiles, Navarre and the Vascongades. The Catalan peasants were particularly remarkable for the tenacity of their struggle with an ungrateful soil, and, as the proverb ran, made bread out of stones. Finally, in Italy, not only in the two Sicilies, but in the northern and central districts, the forest fell before the axe of the pioneers. Uncultivated land was ploughed or irrigated, and at the end of the thirteenth century no one would have recognized this land covered with farms, vineyards, and plantations for the wooded and half-desert country of the end of the tenth.

To this magnificent work of colonization, which is one of the glories of Western Christendom, and in which France, through her monastic Orders, her princely dynasties, and her emigrants, played the leading rôle, is due the economic hegemony of the Western lands, and the splendid development of their agricultural production, which was so fruitful in results. The West took up again and carried further the work of the Roman Empire.

A tremendous access of activity was, indeed, manifest in all the domains of agricultural production. The people of the West strove to make the most of all sources of natural wealth in order to fulfil the growing needs of consumption.

Side by side with the primitive fisheries along the sea coasts and the rivers, monks and great lords practised pisciculture in the interior by means of reservoirs and stewponds. Deep-sea fisheries arose and developed rapidly, to the profit of the Netherland sailors, the Flemings, and the English; in the Baltic and the northern seas they fished for cod, stock-fish, mackerel, and, most important of all, herring, that essential food of the lower classes, while in the Channel and the Atlantic, Norman, Breton, Basque, and Galician fishermen pursued the whale, the salmon, the sardine, the lamprey and the dolphin. On the coasts of Picardy, Bas-Poitou, and Aunis the cultivation of oyster-beds and of mussels was organized. In the Western Mediterranean men fished for tunny fish and brought up coral and sponges.

LIFE AND WORK IN MEDIEVAL EUROPE

In spite of clearances, so many forests had been preserved in the majority of Western lands that the produce of the chase, reserved especially for the upper classes, still counted for a great deal in the general food supply. Careful regulations were made to protect these reserves against destruction, providing for the maintenance of woodland and coppice, the planting of trees and their felling at long intervals, and limiting the abuse of customary rights of pannage and pasture. A pitiless war was waged against wild beasts, and wolves now disappeared from certain countries, such as England. Germany, France, the eastern districts of the Low Countries, and Southern Italy were the parts of the West in which the wealth of the forests was best preserved. In the north they were exploited for ashes, potash, wax, wild honey, the skins of animals, and everywhere for fuel for the domestic hearth, the forges, and the glassworks, and also for timber. Timber rafts appeared, notably in the Low Countries and France; wood was despatched down the rivers to rural saw-mills and urban timber yards, while the naval dockyards received by sea or by river the wooden material which was indispensable for them. In the south the cultivation of cork-oaks was carried on.

A great impetus was given to cattle-farming. " If your land is well furnished with live-stock," wrote an Anglo-Norman agricultural writer in the thirteenth century, " it will return you thrice as much as if you confine yourself to agriculture." Farmers were no longer content with the common pasture, in which pasture rights were stinted; they developed grasslands by irrigation, and hayfields, yielding an aftermath hitherto rare, began to be numerous. In the Low Countries the first fodder crops appeared. An empirical veterinary art arose, but it was powerless to prevent the terrible murrains of the period. The first experiments in the crossing and acclimatization of breeds were made at this time. Model farms were organized. Monastic Orders and rich burgesses began to put capital into cattle-rearing businesses and under-took contracts to fatten beasts or to convert land into meadows. The force of tradition, however, and the general lack of capital gave small live-stock still the first place in the rural economy. In certain Norman properties in 1307 there were 900 to 1,500 sheep and 180 to 200 pigs, as com-

PLATE V

PLOUGHING, SOWING AND HARROWING
(Early 16th Century)

[face p. 232

pared with 100 to 140 horned cattle and less than 100 horses. The pig was found everywhere, and goats were often kept. Common poultry was very abundant, and was increased by the acclimatization of the guinea fowl or Indian fowl in the thirteenth century. The peacock and the pheasant or Limoges cock are frequently to be met with. Bee-keeping, practised everywhere, rendered great services, for the honey took the place of sugar, and the wax served for lighting purposes.

Sheep were the most valued of all the different kinds of smaller live-stock. A variety with particularly fine flesh, known as *présalé* (because fed upon the salt marshes), was already well known in the West of France. Sheep farms were created in all parts of the Low Countries, and Germany and France possessed millions of sheep, whose fleece was much sought after for the common or less fine sorts of cloth, and whose meat was valued for the people's food. Spain and Southern Italy reared immense migratory flocks, which passed from hill pasture to plain pasture, and were valued for the same products. England, like Australia to-day, was a huge sheep-run, which furnished the best fine wool in the world; no less than half her landed wealth was founded upon her flocks of sheep, and from the Customs on fleeces she drew as much as a fifth of her public revenues. In Artois attempts were made to acclimatize the Cashmir sheep with their fine wool, in Spain the merinos of Maghreb, in Southern Italy the ewes and rams of Barbary.

The larger live-stock, particularly on the big estates, played a more considerable part than they had done in the past. In order to meet the needs of commerce and of war, studs were created and crossings with foreign breeds were undertaken. In Germany, the Low Countries, the Boulogne country, Normandy, and Lombardy battle-horses (*destriers*) were reared; in England, Gascony, Spain, and Southern Italy saddle-horses. Poitou, Provence, and Spain specialized in mule-breeding; the ass was to be found everywhere and was the great burden-bearer of the people. The Alpine regions increased the value of their fine indigenous cattle. Low Germany, the Netherlands, and Flanders enriched themselves by the improvement of their Frisian and Flemish cows. England and Ireland, like the Argentine and the United

States to-day, drew a good revenue from the export of bacon, ham, lard, and tallow, which they got from their numerous herds of cattle, and so also did Roussillon and Northern Spain. France and Upper Italy possessed fine breeds for draught and for meat; their cheeses and butters were already much sought after.

The superior forms of cultivation were more and more honoured, particularly that of cereals, which had to meet the demands of a growing population, and was carried on everywhere in order to prevent the menace of local scarcity, ever present by reason of the difficulty of communications and the small returns of medieval harvests, which were four to seven times less than those of our own day. The élite of the farming community, recruited particularly among the monastic Orders and the Italian, Flemish, and Anglo-Norman agriculturalists, was at pains to recover the methods of the ancient Roman agricultural science. Upon this and upon their own experience they founded a new agricultural science, which was already remarkable. To vegetable manures they added animal manures in increasing quantities, notably in the Low Countries. In England they devised the manuring of land by means of folding sheep on it for eight weeks. Attempts were made, especially in France, to improve the soil by complementary manures, such as chalk, marl, ashes, turf, and calcareous sand. It is true that in the greater part of the West the extensive method of cultivation, with its enforced rotation of crops (a triennial rotation and fallow), persisted; but already in certain regions—the Low Countries, the North of France, and the South of Italy—intensive culti-vation had appeared, in which the fallow year and the forced rotation were suppressed, and in which an alternation of crops was practised, by which the soil was permanently in use, and its nutritive power was kept up by fodder or leguminous crops, introduced every third year. Side by side with the labour of hoe and spade, the use of the iron ploughshare allowed the earth to be ploughed deeply, some-times seven or eight times on end; it was drawn by powerful teams of horses or oxen. The Western peasant, under the guidance of a group of enlightened agriculturalists, was now beginning his fruitful and obstinate struggle for the enrich-ment of the soil.

COLONIZATION AND AGRICULTURE

His activity displayed itself, first of all, in the cultivation of cereals, which was general everywhere; to rye, barley, oats, and millet there was added " Saracen corn " or buckwheat. Wheat was produced for export in the rich clay soils of the Rhineland, Low Countries, and Western France, the *campos* of Castile, Lombardy, Campania, Apulia, and Sicily. The midland and south-eastern counties of England were producing as much as two and a half million quarters in 1314. Rice cultivation was introduced into Lower Aragon, Lower Lombardy, and Sicily in the twelfth and thirteenth centuries. Under the influence of the French monastic Orders and of the Italians and Spaniards, market gardening and horticulture made great progress; the usual vegetables were grown, together with shallots, artichokes, spinach, tarragon, and aubergine, which were imported from the East. The countries of the Mediterranean zone, in which the fertility of the gardens was maintained by irrigation, supplied and taught the rest of the West. Italy, Eastern Spain, and the South of France, full of flourishing orchards, provided the rest of Christendom with oranges, apricots, figs, pomegranates, lemons, and almonds. The cultivation of the olive became widespread in Sicily and Tuscany, Castile, Lower Aragon, and Lower Catalonia, and throughout the East of Spain; they exported oil everywhere.

Everywhere were sold the nuts and chestnuts or the oils, almonds, and plums of Southern Italy and the Apennine marches, Provence and Lower Languedoc, Auvergne, Angoumois, Agenais, Touraine, and Dauphiné, while Normandy and Picardy exported apples, which were as yet not much used for the making of cider. Eastern Spain and Languedoc traded in dried raisins, which rivalled those of Greece. Vines became, with corn and live-stock, one of the great sources of wealth of the West. Monastic Orders cultivated them, and peasants and proprietors united in planting them. Vineyards even appeared in regions which were least favourable to their cultivation, such as the Low Countries, England, Germany, and the North of France, where nothing but uncertain and defective vintages could be obtained from them. They were created or reconstructed successfully in the Rhine and Moselle lands and on the slopes of French Switzerland and of the county of Burgundy.

They prospered in France, of which they formed, together with corn, the chief agricultural revenue. The vineyards of Upper Burgundy and Soissonnais, Limagne, and the Loire Valley, Aunis, Languedoc, the hills of the Rhône country, and Avignon acquired a European renown. In 1330 the port of Bordeaux alone exported wines of Guienne to the value of £50,000 sterling, and La Rochelle exported 30,000 to 35,000 tuns. Only Spain, Portugal, and Italy could rival French production. Their vineyards received an enormous extension from the twelfth century, and their wines soon supplanted the most famous brands of Greece and Cyprus.

Finally, the renaissance of industry brought about a great development in industrial crops. The cultivation of the sugar-cane was attempted in Sicily, Spain, and Provence, that of aniseed and cummin had some success in Aragon, Catalonia, and Albigeois. The hop gardens of the Rhineland and Bavaria now began to be famous. Normandy, the Low Countries, and Northern France set to work to cultivate oleaginous plants for purposes of lighting and of food. Everywhere in the West the cultivation of hemp and flax was developed in the best soils; it went on in Germany and England as well as in the Low Countries, France, Spain, and Upper and Lower Italy. In Sicily, Calabria, and Basilicata an attempt was made to acclimatize the cotton plant of the Levant and indigo. Southern Italy and Eastern Spain wrested from the East its monopoly in the cultivation of mulberries and the raising of silkworms. In Burgundy, Normandy, and Spain the cultivation of teazles, and in Upper Italy, the South and North of France, the Low Countries, and Germany that of dye plants, woad, madder, and saffron was developed; the latter enriched more particularly the Aquitanian provinces, the "cockayne" lands of Albigeois and Lauraguais.

The magnificent effort thus made by intelligent leaders and by the rural masses of the West was not without fruit. The result of this colonization, which is one of the principal claims of the Middle Ages to honour, was that the soil of the Western Christendom was brought under cultivation. It helped to bring about the transference to the Western countries of the economic hegemony hitherto possessed by the East, and gave them an unprecedented prosperity, greater even than that of the Roman period. The greater part of Italy and of Spain now reached a high degree of wealth in the sphere of agricultural production. But France outshone them both; she became the "fairest kingdom of the world after the kingdom of heaven," which Froissart described before 1345—"rich and hardy, with great abundance of rich and powerful folk, having great possessions." England, civilized by the Normans, was held, in the thirteenth century, to be a happy isle, fertile with all the fruits of the earth (*terra ferax, insula prædives*). But the greatest triumph of colonization was the transformation of the Low Countries and Germany, wild and half-barbarous regions in the tenth century, into opulent lands which could rival the foremost agricultural centres of Christendom. By the immigration of French, Flemings, Frisians, and Germans, by the fecundity of the pioneer peasants, the West, which had been depopulated by the invasions, was peopled again with extraordinary rapidity in the space of 300 years. If one may judge by England, for instance, the population of the Western states doubled. Instead of 1,200,000 souls, the figure reached in 1086, the English counties (excluding Wales and the West) numbered 2,355,000 towards 1340. The Low Countries, almost empty in the tenth century, reached a higher figure yet; their villages contained on an average 1,500 souls, thrice as many as the majority of rural groups in the West. Germany, between the Rhine and the Oder, a sort of European Far East in the Dark Ages, became peopled with a hardy race of pioneers. The population of the Rhine and Danube lands became more and more dense; in the region between the Rhine and the Moselle it increased tenfold between the tenth and the thirteenth centuries. Spain repaired the gaps caused by the eternal war against the infidel. Italy, happier still, made such progress that in the fourteenth century she numbered, perhaps, some 10,000,000 souls, while in the two Sicilies a census in 1275 showed 1,200,000 souls—twice as many as at the height of the modern period. Finally, France, outstripping all the other countries of the West, attained a population of twenty to twenty-two million inhabitants (thirty-eight to forty-one to the square kilometre), almost as many as in the eighteenth century. The six states of the West contained together, perhaps, 60,000,000 souls before the Black Death—twice as many as they had numbered before the fifth century.

Thus this great work of agrarian colonization did more than merely increase material wealth; it also greatly increased human capital. Moreover, it brought about profound changes in the distribution and value of landed property and also in the condition of the rural masses.

CHAPTER IX

CHANGES IN THE VALUE AND DISTRIBUTION OF LANDED PROPERTY AND
EMANCIPATION OF THE RURAL CLASSES IN THE WEST FROM THE
ELEVENTH TO THE FOURTEENTH CENTURIES.

THE influence of the colonizing movement of reclamation, together with the appearance and progress of a money economy, brought about a veritable revolution in the old feudal agrarian economy.

The first result was a notable rise in the value of the soil and of landed revenues. The reclaimed lands increased enormously in value in a few centuries, enriching the owners who had been wise enough to bring them under cultivation and at the same time to retain possession of them. It has been shown, for example, that in the valleys of the Rhine and Moselle the value of the land had increased on an average sevenfold, often tenfold, and sometimes sixteen to twentyfold, since the end of the Dark Ages. In Roussillon an estate, which was valued at 100 sous in the eleventh century, was worth 3,000 in the thirteenth. In France the price of a hectare of ploughland—which had already risen greatly by the twelfth century—doubled in the thirteenth, as also did that of meadows, vineyards, and woods; for the ploughland it reached 222 fr., and for the others 616, 636, and 104 fr. respectively. At the same time rents rose with the rise in the value of agricultural produce. In France a hectolitre of corn rose between the years 1200 and 1335 from 3 fr. 80 to 8 fr. 56, and a hectolitre of wine from 5 fr. 12 to 25 fr. 66. An ox, which sold for 21 fr. at the first of these dates, fetched 52 fr. at the second; a sheep, instead of 3 fr., cost 4 fr. 50; a pig 12 fr. instead of 6 fr.; butter was worth 0 fr. 65 instead of 0 fr. 45 the kilogramme; poultry 0 fr. 50 instead of 0 fr. 32. By calculations which seem plausible it has been found possible to rate the level of the ground rent in France during the first third of the fourteenth century at between 5 per cent. and 8½ per cent.

A large part of this increase of capital and income fell to

the lot of the large landowners; but small landowners and the cultivators of the soil also benefited more or less proportionately. As a whole the movement of reclamation was chiefly favourable to private property and to great royal or ecclesiastical properties, rather than to the feudal estates, which were gradually broken up for the profit of the bourgeoisie and the peasants.

Collective property and seigniorial property were thus the two chief victims of this peaceful agrarian revolution. Except in those parts of the British Isles which were inhabited by Celts, where it was partially maintained for the profit of the clans, the former decreased in all the states of the West, as a result of the progress of colonization, which fitted ill with a régime of indivisibility and periodical partitions, unfavourable as they are to the cultivation of the soil. Sometimes the common lands were entirely usurped by the lords or restricted by means of the enclosures which they made therein. Sometimes the reconstituted royal power claimed them in the name of the imprescriptible sovereignty of the state. Sometimes, finally, the peasants appropriated them, allocating them in private ownership or bringing them under cultivation. In the ancient Germanic lands, the Low Countries, England, and Germany the periodical divisions of ploughlands ceased. The village communities often alienated undivided lands. Of the old agrarian collectivism there remained only occasional vestiges, commons or wastes, *marches* or *devèses*, formed in general of land which was unsuitable for cultivation, and upon which the peasants, with the agreement of the state and the lords, could continue to exercise customary rights.

On the other hand, seigniorial property also found itself the object of attack. At the very time when the military class was tending to organize itself into a close hereditary military caste, its landed property, the principal basis of its social influence, was diminishing. In many of the Western lands it lost, with its political prerogatives, some of the sources of revenue which derived from them, such as rights of justice. But it was, above all, social and economic causes which brought about a crisis in the fortunes of feudal property. In the majority of states "noble" land, at first inalienable and indivisible, became susceptible of alienation and division; indeed, it became subdivided to an infinite extent. In Italy feudal estates were cut up between seven, ten, and sometimes a hundred co-heirs; in Languedoc fifty gentlemen were sometimes living on one fief. Poverty forced a large number of the holders of these lands to get rid of them by degrees. Moreover, the prodigality and mad wastefulness of the members of the feudal class, their taste for luxury and warlike adventures, their quarrels and their lawsuits, drove them at an early date to ruinous expedients for raising money, such as loans raised upon mortgages or land rents, which rapidly led to the final alienation of their possessions.

On the other hand, the feudal lords, usually unversed in business affairs, had no idea of how to profit from the reclamation which was going on under their eyes, nor from the increased value of landed property and produce. In most cases they consented to the clearance of their land and the emancipation of their tenants, in return for the payment of rents or fixed dues. Frequently they even stipulated that these dues or *cens* should be partly paid in money, the value of which fell. To spare themselves the trouble of farming the land themselves, they willingly let out their demesnes at a rent, with the result that they sacrificed the future to the satisfaction of their present needs. In Normandy, for example, from the twelfth century, noble estates began to disappear, submerged beneath money rents, which in practice transferred them to the peasants. Indeed, wherever the urban bourgeoisie prevailed, a mortal war was waged against the feudatories and despoiled them of their possessions. The peasants, on their side, multiplied their attempts at usurpation and profited by the frequent disappearance of written title-deeds to legitimize their hold on seigniorial property, with the approval of the royal courts, especially in France. With the exception of England—where the gentry, ceasing to be a knightly class and amalgamating with the small freeholders, renounced the profession of arms in order to administer their own estates, and thus escaped poverty— the mass of the nobles degenerated everywhere into a needy and sometimes starveling class, which possessed no more than a wretched remnant of the old seigniorial property, insufficient to support them.

LIFE AND WORK IN MEDIEVAL EUROPE

In Italy one section of the nobility turned to industrial and commercial careers and thus escaped ruin; but the other section, incapable of adapting itself, vegetated and sometimes sank into destitution. In Siena in the thirteenth century descendants of ancient aristocratic families were to be seen begging their bread. In Spain many gentlemen suffered a like fate; the wisest of those in the towns (*caballeros de villa*) opened their ranks to labourers and prosperous artisans and with them formed an influential municipal class. In France they lived wretchedly upon the meagre rents of their *censitaires*, or were obliged to enter the service of the king or the nobles. The same thing happened in the Low Countries; in certain parishes, notably in Brabant, the number of knights fell from sixty to one or two, and a whole category of inferior nobles—the so-called *ministeriales*—ceased to exist. In Germany a new nobility, which had grown up out of the fusion of the knights and the *ministeriales*, vegetated miserably; occasionally it became merged with the peasantry; for the most part it lived by robbery. The German noble was a boor (*junker*) or, worse still, a brigand (*raubritter*).

Nevertheless, the élite of the military class, the great nobles, were able to maintain and even to increase their landed property. France had its appanaged fiefs and its nobility of the first rank; the two Sicilies had their baronage; Spain had its oligarchy of 380 victorious Valencian gentlemen, its wealthy lords of Aragon, its proud lords of Castile; Germany had its princes, dukes, margraves, burgraves, counts palatine, enjoying both political sovereignty (*landesherrschaft*) and territorial possessions (*grundesherrschaft*). England had her great barons and landlords. All tried to increase and preserve, sometimes by means of primogeniture and the prohibition of alienation and subinfeudation, the considerable portion of landed property which had fallen to their share. But, on the whole, feudal property lost its former preponderance in the West.

The state, however, tended to reconstitute its domains. It added to them in some countries by conquest, as in Spain, the two Sicilies, and England, in others by confiscations, acquisitions, or disinheritances, and by the part which it took in the work of reclamation, as in France, the Low Countries, and certain parts of Germany. In the time of his greatest power the Holy Roman Emperor had immense imperial estates (*reichsgüter*), spreading from the Mediterranean to the Baltic, the revenues of which brought him in in 1180 as much as six million thalers. Similarly in France the royal domain doubled in extent under Philip Augustus, and its revenues reached 438,000 Paris livres, which grew to 525,000 livres (about twelve million francs) in 1825, in the time of Charles IV. Nevertheless, state property suffered continual fluctuations by reason of pledges, alienations, donations, the prodigality or weakness of sovereigns, and the constant usurpations which diminished it. Thus the imperial domain after the great interregnum was diminished by two-thirds (1280).

More persevering in its policy and more successful in its administration, the Western Church continued to extend its dominion over the soil. It is true that old religious Orders like the Cluniacs (which had fallen into decadence), or unthrifty ecclesiastical dignitaries and chapters, sometimes, by their carelessness and rash expenditure, compromised the patient work of piling up possessions pursued by their corporation. But in general the Church profited, steadily increased its territorial power, taking advantage of the reclamation of which it was the chief promoter, the piety of the faithful who poured gifts upon it, and the increase of movable capital, in which it was able to share, and which it often invested in land. The new religious Orders—Cistercians, Carthusians, Premonstratensians, Templars, Teutonic knights, the Brotherhood of the Sword-Brethren—took their place among the greatest landed proprietors of Christendom. The Cistercians made their farms or *granges* into magnificent estates, the objects of admiration and of scandal, and their own chapters admitted that the passion for property had become an ulcer among them (1191). The 13,000 Knights Templars in the thirteenth century were proud of their 10,000 manses, and the Abbey of Prüm boasted of its 1,466 estates. The Teutonic knights had appropriated the soil of Prussia, the Sword-Brethren that of the Baltic provinces. A Cistercian abbey, Las Huelgas, near Burgos, had the land of sixty-four townships in its possession.

Chapters and bishops rivalled the monks. The Archbishops of Cologne, Mainz, and Treier had seized imperial possessions; the Archbishop of Riga had appropriated half the soil of Livonia; the Archbishop of Toledo drew 80,000 ducats of revenue from his estates. Even the mendicant Orders, Franciscans and Dominicans, were not slow, in the words of Jacopone di Todi, one of their members, to " banish poverty to heaven," in order to take their share in the riches of this earth. In Castile the conquest had given the Church possession of a quarter of the soil, in England of a fifth. In spite of their deep faith, the princes had begun, by the thirteenth and fourteenth centuries, to take restrictive measures to try to prevent this growing monopolization of the soil of the West by ecclesiastical bodies. Mortmain, that fixed and inalienable form of property, had ended by becoming a danger to lay society.

The attraction of landed property, as a source of wealth and of social consideration, even seized upon the new powers which were arising in medieval society. The urban communes built up for themselves on all hands more or less extensive domains, either by purchase or by usurpation, at the expense of the feudatories. By acquisitions and by reclamation their estates grew. They had their subject and rent-paying peasants, their *contadini* in Italy, their *pfahlburgen* in Germany, whom they protected, and whose work they supervised. Arles, for instance, owned a lordship, several castles, lands, vineyards, and ponds in Camargue.

The bourgeois, on their part, aspired to take their place among the landed gentry; they managed it easily, by employing a large part of the capital which they had acquired by the exercise of commerce and industry in the purchase of estates alienated by the nobility, and the appropriation of uncultivated lands, which they proceeded to have cleared. Henceforward there began a slow transference of the rural soil into the hands of the middle class. Moreover, now, for the first time, the rural masses profited by the movement of reclamation and emancipation, to win, in their turn, the ownership or quasi-ownership of that landed capital which up till then it had been their part merely to make fruitful by their work for the profit of others.

An event of the first importance was then, indeed, transforming the structure of Western society and of human society in general. This was the accession of the agricultural classes, who formed nine-tenths of the population of the West, to liberty and to higher conditions of life. For the first time in the history of the world the mass of the peasantry succeeded, like the mass of the working folk in the towns, in winning recognition of the social value of manual labour and of the labourer.

Their enfranchisement was to some slight extent the work of the equalizing tradition of Christianity and of Roman Law. Sometimes, indeed, villeins were enfranchised in the name of " Christ, who ransomed all men from the yoke of slavery," as a charter of 1233 expresses it, or, yet again, for " the salvation of the soul " of the master who emancipated them, as a number of acts recite. Often, too, kings and lawyers proclaimed the imprescriptible rights of man to liberty, founded on natural equality, as was done by the Capetian kings of France, Louis VII in 1170, and Louis X in 1315, and by the celebrated legist Beaumanoir. But these idealistic sentiments usually only influenced a few enlightened rulers, or were used merely as a rather imperfect disguise for more realistic motives. It was, in reality, a series of economic and social necessities which made the movement of emancipation irresistible.

The advent of monetary wealth was a grave menace to the preponderance of fortunes based upon land. In order to maintain and increase the value and revenues of the latter, it was essential to keep the peasants on the land, to increase their labour services, to prevent the exodus of serfs to the towns, to attract settlers, finally to give peasant labour the remuneration and the guarantees which had been for so long refused to it. Charters sometimes avow this quite openly. Emancipation, says one of these, has as its object " the multiplication " of cultivators. It makes, say a large number of others, " for the interest (*ad utilitatem*) of the owners and the improvement of their estates (*ad emendationem villarum*)." Often it was pressing and immediate necessity which determined the lords to emancipate their villeins. They sold liberty for fair silver coins, either outright for a commutation fee or for an annual rent, in order to meet the claims of their creditors, or of their own lives of luxury and warlike adventures, or to ensure themselves a regular revenue without further trouble. Hence in Champagne (1248) and the Toulouse district, and in Albigeois (1298), and even on the domains of the Capetian and Plantagenet kings, the obligatory enfranchisement of serfs was decreed as a fiscal expedient, more advantageous for the lord than for the tenant.

Political considerations also favoured the movement towards emancipation. Kings, usually in the twelfth century unfavourable to the enfranchisement of peasants on the royal domain, were very willing to assist them to emancipate themselves upon seigniorial or ecclesiastical estates, in order to weaken the rival authority of the feudatories. The Church, at first violently hostile to the emancipation of the peasant, as she had been to that of the artisan, because its immediate result was a diminution of her revenues, gradually rallied to the movement, when its power as a lever for the colonization or improvement of her immense estates became manifest. The urban bourgeoisie promoted rural liberty with all its strength, and the communes declared decisively for the peasants against nobles and churchmen, their common adversaries. Their first care after their victory, notably in Italy, was to proclaim the emancipation of rural tenants, in virtue of the rights of man, inalienable despite " the deceit or force " upon which serfdom rested, and in it they themselves led the way. At last even the landowners perceived that the true method of preserving their social preponderance was to exploit an irresistible movement to their own advantage, by turning the concession of rural liberties into a new source of direct or indirect profit, and a new means of restoring by the prestige of wealth an authority which neither tradition nor birth any longer sufficed to retain for them.

In any case, resistance soon became impossible or dangerous, in face of the effervescence which began to take place from the twelfth century onwards in the Western countryside. The peasants, resolved to be free, stopped at no sacrifice, no ruse, no means of coercion. Sometimes they offered their needy lords large sums of money, the fruit of long economies, for the purchase of a charter of enfranchisement. Sometimes they usurped clerical privileges to escape from the jurisdiction of lay lords. Sometimes they stole or burned the seigniorial charters, or else by innumerable quibbles contested the validity of feudal rights. More often still they evoked their customary privileges; they disavowed the lord; they threatened to abandon his land and fly to the neighbouring town or to a royal domain, upon which peasants were free. Finally, like the bourgeois and the artisans, they had recourse to the invincible weapon of association. They formed rural unions, fraternities, *confréries*, and *conjurations;* they bound themselves together by oaths. They rose against lay or ecclesiastical lords and dragged liberty from their masters by veritable *jacqueries*, accompanied by the burning of castles and acts of violence against their oppressors. Everywhere, from the two Sicilies to Germany, a number of such revolts took place at this period, episodes which the chroniclers in general disdained to record. But those of which they have handed down the memory, and which took place upon the domains of the Church, such as the risings at Sahagun in Castile, at Arles in Roussillon, against the Chapter of Notre Dame of Paris, and the Abbeys of Corbie, St. Martin of Tours, Saint-Denis and Vézelay, and in the bishoprics of Soissons and Laon, suffice to show that the peasant, like the *roturier* of the town, could conquer by force the independence which a blind resistance refused to him.

The movement began in the eleventh century by a series of agreements, often individual, which fixed the obligations and lightened the duties of the villeins; it proceeded more widely by dint of collective agreements, in which large rural groups were concerned. This became general in the twelfth and thirteenth centuries. Typical charters or " customs " began to spread, such as those of Lorris in Gâtinais and Beaumont in Argonne, which were adopted by nearly 600 villages or townships in France and in Luxemburg, those of Breteuil in Normandy and England, of Flumet in French Switzerland, of Freiburg in Germany, of Mons in the Low Countries, and of Santiago and Logroño in Spain. To the long leases known as *baux emphytéotiques*, the fee farms, the *baux à complant*, and the grants of *hostise* or colonization, which assured to individual cultivators special advantages in the enjoyment of their tenures, there were added general liberties, recognized by the *fueros*, laws, customs, charters, granted to thousands of settlers in the reclaimed lands. They grouped themselves into villages or townships called new or free towns—*villes neuves, villes franches, sauvetés, bastides, salvetats, bourgs neufs, bourgs francs*—which may be found all over the West under analogous names.

There, within regular enclosures, protected by moats or thick walls, under the shelter of their churches and of the cross, symbol of the peace of God, the peasants found a refuge for their new-born liberty. The greater part of Italy, particularly Tuscany and Lombardy, the Castiles, Navarre, the Basque provinces, Western France, the Low Countries, and the German Rhineland were the first regions in which the rural populations received their franchises, and in which, from the twelfth and thirteenth centuries, emancipation made the greatest strides. Eastern and Central France, the two Sicilies, Aragon, and Catalonia, the Eastern Netherlands, Northern and Central Germany, and England, followed more slowly. But in general the greater part of the rural population of the West had almost completed its emancipation by the first half of the fourteenth century.

There was considerable variety in the conditions under which enfranchisement was granted; in some places it was very wide, in others surrounded with restrictions; sometimes concessions were made in a body, sometimes only bit by bit. But in general emancipation gave the peasants precious guarantees, whether obtained *en bloc* or separately.

The first benefit which it brought was that of personal liberty. The peasant could dispose of himself. Laws and customs henceforward recognized that man is born and should remain free, and that he cannot be an object of property. The charters of the " new towns " even went so far as to declare the villein's person inviolable. The master's right of coercion disappeared or was limited. Liberty of domicile was admitted, and the lord could no longer bring back by force the peasant who had left his estate, provided that the latter had given him notice, ceded to him a part of his movable possessions, and furnished him with a substitute, or paid a special tax. Barriers placed upon freedom to marry were suppressed or lowered, in return for special payments or in virtue of conventions concluded between lords (*traités d'entrecours*). The legal personality of the villein was recognized; he could sue in a court of justice, and, together with his wife and children, enjoyed legal protection against ill-treatment. The right of peasants to bequeath their movable and immovable property was recognized; where the *mainmorte* survived, its prescriptions were successfully evaded by a series of legal fictions, as in Auvergne and Nivernais; most frequently it was bought off and abolished or replaced by light money taxes—twelvepence, for instance, in the Low Countries. In the same way the most vexatious inheritance rights were suppressed—such, for instance, as the " best chattle," which enabled the lord to seize half of the inheritance in Germany, England, and the Low Countries. Almost everywhere the villeins could henceforth freely alienate, exchange, sell, or bequeath their possessions of all sorts.

The law protected the property of the emancipated peasants; it often forbade the seizure of their tools, their live-stock, their harvests, or their furniture. In general all unjust charges, called " exactions " or " evil customs," were abolished, as well as all those which belonged to the state of serfdom, notably the capitation tax, with or without a redemption fee. The other payments, the dues in kind which represented a sort of rent, the *cens* and *champarts* and *terrages*, were sometimes partially redeemed, more generally fixed or converted into pecuniary rents, so that their weight grew less as the revenue of the land rose and the value of money fell. Tithes, forced gifts, and dues were fixed, transformed, or limited. The arbitrary *corvée* was abolished or commuted or replaced by money taxes. Most frequently the number and duration of the days of labour due from the villeins were limited and their conditions of work fixed. In Beauvais, which was, however, exceptional, the peasants from whom the *corvée* could be exacted had to furnish only one day's labour and three days' ploughing each year, and in many places the lord had to feed them on such occasions. The tallage or *queste* was sometimes suppressed and sometimes replaced by a fixed poll or hearth tax, proportioned to the peasant's fortune and levied according to an invariable and moderate rate. " Aids " were commuted, abolished, changed into fixed payments, or limited, as also were the seigniorial monopolies which were so harmful to economic liberty, and the seigniorial rights which impeded freedom of movement.

The rural populations obtained commercial franchises and freedom to trade in their fairs and markets. Fixed weights and measures, and sometimes also a fixed coinage, were guaranteed to them. In Central France they received the rights of hunting, fishing, and free warren. They obtained the recognition of advantageous customary rights over the common lands, and were sometimes even allowed to appropriate the assarts which they made themselves. The abusive privileges which the lord had exercised in virtue of his rights of sovereignity, such as hospitality (*gîte, albergue*), *prise*, and *procuration*, were commuted or limited. The military obligations of villeins for local defence were restricted; they were allowed to commute them or to convert them into pecuniary rents, and the same held good of the seigniorial *sauvement* or police services.

In addition to these civil and economic liberties the rural classes won administrative and political privileges, guarantees against the arbitrary powers of the feudal court, its fiscal demands, and its officials. They often stipulated that they should be subject to the jurisdiction of only one tribunal, and that cases should be tried on the spot and by a jury of their peers or chief men (*boni homines, notarii*), according to fixed rules of procedure, which protected them against arbitrary arrests, confiscations, and abusive fines. They received the right of release on bail, of fleeing to sanctuary, of appealing to superior courts, and of pleading against the lord himself. Sometimes, notably in the new villages of the reclaimed districts, the peasants intervened in the choice of the seigniorial officials, bailiffs, provosts, and podestats. Most often they contented themselves with gaining recognition by charter of the right of meeting in their village and district assemblies to discuss common interests and to nominate magistrates, *prud'hommes*, mayors, provosts, consuls, judges, *jurats*, inspectors (*veedores*), who were invested with certain duties of police and justice, proctors who were charged with defending their cases before the law-courts, inferior agents, sergeants, foresters, reeves, woodmen, on whom devolved the duty of securing observation of the local regulations or *bans*. The rural communities had their property, their common lands, their churches, their hospitals. They participated in the administration of the parishes. Sometimes they rose higher still and attained possession of full political rights, as in certain regions of Northern France and Flanders, in the valleys of the Alps and Pyrenees, in which they formed real communes (*universitates*) and even leagues, such as the *hermundades* of Northern Spain, and confederations, such as those of the forest cantons of Switzerland (1291-1350).

Extending to a much larger mass of people than did the emancipation of the towns, this emancipation of the peasantry was one of the greatest events of history. It endowed the rural multitudes, who had never in the past known such a régime, with the most precious prerogatives. For the first time, liberty of person and of contract was proclaimed and put into practice among the country people. The peasant won, to a great extent, the free disposition of his labour. He had a legal place and a recognized value in society, and with the sense of his independence he soon acquired that of his strength. The rural masses ceased to be passive herds and became groups of men, proud of their liberty and determined to have their rights respected. A new era began in the history of the peasant, and the conditions of life of the rural classes were improved to an extent hitherto unknown.

CHAPTER X

In the rural districts of the West, as in the towns, emancipation and colonization brought about the formation of new social categories, and determined the birth of classes different from those which had characterized the previous age. Distinctions began to appear between the free peasant proprietors, the *censitaires*, tenants who paid dues and were not proprietors, though they enjoyed a sort of semi-ownership, and the associates and organizers of cultivation. Above the survivals of the old social and economic régime, serfdom, and even slavery, there appeared a class of agricultural wage-earners.

At the head of the mass of peasants there grew up a true bourgeoisie, a rural third estate, which attained enjoyment of the full and entire ownership of its land, and even, by dint of economy, bought up the lands of nobles; a class which thrust its children into the ranks of the clergy and into administrative posts in the service of princes and lords, and which soon acquired both wealth and consideration. It was to this class that the small free proprietors of Germany, known as fief-owning peasants (*lehnbauern*), belonged, as well as those peasants, numerous in the south, who were exempt from the payment of *cens* (*freizinsen*, *parleute*), and the pioneer assarters, who had become hereditary landowners (*erbpachter*). They often amalgamated with the official class, with the country squires (*knechte*), even with the knightly classes (*ritterstand*). A similar élite was also to be found in the Low Countries. In Flanders and France some who were thus privileged managed to slip into the ranks of the nobility, as did that erstwhile serf of Saint-Benoît-sur-Loire, who became, in the twelfth century, one of the best-known knights of Burgundy.

Most often they were the root from which sprang clerks, officials, town burgesses, village " cocks of the walk," who, according to one satire, owned " pasture and land enow and great possessions." In Spain, especially in Roussillon, where there were more peasant owners in the thirteenth century than there are to-day, the fact that they had filled the office of seigniorial bailiff or judge was enough for them to mount on horseback, like nobles, and eat wheaten bread. In England the small peasant proprietors, socagers of ancient origin, or newly founded yeomen and freeholders, swore fealty directly to the king, sat upon juries and county courts, and approximated to the gentry, who led the same laborious life as they. "The toe of the peasant comes so near the heel of the courtier, he galls his kibe," says an English proverb which Shakespeare has preserved. The formation and development of this middle class of small peasant owners, comfortably off or even rich, was a characteristic of this period, and was in a great measure the result of the movement of emancipation.

The mass of villeins in the West formed by far the most numerous class, that of *censitaires* or rent-paying tenants who, under various names, succeeded in obtaining the majority of civil liberties, but remained subject to a variety of obligations, without attaining full proprietary ownership. On the lands which these tenants cultivated the old land-owners preserved their proprietary rights, attested by the payment of quit rents (*cens*). But most of the pre-rogatives of real property passed to the tenants, who thus became quasi-owners of the holdings which they cultivated. They possessed the essential rights of property, to wit, succession, donation, sale, and alienation; they could mortgage or bequeath their holdings. They were secured against eviction, on condition that they regularly paid their rents, which had become invariable and strictly determined by individual or collective contracts. Such was the condition of millions of peasants in the Western world, whose situation was ruled by extremely various conventions and leases.

In Germany the *hörigen*, as they were called, often obtained in virtue of "spade right" (*jus palae*), something like the full ownership of reclaimed lands and fixity of tenure, in virtue of long-term or hereditary leases (*erbpachten*), the lords being unable to refuse them admission or to resume possession of the peasant estate. In the Netherlands the concession of leases for an indefinite period (*beklemregt*) had the same result. In England the tenants obtained legal recognition of their hereditary enjoyment of their lands and took the name of copyholders, or tenants by copy of court roll; they formed a class so numerous that up to quite recent times they held a third of the soil of Britain. In France, the process by which the peasants took possession of the soil was disguised under a mass of conventions and leases drawn up on different terms and under different names, all of which resulted in conferring effectual rights of property upon the cultivator in return for the payment of *cens*. The perpetual lease (*aforamento*) of Portugal and the contract (*livello*) at a land rent (*fitto*), which became usual in Italy, acted in the same way. Under the latter system the peasant even possessed the right of *lods et ventes*, and the landowner retained only a right of pre-emption in case of sale, retaining his title by requiring the contract to be renewed at more or less lengthy intervals. Thus, little by little, there was accomplished one of the most important events in history, the transference of the right of real property, under the form of long or hereditary leases, until such time as the last vestiges of the old subjection should be entirely swept away.

The peasant property which now appeared under these modest disguises still retained the aspect which it had presented in feudal times. It was composed of little holdings, often made up of scattered strips, which tended to become smaller and smaller, as a result of the custom of equal division among heirs or the hazard of sales and alienations. In Germany the average size of the rural *hufe*, which varied from 14 to 120 acres, diminished by three-quarters after the twelfth century. In England it was rare for the copyholder or for the freeholder to hold more than a virgate of land (30 acres); often he possessed only half that amount and a good number of holdings contained only $4\frac{1}{2}$ acres, with a strip of meadow. In Picardy labourers who owned oxen had, as a rule, about 30 acres. The subdivision went so far that there were in Roussillon rural domains or *bordes* formed of sixteen to sixty-two lots, while in Picardy labourers known as *haricotiers* banded together to cultivate their holdings, which were not large enough to support plough-teams, and in Italy the northern communes had to take measures to facilitate the building up again of these small properties by means of exchanges.

Among the rural populations there soon began to appear, during the period of emancipation, new classes exploiting the land, distinct from the small free proprietors and the copyholders or *censitaires*. At first they formed only a small minority, comprising tenant-farmers, *métayers*, and agricultural wage-earners.

The system of tenant-farming allowed peasants of independent and energetic character, who were possessed of some small capital and anxious for the preservation of their freedom, to obtain from the soil returns of which they kept the larger part, on condition of paying a fixed rent to the landowner. On their side the landowners kept full ownership of the land let out at farm, were able to participate in the increment on its capital value, and did not have to take the risks involved in farming the soil themselves, or submit to the disappointments which the system of commutation rents had often carried with it. The tenant-farmer system appeared most generally in regions of advanced agriculture; in Italy from the twelfth century, and in the Low Countries, Northern France, Catalonia, and Roussillon in the thirteenth. But previous to the fourteenth century it spread only slowly in the greater part of the West.

It was a system of speculative enterprise, in which town burgesses took part as well as peasants, who thus undertook the risk of farming seigniorial and ecclesiastical domains, on condition of keeping them in good condition, introducing useful improvements, and paying in money or in kind a fixed part of the produce, which in Italy was called a *canon*. The amount payable varied in Tuscany from a third for cereals to a tenth or an eleventh for wine, olives, and fruit. The landowner sometimes provided the farmer with part of his stock and seed, and with extra labour for the harvest and for threshing the grain; he had to pay an indemnity for unearned increment, if the farmer had notably improved the soil. Landlord and tenant only engaged themselves for a short term—one year, two years, three years, but in the interests of both parties the majority of farm leases varied from six to twenty-nine years, in multiples of three years, corresponding to the triennial fallows.

Side by side with these leases and the class of tenant-farmers, there also appeared leases of *métayage* and the class of *métayers*. The system of free and temporary association between the cultivator and the landowner reserved to the former the free disposal of his work when the contract lapsed, and to the latter the free disposal of his land, while to both it ensured an equitable partition of produce, without risk of loss. This method of farming (*mezzadria*) and class of cultivators arose in Tuscany and Central Italy in the twelfth century and spread through the centre and north of the peninsula in the course of the two following centuries. It is found in Provence, Catalonia, and Roussillon at the same time, and then in Central and Western France and Normandy, where the system of *métayage* was used for clearances, in Flanders from 1220, and in the country round Treier and the Rhineland.

This system allowed poor peasants, who had no holding or who were anxious not to lose their freedom by tying themselves indefinitely to the land, to use their labour in return for a fixed share in the produce of the soil. The landowner provided them with capital in the shape of the land, with their tools, seed, manure, hay and straw, the cost of keeping up buildings, and half of the expense of harvesting, threshing, and winnowing. The *métayer* gave his labour, looked after the beasts, gave *corvées* and carting services, and handed part of the revenue over to the landowner in kind, the amount often varying in Italy from a third to a mere tenth, and only rising as high as a half for fruit, over and above obligatory gifts of eggs, poultry, and cheese. But he had the right to take the whole produce of the smaller live-stock, pigs and farmyard animals. He could not be expelled save for specific cases of ill-behaviour, and he could enjoy the profits of the soil for periods varying from two to five years, or even from twelve to twenty-nine. Henceforth, too, another form of limited co-operation, the stock lease or *bail à cheptel*, frequently associated peasants and land-owners in the purchase of cattle and in the profits of stock-farming, especially in Catalonia, Roussillon, and Provence.

Finally, there was the class of agricultural wage-earners, day labourers, and domestic servants, which began to form about the same time as that of the urban wage-earners, in proportion as emancipation restricted landowners in the use of that unpaid labour, or labour at reduced rates, which the *corvées* had given them, and in proportion as the system of direct cultivation and agricultural enterprise was added to the copyhold system. The number of holdings to be granted no longer corresponded to the demands of a growing population of peasants, who had attained freedom, but no longer had access to land, or who preferred to preserve complete independence without being bound in any way to the soil, making a livelihood instead by hiring out their labour. The formation of a class of day labourers may be observed in Italy from the twelfth century, and their number grew throughout the West with the approach of the fourteenth. They were known in the Italian peninsula as *braccianti*, *pimenti*, or land labourers (*laboratores terrarum*), in Navarre as *villanos asaderos*, in Languedoc and Provence as *brassiers*, in the West of France as *hotteurs* and *bezocheurs*, in England as labourers, and in the Low Countries as *koppers*.

Often, like the German *kotsaten*, the Flemish and Walloon *cossates*, and the English cotters, they had a cottage, a little scrap of land and a few heads of cattle, but they were forced to hire out their labour to procure the supplementary resources necessary for existence. Many others were entirely destitute of landed capital, and lived solely by the wages of their labour. But all of them, whether hired by the day or on piecework, had the great advantage of disposing freely of their persons, bargaining for their wage and engaging their labour only for a short period.

More stable, though less independent, was the situation of another class of wage-earners, which was also being formed at this time, that of the servants in husbandry (*servientes*, *valets*). It became more and more the practice to choose the *personnel* necessary for the direct farming of the land by the owner from among persons of free condition, whether they were entirely destitute of property or not. Ox-herds, carters, goat-herds, shepherds and shepherdesses, swine-herds, servant girls were thus hired by the month, or more often by the year; in Normandy there were servants who hired themselves for nine years on end. They lived in strict dependence upon the landowner, who exercised an extensive authority over them, and even a justice which was not unlike that exercised by the absolute lord of former days; but their subordination never went so far as to involve a loss of liberty.

Small owners, copyholders or *censitaires*, tenant-farmers and *métayers*, and agricultural wage-earners, such were the classes which henceforth made up the rural population of the West. Their fortunes varied, but all of them were free. Nevertheless, the transformation was neither complete nor continuous. Like witnesses to a tenacious past and to institutions which might have been thought dead, serfdom and slavery survived, and sometimes even reappeared. Throughout Northern Germany the old Slav or Pruss populations, who had been allowed to keep their lives, formed a new class of serfs (*tides, smurdes*), "men of naught," despised and ill-treated. In the British Isles the progress of Anglo-Norman feudalism and the partial dissolution of the tribal system often resulted in the aggravation and generalization of serfdom among the Celtic populations of Scotland, Wales, and Ireland. In the Low Countries and in Aragon and Upper Catalonia serfs of the glebe still survived. In the latter regions the serfdom of divers classes of Christians called *mezquinos, pageses de remensa,* and of Moslems (*ejaricos*) was pushed to such a degree of severity that, even as late as the thirteenth and fourteenth centuries, the law recognized the right of their lords " to treat them well or ill, according to their will " (*jus maltractandi*).

Though in the Iberian lands and in the two Sicilies Jews and Moslems were often favoured, given a certain autonomy and allowed rights of property, it also befell that some of them were reduced to the condition of serfs, subject to *mainmorte*. Even in France, although serfdom in general disappeared, islands of *mainmorte* still persisted in the Île-de-France, the Toulouse country, Brittany, above all in the Dauphiné, Champagne, Lorraine, and a part of the centre. It is true that this serfdom, which fell upon the land and carried with it the payment of special succession duties, left the essential guarantees of civil liberty and of stability to the cultivator. But these milder forms of serfdom were limited to the most civilized countries. In most others the condition of the serfs continued to be very hard, although it is true that they were only a minority. There were even worse things than serfdom.

In the Mediterranean regions of Spain, Italy, and France slavery was partly built up again by war and by commerce, although it never again attained its former proportions.

Nevertheless, on the whole, it is undoubted that the material conditions of the rural classes improved greatly during these three centuries and a half. A fair number of peasants reached a condition of comfort, and some made fortunes. The majority, having gained the effective ownership of the soil, were able to profit by the rise in the price of agricultural produce and in the value of land, sometimes to a greater extent than the landowner, who was bound by customs which fixed the tenants' payments, frequently commuted into money, at invariable sums. It has been held that the *censitaires*—that is to say, the mass of the cultivators in France—succeeded in taking two-thirds of the landed revenue for their own exclusive profit. The extension of the system of tenant-farming is an equal proof that the business of farming presented advantages which attracted peasants gifted with initiative, while the conditions of *métayage* seem to have made agrarian partnership a profitable system for those who preferred to employ their activity thus.

As to the agricultural wage-earners, it is certain that a large number of them—for instance, the day labourers in Italy and Spain—were then classed among the poorest inhabitants of the countryside, even among the indigent. They usually, at least at first, received very low wages. In Tuscany, in the thirteenth century, they earned 2d. during the winter and 3d. during the summer, when they were hired by the day. In England they were paid from 1d. to 2½d. for weeding and mowing, and from 6d. an acre for task work. For women the wage fell as low as a penny a day. But the day labourers soon profited by a continuous rise in the price of labour. In England about 1330 it had risen by about a fifth, and the labourers also received gratuities known as "courtesies." In Poitou about 1307 the basket-bearers and labourers in the vineyards received 8d. to 9d. a day without board, and the wood-cutters 10d. to 12d. Wages had reached this average in France in the first half of the fourteenth century, whereas in the tenth century a harvester only earned a halfpenny. Thus the price of labour must have doubled before 1348. It then rose to between 3 sous and 2 sous and

6 pence, almost half that of urban labour, and almost equivalent to the rural wage at the beginning of the nineteenth century. The servants, more favoured still, for they were protected from unemployment, and provided with food, lodging, laundry, light, and a part of their clothing, earned in Catalonia and Roussillon from 25 to 75 sous a year, and in France, before 1348, from 5 to 7 fr. a year, as much, having regard to the value of money, as they earned in the first quarter of last century.

The diminution in feudal warfare and brigandage as a result of monarchical government, and in the number of great famines, which were six times less numerous in France in the thirteenth century than in the tenth (10 as against 60), the absence of great economic crises in a society in which excessive competition did not yet play havoc, and the simplicity of life, all contributed to the growing well-being of the mass of the rural classes in the West.

Never had the material existence of the peasants been so favourable, and to find such conditions again one must look onward to the middle of the nineteenth century. A multitude of new villages, townships, hamlets, homesteads, and farms sprang up, and a crowd of parishes. In France their number was unsurpassed for 500 years, and even diminished in certain parts during the centuries which followed. Here the peasants lived, sometimes in groups protected by hedges or walls of earth and rubble, furnished with watch-towers, sometimes scattered along the roads or in the midst of their fields, near their well or spring or pond and in the shelter of some valley or grove of trees. Their houses, made sometimes of wood and sometimes of mud, stones, or rubble, and occasionally of bricks, or even hollowed like caves out of the soft limestone hills, had usually but a single story, and were covered with thatch or tiles, destitute of window-panes and chimneys, dark, dirty, smoke-laden, esteemed of so little value that at the end of the tenth century a country cottage was only worth from 8 to 10 sous. The family was crowded together in a few rooms, hardly separate from the stables and barns. The furniture was scanty, and consisted of beds with straw mattresses, tables, stools, massive benches, a " hutch " or trunk, a box or coffer, and a collection of kitchen utensils made of earthenware, or of pewter or copper among the more prosperous. Nevertheless, in proportion as comfort spread, rural inventories bear witness to the appearance in rustic homes of a more considerable collection of utensils, and more comfortable furniture, of pewter pots, and even of silver plate. The peasant in this interior could only light himself by the aid of resin candles, or by more elementary procedures still; for a pound of tallow candles cost the price of a day's work. But he warmed himself like a king, so abundant was wood and so low its price.

He dressed simply in clothes made from the wool and flax which he raised upon his land, spun by his wife and daughters, and woven by himself or by the neighbouring village weaver. Usually he wore garments of linen cloth on weekdays, and, of course, woollens, or mixed wool and thread fabrics on Sundays; one of these coats cost him from 4 to 20 sous. In the thirteenth century an ox-herd had a tunic valued at 3 sous and 4d. He often went barefoot, but when he wished to be shod he could have a pair of clogs or sabots for 7d. or 8d., and shoes, boots, or hose of cowhide or dressed leather for from 18d. to 4 sous (1325). In place of furs he used sheepskins, and the skins of rabbits, hares, and foxes. The peasant woman, however, was beginning to take care of her clothes and to own a few ornaments, and when they reached easier circumstances, the peasants took particular pride in the accumulation of body and household linen, to the great advantage of hygiene.

The greatest improvement of all took place in their food. It become at least abundant and substantial, if not more varied. Besides vegetables, milk, cheese, and fruit, the peasant also ate rye and barley, and even wheaten bread in the thirteenth and fourteenth centuries. To this he added a great deal of fresh and, still more, of salt fish, bacon, fresh or salted pork, a little beef, mutton, and an increasing amount of poultry. In Flanders and England meat became enormously plentiful in the country districts. The villeins used few spices, but a great deal of salt; they had plenty of honey instead of sugar. In the countries of the north-west their drink was beer brewed from barley or corn, and ale; cider was as yet reserved for the poorest of the poor.

LIFE AND WORK IN MEDIEVAL EUROPE

In the French, German, and Latin countries the peasants drank a great deal of wine, and the consumption thereof spread far and wide in village taverns throughout the West.

The peasant had for long retained such filthy habits that *fabliaux* were wont to assert that the smell of the dung-heap was his favourite scent, and to define the villein as " a stinking creature, born from an ass's dung." But from the twelfth and still more from the thirteenth century, the custom of hot and cold baths spread in the country districts, and bath-tubs were often to be found in houses, and stews, or public baths, in the villages. Precautions were taken against contagious diseases by the foundation of large numbers of lazar-houses, which formed a fifth of the hospitals in England. Medicine and surgery spread to the country townships, where sworn surgeons, and sometimes even apothecaries, were often to be found in the fourteenth century. The rural folk of the West then appeared heavy and clumsy, " ugly brutes," as the satirists called them, but full of vigour, hardened by their open-air life and physical exercises; often, as in England, France, and Flanders, over-flowing with a gross and sensual gaiety.

The rural classes had also acquired in the new atmosphere of liberty and comfort a moral physiognomy, the characteristics of which gradually became more precise. They were not at all refined in their tastes, but they were cheerful and full of activity, loving the tavern, festivals, dancing, sometimes also dicing and games of chance. They loved to listen to the tales and songs of minstrel or *jongleur* on the village green; on fair days they marvelled at the juggler and the charlatan; and they lent a greedy ear to the sermon of the wandering friar or the gossip of the pedlar, that living newspaper. From their servile past the peasants inherited habits of brutality, grossness, and dishonesty. Their sexual morality was low, and they had but slight respect for woman, in whom they saw only the mother of their children and the companion of their labours. They were miserly and avaricious, superstitious and credulous. But they had already acquired those social virtues which made them one of the regenerating forces of the medieval state. The classes which mocked and despised them owed it to these peasants that they never lacked the bread which they had not sown, and could live in idleness upon the fruits of a labour of which they were incapable. Attached heart and soul to the earth which nourished them, the peasants delivered it from sterility and made the soil of the West fertile by their sweat.

Respecting religious authority without servility, they knew, on occasion, how to oppose a Church too much pre-occupied with temporal power. Little by little they awoke to the life of the mind, and their adroit and mocking wit made itself felt in Italy, France, the Low Countries, and Spain. The low-browed torpid creature depicted in the *fabliaux* soon learned to appreciate the benefits of education, some-times drove his children to school, and succeeded in emancipating his intelligence and reason. In certain countries, such as France, a spirit of sociability appeared among the country folk. Everywhere the peasant showed by innumerable works of poor relief how powerful was his sense of charity, while his vigorous sense of solidarity was manifest in the innumerable family communities and associa-tions for ploughing, cattle-rearing, and mutual protection which he formed. A rural élite even proved capable of generosity, devotion, bravery, and liberality, and more than one peasant showed himself at heart the equal of a gentle-man. These men acquired, notably in England and the Low Countries, a sense of their own value; "The Flemish peasant," ran one song, "thinks that the world belongs to him when he is drunk." Emerging from his humility, the villein reasoned, discussed, pleaded. A new force was born, of which medieval society did not, at first, suspect the power, but which, revealing itself by slow degrees, pro-foundly changed the Western world. It gave an irresistible impulse to material wealth and increased comfort and well-being. For the first time the multitudes who lived in the countryside knew not only freedom, but the sweetness of life. They endowed the society which emancipated them with the treasure of those rustic virtues—love of labour, economy, foresight, and energy—which established Western civilization upon the most solid foundations.

DURING the first six centuries of the Middle Ages it was the East Roman Empire which had been the great home of civilization and the chief centre of production of civilized peoples. But after the end of the eleventh century its rôle was ended and its supremacy passed to the West, the activity of which became preponderant and was exercised in precisely those regions in which Byzantine influence had before predominated.

Indeed, the East Roman Empire grew weaker and weaker; it lost Southern Italy in the eleventh century; then it lost Asia Minor, the chief reservoir of its soldiers, sailors, and wealth. It died slowly of inanition, despite the efforts of the new government of the Commeni, under which it had a last flash of brilliance in the twelfth century. But its weakness was already manifest, and little by little it was despoiled of the superiority which the strength of its political, administrative, financial, and military institutions had hitherto bestowed upon it. Overthrown by the Latins in 1204, and restored in 1261 by the Palæologi, it dragged out a long death-agony for 200 years. It no longer possessed either administration, or money, or an army, or even that moral unity which patriotism had once given to it.

Social and economic power passed from the state to a feudal class of great landowners, bishops, and monks, who seized possession of the land. The imperial domains, which the Commeni succeeded in restoring for a brief moment, by means of confiscations, conquests, and the secularization of ecclesiastical possessions, soon fell into the hands of soldiers in the form of military benefices (*pronoiai*), or of the Church, by gifts, or even of the nobles. It was the latter who prevailed and who towards the end of the eleventh century formed themselves into a territorial feudal class analogous to that of the West. Formed by a fusion of the ancient territorial nobility with the new administrative nobility, this feudal class of *archontes, dunatoi, sebastades, primates,* and *toparchs* built up great domains in Greece, Macedonia, and Thrace, by means of concessions from the imperial treasury, usurpations at the expense of small free properties, inheritance, and purchase. By degrees they laid hands upon local government, surrounded themselves by a body of vassals (*stratiotai, kaballarioi*), and made themselves a nuisance to the state by their turbulent temper. Side by side with them the secular and monastic Church, eluding the imperial constitutions which sought to prevent the formation of estates in mortmain, grew rich by public and private gifts, by usurpations, and by the skill with which it cultivated its lands, until at the end of the twelfth century it was in possession of the major part of the landed wealth of the empire. Furthermore, the Church was exempt from most of the public taxes, and, having become richer than the state, obtained the right to exercise some of the attributes of government.

On the other hand, that middle class of rural *petits bourgeois* and free peasants (*chorites, eleutheroi, eutourgoi, mesoi*), whose energetic labour had been one of the main strengths of the empire, disappeared, submerged beneath the flood of feudalism, after a struggle, which for a short time procured for it a certain local autonomy under elected heads (*demogerontes, epitropoi, proestai, phylarchs*) and the preservation of its common lands. In the thirteenth century the mass of the rural populations of the East Roman Empire were reduced to the condition of villeins (*moteles*), preserving personal liberty in dependence upon *archontes*, or, worse still, to that of serfs (*paroikoi*), fixed to the soil and bound to pay to the landowner a land tax (*canon*), a third of the harvest, and a succession duty of a third of their inheritance, and to furnish him with two days of labour weekly, without prejudice to the military service, the poll tax, and the other crushing requisitions of the state. At the very moment when the villeins of the West were rising to liberty and well-being, those of the East were falling into an abyss of servitude and misery; they became those mournful herds over whose indifferent heads so many different dominations came, held their brief sway, and passed away.

LIFE AND WORK IN MEDIEVAL EUROPE

As long as the central power remained fairly strong—that is, until the twelfth century—this social retrogression had little effect upon agricultural production, which continued to be abundant. Cattle-raising, the cultivation of cereals, vines, fruit-trees and industrial plants, remained flourishing for another hundred years. Travellers such as Edrisi and Benjamin of Tudela still vaunt the abundance " of all kinds of natural products " in Romania. But the prosperity of the countryside did not survive the troublous times which followed the end of the dynasty of the Commeni, and the wars which set the empire at grips with Latins, Bulgars, and Turks. In the thirteenth century the state, which had been the envy of the West, became an object of contempt and pity to its rivals, and its soil was no longer able to suffice even for the needs of a decimated population.

In the preceding century it still had a numerous urban bourgeoisie and an active industry. Byzantium was still the wonder of the world, the centre of wealth and of splendour, whose brilliance the Crusaders were not slow to admire, wherein were heaped up, in the words of Villehardoin, " all the riches of the world." Salonica, although sacked in 1185, still seemed to this country baron " one of the strongest and richest towns in all Christendom." But these were the last gleams of a great fire, which burned lower from century to century. Soon the industries of the West took its old lucrative monopolies from the East. The old corporations, once the strength of the commercial and industrial classes, became a prey to the suspicions of imperial despotism and disappeared. Economic activity was ruined by the exactions of the treasury and by foreign competition.

Trade passed completely into the hands of Venetians, Genoese, Pisans, Catalans, and the traders of Provence and Languedoc. Italy, wrote Nicelas, " is penetrating Byzantium with spread sails." After the restoration of the Palæologi, Genoa became the real mistress of trade, in competition with Venice. " She shuts all trade routes to the Romans," observes a Byzantine historian. In the towns, as at Salonica and Adrianople, intestine struggles set the artisans in conflict with the rich, and social war completed the ruin of urban prosperity. The empire, which had for a space held " two-thirds of all the wealth of the world " and the economic hegemony thereof, lost both its wealth and its supremacy in less than 200 years.

It was the West which supplanted it as the leader of civilization. French barons carried the feudal régime of the West into Romania, the Archipelago, and Greece. For a brief space in the thirteenth century they revived the material prosperity of Achaia, but they did not succeed in rescuing those regions from anarchy, and as a rule they precipitated their ruin.

Nevertheless, in Central and Eastern Europe the civilizing mission of the West, sometimes taking up and continuing that of the East, obtained better results. In the eleventh century the Slav, Roumanian, and Magyar peoples who inhabited these vast countries had, for the most part, not yet emerged out of barbarism, or left behind the stage of primitive economy. They lived by the chase, by fishing, and by cattle-raising; agriculture was little developed among them, and they knew only the most elementary forms of trade. In general they possessed no towns. Some, such as the Serbs, the Bulgars, the Russians, and the Vlachs or Roumanians, had been converted by Byzantium and had undergone its influence, to which, from the twelfth century onwards, was added that of the West. Others, such as the Magyars, Croats, Czechs, Slovaks, and Poles, had received Christianity from Western apostles, and it was under the auspices of the West that they were won to a civilized existence. Greek missionaries and merchants spread far and wide in the Balkans, and French monks, Italian merchants, above all, a crowd of colonists, artisans, soldiers, and traders of German origin, penetrated Central Europe.

Byzantine colonization assisted the Bulgarians and the Southern Slavs to exploit their natural resources, but Western colonization far surpassed it in activity and influence. It was thanks to these Western settlers, who came in crowds from Germany and the Low Countries, and thanks also to the French monks, that Bohemia, Moravia, Slovenia, Hungary, Transylvania, Poland, Lithuania, Prussia, and Livonia began the great work of clearance and population which was the outstanding event in the history of these regions during this period of the Middle Ages. Summoned by kings, bishops, and abbeys, thousands of

LIFE AND WORK IN MEDIEVAL EUROPE

energetic Western peasants, often accompanied by officials (*ministeriales*) or country gentlemen in search of estates, and clerks in search of benefices, cleared forests, drained marshes, and founded a multitude of villages or "new towns." Unhappily they did not intermingle with the indigenous population; they obtained for themselves not only freedom, but the recognition of privileges which were often exorbitant, and it was not long before they came to be looked upon as parasites—"lice," as the Czechs called the German colonists. Sometimes they even extirpated the previous inhabitants, who were still pagans, by sword and famine, as in Prussia, or enslaved them, as in the Baltic provinces. Nevertheless, their example usually acted as a stimulus to the peoples in whose midst they established themselves. Thus in the south, Slavs and Bulgars colonized Macedonia; Vlachs or Roumanians the Danube plain; Magyars Upper Hungary and several cantons of Transylvania, an ancient Celto-Latin country; Poles colonized the plains which stretched between the Oder and the Vistula and Dnieper, and between the Carpathians and the Baltic Sea; and the Russians began their expansion to the east and north, at the expense of Finnish tribes. This obscure work, often unrecognized in traditional history, brought about by slow degrees the economic transformation of Eastern Europe.

To the elementary forms of agricultural production, the fisheries, the hunting of furred beasts, the raising of large and small live-stock, which remained predominant in these regions, colonization made possible the addition of a more considerable amount of corn-growing, which prospered in Bulgaria, Hungary, Poland, and Prussia, and also the cultivation of vines and fruit-trees, introduced and developed among the southern Slavs, the Magyars, and the Czechs, and of the industrial plants—flax and hemp—which received a new and vigorous impulse. Population increased, particularly in the Elbe and Danube lands, to such an extent that in the thirteenth century it was almost as dense there as in the Germanic countries. Commerce developed in proportion as the states were organized and the conditions of order and security necessary to trade realized. Merchants from East and West were attracted and encouraged by privileges. A metal coinage appeared. Jews organized credit, and in their wake came Italians, who founded banking-houses in some of these countries. The great river routes of the Elbe, Oder, Vistula, Dnieper, and Danube were utilized for transport. Itinerant traders multiplied, and great caravans initiated the peoples of Eastern Europe into international trade at the fairs which were organized at Leipzig, Frankfort-on-Oder, Breslau, Prague, Cracow, Kiev, and Novgorod. The land routes once more took on their ancient activity, especially in the south. The two Roman roads which joined the Adriatic regions to the Archipelago and the Sea of Marmora were once more put into working order by the Serbian Empire, and, above all, by the Slav trading republic of Ragusa. They were provided with courier services and depôts or " factories." In the centre there lay open the great road which unites Northern Germany, by way of Bohemia and Hungary, to the East. Commercial centres sprang up in the twelfth and thirteenth centuries; such were Prague, Budapest, Vralislav (Breslau), Gdansk (Danzig), Cracow, Riga, Pololsk, Novgorod the Great, which numbered 100,000 souls and 190 counting-houses, Kiev, which rivalled Constantinople with its 400 churches, its eight markets, and its counting-houses, and, finally, Ragusa in the south. Between these new lands and the states of the East and the West they established active relations, based upon the exchange of natural products against manufactured goods.

Side by side with the primitive forms of industrial activity, domestic and family industry, more progressive forms were introduced into those lands newly opened to civilization, under the influence of the Westerners and the Byzantines, and the workshops of master craftsmen began to appear in the newly risen urban centres, as well as a great capitalistic industry in the mineral districts. Miners and foreign capitalists, chiefly German, Italian, and Ragusan, undertook the exploitation of the argentiferous lead-mines of Serbia, Bosnia, and Hungary, and the seams of mercury and copper of Rascia, the silver and tin of Bohemia, the iron, copper, and calamine of the Serbian, Czech, and Polish lands, and the salt-pans of Transylvania and Greater Poland. They created the first metallurgical businesses in Serbia, Silesia, Moravia, and Bohemia. Byzantine, French, and Italian artists came to initiate these peoples into building and industrial arts. But neither commerce nor this growing industry was on a sufficiently large scale to give urban economy an impulse at all comparable to that which it had received in the Eastern Empire and in the West.

Eastern Europe remained, above all else, a great zone in which agricultural economy prevailed, and in which towns were little more than fortified posts with the appearance of large villages. It was on the great trade routes alone that there grew up the first urban centres destined to have a brilliant future, such as Ragusa, Pesth, Prague, Breslau, Dantzig, Riga, Novgorod, and Warsaw (founded in the thirteenth century), Königsberg and Limburg, Kiev, and, finally, Moscow, the outpost of Europe, founded in the twelfth century. The urban bourgeoisie in these regions was neither important nor influential, whether because of its foreign origin or because of the narrow scope of action of the towns. It remained, as has been said of Poland, like " drops of oil " scattered over the vast ocean of rural population.

Nevertheless, the transformation in the political and economic life of these countries brought about profound changes in their social organization. It accelerated the disappearance of collective tribal property among the majority of the peoples, and led to an alteration in the old communal family property. If the latter survived as a social framework, with its characteristic traits of labour in common, the equal partition of produce, and the authority of the chiefs, nevertheless its land ceased to be inalienable and indivisible. Its acquisitions could be alienated, and the right of dividing, selling, even of giving away the immovable wealth of the family, and the land itself, was recognized, as was testamentary disposition and the succession of women, in the absence of male heirs. Private property increased at its expense and at the expense of tribal property. Kings and princes hastened to build up vast domains for themselves, peopled with cultivators; they appropriated the major part of the forests and wastelands, and claimed possession of the mineral subsoil; but they could not preserve their landed possessions from usurpation and alienation. The Church, by means of gifts, colonization, and purchase, patiently built up immense territorial possessions, comprising in certain countries, such as Hungary, Bohemia, Poland, and Russia, a half or two-thirds of the soil. A nobility was organized, in general neither close nor hereditary, made up of old tribal chieftains on the one hand, and rich landowners, officials, soldiers, and the companions of princes on the other. It approached with increasing closeness in the Balkan countries to the organization of the Byzantine nobility, and in the rest of Europe, even in Russia, to the institutions of Western feudalism. It had its *alleux* and its fiefs, its domains which resembled the English manor, the French *seigneurie*, or the German *grundherrschaft*, and which were divided up into holdings cultivated by the labour of peasants.

The small free property and the class of peasant smallholders, which had been so important in these regions before the thirteenth century, fell under the domination of these new powers, the Crown, the Church, and the feudal lords. The dependence of this class, either under the form of the Byzantine colonate or that of the Western villeinage, left the cultivator his personal liberty and the perpetual usufruct of the soil, but took from him his property in the land and submitted him to poll tax, rents and labour services. Such was the condition of the rural masses known as *meropsi* and *kmetons* among the Serbs, Slovenes, Poles, and Czechs, *drabans* in Roumania, *udvornici* in Hungary, and *moujiks* and *smerdes* in Russia. A part of the vanquished or impoverished population was even reduced to serfdom, under the influence of aristocratic ideas of German or Byzantine origin. In Bulgaria, Serbia, and Slovenia the *obrotsi*, *atroesi*, and *pariki* were assimilated to the Byzantine *paroikoi*. In Hungary, Bohemia, Poland, and Russia serfdom made continual strides from the thirteenth century onwards. Though, under the sway of Christian ideas and a better understanding of economic interests, rural slavery disappeared completely in Croatia and became rare in Hungary, Bohemia, and Poland, it survived and was even extended in the more backward lands, such as Lithuania and Russia.

In the south and centre, among the Serbs, Moldavians, Croats, Czechs, and Poles, the rural population, scattered in hamlets and villages, profited in part, though far less than in the West, from the advantages of colonization and the diffusion of Christian civilization. In the East, in Russia, they remained in a condition not far removed from Asiatic barbarism. Everywhere epidemics and more frequent famines, and the rude conditions of social life which still persisted, made their existence unstable and hard, although its uncertainty was lessened by the powerful solidarity maintained by the old communal institutions of family and village.

In the north of Europe the three Scandinavian states did not begin to make acquaintance with civilized life until the tenth and eleventh centuries, when they were converted to Christianity. Before this time their inhabitants, the Northmen, were divided into a number of tribes and confederations, and lived chiefly by piracy. Their economic and social organization differed little from that of the ancient Germans, their brothers by race. Like these, they practised agriculture hardly at all, and their principal resources came from fishing, hunting, the exploitation of their forests, and cattle-raising. One part of the soil belonged to the tribes, and another to village communities, which enjoyed the undivided land in common. Private property was limited to the family; each family group held in collective ownership an *odhal*, inalienable and transmissible only to males, which was made up of its own property and acquisitions, and comprised only a house (*topt*), with the enclosure round it, and the land (*ornum*) acquired by clearance. In Denmark each of these patriarchal domains usually comprised about thirty-six acres. The rest of the land, which devolved to each family, was composed of a number of parcels, long and narrow strips, which the village community divided annually by a sort of system of lot, and the size of which was measured by the throw of a hammer or axe, or else by means of a cord. In one such village in Sweden twenty families thus divided among themselves 5,600 lots of land. Round each village (*by*) stretched pastures and forests.

An energetic population of freemen, sailors, fishermen, herds, woodmen, cattle-raisers, and farmers lived upon this vast and half-empty stretch of territory, a great part of which was covered with wood, marsh, and heath, under a severe climate. There were little more than a million inhabitants in the whole area, which was twice as large as France. Denmark, the most populous part, contained 550,000 in the eighth century and 900,000 in the tenth. The greater number were freemen, of whom there were 200,000 in Denmark in the ninth century, holding 12,000 domains. They were by nature fierce and disinclined for labour, living by warfare or the chase, and they recognized no superior authority save that of kings, tribal chiefs (*jarls*), nobles (*adelings*), rich landowners, and the *comitatus* of warriors (*huskarls, landemen*), princes who possessed no privileges and who were distinguished from the ordinary freemen only by wealth, tradition, or function. The cultivation of the land and the raising of cattle was left to slaves, descendants of the aboriginal populations, prisoners of war, condemned criminals, or insolvent debtors. The Scandinavians had for long lived in a state of barbarism, aggravated by the bloodthirsty religion of Odin. The terror of Christian Europe, these piratical "sea kings" had carried destruction and death from the Dnieper to the coasts of Spain. They had formed new settlements in the tenth century in Western Europe and Russia. Finally, they created the first stable states of the north, the three kingdoms of Sweden, Norway, and Denmark.

In adopting Christianity, not without difficulty, they came under the influence of Western civilization, which was brought to them by the Anglo-Saxons, the Germans, and the French monastic Orders. The first benefit reaped from this evolution was the conquest of the soil by colonization. Under the impulse of princes and monks, bands of peasants set themselves to protect the low-lying coasts of Zeeland and Jutland by dykes, to drain marshes and convert them into meadows, and to establish fisheries and water-mills on the rivers. On all sides monastic colonies and village communities attacked the immense Scandinavian forest, and established grass farms with huge herds of cows, isolated domains in which pioneers settled—above all, in the north and east—and villages of colonists, Danish *thorpes*, Norwegian *sœters*, Swedish *bodas*. The Danish plain, Jutland, Zeeland, Fuhnen, Southern Sweden, Skaania, Ostrogothia, Nericia, Vermland, and Upland were the first to be colonized, and were soon covered with meadows and ploughlands.

The Norwegian and Swedish pioneers penetrated resolutely into the central and southern regions—Svealand, Dalecarlia, Norrland, and Finmark—the home before the tenth century of wandering tribes of Finns and Lapps, whom they now drove before them. Through the great forest—first along the coast and then inland—were scattered their cattle-farms and their camps of woodcutters. Soon, in the twelfth and thirteenth centuries, the Danes even sent warlike agricultural colonies to swarm over the lands of the Obotrite Slavs in Mecklenburg and Western Pomerania, and among the Esthonians on the eastern shores of the Baltic. On their side, the Swedes colonized the Aaland Islands, Ingria, Carelia, and Finland, where they established villages of free peasants; and the Norwegians scattered fishing stations all along the Biarmic coast as far as the White Sea.

At the same time they exploited the resources of lakes, rivers, and seas, caught the eider-duck, the whale, the cod, and the seal in the north, and salmon and herring in the Baltic. From their forests, which were still abundant in spite of clearances, they obtained timber, pitch, tar, potash, ashes, and the furs of wild beasts, with which they supplied the West. Model farms were created, notably on the Cistercian estates, and cattle-breeding was improved. Denmark bred strong battle palfreys and draught horses, as well as horned cattle, and so also did Sweden and Norway. Like England, Scandinavia was one of the most active centres for the exportation of butter, cheese, fats, lard, grease, and strong hides. Even the ploughlands made some progress in spite of extensive methods—the triennial fallow, the compulsory rotation of crops and cultivation in common. The use of farm manure and peat became more general; the iron ploughshare and the practice of ploughing deep appeared. Southern Sweden, particularly Skaania and Denmark, produced rye, oats, barley, and corn. The Cistercians introduced horticulture and perfected aboriculture. Flax, hemp, and hops were cultivated over wider areas.

A regular trade now appeared, and in the twelfth century a money economy; from the eleventh century Denmark had struck silver coins (the *rixdales*), in imitation of Germany. But movable wealth was comparatively small, and credit rare and expensive; the legal rate of interest in the thirteenth century still varied between $10\frac{1}{2}$ and $20\frac{1}{2}$ per cent. Nevertheless, roads were established and internal navigation was organized. An active national marine was created in Denmark and Norway, and, before it was crushed by the Hanseatic monopoly, Scandinavian trade reigned supreme in the Baltic and in the seas and glacial ocean of the north. It even established direct relations with the West and the Levant.

In the newly founded towns—Trondhjem (997), Bergen, Copenhagen (1168), Roskild, Odense, Lund, Wisby (the great port of Gothland) Stockholm (thirteenth century), Calmar, Norrköping, Abo—workshops and associations of artisans arose, and likewise merchant gilds on the German model, over and above the old family and domestic industry. The first metallurgical industries, in the shape of small forges, were created in Sweden, beside the seams of copper and iron, which were uncovered and worked by Scandinavian and German miners in Dalecarlia. Finally, France gave to the Scandinavian states their first architects and the promoters of their industrial arts.

Nevertheless, Scandinavia, like Eastern Europe, remained primarily a region in which natural economy held sway. Private property, it is true, soon took the place of collective property, and the tribes lost their undivided lands, while those belonging to the village community diminished by dint of alienations, partitions under definite titles of possession, and the appropriations which followed upon clearances. Family property itself could be divided among co-heirs, even women. Nevertheless, by reason of the vast extent of forests and uncultivated lands, common lands remained numerous and comprised about half the soil of Sweden and Norway. Kings built up large domains for themselves and claimed the ownership of fisheries and mines. The secular and monastic Church got possession of the greater part of the appropriated soil. One archbishop of Lund alone possessed three-quarters of Bornholm and the district of Aarrhus. A nobility was constituted on the model of Germanic chivalry, provided itself with fiefs, sought to make itself hereditary, and seized a large part of the land.

Nevertheless, it did not succeed in eliminating the class of small peasant owners, who remained numerous and influential until the fourteenth century, except in Denmark and Skaania, where they fell into a condition analogous to that of villeins, and sometimes amalgamated with the ex-slaves, whom Christianity had freed. In the same way tenant-farmers and free day labourers made their appearance. Under this régime the Scandinavian countries were able to attain a certain degree of prosperity. Their material condition improved; there were few paupers among them, and population grew; it almost doubled in Denmark, where in the country districts alone in the middle of the thirteenth century it numbered as many as 1,500,000 souls, and in the six bishoprics of Sweden in 1320 it reached the figure of 384,000. A crowd of new villages (*thorpes*) were created side by side with the old *bys*, apart from the isolated farms (*gaardes*) and châlets (*sätters*). Up to the fourteenth century the rural masses of Scandinavia, whose life was rough and simple, seem to have enjoyed a certain ease of existence and fairly extensive local liberties. Family life remained powerful, and associations of all kinds—religious, charitable, and economic —multiplied. Without attaining as great a height of development as the West, Scandinavia, like Eastern Europe, reached, under the beneficent influence of Latin, Germanic, and Christian civilization, a degree of prosperity unknown to it in the barbarian period, and not even equalled in modern times.

Thus in the history of labour the first three centuries and a half of the Middle Ages is one of those capital periods during which some of the most important works of progress which have transformed human societies were accomplished. The work of Ancient Rome herself and of all antiquity had been surpassed. In the East, North, Centre, and West of Europe the barbarian world had been conquered and civilized by means of the combined action of Christianity and of the new civilization of the West. After the first feudal age, a necessary marking time, in order that the military structure of medieval society might be organized and that it might be preserved from a renewed offensive by the invaders, after two centuries, in which the aristocratic and clerical castes had monopolized landownership, made villeinage and serfdom general, and submitted the rural population to the yoke of a dearly purchased protection, the dawn of a renaissance had shone upon Christendom, at length emerged from its isolation.

The great stream of trade had begun to flow again, more

ample than before. An immense commercial development had brought with it the appearance of a money economy, the transformation of industry, and the formation of a bourgeoisie and an urban civilization. The commercial and industrial classes had, for the first time, united to conquer liberty and even privileges for themselves. For the first time the labouring masses had won for themselves a place in society worthy of their social value and economic rôle. They had become real powers, strong in their associations and had attained a degree of independence and comfort hitherto unknown. On the other hand, it had been necessary to exploit the soil to its utmost, and parallel with the grand work of the industrial and commercial renaissance, accompanied as it was by the emancipation of the urban populations, had gone that magnificent labour of agricultural colonization and the liberation of the rural classes which changed the face of Europe.

The greater production of wealth had allowed the number of human settlements to be vastly increased. Christian Europe had been so effectively renewed at the beginning of the fourteenth century that its people grew and multiplied and everywhere founded towns and villages, while population, double what it had been in the European provinces of the Roman Empire, had reached the figure of sixty to seventy millions. Never in the whole history of labour had such far-reaching results been obtained by the work of man. Then was seen the spectacle, unimagined by all the generations which had gone before, of multitudes of free human beings, enjoying the rights of man, and breathing a new air of liberty, whetting their energies by the conquest of independence and by the play of their multifarious activity, developing all the resources of their strength and initiative, and, above all, tasting the joy and sweetness of life, in the framework of an existence which was still simple enough to escape the economic uncertainties of modern society.

BOOK III

CHAPTER I

POLITICAL, SOCIAL, AND DEMOGRAPHICAL DISTURBANCES AT THE CLOSE
OF THE MIDDLE AGES, AND THE BIRTH OF A NATIONAL ECONOMY
(1340-1453).

DURING the last century of the Middle Ages, between
the beginning and end of the Hundred Years' War, a new
Europe was created in the throes of long and painful birth-
pangs. The different nationalities hurled themselves against
each other from West to East, and grew strong by dint of
their violent struggles. In the East and South-East, Asiatic
barbarism once more began its assaults upon Christendom,
and submerged a large part of Eastern Europe. Civil and
religious wars increased the confusion and added their evils
to those brought about by the conflicts of peoples and races.
At the same time the political and social forces of the past
broke up. The Church, corrupted by wealth and weakened
by heresy, shut itself up in its selfishness and resigned itself
to the rôle of a parasite, abandoning the leadership of the
Christian commonwealth and ceasing to promote economic
progress. Everywhere feudalism showed itself more and
more devoid of the qualities indispensable to the art of
government, and able only to renew and perpetuate
anarchy. It lost its military prestige at Crécy, Poitiers,
Nicopolis and Agincourt, and in the Hussite wars. It became a mere court nobility, vowed to the service of princes,
and lived henceforth only by exploiting its tenants, or, worse
still, by rapine and brigandage.

The urban bourgeoisie, the power of which grew in the
Low Countries and Central and Northern Italy in the fourteenth century and in Germany until the end of the
fifteenth, showed a superior political sense. But the
municipal government was no longer able to give adequate
protection to the various groups under its shelter. Moreover, communal patriotism waned in the midst of the social
struggles which were now let loose, and urban prosperity was
often menaced. The horizon of town life narrowed, and the

commune, which had been in the preceding period the standard-bearer of emancipation and progress, finally became an agent of particularism and tyranny in the realm of economic activity, opposing by its spirit of exclusiveness, monopoly, and excessive regulation the development of new and larger societies.

In place of the old dying feudal economy, and above the decaying urban economy, a national economy was organized and developed. Its framework was the monarchical or princely state, in which were merged the old local sovereignties. With much uncertain groping, under the influence of the maxims of Roman Law, and impelled by the pressure of necessity, the state became conscious of its rights and of its duties towards the community, especially in the West. In the Low Countries, France, Italy, Spain, England, and at times even in other parts of Europe, sovereigns showed themselves possessed of an economic policy, sometimes incoherent, but every day more active. Their power and prestige often depended upon the manner in which they carried it out. The Italian princes, the dukes of Burgundy, certain of the Valois kings, such as Charles V, owed some part of their popularity and their ascendancy to it. This policy had for its object the increase of national wealth, the expansion of all kinds of business enterprises, and the satisfaction of popular needs. It sought to maintain a due proportion between production and consumption, to stimulate the one and to supply the needs of the other. In order to accomplish this the royal power essayed to establish centralized institutions, to rely upon the support of the middle classes, and to submit Church, feudal nobles, and communes to its authority, despoiling them of their economic prerogatives or bringing them under its own control. Not only did it attempt to maintain or restore order and public peace by creating administrative machinery, law-courts, finances, and regular armies, but it also intervened more or less continuously, and with more or less happy results, in the organization of production and in the relations of the labouring classes.

It lent its support to agricultural colonization, to works of embankment and drainage, and to the destruction of wild beasts, as may be seen in the history of Spain, Italy, the Low Countries, France, and Portugal. It was at pains to preserve by protective legislation natural wealth such as waters and forests, preventing their wasteful exploitation and encouraging the clearance of wasteland and the immigration of cultivators. In one place it tried to develop cattle-raising, as in Spain, and in another rich crops, such as rice in Italy; everywhere it encouraged the production of cereals. In the Low Countries the princes of the house of Burgundy favoured the spread of rural industries, and protected them against the intolerance of the towns. Anxious to maintain an abundant supply of labour and low prices in the country districts, the sovereigns helped landed proprietors against the flight and the exactions of agricultural wage-earners by measures of taxation and coercion. At the same time they favoured the emancipation of serfs (for example, in Spain) and almost everywhere they made meritorious efforts to prevent the restoration of serfdom.

Everywhere royal legislation forbade the seizure of ploughshares and beasts of labour, sometimes even of the seed and provisions necessary for the subsistence of the peasant. Often it granted temporary exemption from taxation to cultivators in order to encourage their efforts. The monarchical state sought to establish a protection over the rural masses, which should preserve them from the excesses of its own agents and, above all, of the old feudal powers. Charles V (the Wise) in France went as far as to permit the peasants to beat those royal officials who tried to exercise the right of purveyance of carts and fodder without payment. In Bohemia Charles IV invited all peasants who had suffered wrong by seigniorial exactions to bring their complaints to him, under the guarantee of his protection. The royal power began to exercise a control over excessive tolls and labour services. It allowed the country folk to claim their stolen commons from the lords and to have recourse to royal justice against feudal abuses. Nevertheless, it was careful to maintain the essential prerogatives of the privileged social classes; its economic policy was not at all revolutionary; it was even, as a rule, timid and hesitating, so intent was it upon maintaining a sort of unstable equilibrium between its different classes of subjects, between the spirit of tradition and the spirit of progress.

LIFE AND WORK IN MEDIEVAL EUROPE

The same principles also informed the rising national economy in the domain of industry and commerce. To increase the resources of the state, by augmenting the production of the workshops and the circulation of manufactures, to maintain the authority of the central power over the trading and working classes, while at the same time seconding their efforts and endowing them with privileges, these were the motives with which sovereigns were inspired. In the majority of states, the princes took the initiative in the reorganization or creation of industries, they supported the exploitation of mineral wealth and the establishment of metallurgical works. They called in from abroad entrepreneurs or workers who could introduce new industrial specialities, such as silks in France, fine cloths in England, and the manufacture of mixed fabrics of silk and wool in Italy. Under their protection glass and porcelain works were organized, and, above all, the artistic and luxury industries, to which they lent an intelligent patronage, notably in the Italian states, France, the Low Countries, and Bohemia. Without entirely removing the control of industry from the old powers and, in particular, from the towns, the monarchical state brought the concession of statutes to crafts and the promulgation of economic regulations into increasing subordination to its authority. Sometimes, in order to overcome the abuses of the corporative monopolies, it decreed freedom of profession and authorized any capable artisan to establish himself and " do loyal work or merchandise," as John the Good of France expressed it in his ordinance of 1351, and Richard II of England in that of 1394; at other times, on the contrary, after periods of crisis, it provoked and encouraged the formation of privileged corporations, in order to favour the re-establishment of production. It even began to arrogate to itself the right of authorizing artisans to work independently outside the bounds of the corporation, by virtue of royal letters of mastership. It brought under its control the whole world of workers, free crafts and sworn corporations, regulated their organization and discipline, superintended their administration and police, imposed governors upon them at need, and submitted them to fiscal and military obligations. Representing the general interest, it forced industry and commerce to observe rules of manufacture and sale, intervened, if necessary, to forbid coalitions of masters, rings and monopolies, as well as unions and fraternities of workers, and fixed wages and prices. Thus there grew daily stronger a sort of unconscious state socialism, the manifestations of which were to increase enormously in the course of the modern period.

No less anxious for the progress of trade than for that of production, the royal power showed a more or less effective zeal to secure the position of both. It encouraged by grants of privilege the formation of commercial associations, such as the wholesale mercers and the merchants who frequented the River Loire in France, the Staplers and Merchant Adventurers in England, and the Hansards in Germany. Torn between aristocratic prejudices and the national interest, the princes sometimes forbade the nobles to take up commerce, and sometimes (as under the Valois kings) authorized them to do so. In general, they were so well aware of the power of the merchant class that they often associated it with the government. They dimly descried an economic policy, the principles and direction of which they could not yet distinguish very clearly. They understood the need for a strong organization of credit, and yet they bowed to popular prejudices and to the antiquated suggestions of the canon law, and sometimes prohibited loans at interest, which were confounded with usury, and took measures of intermittent severity against Jews and Lombards.

They guessed sometimes, as did Charles V of France, the English Plantagenets, and the Dukes of Burgundy, how great was the advantage of a stable coinage, yet they occasionally gave way to the deceptive temptations of the old fiscal ideas, and tried to make money by debasing the coinage, as John the Good did eighteen times in a single year. In general, they tried to realize the ideal of a single coinage and to prevent the export of precious metals and of the currency, to regulate exchanges, and to introduce a little order into the chaos of feudal economy. Similarly, they attempted to ordain uniform weights and measures, notably in France and England. They saw the necessity of maintaining and improving roads, and made roadmaking and road preservation one of the essential prerogatives of the central power. They favoured inland navigation and companies for river transport, laid an axe to the sprouting vegetation of seigniorial tolls, conceived the first idea of a public service of bridges and highways, and in Italy, Germany, and France at the end of the Middle Ages even inaugurated public posts and passenger services.

Inexperienced and hesitating, the royal commercial policy picked its way between prohibition, protection, privileges, and monopolies on the one hand, and free competition on the other. Yet if the intervention of the state in the mechanism of trade remained narrow and irritating, incoherent and contradictory, it did have the merit that it favoured the creation and prosperity of markets and fairs, of merchant marines and navies, and opened foreign markets by means of commercial treaties, attracting merchant strangers, and giving a fruitful impulse to commercial relations.

The national economy was nevertheless unable to bear all its fruits in the midst of the political and social crisis in which the whole of Europe was struggling, and to which there was added a severe crisis in population. The latter was brought about by the massacres provoked by the great wars which were then bleeding Christendom white, by the ravages of bands of brigands, and by the excesses of religious fanaticism. Famines reappeared more frequently than ever in the devastated regions. Those of 1343, in Austria, and of 1351, 1359, and 1418, in France, left particularly terrible memories behind. The last carried off over 100,000 persons in Paris, where groups of twenty or thirty poor wretches at a time died of starvation on the dung-heaps, and where wolves came to devour the corpses. Earthquakes shook the ground, and one of them, in 1347-48, destroyed Villach and thirty little townships of Carinthia, while in the Netherlands the sea redoubled its murderous assaults. But worst of all were the ravages of epidemic maladies, leprosy, and typhus, which raged among the masses, who were already weak from want and wretchedness.

The most famous of these epidemics, the Black Death, or bubonic plague, which came from Asia, ravaged all the countries of Europe in turn from 1348 to 1350, and carried off two-thirds of the population of Central Italy; a third, a half, and sometimes two-thirds of the inhabitants of Lombardy, Northern Spain, France, England, the Low Countries, and Germany; a half or two-thirds in the Scandinavian and East European countries. The towns were attacked with special severity. Venice lost two-thirds of its population; Bologna, four-fifths; Florence, 80,000 to 100,000 souls; Majorca, 30,000; Narbonne, 30,000; Paris over 50,000; Strassburg and Bâle, 14,000 each; Vienna, 40,000. There were 300 deaths a day at Saragossa; at Avignon, 400; at Paris, 800; at London, 200. The scourge made new attacks from time to time in different places; it reappeared nine times in Italy, where it carried off 4,000 peasants in 1399, four times in Spain between 1381 and 1444, six times in France between 1361 and 1436, on which last occasion it cost 5,000 Parisians their lives. It paid five visits to England between 1361 and 1391, and in 1382 it is said to have destroyed a fifth of the population and caused a loss of life of 11,000 in York. From 1363 to 1391 it again ran through Germany and Poland, and 30,000 people died of it in one year in Breslau, 20,000 in Cracow, and from a half to two-thirds of the inhabitants of Silesia. It was a disaster for Europe comparable with, and perhaps greater than, that of the late world war. As far as can be calculated it cost from twenty-four to twenty-five million human lives. It brought about an unexampled scarcity of labour, which resulted in a series of economic and social crises of extreme gravity, lasting for half a century. Work was disorganized, and to the confusion engendered by the great changes which had taken place in the states and in society, there was added the confusion resulting from a diminution of human capital and of the productive power of the European peoples.

CHAPTER II

TRANSFORMATION AND PROGRESS OF COMMERCE AND INDUSTRY IN EUROPE
AT THE CLOSE OF THE MIDDLE AGES.

IN spite of these crises and "growing-pains," European commerce developed in the course of the last century of the Middle Ages, chiefly to the benefit of those states which were most free from attack, or which were the soonest to repair the ruin which had been spread by the scourges of war and of epidemics. It was then that the future commercial organization of modern times took shape. In spite of the deep-rooted prejudices which prevailed on the subject of business enterprise, the needs of consumption and of luxury, as well as the growing profits to be drawn from commercial operations, gave a vigorous impetus to the trading powers—Italy, the South of France, Eastern Spain and Portugal, the Low Countries, and Germany.

Large-scale international commerce grew in vitality and initiative, its organization became more complicated, and it withdrew more and more from the bonds of urban economy and engaged by preference in wholesale and commission trade. New and more or less extensive associations were formed, often on the joint share principle, sometimes carrying on only a limited commerce, sometimes engaging in numerous varieties of traffic, sometimes even in banking and exchange, and supplanting the old gilds, which were too set in their limited circle of local or regional transactions. Such were the English livery companies, the six merchant corporations of Paris, the " arti maggiori " of Florence, and, above all, the Florentine arte of the Calimala, the French federation of mercers, the British companies of the Staple and Merchant Adventurers, the Hanses of the carrying or export traders of France, Germany, and Prussia. The most famous, the German Hanseatic League, included fifty-two towns in 1360, and eighty to ninety between 1450 and 1500.

It was under the influence of the great merchants who carried on the export or carrying trade that the mechanism of commercial operations was perfected. Means of information multiplied, in the shape of manuals and treatises on business, exchange, and jurisprudence, as well as accounts of journeys. The systems of account by double entry and of trade-marks which could be granted and transmitted made their appearance. The great commerce collected a whole army of clerks, porters, couriers, commissioners, interpreters, and messengers for its service. It organized meeting-places—bourses or exchanges—splendid buildings such as those of Genoa, Venice, Palma, Valencia, and Bruges. It had its representatives at the courts of princes, and its special justice, which was swifter than that of the ordinary tribunals; it elaborated a special merchant law, which took the place of canon law and approached more nearly to the civil law.

It laboured to improve means of communication. Under its care old roads were repaired; in the fifteenth century there were 25,000 kilometres of them in France alone. The West was henceforth well provided with roads, and communication with the Mediterranean over the Alpine passes was easy. In the fourteenth century the convoys of merchandise allowed no more than thirty-five days for the journey from Paris to Naples via the Mount Cenis pass. Services of carriers and posts were established in Italy, the Low Countries, France, and Southern Germany. River navigation was managed by great transport companies, which dug out and buoyed river beds and established river ports. The first sluice locks were invented in Lombardy, and the first navigable canal was opened between the Baltic and the Elbe. On the Loire alone merchandise worth nine million francs was carried annually.

War had, indeed, destroyed the vitality of the French fairs, notably those of Champagne; but others prospered in Italy, Switzerland, Germany, and Spain, and in particular at Florence, where business to the amount of fifteen or sixteen million francs was transacted every year, and at Geneva, Cologne, Frankfort, and Bruges. In spite of a chaotic Customs system and a régime which was often marked by all the old exclusiveness, colonies of merchant strangers were the recipients of consideration and favour. States were united by treaties of commerce. A money economy spread throughout all civilized countries, and it has been calculated that at this period 15 to 40 per cent. of all business was done in coin, and that the stock of circulating money in the West reached in the fifteenth century the value of a milliard of francs. The anarchy of the monetary system decreased with the increasing employment of the great metallic species and with the diffusion of international coins, florins, and Italian ducats, the standard of which was fixed and invariable.

Loans on pledges, or for short periods at very high rates, were no longer used by any but individual debtors; the rule of Jew and Lombard declined, as a breach was made in their monopoly by the *monts de piété* and the popular banks which were set up in Italy and Germany. Less burdensome forms of credit became general, such as loans on a limited partnership basis or on joint account, and advances on merchandise and on negotiable securities. Bills of exchange became supple instruments of commercial circulation, permitting the operations of merchants and bankers to be carried on without the transfer of bullion, and the value of goods exchanged to be mobilized. In Italy and Germany commerce obtained credit at the rate of 4 per cent. to 10 per cent., instead of the 20 per cent. to 86 per cent. demanded by the Jews and Lombards. Powerful Italian banking companies—Florentine, Sienese, Luchhese, Venetian, Lombard, Piedmontese, and Genoese—covered Europe with a network of counting-houses and spread far and wide an already advanced banking system, by no means limited to exchange operations, but extending increasingly to the recovery of taxes, the negotiation of loans to collective or individual borrowers, the deposit of money, current accounts, clearance, and the discounting of bills. Associations of Spanish, German, French, and Flemish bankers were organized in imitation of these Italians. The first state banks even made their appearance in Venice, Genoa, Barcelona, Strasburg, Nuremburg, Frankfort, Hamburg, and Augsburg. The trade in money became definitely one of the vital branches of European economic organization.

Maritime commerce extended in scope in spite of the obstacles which it met with in customs systems, and in survivals of the old feudal economy. The right of reprisal was regulated; maritime courts or courts of Admiralty were set up; letters of marque were limited; an attempt was made to eradicate the endemic evil of piracy; armed escorts were organized to convoy the merchant fleets. In imitation of the Italian cities, such as Venice, which then possessed 3,300 ships manned by 36,000 sailors, the Western powers equipped navies. Barcelona and the Balearic Isles owned 660 vessels and 30,000 mariners, and France had at one time 200 great warships with 20,000 sailors on the sea.

Western commerce now set out to discover the world; nautical science was perfected, the compass came into general use, marine cartography advanced owing to the work of the Venetians, Genoese, and Catalans. The resources of Muscovy and of Central and Eastern Asia began to be known. The Italians sent their commercial agents as far as the Soudan. The Spaniards and Normans explored the coasts of Africa and discovered the Canaries in the four-teenth century, the Portuguese discovered Senegal, the Azores, Cape Verde, the Congo, and the Guinea Coast in the fifteenth century, the sailors of Dieppe reached the Ivory Coast, and the Bretons Terra Nuova. Already the world saw the beginning of that great movement which was later to reveal to it the marvels of the Indies and the New World.

The Mediterranean remained the chief centre of world commerce, and Italy kept the chief place in it. Venice had replaced Byzantium and had become the greatest entrepôt for merchandise in the world, and the Venetians passed for "lords of the gold of all Christendom." They imported annually from the East at the beginning of the fifteenth century ten million ducats worth of goods, more than a third of which came from India, and they bought in Egypt alone goods to the value of a million pounds. After them other Italian powers—Genoa and Florence—shared in the trade of the Black Sea and the Archipelago, Western Asia and Northern Africa, which was a source of immense profit. To this they added trade with the West, where in the fourteenth and fifteenth centuries they established a crowd of counting-houses at Lyons, Paris, Rouen, London, Bruges, Antwerp, and many other places; and they traded also with the distant lands of Central and Eastern Europe. Side by side with them the Spaniards and Portuguese prepared them-

selves for the great part which they were to play in the age
of discoveries. Barcelona, Parma, and Valencia disputed
the empire of the Mediterranean and the African trade.
Catalans, Castilians, Basques, and Portuguese set up "factories" on all the coasts of the Atlantic, from La Rochelle
to Bruges and London, and also in the interior of the
Continent.

France, whose commerce was ruined by the Hundred
Years' War, recovered her marvellous vitality from the time
of Charles VIII, renewed her commercial relations with all
Europe, and, thanks to Jacques Cœur, once more took up
her trade with the Levant. England herself, awaking at last
to a presentiment of her commercial vocation, persevered
until she had built up a mercantile marine, equipped her
ports—London, Bristol, Hull, and Newcastle—and developed
her trade with her Continental possessions and with the
Low Countries, Germany, and the Northern States.

The Low Countries and Germany disputed with Italy the
hegemony of the commercial world. The former, profiting
by their privileged position at the juncture of the great
international trade routes, almost monopolized the carrying
trade between the north and south and the east and centre
of Europe. Bruges was the hub, and rivalled Venice in its
thronging trade as well as in its beautiful buildings; in
1435, 100 ships sailed into its port daily, and its wealth and
splendour dazzled the world. Antwerp, thanks to its
franchises and to the widening of the Scheldt, began its
career of prosperity, drawing to itself all the trade of
Brabant, and from 1442 began to threaten the supremacy
of Bruges, while in the north the Netherlands ports of
Middleburg, Flushing, Rotterdam, and Amsterdam supplanted the old "staples" of Hardwyck and Dordrecht,
thus preparing the way for the future "carriers of the
sea."

Germany, which had developed a commercial life rather
late, had with her native tenacity succeeded in winning herself an eminent place among the commercial powers. She
had attracted a good proportion of the trade of Europe to
her land routes and her great rivers. On the Rhine a league
of 60 river cities created a fleet of 600 ships; the Rhenish
merchants, like the Flemings, grew rich on the carrying

trade in the " golden city " of Strasburg, in Frankfort-on-Main, and, above all, in Cologne. The Danube towns reached an unprecedented degree of prosperity through their relations with the East, Italy, and the Levant; Ulm drew a revenue of half a million florins annually from this trade, and Augsburg and Nuremburg, more active still, " held the world in their hand," as the emphatic German proverb ran.

In the north, east, and west the Teutonic Hanse made a veritable empire for itself and turned Germany towards sea trade. Formed in 1241 by the free association of a small number of trading cities of Low Germany, chief among which was Lübeck, the League a century and a half later included over a hundred, spread over four districts or " quarters," from the Sudetes to the Baltic, and from the Scheldt to the great lakes of Russia. This powerful federation, which had four capitals — Cologne, Brunswick, Lübeck, and Dantzig—and which contained all the chief trading cities of the Low Countries, Germany, and Eastern Europe, notably Amsterdam, Bremen, Hamburg, Magdeburg, Stettin, Breslau, Königsburg, and Riga, was a real mercantile state. It had its diets and general assemblies which promulgated regulations and decrees (*recessen*), its taxes, its treasury, its tribunals, and even its armorial bearings. It carried on an active and sometimes arrogant diplomacy, concluded commercial treaties, and made its flag known and respected everywhere. It set up its factories in Russia, Scandinavia, Poland, and Flanders—veritable fortresses with garrisons as well as warehouses, inhabited by the members or by clerks (there were two or three thousand of them, for example, at Bergen), who were submitted to an iron discipline and animated by an intransigent sort of mercantile patriotism. Its merchant fleet, with admirably trained crews, was protected by a navy of warships, which secured the safety of the convoys and waged a merciless struggle against piracy.

The Hanse was the rough school in which Germany formed her sailors and her explorers. It pacified the northern seas, founded the first great ports there, and brought about the prevalence of a uniform commercial legislation. It tried to unify measures and to regulate the exchanges. But its ideal was a sort of economic imperialism, selfish, brutal, and coarse, which trampled underfoot the interests and lawful rights of the weaker nations and exercised a kind of tyranny over them, at Bergen, Novgorod, and London, seeking to monopolize all trade and to destroy the national commerce of Scandinavia, Russia, and England, and thus rousing an inexpiable hatred against itself.

Thus Western Europe, continuing its former work, had developed trade everywhere, on sea and on land, had added to Mediterranean commerce that of the Atlantic and the northern seas, and had foreshadowed the new orientation of the great trade routes, which was to appear so clearly in the modern period.

Towards the close of the Middle Ages there also began a new industrial revolution, brought about by the progress of credit, trade, and consumption. Everywhere, side by side with the small industry carried on at home or on the great domains, which maintained its widespread activity, particularly in districts where a natural economy still predominated, the small urban industry spread, with its workshops, its free crafts, and its sworn corporations. It maintained an undeniable superiority all over Europe, especially in the West.

But already the great industry, which had begun its conquests during the preceding period, was continuing them with yet more success in the new age. Better adapted to the exigences of national and international economy, more easily able to furnish wide markets, more remunerative for capitalists in search of profits, it extended step by step, first to the manufacture of cloth, then to mines, then to metallurgical enterprises, glassworks, potteries, printing-presses. Sometimes it made use of pre-existing organizations, and enrolled in its service isolated workmen, or artisans grouped into crafts and corporations, to whom it distributed orders and whose work it regulated. Sometimes it organized veritable factories containing 120 weavers, as at Amiens in 1371, or 120 printers, as at Nuremberg after 1450. Under its influence the new rural industry was organized, out of reach of the rules and hindrances of the urban government and the gild system. The big entrepreneurs favoured it, because they could more easily impose their conditions, increase or reduce production at their will, and diminish their expenses, profiting by the smaller demands of peasant labour, while the peasants, on their side, found in the exercise of a craft, even though intermittent, an occupation for the dead season and an appreciable supplement to their means of existence. Rural industry soon prospered in most European countries, more especially in the Low Countries, France, Germany, England, and the Lowlands of Scotland, and even in Poland and Bohemia, under the direction of great merchants and entrepreneurs. It shared with the towns, and even sometimes lured away from them, the woollen and lace manufactures, many metallurgical trades, glass and paper-works, mines and ironworks, leaving to the urban centres more especially the principal food, clothing, and building trades and the luxury industries.

Industrial technique made considerable advances in specialization and perfection. In a fair number of industries, notably in the textile and cloth-dressing trades, great progress was made in specialization. The field of invention widened, and the employment of mechanical methods increased the productivity of human handiwork. Waterpower, which had already transformed certain industries, such as the crushing of grain or of oleaginous matters, was used more and more for the fulling of cloth and the preparation of tan and woodwork, as well as for the manufacture of paper. It was the power used to pump water out of saltpits and mines, to bring coal and minerals up to the surface, by means of special machinery, to cleanse them in buddles, to sort them on sliding tables, and to crush or break them up in crushing-mills. It was used to move the hammers which moulded metals and the grindstones which made them into tools. At the same time men learned how to regulate the use of wind in bellows, so as to obtain in their high and low blast furnaces a higher and more regular temperature and produce a larger quantity of metal. They learned how to employ the power furnished by vegetable and mineral fuel to better purpose in forges, glassworks, and potteries, and in Styria and in Germany were constructed the first blast furnaces, which were much more powerful than the old Catalan or Swedish hearths. Graduation houses and distillation works were set up in the salt industry. This growing use of machinery and technical innovations gave an already marked superiority to the industry of the last century of the Middle Ages.

The West continued to strengthen its hegemony over the East in the industrial sphere, and this despite the temporary eclipse of French industry. Italy, Germany, the Low Countries, Spain, and even new districts, rivalled each other in activity. The impetus was most marked in the mining, metallurgical, and textile industries. Men were no longer content to exploit the gold-strewn sands of the rivers. They now attacked the seams of yellow metal contained in the rocks of the Bohemian Mountains, the Carpathians, and the mountains of Carinthia and Transylvania. From the first of these gold to the value of 20,000,000 francs was extracted in 100 years, and the last brought the King of Hungary in 100,000 florins a year. Above all, silver-mines and argentiferous lead-mines were everywhere opened—in Italy, France, Sweden, Hungary, Poland, and especially in Alsace, the Harz Mountains, Saxony, Bohemia, and the Tyrol.

Before the discovery of Peru and Mexico, the Saxon, Czech, and Tyrolese mines furnished Europe with silver, which was more and more sought after. The Schwartz mines produced metal to the value of 40,000,000 francs in 200 years, those of Freiburg and Annaburg produced 1,300 to 20,000 kilogrammes a year, and those of Kutnahora, the Potosi of Bohemia, as much as 2,000,000 kilogrammes in three centuries. Everywhere, in the most favoured districts of Italy, France, and the Low Countries, flourished quarries of marble and of calcareous stone for building.

In Italy, Spain, Portugal, and, above all, France, sea salt was actively exploited, and the lagunes of Comacchio furnished 40,000 loads a year for export. The marshes of Saintonge, Bas-Poitou, and Brittany provided a great part of the West with salt. From the rock salt-mines of Transylvania the kings of Bohemia drew a revenue of 100,000 florins a year, and from those of Poland and Galicia the Jagellons derived over 100,000 thalers.

Men sought out and utilized more actively the iron-mines of Italy, Biscay, France, and Germany, the lead-mines of Brittany, the Harz Mountains, Devonshire, and Cornwall, the copper-mines of England and Germany, where the workings at Mannsfeld produced 8,000 to 30,000 hundredweights a year. In Sweden from 1347 the exploitation of the Kopparberg began, and in Hungary copper and sulphates were mined. From Cornwall and Devonshire a growing quantity of tin was obtained and exported, especially to Antwerp, where the trade reached a value of two million francs. The stannaries of Altenberg in Saxony and Ober Graupen in Bohemia quadrupled their output, which finally reached 1,000,000 tons a year and rivalled that of England. Poland exploited calamine and saltpetre, Spain mercury, Tuscany and the state of Rome alum. Coal began to be better appreciated, and the workings round Newcastle, Liège, Aix-la-Chapelle, and Dortmund became active. Pains were taken to develop the Italian, French, German, and Czech mineral and thermal springs.

The progress in metal working and in the military arts stimulated the metallurgical industries. For the first time it was possible by means of the blast furnace to increase the production of cast-iron, to keep the apparatus working from eight to twenty-five weeks in the year, and to produce directly ordinary raw iron. Germany, mistress of the art of mining, took the first place in the great metallurgical industries, and the French metallurgical enterprises, once so flourishing, now declined. A large number of forges were set up in Italy and Northern Spain, Hainault, the Namur district, the principality of Liège, and the German and Scandinavian countries. The use of the rolling-mill and the hydraulic hammer transformed the operations of rolling and hammering, and facilitated metal working. Bell foundries and gun foundries multiplied in Germany and the East of France. The Italian and German founders carried artistic cast-iron and bronze-work to a high degree of perfection. The fabrication of arms and of materials of war prospered in Italian, Spanish, French, and German workshops and in those of Liège. Nuremburg excelled in locksmith's work, ironmongery, hardware, and clock-making, surpassing the French manufactures. If the French invented brass wire, it was the Germans who resuscitated the making of edged tools, of nails, and of iron wire, leaving to Italy a quasi-monopoly of the medallist's and moneyer's art, and to the workshops of the Low Countries, at Dinant, Malines, and Douai, that of copper and pewter-work.

The textile industries enriched Italy above all. In that country Naples, Pisa, Siena, and, chief of all, Florence, Milan, and Venice worked at the fabrication of fine or dyed cloths for export. Florence at the beginning of the fifteenth century had 300 manufactories and 30,000 workmen, wove 100,000 pieces a year, and sold 16,000 of them in the Levant, while a single one of her merchant companies—the *Calimala* —made 300,000 golden florins a year on its sales. In the Milan district the cloth manufacture occupied 60,000 workers, and the export of fabrics brought in 300,000 ducats. Venice employed 16,000 workers to produce the most beautiful fine cloths of the peninsula. The workshops of Catalonia, the Balearic Isles, and Flanders rivalled those of Italy, and the Majorcans exported 16,000 florins' worth of cloth annually. While war meant death to the majority of the French workshops (which preserved a little vitality only in Languedoc, Berry, Brittany, and Picardy), the prosperity of the manufactures of fine cloth in Flanders and Brabant reached its height in the fourteenth century. When it was threatened in the fifteenth century by the rise of prices and the shortage of English wool, it was replaced by another industry—that of drapery made of combed wool, plain or mixed, and known as " bayes and sayes " (*bourgetterie* and *sayetterie*), which took the place of the old and moribund manufacture, and developed with an astonishing rapidity from Picardy to the Netherlands, saving the towns and country districts of Flanders and Brabant from ruin. On its side, Germany made use of its indigenous coarse wools in the fabrication of hundreds of thousands of pieces of coarse cloth, from Silesia and Westphalia to the Rhineland. Finally, England built up round Norwich her first great industry, that of fine cloths, friezes, kerseys, and worsteds, the export of which rose from 5,000 to over 80,000 pieces in less than a century.

The growth of luxury was favourable to the success of the art of silk weaving in Italy, which inherited the supremacy of Byzantium. From the workshops of Sicily and Calabria, and, above all, of Lucca, Siena, Florence, Genoa, and Venice, the last of which numbered 3,000 workers, there came forth the silken thread and the cloth of gold and silver, the brocades, the damasks, the satins, and the velvets, in which the wealthy classes loved to flaunt themselves. Catalonia and Valencia manufactured light silks. In spite of attempts to rival them made at Paris, Zürich, and Basle, Eastern Spain and Italy preserved something like a monopoly of this lucrative silk industry.

The manufacture of fine linens was another Italian speciality, practised in particular at Milan and Venice. That of semi-fine linen and table linen was kept up in Catalonia, Champagne, Languedoc, and Normandy; that of sail-cloth in Brittany and Galicia. In Northern France and the Low Countries were manufactured those famous fabrics in linen thread which have made the names of Cambrai, Malines, Brussels, and Holland illustrious. In the country districts of Germany the manufacture of coarse linen and hempen goods was carried on; Ulm produced 20,000 to 60,000 pieces each year. A new variety of stuff called fustian was made with cotton imported from the Levant, and had an enormous vogue; the chief centres of its manufacture were Milan and Venice (where 16,000 weavers were occupied with it), Catalonia, and, in Germany, Augsburg and Ulm, where 6,000 weavers were employed and produced 350,000 pieces.

Arras in Artois, Oudenarde and Tournai in Flanders, Brussels and Enghien in Brabant, won universal renown in the art of tapestry weaving, which spread to Paris, Venice, and Ferrara; they excelled also in lace-making.

Venice made over 100,000 ducats annually from the export of her gilded leathers. Paris rivalled her in furrieries. Manufactures of chemical and pharmaceutical products, and of confectioneries and syrups, were set up in Italy in imitation of those of the East. The French, Flemish, and German cabinet-makers, the Italian, Catalan, and Valencian potters, the Italian inlayers, the Venetian and Czech glass-makers, rivalled each other in skill. The arts of building, painting, sculpture, and goldsmith's work produced new wonders in the West in an early Renaissance, the forerunner of that of the sixteenth century. Paper-mills began to pour out the new material upon which, at the beginning of the fifteenth century, map-makers exercised their talent and copiers of manuscripts their activity, up to the time when the process of xylographic printing with movable wooden characters first appeared at Limoges (1381) and Antwerp (1417), followed by the invention of typography, based on the use of metal characters, by Gutenberg (1436-50).

In this medieval society, now drawing to its close, industry was manifesting a feverish activity in all directions, multiplying the sources of wealth, and strengthening the power of the labouring classes.

CHAPTER III

CHANGES IN THE ORGANIZATION OF THE COMMERCIAL AND INDUSTRIAL CLASSES.—URBAN REVOLUTIONS AND PROGRESS OF THE TOWNS AT THE CLOSE OF THE MIDDLE AGES.

WHILE commerce and industry were thus taking a new course, the primitive unity of the commercial and industrial classes, already severely shaken during the preceding period, was finally broken up. At the top appeared a growing minority of bourgeois capitalists; in the middle developed the small or medium bourgeoisie of masters, who formed the free crafts and corporations, below were the workmen, who were slowly becoming separated from the class of small masters; and at the bottom of all came the hired wage-earners of the great industry, reinforced by casual elements, who formed a new urban proletariat.

Henceforth the capitalist bourgeoisie, few in numbers and all powerful in wealth, was organized and grew. At Basle out of 30,000 inhabitants these capitalists formed only 4 per cent. of the population, and at Venice, the richest city of the West, they were a mere 2,000 patricians, each of whom owned an income ranging from 200,000 to 500,000 francs. But they held in their hands the greater part of the wealth of their towns; at Freiburg, for instance, thirty-seven burgesses had possessed themselves of 50 per cent. of the movable and immovable capital of the city, so that over a third of the inhabitants were without possessions. The bourgeois capitalists were able to equal and, indeed, to surpass the magnates of the landed aristocracy. A Florentine merchant banker, Cosimo de Medici, left a fortune of 225,000 golden florins in 1440, greater than that of the appanaged princes of France. Dino Rapondi, the banker of Lucca, once advanced two million francs to the Duke of Burgundy, and the famous mercer Jacques Cœur, treasurer of Charles VII, amassed a capital of twenty-seven million francs, which was, indeed, less than that of the *surintendant* Pierre Rémy, who, in the time of Philip VI, was supposed to possess a fortune of fifty-seven millions. In the second half of the fifteenth century the merchant capitalists of Nuremburg and Augsburg were worth from three and a half to five million francs, which had been amassed in part during the first half of the century, when some of them possessed incomes of 10,000 to 15,000 florins apiece; it was then that the ascendancy of the bourgeois dynasties of the Fuggers, the Baumgartners, the Hochstetters, and the Hervaths began.

They owed their success to their business capacity, their activity or their audacity, and to the spirit of enterprise which led them to spy out all possible sources of profit. They accumulated land rents; they got into their hands the greater part of the urban house property, which, in Venice in 1420, represented a capital of nearly 100 million francs; they bought lordships and lands in the country. But it was, above all, banking, commercial, and industrial enterprises which enriched them. Through their associations they were the masters of credit and of money, and they even began to tap the savings of private individuals on the pretext of increasing them. They monopolized the great international commerce, the trade in foodstuffs and in luxuries, corn, fish, wine, cattle, and spices. They speculated in the raw materials necessary to industry and in manufactured goods, in lard, potash, tar, wood, hides, skins, furs, cotton, silk, wool, as well as in woollen and silken fabrics, fustians, coverlets, mercery, and soap. They undertook the exploitation of mines, set up metallurgical and textile manufactures, and everywhere the capital which they engaged bore fruit.

These great manipulators of money and men of affairs were animated by a cosmopolitan spirit and detached from narrow urban interests. They were, on the contrary, glad to become the agents of kings and princes, and were the best auxiliaries of absolute monarchy, whose interests they served in serving their own. Often they adopted the magnificent and luxurious way of life of the high aristocracy. Men such as the patricians of Venice, Jacques Cœur, or the Portinari at Bruges, dwelt in palaces or mansions worthy of princes. They took a pride in playing the part of Mæcenas, and they were among the intelligent promoters of the Renaissance. But into medieval economic organization they brought unrest and pernicious ways: reckless speculation,

PLATE VI

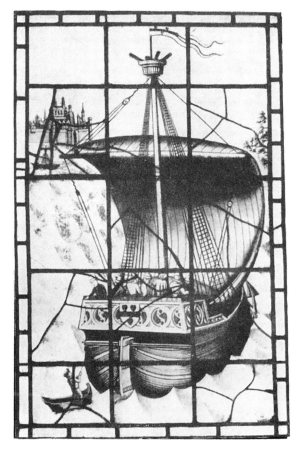

Bourges

JACQUES COEUR'S SHIP
(15th Century)

the practice of rings and monopolies, even of Cartels, the most complete absence of scruples and a contempt for every law of morality. They were reproached (as in one of the German diets) with "destroying all chance of work for small trade or trade on a moderate scale," or, as a contemporary wrote concerning Jacques Cœur, with "impoverishing a thousand worthy merchants to enrich a single man." By their manœuvres and their failures, which harmed "their opulence" not at all, as a contemporary pamphlet complained, they overthrew all honest labour and trade. They upset the harmony of the old urban organization, shaking or annihilating it by making the protective regulations which it enforced illusory. They forced a large part of the industrial and commercial population to submit to their domination. They established a veritable dictatorship over certain forms of work, and contributed to the creation and development of those redoubtable evils inseparable from hired labour and an urban proletariat, which they bequeathed to the modern world.

If the struggle born of the formation of the capitalist bourgeoisie and its acquisitive spirit was then less serious than it became in the following centuries, the reason was that it was modified by the power which force of numbers and association gave to the small and middle class of bourgeois. This class, composed of small urban proprietors, of the mass of officials and, above all, of the traders and masters of the crafts, formed the great majority of the population in most towns; at Basle, for instance, they formed 95 per cent. They were content with modest fortunes; in Germany, in the fifteenth century, the middle class of the bourgeoisie frequently owned from 2,000 to 10,000 florins. At Basle one-fifth of the bourgeois possessed on an average 200 to 2,000 florins, and one-third, among whom were many artisans, from 30 to 200 florins. In France the bourgeois of this category usually gave their daughters dowries equivalent in value to 500 to 2,000 francs. This numerous class, not very adventurous, but often independent enough in character, was the object of the fostering care of the state, which often associated it in the work of government and abandoned to it a considerable part of urban administration, in which it allowed popular elements to participate.

LIFE AND WORK IN MEDIEVAL EUROPE

It was, indeed, a precious element of vitality and stability in society. It never for an instant slackened its work, and at every moment new professions arose within the framework of the small commerce and the small industry. At Frankfort-on-Main, in the fifteenth century, for instance, there were 191 organized crafts, 18 of them engaged in the iron industry alone; at Rostock there were 180; at Vienna and Basle, 100. Even in centres where the great industry seemed to exercise an undisputed sway, as at Ypres, its supremacy was challenged by the small industry, which occupied 48˙4 per cent. of the workers, as compared with 51˙6 per cent. who were employed in the cloth manufacture. In the immense majority of towns the greater part of the inhabitants were grouped in the crafts of the small industry; at Frankfort, which may serve as a type, they comprised 84 per cent. of the working population, and the great industry only 14 per cent.

The organization which had assured independence, dignity, and equitable conditions of labour to the working classes still prevailed with all its distinctive characteristics. The small crafts predominated, requiring neither great capital nor costly tools, giving the producer the possibility of enjoying the full fruit of his labour and securing a certain equality in the way in which the produce of the collective activity was divided. The majority of the working population was grouped into free crafts, which exacted neither a *chef d'œuvre*, nor a long term of apprenticeship, and which governed only by means of simple rules, which promoted rather than harmed the cheapness and good reputation of the manufactures. Up to the middle of the fifteenth century great towns like Bordeaux, Lyons, and Narbonne were living under this régime, and even in those in which sworn corporations existed, the proportion of free crafts might be as high as a half (as at Poitiers) or two-thirds (as at Paris and Rennes) of the total number of occupations.

Nevertheless, at this period sworn or privileged corporations were increasing with extreme rapidity, whether in order to stimulate the languishing activity of labour, or to institute a satisfactory method of regulating industry and commerce, or to discipline the working classes, or to exploit their fiscal and military resources for the profit of the Government.

Such corporations appeared at this time in France, at Tours, Besançon, Rennes, and many other towns, at Douai and Tournai and in the majority of towns in the Low Countries, England, Germany, Italy, and Spain, whence the movement spread to the rest of Europe. At Frankfort in a hundred years their number rose from 14 to 28, at Vienna from 50 to 68, at London from 48 to 60, and at Venice from 59 to 162. The corporations themselves subdivided and gave birth to new sworn crafts. The corporative régime was applied in some countries so widely as to include fiddlers, blind men, beggars, nay, even rogues and courtesans. Federations or unions of trades were organized, such as the *safran* at Basle, into which were grouped 100 crafts, or the brotherhood of tailors in the county of Hohenzollern, or the *nations* and *liden* of the towns of the Low Countries. Privileged corporations even arose in the little towns and townships. Without entirely submerging the free crafts, the sworn corporations enormously increased the extent of their own dominion.

In some respects this régime continued to exercise the beneficial influence which it had exerted in the preceding period. It contributed towards maintaining the tradition of probity and technical capacity, of stability and social equilibrium in the world of labour. But the corporations were not slow to show themselves also possessed of that spirit of selfishness, exclusiveness, and even of dead routine, which in the end animates all privileged bodies. They carried monopoly and regulation to an extreme point, multiplied lawsuits between rival trades, pursued all independent labour with their hatred, exaggerated the minutiæ of their rules. They established an inquisitorial police, and became fortified Bastilles of privilege, in which a minority of employers ambushed themselves. The ill-advised policy of the municipal and central authorities allowed them to multiply enterprises, which were against the general interest, under all sorts of fallacious pretexts.

Worse was yet to come, for division spread to the world of labour. In each centre rich or powerful corporations were striving to bring into dependence those which were less fortunate or weaker. In Florence the *major arts* trampled upon the *middle arts*, and yet more upon the *minor arts*.

LIFE AND WORK IN MEDIEVAL EUROPE

In London the twelve great livery companies, which had the right to bear coats-of-arms, separated themselves from the fifty crafts which did not enjoy this right. In Paris the six merchant bodies, among which were the drapers and mercers, erected themselves into an aristocracy, and in Basle the corporations of " gentlemen," the *herrenzünfte*, did the same. In each sworn craft itself the old masters tried to monopolize the government at the expense of the young. In London, for instance, the 114 masters who were known as the Livery of the Brewers' Company ruled the 115 others.

This spirit, so hostile to liberty and so different from that of the preceding epoch, was particularly marked in the relations between the masters and the workmen or journeymen. In a large number of crafts the workman was evicted from all dignities and responsibilities and reduced to playing a silent part in assemblies. Worse still, he was excluded from the mastership, which the masters made a property transmissible from father to son, accessible to sons-in-law, open to rich journeymen, but closed to the poor. The proof of technical capacity, the masterpiece, became for this reason obligatory, and its conditions were purposely made more complicated. All these regulations, which were aggravated by high entry fees, or the obligation to give costly banquets, were intended to put the mastership out of reach of the great mass of the workers. A simple tinker in Brussels found himself asked to pay 300 florins for permission to set up shop. The stages through which the aspirant to mastership had to pass became more numerous and longer. Both the apprentice stage and the journeyman stage became obligatory, and sometimes lasted for as long a period as twelve years for all save the sons of masters, for whom it was reduced. Journeymen and apprentices were subjected to examinations, entry fees, and payments, which allowed the masters to exercise a despotic authority over them. Everything combined to keep the mass of the workmen in a situation from which there was no escape, for the advantage of a small number of privileged persons, for whom the rewards of labour were reserved. It was only in the free crafts and in a few corporations that communal life, a modest scale of business, and a small number of journeymen and apprentices were still the rule and kept alive the old relations of cordiality and equity.

But on all sides where the monopolistic policy of the masters triumphed, the journeymen entered into conflict with them, or else became consolidated into a class, whose interests were distinct from those of their employers. The gild regulations now only served to bow the worker beneath an intolerable yoke, preventing him from working for anyone but the master, who kept him in strict dependence, refused him any legitimate rise in wages (as happened after the Black Death), and allowed him only a humble place in the meetings of the craft and even in the fraternities.

Wounded alike in his self-esteem and in his interests, the journeyman sought in rival corporative organizations the guarantees of liberty, equality and equity, and the means of protection which the privileged craft no longer gave to him. In the last century of the Middle Ages there began to appear a number of journeymen's gilds, called associations of *compagnonnage* in France and *bruderschaften* in Germany. These workmen's unions were founded and often obtained recognition under cover of piety, charity, or technical instruction; they were sometimes set up without permission as secret societies practising mysterious rites. They broke from the rigid framework of the city, spread to whole regions and countries, formed (for example, in the Rhineland) regular federations, and concluded treaties of alliance and reciprocity among themselves.

They made the acquisition of technical instruction easier for their members by organizing journeys from town to town and country to country, tours of France and tours of Germany, which in the latter country sometimes lasted for as long as five years. They had correspondents everywhere, and could secure lodgings and jobs on equitable terms for the workers. They were able, at need, to impose advantageous wages contracts upon masters, and sometimes they even admitted women to the benefits of their association. They had their officials, assemblies, subscriptions, treasuries, fêtes and banquets, even their police and their secret meetings, such as those of the builders or " freemasons," with romantic rites of initiation, oaths, and means of correspondence. Moreover, they were intolerant and exclusive, and made war on the independent workman (the " fox " or " savage," as the French were wont to call him) in order to force him to enter their association. They claimed the sole right of placing workmen and fixing conditions of work and wages. Thus they sketched, as it were, the first Workers' International, which coexisted with innumerable other local groups, brotherhoods, *confréries*, the object of which was primarily religious, but which the journeymen could use to organize mutual understandings and defence, in spite of the disapproval and prohibition of the Church and public authorities.

Some of the workers in the small industry, in spite of the journeymen's organizations, had to resign themselves to living in a perpetual state of subordination under the rule of the masters, and to accept the rates of wages which were often imposed upon them by the gild or municipal regulations. These men went to swell the ranks of the urban proletariat, the chief element in which was, however, formed by the hired wage-earners of the great industry.

The latter, more numerous now than in the preceding era, were more than ever subject to the domination of great entrepreneurs, who distributed orders to them at will, bought the produce of their labour, paid them famine wages, obliged them to take part of their payment in truck at arbitrarily fixed prices, kept them in dependence by means of an ingenious system of advances, which lured them into debt, and exposed them to crises of over-production and unemployment. Hence these proletarians lived in a permanent state of discomfort and discontent, which found vent in strikes or unions, accompanied by boycotts, when it was found impossible to settle them by arbitration or to suppress them by force. Hence also attempts at risings and revolutions which more than once brought trouble and bloodshed into the towns. The proletariat usually gained only ephemeral successes, which they compromised by their violence, intolerance, and tyranny; the final victory remained with those powers which were the traditional defenders of order and of the privileges of the masters.

Henceforth, too, began the development of those two endemic ills of the proletariat—tramping and begging. Numbers of workmen, discontented with their lot, wandered from country to country in search of work. Thus it was that during the Hundred Years' War 20,000 Norman workmen emigrated to Brittany, and others as far as Germany, while Flemish workmen crossed the Channel and the Rhine in large numbers, and German workmen spread over Italy, France, and England. At the same time the transformation of industry, the competition of rural and female labour, which the great entrepreneurs preferred to employ, and of foreign labour, which grew in spite of the gild regulations, brought with them prolonged crises of unemployment, and developed pauperism among the proletariat. Bands of unemployed workmen and other poor wretches crowded the poorer quarters and outskirts of the industrial towns to such an extent that at Florence there were 22,000 beggars, or else took to the roads, begging their way from town to town and from city to city. In France they were called *quémans* or *quaïmans*.

Capitalism above and pauperism below were the two disturbers of equilibrium which crept into the closing years of medieval life; but happily their range of action was still limited. The great mass of the industrial and commercial classes, outside the capitalist bourgeoisie, on the one hand, and the proletariat, on the other, enjoyed conditions of life which were nearer comfort than poverty, at least, in those countries which were not the prey of war or other crises. Small fortunes were widespread among the middle and smaller bourgeoisie. The organization of the small industry was always in favour of stability, and guaranteed a certain level of comfort to the majority of artisans and small masters. The workman himself continued to benefit under this régime by the rules which protected him against competition, secured him the right to work, and guarded him from overwork.

Better still, he benefited by the general rise of wages which followed upon the scarcity of labour resulting from the great epidemics, which all the ordinances of the governments were powerless to prevent. In Italy and Spain the rise varied from double to triple the previous rates. The average daily wage of the Italian workman rose from 0 fr. 41 to 1 fr. 54. In France the ordinance of 1350 sought in vain to limit the rise to a third as much as the former wage, and to fix the daily wage of the builders at 16d. to 32d., according to the winter or summer season. It was so unsuccessful that the carpenters who were earning two sous at Poitiers in 1349 were making five in 1422 and six in 1462, while at Paris the builder was receiving in 1450 the equivalent of 4 fr. 60, as much as the wage-earner of the same union earned in the middle of the nineteenth century. In England the workers in this trade were earning 6d. instead of 3d. a day, and others were receiving 5½d. instead of 3½d. Thorold Rogers asserts that the real value of the English workman's nominal wage was then twice what it was in the twelfth or in the seventeenth century. In Germany wages in certain classes of trades rose during the fifteenth century from 13d. to 25d., and the boatmen of the Rhine were making as much as a florin a day. In Westphalia and Alsace the nominal and real wage became equivalent; it exactly sufficed, that is to say, to meet the cost of living.

For the masters and workers in the small industry in most countries the conditions of material life remained, to say the least of it, advantageous. They were, indeed, exceptionally favourable in Italy, the Low Countries, and Germany, which rapidly recovered from the population crisis and enjoyed an economic prosperity superior to that of other regions. As in the preceding period, although the wage-earners in the great industry usually lived miserably in the hovels and outskirts of the towns, the masters and journeymen of the small trade and industry lived an easy enough life, in which the chief element—food—seems to have been plenteous, not to say abundant, notably in the Rhineland, Flanders, and England. In Frankfort, in the fifteenth century, the consumption of meat was as high as 125 to 150 kilogrammes per head; as much as it was at the beginning of the nineteenth century. A traveller of this period remarks that in the Low Countries and England " more folk die of too much eating and drinking than of the pains of hunger." In the towns there were never more fêtes and taverns, more furious gaming, and more moral licence; Florence and Venice each supported from 12,000 to 14,000 prostitutes. Never, also, was the urban population more mobile, more given to works of solidarity and charity, more inclined to welcome the new ideas which were working underground among the masses in the guise of religious reform. Never, finally, did it show a more vivid consciousness of its rights and a greater boldness of spirit and strength of character in taking action to vindicate them and bring about their triumph.

The last century of the Middle Ages is, indeed, *par excellence* the century of great urban revolutions. Although the pressure of the working classes had, in general, modified urban organization in the West during the preceding period in the direction of democracy, the popular elements were far from preponderating. Sometimes, as in Germany, the patriciate had been partly successful in maintaining itself in power; sometimes, as in Flanders, the working democracy had had to share the power with the bourgeoisie; sometimes, as in France, the bourgeoisie of officials and merchants or of masters of the chief crafts formed the governing body of the town; sometimes, as in Bohemia, the municipal offices were seized by a middle class of alien origin; sometimes, as at Florence, the greater and lesser bourgeoisie united to drive the wage-earning proletariat from the urban government.

The conquest of political power was thus the objective pursued by the lower classes, who desired to make use of the wide prerogatives of the urban authority, to alleviate the fiscal and military charges which the bourgeoisie preferred to heap upon their shoulders, and to prevent capitalists and bourgeois from regulating the conditions of labour at their own will. Indeed, these classes were sometimes not content with claiming equality and justice in the communal administration, but more than once cherished a dream of syndicalist government, class domination, a dictatorship of the proletariat exercised in their favour and at the expense of other social grades. Hence the bitter, violent, tragic aspect of most of these urban revolutions, some of which were, indeed, no more than blind explosions of popular hatred or misery.

From East to West, in the last half of the fourteenth century, the hurricane of revolution rose with violence on every side. At Salonica (1342-52) the sailors and artisans set on foot a sort of red terror, accomplished by massacre and ravage, under which the rich (*archontes*), landowners, captains of industry, and clergy bent for ten years. In Italy there was unchained a struggle between the *fat* and the *thin*, between the plebeians of the small crafts and the proletariat, on the one hand, and the great bourgeoisie of masters and capitalists, on the other. In the two Sicilies the Crown put a stop to it by closing access to the urban government to artisans; but while at Rome the visionary tribune Cola di Rienzi (1347) tried, with the support of the people, to break down the authority of the noble patriciate, at Bologna (1376), Genoa (1339), and Siena (1355-70), the masses sought to obtain the absolute mastery of municipal power. At Florence the wage-earners of the great industry, the *piccolini* or *popolani*, deprived of political rights, rallied, at first, round a dictator, the French adventurer Gauthier de Brienne, Duke of Athens (1342). Then, pushed to extremes by a law of 1371, which took from them all hope of paying off their debts to the entrepreneurs, they organized the celebrated revolt of the *Ciompi*. Under the direction of an intelligent and energetic wool-carder, Michel Lando, they forced the bourgeoisie to admit them to the ranks of the official corporations or *arti*, to give them a share in the government, to free them from the jurisdiction of the agents of the great industrialists, and to decree a twelve years' moratorium for the debts of all wage-earners. But they were soon carried away by extremists, proclaimed an anarchical and bloody dictatorship for the profit of the proletariat alone, whom they dignified by the name of " God's people," and thus provoked a reaction which swept away the proletarian revolution in a few weeks (July, 1378). The sole result of these disturbances was to throw the Italian bourgeoisie into the arms of an enlightened despotism, which, under the name of principate, pacified the communes in the fifteenth century by dint of enslaving them.

Nowhere did the revolutionary spirit display a more mystical ardour, a greater spirit of international propaganda, and a more violent pursuit of class demands and the dictatorship of labour than in the Low Countries. There hundreds of thousands of men struggled with fierce energy and an extraordinary bravery (sullied by hideous excesses) against nobles, clergy, and, above all, bourgeoisie, for the triumph of their ideal. They cherished the dream of an equality of fortunes and the suppression of all hierarchy, all authority, beyond that of the people who lived by manual labour. A first experiment had already been tried at Ypres and at Bruges (1323 and 1328) in the *jacquerie* of maritime Flanders, under the leadership of two workers, Guillaume de Decken and Jacques Peit, who proclaimed war on all rich men and priests, and maintained a reign of terror, until the bourgeoisie united with the nobles, and inflicted upon them the disastrous defeat of Cassel (1328). A second attempt, longer and still more serious, was made by a bold and eloquent tribune, himself a member of the great bourgeoisie, the draper James van Artevelde. By means of an alliance between the working classes and a section of the bourgeoisie, he succeeded in realizing his plan of setting up a hegemony of Ghent in Flanders, with the support of the King of England (1338-45). But he was soon outrun by the democracy of weavers, impatient to establish the sole government of the working class. This last dictatorship, which began with the rising in which Artevelde perished, employed as its methods forced loans, massacres, confiscations, and pillage; it set workers against workers, and ranged the fullers (who were crushed on March 2nd, 1345) against the weavers. It ended in the fall of the latter (January 13th, 1349), against whom princes, nobles, clergy, peasants, bourgeois, and small artisans were all united. A number of the vanquished emigrated to England; the others prepared their revenge, and attempted it in 1359 and, above all, in 1378.

This time the movement of the workers of Ghent only just missed having an immense repercussion in the West and unchaining an international revolution. The leaders of Ghent sought to set on foot a pure workers' dictatorship to despoil and destroy the bourgeoisie, and to raise journeymen against masters, wage-earners against great entrepreneurs, peasants against lords and clergy. It was said that they had contemplated the extermination of the whole bourgeois class, with the exception of children of six, and the same for the nobles. Masters of Flanders under their two leaders, Philip van Artevelde and the weaver Ackerman, the workers of Ghent for four years made established governments tremble. The Battle of Roosebecque brought this nightmare to an end in November, 1382, and cost 26,000 proletarians their lives. No other movement attained such proportions, but sporadic attempts at Liège in 1330 and 1343, at Louvain in 1340, at Brussels in 1359, 1366, and 1368, and at Bruges in 1359, 1366, 1367, showed how tenaciously the working classes of the Low Countries clung to the hope of a renovation of society. Little by little, in the fifteenth century, the movement became confined to Bruges and, above all, to Ghent and Liège, where, as in Italy, it was destined to be stifled by the princely power.

In the rest of Europe, particularly in the West, the working classes indulged in less audacious visions. They were content, with more or less success, to claim a share in municipal power or to try and reform the organization of urban government. Thus in Germany a series of risings at Cologne (1396), Strasburg (1346-80), Regensburg, Wurzburg, Bamberg, Aix-la-Chapelle, Halberstadt, Brunswick, Magdeburg, Lübeck, Rostock, and Stettin, forced the bourgeois patricians to yield up their monopoly and to hand civic offices over to the crafts. These displayed a certain sense of equity and balance, so that the German towns enjoyed a really liberal régime. In Spain, on the contrary, although the great bourgeois, the " honourable citizens " of the Eastern towns, Palamos, Figueras, Barcelona, Valencia, and Palma, had to resign themselves (not without a stubborn resistance) to sharing their power with the artisans (*menestrals*), the latter failed to wrest the civic offices from the nobles and wealthy bourgeois in Castile. In Bohemia and Poland, France and England, the democratic urban governments in most cases declined, as happened at Paris, Rheims, Rouen, Verdun, Montpellier, and Nîmes, or only with difficulty clung to a few of their conquests, as at Amiens and London.

For the rest the commercial and industrial classes were not usually successful in endowing the towns with stable and equitable institutions. Working democracies or bourgeois aristocracies had in their hearts only one common sentiment, municipal patriotism, which often inspired them with an admirable zeal to preserve the autonony, greatness, and glory of their cities. But, except in those centres in which mixed governments were established, urban administrations were animated by a rigid caste selfishness, which was contrary to all spirit of justice and true equality. They sought to monopolize power and office, now on behalf of the bourgeoisie, now on behalf of the people. Their despotism was exercised here against the rich bourgeoisie, there to the detriment of artisans and wage-earners. The workers themselves, when they got the upper hand, were not content with oppressing the bourgeoisie, but tore each other to bits. Each class governed in its own exclusive interest, trying to direct labour and regulate the production and sometimes the distribution of wealth to its own advantage. The spirit of intrigue and the lust of power showed itself in bourgeois and proletarians alike. The former often gave more heed to wealth than to talent in the apportionment of municipal dignities; the latter showed a blind faith in the most unworthy adventurers and the lowest demagogues; at Paris they hailed a skinner as their leader, at Ghent a street-singer, and at Liège a pavior. Neither the one nor the other knew how to maintain good order and probity in their dealings.

Nor did they think of breaking away from the narrow spirit of the old urban economy. They had but one ideal, to preserve and increase the particular privileges of their city and of its constituent groups. Thus they were ready to defend their commercial and industrial monopolies even by force of arms. Bruges claimed to reserve for herself the import trade in wool and spices to the Low Countries; Ghent, that of corn; Malines, that of salt and fish. Economic rivalries set Venice and Genoa, Bruges and Sluys, Ghent and Bruges, Malines and Antwerp, Dordrecht and Amsterdam, Paris and Rouen, at grips with one another. Sometimes towns aspired to build up an exclusive colonial or commercial domain for themselves, like that of the Venetians, the Genoese, and the Hansards. Sometimes they extended their dominion over the small towns in their neighbourhood, as Ghent, Ypres, and Bruges did in Flanders, Genoa in Liguria, Florence in Tuscany, Venice in Lombardy, and Barcelona in Catalonia. Everywhere they subjected the neighbouring countryside and tried to make the peasants their docile purveyors, while at the same time forbidding them to exercise any industry in order that it might be reserved for the urban crafts.

The towns thus opened the way for the encroachment of the princely power, which undertook the re-establishment of order and social equilibrium in the towns by submitting them to a more or less rigid control. This new power in its turn, however, provoked a fresh series of revolutionary movements, by reason of the partiality which it showed to the wealthy classes, the encroachments of its fiscal policy, and the arbitrary actions of its administrative agents. The most famous of these risings were those which agitated the great urban centres of France and the Netherlands. At Paris, in 1356 and 1358, the revolution led by the rich draper Etienne Marcel had as its chief supporters the mercantile bourgeoisie and the gilds of artisans, who lent their aid on the famous day of February 22nd, 1358, and inspired certain articles in the great ordinance of reform, by which an attempt was made to repress the abuses of royal administration.

Twenty-two years later, in 1379-82, from Languedoc to Picardy, from Montpellier, Carcassonne, and Béziers to Orleans, Sens, Châlons, Troyes, Compiègne, Soissons, Laon, Rouen, Amiens, Saint-Quentin, and Tournai, a whirlwind of revolution, with Paris as its centre, once more hurled the urban classes, weary of royal fiscal and administrative despotism, against the central power. The movement collapsed; the political privileges of the craft gilds were attacked, and in some places, as at Amiens, they were dismissed from the chief municipal offices. At Béziers forty working weavers and cordwainers were hanged, and at Paris and Rouen the crafts were severely treated. A third attempt, the Parisian revolution of 1413, once more brought the working democracy into power, in brief alliance with the bourgeoisie, and gave rise to a fresh attempt at administrative reform, the " Ordonnance Cabochienne," which was rendered fruitless by civil war and a terror, led by the skinner Caboche and the hangman Capeluche (1413-18). The central government finally prevailed, and henceforth, the communal bourgeoisie having grown wiser and the common folk of artisans somewhat calmer, the direction of urban policy was left in its hands. The same thing happened in the Low Countries, when the Dukes of Burgundy repressed the last particularist rebellions of Bruges (1436-38), Ghent (1431-36-48), Liége and Dinant (1408-66-68). For the Middle Ages were now drawing to a close, and, except in Germany, the urban economy was finally disappearing before the triumph of a national economy.

PLATE VII

THE HÔTEL DE VILLE AT YPRES
(*From a photograph taken before the Great War*)

[*face p. 314*

THE URBAN REVOLUTIONS

Nevertheless, despite revolutions and internal conflicts, the movement of commercial and industrial expansion was so powerful that urban life, far from declining, took on a renewed vigour. In the East, Byzantium, Salonica, and Athens threw out a last flicker of glory. France, though crippled by the English wars, still kept great and vital centres, such as Paris (with 300,000 inhabitants in the fifteenth century), Lyons, Bordeaux, Rheims, Rouen, and Amiens. In Central Europe, Prague numbered, perhaps, 100,000 citizens; London reached a total of 35,000; and in Spain, where small towns abounded, Barcelona, the queen of Iberian cities, attained to 60,000 or 70,000 souls, followed closely by Valencia and Palma.

But the chief centres of urban life were, on the one hand, and above all, Italy, where Venice had 190,000 inhabitants, and Florence 100,000, only just outstripping Milan and Genoa, and supreme among 120 other cities both large and small; and, on the other hand, the Netherlands, where beside Bruges, with its 100,000 inhabitants, Ghent seems to have had 80,000, and Ypres 40,000. Flanders had the aspect of " a continuous town," so preponderant was the urban population; in Brabant it comprised no less than a quarter of the whole. This was likewise the golden age of the urban republics of Germany, those 96 free German towns, chief among which were Cologne, with its 40,000 souls, and Basle, Strasburg, Augsburg, Nuremburg, Regensburg, Vienna, Constance, Speier, Treier, Frankfort, Mainz, Magdeburg, Erfurt, Lübeck, and Breslau, in which the population normally ranged between 5,000 and 20,000.

The towns, above all those of the West, were filled with a generous spirit of emulation; they adorned themselves with magnificent monuments, dowered themselves with a host of charitable institutions, developed all the grades of education, and became more than ever before the homes of literary and scientific culture, playing an eminent part in the literary and artistic renaissance of the fourteenth and fifteenth centuries. Before going down beneath national economy and monarchical rule, urban civilization, thanks to the economic activity of the bourgeois and working classes, blazed out in a last magnificent brilliance, the forerunner of the splendour of modern civilization.

CHAPTER IV

VICISSITUDES OF COLONIZATION AND AGRICULTURAL PRODUCTION.—
CHANGES IN THE DISTRIBUTION OF LANDED PROPERTY AND IN THE
CONDITION OF THE RURAL CLASSES AT THE CLOSE OF THE MIDDLE
AGES.—THE PEASANT REVOLTS.

THE end of the Middle Ages was a period of marked contrasts
in the domain of agriculture. Certain regions, such as the
old Eastern Empire, Bohemia, and Hungary, grew poorer and
more depopulated, and others, such as Sweden, Ireland, and
Scotland, were unable to emerge from their condition of
poverty. France, the most prosperous country in the West,
became, in Petrarch's words (1360), " a heap of ruins ";
from Loire to Somme nothing was to be seen but " uncultivated fields, overgrown with brambles and bushes," as
Bishop Thomas Basin said in 1440, when a third of her territory lay uncultivated. But other more favoured regions continued to exploit their soil to its utmost value. In Italy
the embankment of the Po was carried on from the place
where it joined the Oglio; a number of marshes (*polesine,*
corregie) were converted into cultivated " polders " in
Lombardy and Tuscany, irrigation canals or trenches fed
from the Naviglio Grande and the Naviglio Interne, besides
those of Martesana, Panarello, and Chiaro, fertilized the
fields of Lombardy and Modena. A similar work was being
carried out in Eastern Spain.

In the Low Countries the work of defence against the sea,
which, in 1377 and 1421, had swallowed up ninety townships
and increased the area of the Zuider Zee, went on. The
dykes were reinforced at the end of the fifteenth century,
and 1,100 square kilometres of " polders " were conquered.
From the Vistula to the Niemen, under the auspices of the
Teutonic Order, the formation of " werder " was accelerated.
In Hungary, under the Angevins, and in Poland, under the
Jagellons, the clearing of the land made active progress, as
also in those Baltic territories which were occupied by the
Scandinavians. Finally, in the East, the merchants of
Novgorod and the Great Russian monks and peasants of

Muscovy carried across marsh and forest that great work of colonizing Finnish and Tartar lands, which was to make Russia mistress of the immense stretch of territory which lies between the middle Volga, the Arctic Ocean, and the Obi (1363-1489).

Popular activity tended to turn in the direction of the most advantageous forms of production, to follow variations in demand and in foreign markets, and to be governed by the natural aptitude of each region. The maritime populations of the North-West and North of Europe—Norwegians, English, Scots, Hansards, Netherlanders—drew increasing revenues from their fisheries, especially from that of the herring, which was *par excellence* the food of the people. The Netherlands employed 40,000 boats in this work, and benefited by the discovery of a new method of preserving the favourite fish of the masses, by packing it in kegs or barrels, which facilitated export, and was due to the Zeelander, Gilles Beucholz. From the North Cape to Galicia, sailors pursued the whale, the seal, and, above all, the cod, which, swept on by the Gulf Stream, they sought even as far as the " new-found land."

While deforestation was going on apace in England, the Low Countries, Italy, and Spain, the lands of the North, East, and Centre of Europe were turning their forest resources to more and more profitable account. Princes and lords increased the number of their studs in Italy and England. The raising of sumpter-horses, battle-horses, and race-horses prospered in regions rich in grasslands, as did that of horned cattle in the Alpine zone and in the Western countries, which furnished meat, bacon, and lard to the rest of Europe. In the Low Countries the art of fattening cattle on turnips and leguminous plants was first invented. Elsewhere milch cows were the chief speciality. The scarcity of labour after the Black Death, combined with the fact that sheep required but little labour and expense, and with the growing demand for and high price of wool, led to an extraordinary development in one form of pasture-farming, that of sheep-rearing. In the majority of European countries this business became once more extremely popular, and pasture-farming even took the place of corn-growing in Central Italy, the Roman Campagna, the Castiles and Upper Aragon, and finally, in England. In Spain, in the fifteenth century, the great association of sheep-farmers known as the Mesta grouped into a single organization 2,694,000 sheep, out of the 10,000,000 then kept in the peninsula. In England the great landowners, attracted by a system of rural economy which gave them ten or twelve times as high a return as corn-growing, kept flocks of 4,000 to 25,000 sheep. In 1400 the English were exporting as many as 130,000 packs of fine wool, weighing 364 pounds apiece, and had ousted the Spaniards as masters of the market.

On their side new countries began to turn their attention to corn-growing. Prussia, Poland, and Hungary henceforth took their place as the great producers of cereals, side by side with old centres of production, such as France. In the Low Countries and in England, where methods of intensive cultivation were used, farmers succeeded in getting returns of seven to one, instead of four to one. Horticulture, floriculture, and arboriculture developed in the rich lands of the West, and it was now that the reputation of the Flemish florists and the nurserymen of Nuremburg and Augsburg was founded. The cultivation of the vine tended to become localized, and to increase in Italy, Spain, France, the Rhineland, and Hungary. Italian and Spanish wines supplanted those of the East, and the wines of France kept their popularity. At the beginning of the fifteenth century Bordeaux was still exporting from 28,000 to 30,000 casks a year. The cultivation of textile and dye plants benefited by the progress of industry.

The decline of production in one part of Europe was counterbalanced by its increase in another. The rise in the price of agricultural produce was in favour of the development of landed property in privileged regions. While in France, a prey to war, the value of land fell to a half between 1325 and 1450, and in Normandy even reached as low a figure as from 325 to 23 francs the hectare, it rose in the inverse direction in the states of the Dukes of Burgundy, and in Italy, England, the Low Countries, Southern Germany, and Eastern Spain.

The break-up of landed property continued along the lines laid down in the preceding period. Agrarian collectivism finally disappeared, even in the Germanic countries, and in general the only traces left of it were the commons, which were still numerous in the Scandinavian countries, Eastern and Central Europe, and the hilly districts of the West, such as Upper Italy, where they covered a sixth or a seventh of the soil, or even in the North of Spain. Everywhere communal property was enclosed and the major part of it appropriated. The large properties of the state, the greater aristocracy, and the Church continued to spread. Everywhere princes sought to build their domains up again. In Muscovy they claimed three-fifths of the land for themselves, and in Moldavia and Wallachia the whole. In France the Valois kings, despite their prodigality, drew a revenue of 4 million livres from the state lands, and the Dukes of Burgundy 160,000 *écus d'or*. In England the Yorkist kings, in 1460, laid hold of a fifth of the soil. But the sovereigns were unable to maintain this property intact, and it was continually breaking up to the profit of the Church and the nobles.

In spite of measures taken everywhere against the extension of mortmain, ecclesiastical property grew to a monstrous extent, which aroused the cupidity of lay lords and the desire for secularization. In the two Sicilies and Central and Northern Italy, the clergy, in the fifteenth century, held two-thirds and sometimes as much as four-fifths of the land; in the state of Venice their landed capital was worth 129 million *écus*. In the Castiles, where the Church held from a third to a fifth of the land, it had a revenue of 10 million ducats. In France, ruined by the war, it was so successful in building up its landed wealth again in fifty years that it recovered from a quarter to a half of the land, and drew from it a revenue greater than that of the state—to wit, 5 million livres *tournois* (100 million francs). The revenue of the English clergy was twelve times greater than that of the king, and they held about the same proportion of the land as in France. In Germany, the Scandinavian countries, and Eastern Europe that proportion was as high as a third or a half, and even two-thirds.

A minority of great lords, barons, landlords, magnates, sovereign lords (*landesherren*), sometimes owned immense domains which they called " states " (*estados*, estates) in Spain and England, sometimes scattered, and sometimes concentrated. In Italy a Colonna, in the fifteenth century, owned 97 fiefs and had 150,000 vassals; a Villena at Castile had 30,000 *censitaires* and a revenue of 100,000 ducats; a Duke of Orleans had an income of 540,000 livres; a Duke of Anjou, 400,000; a la Trémoille, 336,000; a Rohan, 280,000. In England Lord Cromwell drew £66,000 sterling from his possessions, and the German princes each owned lands yielding on an average 240,000 marks, a tenth of the revenue which was later to be enjoyed by Charles V. But they formed only a very small minority. The mass of noblemen, save in a few countries, such as England, neglected the cultivation of their estates, and alienated them one by one to pay their debts or to meet their expenses.

It was usually the rich bourgeoisie which stepped into their shoes and laboured to build up a fortune in land, accumulating it by means of copyholds or *accensements* and reclamations, as well as by purchase. They owned fine farms well stocked with cattle, like the one which belonged to the Chancellor d'Orgement at Gonesse (1358). They sometimes even rivalled the great nobles; Jacques Cœur possessed twenty-five lordships, and the Chancellor, Nicolas Rolin, was one of the greatest landowners in Burgundy. Bladelin, the Treasurer of Philip the Good, employed a large part of his fortune in draining " polders." The middle and lower ranks of the bourgeoisie, and even the urban artisans, followed the example of these great bourgeois, coveted land, and appropriated numerous holdings; the communes did the same. Thus a London mercer, in the fifteenth century, leaves several manors to his children, and a cook, a blacksmith, and a dyer of York all have small landed properties. This state of affairs was still more frequent in France, the Low Countries, Italy, and the Rhineland, where there was no burgess, however humble, who did not dream of a little estate and a country house.

Among the rural classes the number of small proprietors also went on increasing in the West, although it diminished in Eastern and Northern Europe, where they had been very numerous. In the West of Europe a rural third estate came into being, sometimes, as in Central and Northern Italy, favoured by the public authorities, who reserved to it the right of pre-emption in the purchase of non-noble lands.

THE PEASANT REVOLTS

In France so greedy was the peasant for land that, in the fourteenth and fifteenth centuries, 60 per cent. of the changes in landownership in certain provinces took place in his favour, and in the end peasant proprietors occupied a fifth, and in some parts as much as a third, of the soil. It is true that the peasants were able to build up only very small properties; peasant owners, holding from ten to fifty hectares with several yokes of oxen, formed in some regions no more than a sixth of the total peasant population. In England these freeholders or franklins, whose jolly countenances live again in the pages of Chaucer, dwelt on estates averaging eighty acres, which brought them in about £20 a year. In the German Rhineland the little peasant estates contained no more than about twenty to thirty acres each. Most of the small peasant proprietors had only moderate incomes, to which the growing *morcellement* was a constant menace. In the Rhineland, for instance, the size of the holding diminished by three-quarters in the course of this period. All the tenacity and economy of the peasants was needed to prevent the dissolution of these small rural properties, which they, nevertheless, consolidated and extended by slow degrees.

The great mass of the rural populations was then composed of *censitaires* who had not an absolute property in the land, but held it in perpetual usufruct. In the West of Europe they had gained their liberty, and no one dared any longer to contest it. In England hardly one per cent. of the rural population was unfree. In France it was a sacred maxim that every Frenchman was born free. In the Low Countries the *échevins* of Ypres declared proudly that among them "never was there heard tell of folk of servile condition nor of *mortemain*." Commutation spread with renewed activity; for example, in France after the Hundred Years' War, and in all regions in which there prevailed the old systems of mixed farming, which required a great deal of labour. Free *censitaires* or copyholders were by the end of the Middle Ages cultivating five-sixths of the soil in different parts of France, and a third of it in England. It was rarely that they were unable to obtain advantageous terms, which assured them, together with the divers prerogatives of civil liberty, the majority of the effective rights of property, such as alienation and succession, while limiting their labour services and dues.

But even in the West a social and economic evolution was on foot, which was, in part, unfavourable to them. On the one hand, landowners, clergy, lords, and burgesses took advantage of the troublous times to try and increase the obligations of their tenants, or to take away the guarantees and advantages which had been granted to them, to the point of menacing them with a return to villeinage or serfdom. On the other hand, they deprived the villeins of that stability which they had always enjoyed. The fact was that the new practices—the substitution of pasture-farming for mixed farming, and that of *métayage* or lease-hold farming or the direct farming of the estate by the lord for the old method of *accensement*, the appropriation of commons by great landlords by means of the enclosure system — all contributed to make the assistance of *censitaires* less indispensable. They soon became a positive nuisance to all the large landowners who wanted to increase their revenues and diminish the cost of labour. Attempts were, therefore, made to evict them, to profit by their temporary difficulties, or by their failure to execute the clauses of their contract, as well as by their impoverishment or desertion, to take back their holdings into the lord's hands. All over the West a considerable number of these *censitaires* and copyhold tenants, thus deprived of the land which they cultivated, went to swell the ranks of the agricultural wage-earners or proletariat, notably in England. A vast number of others, in Central and Eastern Europe, were even more unfortunate, and fell back into the condition of the villeins, or, worse still, of the serfs in the previous period.

In Western Europe, where such a retrogression was no longer possible on account of the level reached by manners and civilization, new classes grew up at the expense of the *censitaires*, some farming by themselves or in partnership, others seeking a means of existence in the sale of their labour.

Farming as a free business enterprise, the so-called *fermage* or tenant-farming, became a speculation which was readily taken up by the rich bourgeoisie, who contracted for

PLATE VIII

HARVEST
(Early 16th Century)

[face p. 322

the cultivation of the lands of the Church and the nobility, and made themselves administrators of *fermes générales*, vast domains belonging to individuals or to corporations. Soon the most enterprising section of the rural third estate developed a taste for this system, and side by side with these big contract farmers, there appeared a growing number of small farmers, farming landed estates less wide in extent. In Italy, the Low Countries, the German Rhineland, England, and France (where it became general in the provinces of the Parisian basin, Champagne, Picardy, and Orléanais), and in the East tenant-farming made considerable progress under the two forms of agricultural leases and stock leases (called *bail à cheptel* in France, and *socida* in Italy). The latter were signed for one year, or sometimes for three to five years; the former were sometimes concluded for life, and sometimes for one or more generations, but tended to become restricted to shorter terms: seventy years in England, thirty to fifty years in France, six to twenty-nine years in Italy. Sometimes the rent payable by the farmer was fixed, sometimes it varied with the produce of the farm, and the rate was more or less high according to agreement. It was as low as a quarter or even an eighth of the land rent in Provence, and stood at 3˙13 per cent. and 2˙33 per cent. of the revenue in various other districts of France; while in England, where, from the fifteenth century, the farmers were, above all, big graziers, the figure mounted steadily, enriching landlords and tenants alike.

Co-operative farming (*mezzadria, colonat partiaire, métayage*) grew in some districts more widely than tenant-farming, notably in Italy, the South and West of France, Eastern Spain, and the Rhineland. It was a method more easily accessible to peasants without capital, and it sometimes gave them appreciable advantages, in cases where the demand for labour was greater than the supply, and where it was necessary to bring uncultivated or ill-cultivated lands under the plough. In Provence and Italy there were a number of *métayers* who had to pay only a fifth, a fourth, a tenth part of the produce of their farms, or even a rent which varied from year to year with the harvest. But more often they had to pay a strict half of the land rent to the lord, and their economic independence was far less than that of the *fermier* or ordinary tenant-farmer. In Tuscany they were forbidden to emigrate to the towns and to leave the land without having paid their debts, and the disciplinary powers of the landowner over them were not sensibly dissimilar from those formerly exercised by the lord over the free villein. It is true that the *métayer* only alienated his liberty for a short period, a year, or sometimes longer—for instance, ten years in Provence; but, on the other hand, he enjoyed neither the stability of the old *censitaire* nor the privileged position of the independent farmer.

The different forms of agricultural wage labour developed yet more widely than tenant-farming and *métayage* towards the close of the Middle Ages. The ranks of the free day labourers, who had appeared during the preceding period, were swelled by evicted *censitaires* and peasants who had no resources other than the sale of their labour, and by others, like the German *kossaten* and the English cotters, whose tiny holdings (sometimes only three or four acres) were too small for their entire support. Hiring themselves out by the day or the week, or on taskwork, these *brassiers*, *varlets*, labourers, servants in husbandry (as they were called in different places), often set a high price on their services, when labour became scarce after some great epidemic, such as the Black Death. But although free they were still subject to strict regulation. In Italy, France, Spain, and England, Draconian laws, such as the Italian municipal statutes, the French ordinance of 1350, and the famous English Statutes of Labourers (1350-1417), punished all who refused to work by heavy fines and even by imprisonment, allowed them to be taken by force, and sometimes to be thrown into chains if they left their work, forbade them to change their domicile, or to apprentice their sons, and fixed their wages. The theoretical freedom of these wage-earners did not prevent them from being tied hand and foot by iron laws, which the public authorities claimed the right to impose upon them, laws from whose clutches they only succeeded in escaping when the urgent need for labour obliged their employers to capitulate.

The class of domestic and farm servants also grew in numbers; hired by the month or year, they enjoyed more stable conditions, and were protected from unemployment and from the rise in price of the necessities of life, since they were lodged, fed, and clothed; but domestic service in those days, although based upon freedom of contract, was exceedingly restricted by the authoritarian traditions of the past, which obliged the servant to remain in his place until he had obtained permission to leave, and which even conferred upon the master the right of corporal punishment.

Finally, the more undisciplined and adventurous elements, or those less apt for labour or less industrious, formed henceforth a rural proletariat analogous to the urban proletariat, and, like the latter, often became tramps and beggars. Medieval society bequeathed to the modern world these two evils, destined to grow worse, and the redoubtable problem of pauperism was already appearing in the country in as acute a form as in the town.

Sporadically in the West and in enormous proportions in the Centre, North, and East of Europe, a real retrogression was, indeed, going on. Serfdom, which had been declining and seemed on the point of extinction, took on a new vigour when the scarcity of labour made itself felt. It was extirpated with greater difficulty in the less populous districts of Western Europe, where it had survived, and it established itself and advanced in a great part of the continent to the East and North.

In the West, where it survived in the attenuated form of *mainmorte*, which fell rather on the land than on the person of the serf, it maintained itself obstinately in Friuli, Montferrat, Piedmont, Aragon, the Balearic Isles, and Upper Catalonia, the Limousine March, Champagne, the Nivernais, and divers regions in the East of France, in Luxemburg, Namurois, Drenthe, Guelders, and Over-Yssel; and it still lay upon one per cent. of the rural population of England. In the Spanish states the hard-working Moslem population of *mudejares*, as well as the Jews, who, in the preceding period, had enjoyed extensive franchises, were now reduced to serfdom.

But it was, above all, in the rest of Europe that a renaissance of serfdom took place, favoured by the rising influence of the feudal classes. In the North of Germany, notably in Pomerania, Mecklenburg, and Brandenburg, and even in the Austrian lands, Styria, Carinthia, and Carniola, not only the old Slav populations, but also a large number of villeins (*hörigen*) of other race fell into serfdom (*leibeigenschaft*). It often happened that the mere fact of living on servile land was sufficient to bring about the loss of liberty. " The air alone makes serfs," ran a German saying. The peasant, thus pushed into serfdom and despoiled of his old customary rights and commons, was reduced, as a proverb of Brandenburg expressed it, to wishing long life to the junker's horses, lest he might conceive the notion of riding on his tenants.

In Hungary, Transylvania, Poland, and Denmark the rural populations, among whom freemen had once predominated, were reduced to serfdom by the invading aristocracies. In Serbia, Roumania, and Bulgaria and in the old Eastern Empire the liberty of the peasant disappeared in like manner, and the cultivator, assimilated to the Byzantine *paroikos*, became the most miserable peasant in Europe, the forerunner of the Turkish *rayah*. In Muscovy alone the necessities of colonization were able to maintain the inhabitants of the countryside in a condition analogous to that of the villein or *colonus*. Russian serfdom is a modern institution. But, on the other hand, the Muscovites, Lithuanians, and Poles reduced all their prisoners to slavery— pagans or Moslems, Finns, Tartars, or Turks. At the same time the slave trade woke into life again in the South of Europe, Italy, and Spain, even in the French provinces of the Mediterranean littoral, at the expense of the paynims, and sometimes provided landowners with a considerable contingent of cultivators. There were as many as 20,000 of these slaves in Majorca, and Italian statutes show that in Sicily, Tuscany, Venetia, and Istria slave labour was more than once called in to supplement the scarcity of free labour.

The many crises of all kinds which marked the close of the Middle Ages and gave rise now to anarchy and misery, now to conflicts between landlords and labourers, aristocrats and peasants menaced with serfdom, filled the rural world at this period with an effervescence similar to that which was disturbing the towns. The second half of the fourteenth century, and to a less extent the first half of the fifteenth, were marked by constant risings, usually without either programme, unity, or direction, mere anarchical and bloody manifestations of the suffering and hatred of the people.

THE PEASANT REVOLTS

Such, in particular, was the character of the famous revolt of the French peasants, the *Jacques*, as they were called, whom the nobility mocked and despised and drove to desperation by their brigandage. In the spring of 1358, at a time when the prestige of the nobles had been shaken by the disaster of Poitiers (1356), the peasants of the North of France, Normandy, the Île-de-France, Picardy, Brie, Eastern Champagne, and the country round Soissons, rose under the leadership of an old soldier, Guillaume Cale, burned hundreds of castles, spread pillage, fire, and sometimes murder far and wide, and even aroused the sympathy of the lesser bourgeoisie in towns such as Rouen, Senlis, Amiens, Meaux, and Paris itself (May 28th to June 16th). According to Froissart 100,000 men took up arms, but the peasants were crushed by the nobles at Meaux and at Clermont-sur-Oise and fell back again into their miserable state. The aristocratic classes revenged themselves by executing 20,000 hapless creatures in cold blood, and crushed the rebellious villages beneath fines. The Jacquerie seems to have formulated no precise demands. The same thing happened twenty years later in the revolt of the *Tuchins*, which spread from Upper Italy as far as the central plateau of France and Poitou, though its chief centre was in Languedoc. Peasants and artisans made common cause, and organized a sort of guerilla warfare in heaths and woods, which dragged on for six years (1379-1385); they ill-treated all who had not horny hands, and, finally, succumbed to a pitiless repression. The English, in their turn, for a brief space masters of Western France, where they ravaged the countryside, provoked jacqueries in Maine, Cotentin, and Normandy, the best known of which was directed by the peasant Cantepie (1424-1432), and drowned the land in blood.

Other rural revolutions had a better defined and sometimes a more widely socialistic character than those of France. In Spain the serfs (*pageses de remensa*) of Upper Catalonia thrice took up arms between 1395 and 1479 against the nobles and clergy who oppressed them, and finally succeeded in winning their freedom, thanks to the intervention of the Crown. Less fortunate, the peasants (*foreros*) of Majorca, in spite of four insurrections (1391-1477), the most violent of which was directed by a labourer named Tort

Ballester, did not succeed in preventing the appropriation of rural property by the bourgeoisie, nor in obtaining better conditions of labour for *censitaires* and day labourers. Some were massacred or left the country, the rest were obliged to submit.

In the Low Countries the jacquerie of maritime Flanders, which lasted from 1322 to 1328, had already displayed all the characteristics of a class war, which ranged the free peasants, menaced with serfdom, against the nobles, and was accompanied by unexampled violence on both sides. The rural populations, though beaten, succeeded in consolidating their freedom. Henceforth they upheld the princely power against the towns, and thus increased their influence and won a right to exist for rural industry. But in the East the principality of Liège was, in 1458, the scene of the strange revolt of the *cluppelslagers*, who took a ploughshare for their badge and wore it on their caps, and whose complaint was against the abuses of feudal justice and taxation.

The two most original rural revolutions were those of the English labourers and of the peasants of Bohemia. The English Peasants' Revolt, provoked by oppressive legislation which obliged labourers and artisans to work for fixed wages and to remain in their jobs, was fanned by the preaching of revolutionary mystics, poor priests imbued with Wycliffite doctrines, such as John Ball and Jack Straw. Villeins discontented with their labour services also joined the movement, and the government, by imposing a graduated poll tax, which fell heavily on the poorer classes (1377-80), set a light to the terrible conflagration which made every owner of property tremble. A village artisan, an old soldier named Wat Tyler, led the rebels, who raised the eastern and south-eastern counties and even part of the north. Straw and Ball were the theorists of the revolution. In the name of the Bible they preached the spoliation of the nobility, clergy, and bourgeoisie, the abolition of serfdom and of all social distinctions, the equality of rank and the community of property. But the rebels had, in reality, no common programme or uniform line of conduct; in one place they confined themselves to abolishing labour services and pulling down enclosures; in another they condemned themselves by acts of pillage and anarchy. At one moment

THE PEASANT REVOLTS

they were masters of London and of King Richard II
(June 13-14, 1380); but they allowed themselves to be dis-
armed by the promise of charters of enfranchisement, and in
a few days the revolt collapsed, to be followed by a bloody
repression. The crown, satisfied with the annulment of concessions which had been wrung from it by violence, contented itself with executing the revolutionary leaders, but
was not always strong enough to arrest a blind reaction.
Calm was re-established for sixty years. The short rising of
the Kentish peasants, led by the adventurer Jack Cade
(June 12th, 1450), was not as serious as that of 1380,
although it gave rise to grave disturbances in London.

Bolder still, and of far longer duration and wider scope,
was the Hussite Revolt, which was in part a religious and
in part a social movement. Under cover of the religious
reformation preached by John Huss, and of a national reaction against their German aristocracy, the Czech peasants,
joining forces with the lesser nobility and led by two illustrious warriors, Ziska and Procopius the Great, dominated
Central Europe for twenty years (1418-1437). They created
a Puritan democracy which proclaimed the equality of man,
the liberation of the country districts from the yoke of
feudalism, and the secularization of the goods of the clergy.
But this democracy brought about its own ruin by falling
under the influence of the extreme radicalism of the sect of
Taborites, who ordained the absolute levelling of all social
distinctions, whether of fortune, birth, or intelligence, the
full emancipation of women, the suppression of private
property, marriage and the family—in fact, a complete
system of communism. The Hussite Revolt, abandoned by
the native bourgeoisie and the lesser nobility, who had at
first supported it, was then crushed at the Battle of Lipany,
leaving the ground clear for feudal reaction and serfdom.

It had given rise to an immense effervescence in the
heart of Europe, which spread to the East of France and,
in particular, to Germany, where the peasants rose without
success in Saxony, Silesia, Brandenburg, the Rhineland
(1432), and in Carinthia, Styria, and far Transylvania
(1437). Finally, in the Scandinavian countries, although
the free peasants of Sweden, in alliance with the local
nobility, and led by Engelbrechtson, carried out a success-

ful revolt against the establishment of serfdom (1437-40) and even seized the reins of government, in Denmark three great peasant risings, between 1340 and 1441, resulted only in fixing the yoke of the German aristocracy still more heavily upon the Danish peasant, who was reduced first to villeinage and then to the harshest serfdom.

Thus in the greater part of Europe, as a result either of these social changes or of the scourge of war and disease, the condition of the rural classes would seem to have grown worse, especially in the East, Centre, and North of the Continent, and even in certain parts of the West, in Scotland, Ireland, Navarre, Aragon, and, above all, in France. Most of the French provinces were ruined; the population diminished by a half; and even Languedoc, although far from the scene of hostilities, lost a third of its inhabitants. In the days of Charles VII, the Bishop of Lisieux describes the frightful misery of the northern countryside, where emaciated peasants, covered with rags, wandered in the midst of the deserted fields. The Englishman Fortescue boasts, in 1450, of the contrast between the destitution of the cultivators in the most fertile country in the world and the well-being of the peasantry across the Channel.

In a few countries, however, the rural districts were more favourably situated; for instance, in Bohemia before the Hussite wars, and in Poland, under Casimir the Great and the Jagellons. It was, above all, Italy, Spain, the Low Countries, Germany, and England which were most successful in preserving and increasing their former prosperity. In these countries the different classes of the rural population enjoyed, in general, a certain degree of ease and comfort. The day labourers themselves benefited by the higher wages, which had doubled and trebled in Italy, as in France, England, and Germany. In England they demanded to be paid in money, and to work only five days a week. In the Rhine and Danube lands the daily agricultural wage was equivalent in purchasing power to the price of a pig or sheep, nine to seven pounds of meat, or a pair of shoes, and the annual wage of a servant to the price of an ox or twenty sheep. In England the small peasant proprietors, yeomen or franklins, and the small tenant-farmers often enjoyed an annual income of £70 or £80, and sent their sons to college. The conditions of material life were still further improved, if not in respect of housing and furniture, at any rate, in respect of clothes, and especially of food, which was plentiful and even abundant in the country districts of England, Flanders, and the Rhineland.

One of the most striking indications of this prosperity in the rural districts was the prompt reconstitution of the population in these favoured areas. Between 1450 and 1500 Italy, that "full fair and pleasant land," reached a total of nine to eleven million souls, a third of whom dwelt in the two Sicilies, more than a third in Upper Italy, and a tenth in Tuscany. The Castilian states numbered seven and a half million inhabitants; Catalonia and Roussillon, 300,000; and the whole Spanish peninsula about ten million. The Southern Netherlands, in which the marvellous fertility of the soil and the prosperity of the people were admired by all beholders, contained over three million souls, a half of whom belonged to Flanders and Brabant. England recovered the two and a half million inhabitants whom she had had before the Black Death, and her peasants were among the most prosperous in the Western world. While Bohemia lost half a million out of her three million inhabitants in the Hussite wars, Germany, in the fifteenth century, numbered some twelve millions, and was not to know such prosperity again for three centuries and a half. The progress of this part of the West sufficed to preserve for Western Europe the economic supremacy which it had already won in the domain of rural labour.

It was in this direction that there was to be continued in modern times an evolution which had little by little profoundly transformed the lot of the working classes, an evolution of which the birth and progress are, perhaps, the most important events in the history of the Middle Ages.

CONCLUSION

THE history of labour in the Middle Ages began with a far more terrible shock than that which marked the end of this long period. The latter was only an accident of growth, whereas the former very nearly brought about a complete stop in the march of civilization. The barbarian invasions let loose a real disaster. In two hundred years the ordered edifice of the Roman and Christian Empire, under the shelter of which labour had grown and prospered, was overset from roof to foundation in the West, and formidably sapped in the East. Ruins lay everywhere; anarchy took the place of order, and the reign of force succeeded to that of law; production in all its forms was arrested, the treasury of wealth accumulated by former generations was scattered; economic and social progress ceased. A blind work of destruction was all that was accomplished by these barbarians, whose sole useful influence was to provoke a salutary reaction among the chosen few who preserved the tradition and the remnants of civilization.

It was in the East that those few took up once more the work of Rome. The Byzantine Empire, opposing to barbarism a bulwark which remained for long insurmountable, brought the people back to the land, gave an immense impetus to colonization, commerce, and industry, once more opened the sources of wealth, abolished slavery, fixed men to the soil, and set light once again to the smouldering hearth of civilization. In four centuries it won the barbarian populations of Eastern Europe to civilization, and acted as the teacher of the West, which had sunk halfway back into barbarism. The West itself undertook a more obscure task, but one which was fertile in results. It set on foot the first agricultural colonization which carried the frontiers of a new Christendom to the Elbe and the Lowlands of Scotland. In the framework of a natural and manorial economy, it sought to revive economic activity, substituting serfdom for slavery and, like the Eastern Empire, establishing the mass of the population in great domains, under conditions of stability and relative security. But it was unable to give to trade, industrial production, and urban economy the same vitality as its rival.

On all sides the aristocracy had grown and taken possession of the greater part of the land, which, for the most part, passed from collective to individual ownership. In the East this aristocracy did not succeed in obtaining complete political power as well as social influence and economic supremacy. In the West, collecting in its hands all the forms of authority, it became a feudal class. The clerical and military caste, which saved the people from the dangers of the last invasions in the ninth and tenth centuries, brought about the triumph of a new form of organized labour—to wit, the feudal economy, which grew out of the economy of the previous period, and was every whit as oppressive. In the name of the protection which they claimed to secure for the masses, the feudal classes chained men to the soil or to the workshops, claimed to regulate every sort of activity, divided the fruits of labour as they pleased, and weighed down the multitudes under the yoke of a capricious and tyrannical authority, though obliged to allow them a minimum of material advantages. At the end of two centuries Christendom emerged from the isolation, in which it was kept by these thousands of local governments with their narrow horizons, and the framework of feudal economy began to break up in all directions.

There followed the golden age of the Middle Ages, and one of the finest periods in the history of human labour. It lasted for 250 years (twelfth to fourteenth centuries). Commercial activity began again and increased enormously, as also did industrial production, and they gave an immense impulse to movable wealth and to town life. The working classes, grouped in the towns, set to work the irresistible force of their revolutionary unions, and conquered both liberty and power. They encased industrial production in a strong armour of free crafts and sworn corporations. For the first time millions of emancipated workers learned the formidable power of association, won recognition for the social value of their labour, and raised themselves to a level of material and moral existence unknown to their forebears.

Following their example and impelled by new needs, the

rural classes, whose co-operation assured the success of one of the greatest works accomplished in the whole history of mankind, the colonization of Christian Europe, emancipated themselves in their turn and conquered all those civil and economic liberties, of which they had hitherto been deprived. They began to gain access to the ownership of property, they improved the conditions of their existence, they often attained to ease and well-being. They were associated in the work of local administration, and they rose in the social hierarchy. Finally, taking up the rôle which the enfeebled East was no longer able to perform, Western civilization transformed in its own image the economic and social régime of the young countries in the Centre, North, and East of Europe, the new provinces of Christendom.

But during the last hundred years of the Middle Ages, a crisis threatened the solidity of the new edifice, in which labour was prospering. Nations and states strove with one another; anarchy reappeared; and in the midst of the disorders national economy reaped the heritage of feudal and urban economy. Terrible natural scourges, carrying off half the population of Europe, brought about a momentary scarcity of labour. The primitive unity of the urban classes was more and more shaken. The formation and steady advance of the capitalist bourgeoisie, of international commerce, and of the great industry, accelerated industrial production and trade, but gave rise to the formidable problems of wage labour and pauperism. The interests of master craftsmen and journeymen fell apart, and they opposed union to union. The class war raged in the towns, where revolutions broke out, which had for object now the reform of abuses on the part of the authorities, now the conquest of power, now a new social order. They died out by degrees; the central power re-established order; in one part of Europe the rise of wages and the increase of wealth allowed the masses, the small masters, and the workmen to retain or recover the prosperity of the preceding period.

At the same time agricultural colonization, arrested in a certain number of regions, which were a prey to war and anarchy, went on apace in others. The activity of production was sometimes turned into new channels. Land finally passed into the hands of the state, the great proprietors, the bourgeoisie, and even to a small extent into that of the peasants, while the feudal class grew poorer, and the class of *censitaires* gained a partial hold upon the soil. New forms of agricultural exploitation, tenant-farming, *métayage*, and hired labour received a certain extension. Serfdom, which died out in the most civilized part of Europe, revived again elsewhere. A proletariat and a problem of pauperism appeared in the country districts. Peasant revolts, blind risings, due to misery, or violent attempts to bring about social changes, broke out on many sides, incoherent and ineffective manifestations of the distress of the rural classes. Nevertheless, calm reappeared. In the more privileged regions of the West the prosperity of the country districts equalled that of the towns. But in the greater part of Europe the horizon was dark, and the world of labour lived in the midst of inquietude, on the eve of new shocks, which were destined to retard its ascendancy in modern times.

The work accomplished by medieval civilization nevertheless remained intact in all its main outlines. During this millennium two-thirds of the soil of Europe was conquered by colonization; population doubled; agricultural production increased to vast proportions; individual ownership in its diverse forms replaced the primitive system of tribal, village, or family property. The bourgeois and rural classes themselves attained to the possession of landed capital. Movable wealth, as a result of the increase of commerce and of industrial production, developed anew, and was scattered among a crowd of possessors. But the capital fact which emerges, and which gives to this age its unforgettable importance, is the attainment of freedom by the urban and rural classes.

For the first time the masses, ceasing to be mere herds without rights or thoughts of their own, became associations of freemen, proud of their independence, conscious of the value and dignity of their labour, fitted by their intelligent activity to collaborate in all spheres, political, economic, and social, in the tasks which the aristocracies believed themselves alone able to fulfil. Not only was the power of production multiplied a hundredfold by their efforts, but society was regenerated by the incessant influx of new and vigorous blood. Social selection was henceforth better assured. It was thanks to the devotion and spirit of these medieval masses that the nations became conscious of themselves, for it was they who brought about the triumph of national patriotism, just as their local patriotism had burned for town or village in the past. The martyrdom of a peasant girl from the marshes of Lorraine saved the first of the great nations, France, which had become the most brilliant home of civilization in the Middle Ages. They gave to the modern states their first armies, which were superior to those of feudal chivalry. Above all, it was they who prepared the advent of democracy and bequeathed to the labouring masses the instruments of their power, the principles of freedom and of association. Labour, of old despised and depreciated, became a power of incomparable force in the world, and its social value became increasingly recognized. It is from the Middle Ages that this capital evolution takes its date, and it is this which makes this period, so often misunderstood, and so full of a confused but singularly powerful activity, the most important in the universal history of labour before the great changes witnessed by the eighteenth and nineteenth centuries.

BIBLIOGRAPHY

THERE are thousands of works relating to the economic history of the Middle Ages. The three following bibliographies will give some idea of their number in the case of France, Spain, and England :

P. BOISSONNADE, *Les Études relatives à l'histoire économique de la France au moyen âge* (141 pp., Paris, 1902).—*Les Études relatives a l'histoire économique de l'Espagne* (153 pp., Paris, 1913).—H. HALL, *A Short Bibliography of English Medieval Economic History* (350 pp., London, 1914).

GENERAL WORKS

G. ALEXINSKY, *La Russie et l'Europe* (Paris, 1917).

C. ALLEN, *Histoire de Danemark*, trad. Beauvoise (2 vols., Paris, 1889).

R. ALTAMIRA, *Historia de Espâna y de la civilización española* (4 vols., 2nd ed., Barcelona, 1909).

————, *Historia de la propriedad comunal* (Madrid, 1890).

J. BELOCH, *Die Bevölkerung Europas im Mittelalter* (1888).

P. BLOK, *History of the Netherlands*, vol. I (1904).

K. BÜCHER, *Die Entstehung der Volkswirthschaft* (Leipzig, 1906). French translation by Hansay (Brussels). English translation by S. M. Wickett, *Industrial Evolution*.

J. CARO, *Geschichte Polens* (Gotha, 1840 ff.).

F. CHALANDON, *Histoire de la domination normande en Italie* (2 vols., Paris, 1907).

W. CUNNINGHAM, *Western Civilization in its Economic Aspects* (Cambridge, 1908).

CH. DIEHL, *Byzance* (Paris, 1919).

E. GEIJER, *Histoire de la Suède* (French trans., Paris, 1840).

E. DE GIRARD, *Histoire de l'économie sociale jusqu'à la fin du XVIe siècle* (Paris, 1900).

K. INGRAM, *History of Slavery and Serfdom* (1896).

K. JIZEČEK, *Geschichte der Bulgaren* (Prague, 1876).

————, *Geschichte der Serben* (Vienna, 1912).

337

BIBLIOGRAPHY

M. KOVALEVSKY, *Die ökonomische Entwicklung Europas* (6 vols., Leipzig, 1896-1910). [Deals only with the six great countries of the West, and treats only the juridical side, excluding commerce and the phenomena of production; nevertheless, the best work of this nature.]

P. LACOMBE, *Essai sur le passage de la propriété collective à la propriété privée* (Paris, 1900).

H. PIRENNE, *Histoire de Belgique*, tomes I-II (2nd ed., Brussels, 1910-12).

A. RAMBAUD, *L'Empire grec au Xe siècle* (1870).

————, *History of Russia*, trans. L. B. Lang (1886).

G. SALVIOLI, *Storia del diritto di proprietà* (Milan, 1914).

E. SAYOUS, *Histoire générale des Hongrois* (6 vols., 2nd ed., 1900).

H. TRAILL (ed.), *Social England*, vols. I-III (1896 *ff.*).

A. XENOPOL, *Histoire des Roumains* (2 vols., Paris, 1896).

WORKS RELATING TO THE ORGANIZATION OF PROPERTY, AGRICULTURE, AND THE RURAL CLASSES

A. ABRAM, *Social England in the Fifteenth Century* (1909).

P. ALLARD, *Les origines du servage en France* (Paris, 1913).

J. BACHFAHL, *Zur ältästen Wirtschaftstand und Socialgeschichte Böhmens* (Leipzig, 1891).

L. BEAUCHET, *Histoire de la propriété foncière en Suède* (Paris, 1904).

V. BRANTS, *Histoire des classes rurales aux Pays-Bas, etc.* (Louvain and Paris, 1880).

J. BRUTAILS, *Étude sur la condition des populations rurales du Roussillon au moyen âge* (1891).

R. CAGGESE, *Classe e comunì rurali nel medio evo Italiano* (2 vols., 1909).

F. CARDENAS, *Ensayo sobre la historia de la propiedad territorial en España* (2 vols., Madrid, 1873).

E. CHÉNON, *Étude sur l'histoire des alleux en France* (1888).

L. DELISLE, *Études sur la condition de la classe agricole et l'état de l'agriculture en Normandie* (2nd ed., Paris, 1912).

E. DENIS, *Huss et la guerre des Hussites* (Paris, 1878).

A. DÖPSCH, *Die wirtschaftsentwicklung der Karolingerzeit* (Innsbruck, 1912).

N. FUSTEL DE COULANGES, *Histoire des institutions politiques de l'ancienne France*, tomes III-IV (Paris, 1887-90).

TH. VON DER GOLTZ, *Geschichte der deutschen Landwirtschaft* (Leipzig, 1909).

BIBLIOGRAPHY

R. Grand, *Le contrat de complant* (Paris, 1917).

Hanauer, *Les Paysans de l'Alsace au moyen âge* (Paris, 1865).

L. Hartmann, *Zur Wirtschaftsgeschichte Italiens im frühen Mittelalter* (Gotha, 1904).

E. de Hinojosa, *El Régimen Señorial en Cataluña durante la edad media* (Madrid, 1905).

K. Inama Sternegg, *Deutsche Wirtschaftsgeschichte* (2nd ed., 6 vols., Leipzig, 1909).

P. W. Joyce, *Social History of Ancient Ireland* (1906).

J. Klein, *The Mesta: a study in Spanish economic history* (Harvard Econ. Studies, 1920).

K. Lamprecht, *Deutsches Wirtschaftsleben in Mittelalter* (3 vols., Leipzig, 1879-99).

————, *Études sur l'état économique de la France au XIe siècle*, trad. Marignan (Paris, 1889).

E. Lesne, *La propriété ecclésiastique en France pendant la période mérovingienne* (Paris, 1910).

S. Luce, *Histoire de la Jacquerie* (2nd ed., Paris, 1894).

J. Mackintosh, *History of Civilisation in Scotland* (2nd ed., 1900).

F. W. Maitland, *Domesday Book and Beyond* (1897 ; 2nd ed., 1907).

H. Marczali, *Ungarische Verfassungsgeschichte* (Tübingen, 1910).

E. Martin, *Histoire économique de l'Angleterre* (2 vols., 1912).

J. Mortreuil, *Histoire du droit byzantin* (3 vols., Paris, 1843).

P. Meitzen, *Siedelung und Agrarwesen der Germanen, etc.* (3 vols., Leipzig, 1895 ff.).

P. Milyukov, *Essais sur l'histoire de la civilisation russe* (Paris, 1901).

P. Negulesco, *Histoire du droit et des institutions de la Roumanie,* tome I (Paris, 1898).

C. Neumann, *L'Empire byzantin et sa situation mondiale (X^e-XIe siècle)* (French trans., Paris, 1895).

M. Novakovitch, *La zadruga chez les Serbes* (Paris, 1906).

A. Palmieri, *Laboratori del contado Bolognese durante le signorie* (1909).

Paparigopoulos, *Histoire de la civilisation byzantine* (Paris, 1876).

E. Perez Pujol, *Historia de las instituciones sociales de la España Goda* (4 vols., Valencia, 1896).

K. Rakovski, *Entstehung des Grossgrundbesitzes in Polen* (Posen, 1899).

A. Réville and C. Petit-Dutaillis, *Le soulèvement des travailleurs d'Angleterre* (Paris, 1898).

J. E. Thorold Rogers, *History of Agriculture and Prices in England* (7 vols., Oxford, 1866-1902).

G. Salvioli, *Storia economica d'Italia nel alto medio evo* (Naples, 1913).

BIBLIOGRAPHY

H. Seé, *Les classes rurales et le régime domanial en France* (Paris, 1901).

F. Seebohm, *The English Village Community* (1883).

————, *The Tribal System in Wales* (2nd ed., 1904).

L. Verriest, *Le servage en Hainaut* (Brussels, 1910).

P. Vinogradoff, *English Society in the Eleventh Century* (Oxford, 1908).

————, *Growth of the Manor* (2nd ed., 1911).

————, *Villainage in England* (Oxford, 1892).

Wrainatz, *Die agrarverhältnisse mittelalterlichen Serbiens* (Jena, 1905).

Zachariæ, *Historiæ Juris Græco-Romani delineatio* (Heidelburg, 1839).

M. Dounar-Zapolski, *Economic History of Russia*, vol. I (Kiev, 1911) [in Russian].

WORKS RELATING TO THE HISTORY OF COMMERCE

F. Barthold, *Geschichte der deutschen Seemacht* (2 vols., Magdeburg, 1850-1).

A. Beer, *Allgemeine Geschichte des Welthandels*, vol. I (5 vols., Vienna, 1850-4).

M. Canale, *Nuova Istoria di Genova, del suo commercio, etc.* (1866).

Capmany, *Memorias Historicas sobre Commercio y Artes de Barcelona* (4 vols., 1779-92).

H. Cons, *Précis d'histoire du commerce*, tome I (Paris, 1896).

L. Delisle, *Les opérations financières des Templiers* (1889).

Ch. Diehl, *Venise* (Paris, 1915).

J. Falke, *Geschichte des deutschen Handels* (2 vols., Leipzig, 1859-60).

W. Heyd, *Histoire du commerce du Levant au moyen âge*, trad. Furcy Raynaud (2 vols., 2nd ed., Leipzig, 1923).

P. Huvelin, *Essai historique sur le droit des foires et marchés* (1897).

L. Levi, *History of British Commerce* (1880).

S. Peruzzi, *Storia del Commercio e dei Banchieri di Firenze* (1868).

H. Pigeonneau, *Histoire du commerce de la France*, tome I (Paris, 1885).

A. Schaube, *Handelsgeschichte der romanischen Völker des Mittelmeergebietes* (1906).

W. Shaw, *History of Currency* (1896).

E. van Bruyssel, *Histoire du commerce et de la marine en Belgique* (2 vols., Brussels, 1881-5).

H. van der Linden, *Les Gildes marchandes dans les Pays Bas au moyen âge* (1896).

BIBLIOGRAPHY

WORKS RELATING TO THE HISTORY OF INDUSTRY AND THE INDUSTRIAL CLASSES

W. Ashley, *Introduction to English Economic History*, 2 parts (1893-1906).

M. Bofarull, *Coleccion de documentos, etc., de la Corona de Aragon*, vol. XL, *Gremios y Cofradias, etc.* (1876).

W. Cunningham, *Growth of English Industry and Commerce*, vol. I.

A. Doren, *Studien aus der Florentiner Wirtschaftgeschichte* (1908).

————, *Entwickelung und Organisation der Florentiner Zunfte* (1896).

R. Eberstadt, *Das französische Gewerberecht, etc.* (Leipzig, 1899).

————, *Der Ursprung des Zunftwesens* (2nd ed., Leipzig, 1915).

G. Espinas et H. Pirenne, *Recueil de documents relatifs à l'histoire de l'industrie drapière en Flandre* (tomes I-II, Brussels, 1906-20).

G. Fagniez, *Documents relatifs à l'histoire de l'industrie et du commerce en France* (2 vols., Paris, 1898-1901).

————, *L'industrie et la classe industrielle à Paris au XIIIe siècle* (1877).

L. Gambirasio, *Le corporazioni milanesi nel medio evo* (1897).

T. Geering, *Handel und Industrie der Stadt Basel* (1886).

Gogioso, *Il contratto di lavoro Ligure* (1899).

Huybrecht, *Histoire du commerce et de l'industrie en Belgique* (Bruges, 1888).

J. Huyttens, *Recherches sur les Corporations Gantoises* (1861).

E. Levasseur, *Histoire des classes ouvrières et de l'industrie en France avant 1789*, tome I (Paris, 1900).

G. des Marez, *L'organisation du travail à Bruxelles au XVe siècle* (1904).

Michele, *Le corporazioni Parmesi* (1897).

J. Mundello, *Beiträge zur Geschichte der Arbeitslohn im Mittelalter* (Budapest, 1903).

W. Ochenkowski, *Englands wirtschaftliche Entwickelung im Ausgange des Mittelalters* (Jena, 1879).

O. Peterka, *Das Gewerberecht Böhmens im XIV Jahrhundert* (Vienna, 1909).

G. Renard, *Histoire du travail à Florence* (2 vols., Paris, 1913).

————, *Syndicats, trade unions, et corporations* (Paris, 1900).

E. Rodocanacchi, *Les corporations ouvrières à Rome* (2 vols., Paris, 1896).

G. Martin Saint-Léon, *Histoire des corporations de métiers en France* (3rd ed., 1922).

J. Sarthou, *Las asociaciones obreras en España* (1900).

G. Schanz, *Zur Geschichte der deutschen Gesellenverbände* (Leipzig, 1877).

341

BIBLIOGRAPHY

G. SCHMOLLER, *Die Strassburger Tucher- und Weberzunft* (1879).

STRICKER, *Studien zur Genesis des moderne Kapitalismus* (1908-19).

L. TRAMOYERES BLASCO, *Institutiones gremiales en Valencia, etc.* (1889).

J. VENTALLO VINTRÓ, *Historia de la industria lanera catalana* (1904).

WORKS RELATING TO URBAN EMANCIPATION AND THE SOCIAL RÔLE OF THE COMMERCIAL AND INDUSTRIAL CLASSES

G. ARIAS, *Il Sistema della costituzione economica e sociale italiane nell' età* (1905).

G. BOURGIN, *La commune de Soissons* (1908).

F. CARRERAS Y CANDI, *Hegemonia de Barcelona en Cataluña* (1893).

A. DOREN, *Untersuchungen zur Geschichte der Kaufmannsgilden des Mittelalters* (Leipzig, 1890).

G. ESPINAS, *La vie urbaine de Douai au moyen âge* (4 vols., 1912).

A. GIRY, *Histoire de la ville de Saint-Omer* (1877).

————, *Les Établissements de Rouen* (2 vols., 1883-5).

GONZALEZ, *Coleccion de fueros concedidos á varios pueblos* (2 vols., 1833).

A. S. GREEN, *Town Life in the Fifteenth Century* (2 vols., 1894).

C. GROSS, *The Gild Merchant* (1890).

L. HALPHEN, *Paris sous les premiers Capétiens* (1909).

K. HEGEL, *Die Entstehung des deutschen Städtewesens* (1898).

————, *Städte und Gilden der Germanischen Völker im Mittelalter* (2 vols., Leipzig, 1891-2).

K. LAMPRECHT, *Deutsches Städteleben am Schluss des Mittelalters* (Leipzig, 1884).

A. LUCHAIRE, *Les Communes françaises* (2nd ed., 1911).

J. LUCHAIRE, *Les Démocraties italiennes* (1915).

E. MAUGIS, *Histoire de la commune d'Amiens* (1906).

L. MIROT, *Les Insurrections urbaines au début du règne de Charles VI* (1900).

F. PERRENS, *Etienne Marcel, etc.* (1875).

H. PIRENNE, *Les démocraties urbaines aux Pays-Bas* (1912).

————, *Histoire de Dinant* (1896).

A. SOLMI, *Le classe soziali in Firenze* (1900).

L. VANDERKINDERE, *Le siècle des Artevelde* (1879).

INDEX

ABBEYS, organisation of, 129-30
Abo, 275
Achaia, 267
Ackerman, 311
" Acquisitions," 81
Acre, 168
Adalbero, Bishop, quoted, 119, 146
Admiralty courts, 174, 288-89
Adrian IV, Pope, 155
Adrianople, 55, 266
Adriatic, Venetian conquest of, 175
Adscriptitii, 43, 44
Africa, trade with, 111, 289; Italian banking agency in, 168; European exploration of, 289
Agreements, 247-48 (and see Charters)
Agriculture:
  Bulgarian prosperity in, 59
  Byzantine care of, 32-35, 116
  Churches' services to, 36, 65, 68-69, 157
  communes, agricultural, in Byzantine Empire, 41
  co-operative farming, 323
  corn-growing. See that heading
  day labourers. See subheading, Wage-earners
  decay of, under barbarians, 26; 14th cent. decline, 316
  development of (10th to 13th cents.), 231 *seq.*, 236-38
  Eastern Europe, preponderance in, 270
  encouragement of, under Carolingian and Anglo-Saxon monarchies, 64
  England pre-eminent in, 176
  " extensive " methods, 10, 234, 255, 274
  feudal system, as affecting, 140-41, 152, 159
  German, 12
  Gewaanne, 10
  industrial crops. See that heading

Agriculture (*continued*):
  industry an annexe of, 102
  intensive methods introduced, 234
  iron ploughshare introduced, 234, 274
  live stock, small, preponderance of, 141, 232-33
  manures, 234, 274
  métayage. See that heading
  methods of, Carolingian, 74, 75, 79
  model farms, 153, 157, 232; Scandinavian, 274
  ploughlands, division of, 79; cessation of, 240
  Scandinavia, in, 273
  servants in husbandry (*servientes, valets*), 257-58
  Slav, 7
  soldier cultivators, 41
  State promotion of, 153
  strips of field, 10, 79, 141
  tenant-farming (7th to 10th cents.), 90; nature of, 255; success of, 259; (15th cent.), 322-23; development of, 335
  towns' concern with, 201
  trade development stimulating, 177
  triennial fallows, 10, 255, 274
  wage-earners in, elimination of, in Byzantine Empire, 42; survivors in Gaul, 90; beginnings of, 252, 255; day labourers, 255-57, 276; earnings of (13th cent.), 259; classes of, 324
Ahrimanns, 88, 91, 114, 122
" Aids," 249
Aix-la-Chapelle, 113; mineral springs of, 106; fair at, 170; coal mining in, 295; risings at (14th cent.), 312
Alamanni, 9; influence of, 18; savagery of, 23; spoliation by, 24
Alamannia, colonisation of, 68, 70; royal domains in, 82

343

INDEX

INDEX

INDEX

Basle, 113, 315; woollen industry of, 187, 210, 285; democratic risings in, 217; silk industry of, 297; upper and middle classes in, 299, 301; crafts in (15th cent.), 302; *Safran* at, 303

Basque provinces, 122, 248

Bastides, 191

Baths, 222-23, 262

Baumgartner family, 300

Bavaria: royal domains in, 82; non-feudal property surviving in, 121; hop gardens of, 236

Bavaria, Duke of, 83

Bavarians, 9; influence of, 18

Bayonne, 176

Béarn, 122, 194

Beaucaire, 170

Beaumanoir cited, 245

Beaumont, charter of, 196, 247

Beauvais, cloth industry of, 187; revolt at (1074-79), 194; riots in (1233), 217; *corvée* in, 249

Bee-keeping, 74, 233

Beer, 222, 261; German, 12, 100; English and Flemish production of, 186

Beggars: at Rome (410), 28; laws against, 101; corporations of, 303; increase in, 306-7; rural pauperism, 325

Belgium (see also Low Countries): Frankish occupation of, 16 land reclamation in, 228; forest clearance, 230 villeinage in, 133

Bell foundries, 295

Benedict of Aniane, 69

Benedict of Nursia, 68

Benedictines, 69, 154

Beneficia. See *Precaria*

Benevento, Duchy of, 18

Benjamin of Tudela quoted, 266

Berbers, 115

Bergamo, 184, 211

Bergen, 275, 291-92

Bernard of Clairvaux, 194

Berry, 184

Besançon, 303

Bezants, 51, 165

Bézier, 187, 195, 314

Bigorré, 122

Bills of Exchange, 52, 288

Birth rate, low (7th to 10th cents.), 76

Biscay: sea traffic to, 176; iron mining in, 184, 185, 294

Bishoprics, towns identified with 112

Black death, ravages of, 284-85 labour shortage after, 285 317, 324

Black Sea trade, 289

Blast furnaces, 293, 295

Blind men, corporations of, 303

Bobbio Abbey, 69, 74, 87, 92, 93 96, 107

Bohemia:
Church lands in, 270-71
civilising of, 267-68
crusades as affecting, 160
democracy in, decline in, 312
Hussite wars, 329, 331
luxury industries of, 282
mines of: tin, 184, 269, 295; gold and silver, 294
peasant protection in, 281
poverty of (14th cent.), 316
rural conditions in (15th cent.), 330; rural industries, 293
serfdom in (13th cent.), 271
Slav occupation of, 6

Bologna:
artisans' corporations in, 211
Bishopric of, 83, 124
black death in, 285
cloth industry of, 186
democratic success in (1257-71), 219
feudal power at, broken, 194
marshes of, drained, 229
merchant bankers of, 167
palaces in, 205
restoration of (9th cent.), 113
revolutionary temper in (14th cent.), 310

Boon payments, 92

Bordars, 92, 136

Bordeaux:
administration of, 199
fair at, 170
free craft régime in, 302
importance of, 315
revival of (12th cent.), 176
trade of, 111
wine exports of (14th cent.), 236

Bosnia, 57, 269

Bosphorus, Venetian mastery of, 175

Bottomry, loans on, 52, 166

Boulogne, 111

348

INDEX

Catalonia (*continued*):
  peasant risings in (14th-15th cents.), 327
  population increase in (15th cent.), 331
  riots in, 217
  rural emancipation in, 248
  serfs in, 136; serfs of the glebe, 258; persistence of serfdom, 325
  servants' wages in, 260
  stock leases in, 256
  tenant-farming in (13th cent.), 255
  trade rivalry of, 175-76
Cattle: co-ownership of, 78; trade in, 162, 172; murrain among, 232; scarcity of, compared with sheep, 233; fattening of, 317
Cattle-breeding, in the Roman Empire, 4; among the Slavs, 7; among the Germans, 12; barbarian ignorance of, 26; Byzantine success in, 34-35; prevalence of, 73, 74, 266; in Spain, 153, 281; scientific methods of, 153, 157; development of (13th cent.), 232; in Scandinavia, 273-74; royal encouragement of, 281
Caux, 228
Cecaumenus cited, 40
Celtic Church, lands of, 79
Celtic countries, cattle farmers in, 90; peasant life in, 98; towns non-existent in, 112
Celts: conversion of, 65; food of, 99; communal lands of, 78-79, 240; Anglo-Norman enslavement of, 258
Cens. See under Leases
Censitaires, 253, 255, 321-22, 324, 335
Ceorls, 87
Cerdagne, 229, 231
Cereals, cultivation of, 141, 266; increase in, 75, 234; rent levy on, 255; royal promotion of (14th-15th cents.), 281
Châlons, 187, 314
Chalon-sur-Saône, 170
Champagne:
  cutlery manufacture of, 186
  drainage of, 228
  fairs of, 163, 168, 170-72
  forest clearances in, 230

Champagne (*continued*):
  industries of, 187, 188, 297
  iron-mining in, 184
  peasant rising in, 327
  serfs enfranchised in, 246; persistence of serfdom, 258, 325
  tenant farming in (15th cent.), 323
Champart, 133-34, 140, 249
Charities, burgesses' associations so called, 193
Charity, Church organisation of, 65, 156; urban provision of, 203, 208
Charlemagne, Emperor, 106; reconstructive achievements of, 63, 67, 111; forestry inculcated by, 73; Church grants of, 82; *De Villis* cited, 86, 103; manner of life of, 87
Charles the Fat, 109
Charles IV, King of France, 169, 243, 281
Charles V, King of France, 280, 281, 283
Charles VII, King of France, 330
Charles VIII, King of France, 290
Charroux Abbey, 70
Charters of enfranchisement, 101, 196; cited, 245; purchases of, 246; rural, 134, 247-48, 250, 253, 259
Chartres: cloth industry of, 187; serfdom surviving in, 198; growth of artisans' associations in (11th-12th cents.), 210; craft chapel at, 214
Chase, rights of the, 73
Châtellerandais, 186
Cheese, 261; trade in, 163, 234; rent levy on, 256
Chemical manufactures, 297
Chestnuts, 87, 235
Chevage, 139
Chiaravalle Abbey, 157
Chiari, 167
Chinchilla, 188
Chio, 175
Chivalry, 150, 155
Chorites, 265
Christianity, influence of, in Roman Empire, 2, 3; among Slavs, 8; slavery opposed by, 43, 271, 276

INDEX

Church, Eastern:
  benefices, etc., in, 36
  civilising influence of, 57, 59-60
  imperial relations with, 37
  lands of, 36-37, 265, 270-71
  slavery opposed by, 43
  taxation not levied on, 265
Church, Latin:
  ability in, 156
  agriculture encouraged by, 157
  civilising achievements of, 64-66, 116
  colonisation promoted by. See under Colonisation
  demoralisation of, 279
  economic influence of, 156
  educational work of, 156
  emancipation of peasants and artisans opposed by, 157, 246
  emancipation of slaves encouraged by, 95, 271, 276
  excommunication, 156
  feudal abuses checked by, 154-55
  Frankish Empire supported by (486-521), 16
  Fraternities of Peace, 155-56
  ideal of, 155
  industry and commerce encouraged by, 157 - 58; attitude to industrial combinations, 306
  insurrections against, in Spain (12th cent.), 195
  lands of: monastic organisation of, 37, 65, 85-86, 103; peasants' privileges on, 45, 98, 135, 137, 156-57; development of, 65, 246; methods of acquiring, 82, 123, 243, 270; extent of, in 9th cent., 82; in feudal times, 124, 243, 271; later, 319; schools for art on, 103, 157; diffusion of, 128; reclamation movement as affecting, 240; tenant farming on, 255; in Scandinavia, 275
  Lateran Council, 155
  Mendicant Orders, 156
  monarchical government's re-establishment assisted by, 154
  Monastic Orders as colonists, 230-31; agricultural science of, 234; market gardening and horticulture by, 235

Church, Latin (continued):
  political economy developed by, 156
  Pontiff Brothers, the, 164
  popular alliance with, against nobles, 218
  royal policy regarding, 280
  transport promoted by, 157, 163-64
  truce of God spread by, 155
  usury condemned by, 158, 166
Church buildings, 224
Cider, 100, 235, 261
Cilicia, 175
Cistercians, 154; cloth industry carried by, into Germany, 188; colonisation effected by, 227, 228; land reclamation by, 230; status of, 243; Scandinavia civilised by, 274
Cities. See Towns
Civil liberty, spread of, in 12th cent., 196-98
Clergy (see also Church):
  burgess rights denied to, 197
  luxury and idleness of, in Eastern Church, 36
  peasant members of, 252
  serfs barred from ranks of, 138
  townships' and peasants' struggle against, 246-47
  trade encouraged by, 109
  villeins among, 143
Clerks, 183
Clermont-sur-Oise, battle of, 327
Clockmaking, 186, 295
Cloth manufacture, Frisian, 106; development in the West, 186-88; cloth dressing, 293. See also Woollen industry
Cloth trade, 186-87, 208; in fine cloths, 282
Clothes, coarseness of, 106; of villeins, 145; of the working class (11th to 14th cents.), 222; prices of (14th cent.), 161; improvements in (15th cent.), 331
Clovis, 62
Cluniacs, 227, 243
Coal-mining, 185, 295
Coblenz, 210
Cod, 317
Cœur, Jacques, 290, 299, 320
Coinage (see also Money changers, Money economy)

353

INDEX

Coinage (*continued*):
  debasing of, 283
  diversity of, 159
  general use of (15th cent.), 287
  German ignorance of, 12
  gold and silver (12th cent.), 165
  gold or silver *sou*, 109-10
  international: Byzantine, 51, 165; Italian, 288
  metal, in central Europe (13th cent.), 268
  re-establishment of, under Carolingians, etc., 64
  royal policy regarding (14th to 15th cents.), 109, 283
  Royal *v.* Feudal, 154
  scarcity of, under feudalism, 159
  silver, in Scandinavia (11th cent.), 274
  stabilisation of, 165, 202, 250; encouraged by the Church, 158
Collegia, 3, 104
Colliberti, 136, 137
Cologne, 113; river trade of, 164, 290-91; woollen industry in, 187; merchant aristocracy of, 192; insurrection in (12th cent.), 195; burgesses of, 209; artisans' corporations in, 211; democratic risings in, 217, 312; prosperity of fair in (15th cent.), 287; golden age of, 315
Cologne, Archbishop of, 169, 194, 243
Colonate. See *Coloni*
Coloni :
  barbarian appropriation of, 19
  barbarian immigrants as, 15
  Carolingian protection of, 64
  classes of, 44
  elements composing the class of, 43; variety established in Byzantine Empire, 33
  growth of the class under the Germans, 21
  preponderance of, in France, 91, 132
  produce rent paid by, 90
  rural population of, in Byzantine Empire, 42
  seigniorial domains, on, 86
  settlements of (7th and 8th cents.), 67

Coloni (*continued*):
  Slav employment of, 7; Slav intermingling with, 57
  status and conditions of, 271; in Roman Europe, 3; in Byzantine Empire, 43-44; (7th to 10th cents.), 92-93; degradation of, to serf class, 21, 44, 59, 93, 117, 136
  war prisoners as, 14, 43
Colonisation, agricultural:
  barbarian kings' encouragement of, 63
  Byzantine Empire, in, 332
  Central Europe, of, 267-68
  Church's encouragement of, 65, 68-69, 226-27, 243, 246
  far-reaching effects of, 67
  first attempt at, 116
  Hostise : meaning of, 134; special advantages accruing to, 91, 247
  importance of, 334
  military aid in, 33, 68
  privileges attaching to, 90, 91
  progress in (11th to 12th cents.), 225
  Roman Empire, under, 4
  Scandinavian, 273
  State promotion of, 153, 280
  trade development stimulating, 177
  urban communities' encouragement of, 201
Columban, 68, 70
Commachio, 104, 105, 294
Commerce. See Trade
Commons. See under Lands
Communes (merchants' federations), rise of, 194; land purchases by, 320
Communism: Mendicant Orders and, 156; Taborite, 329
Communistic régime on monastic domains, 85-86
Community of labour, 74-75, 79
Community of property, survival of, to 15th cent., 121
Comneni, 264
Compass, use of, 174, 289
Compiegne, 195, 314
Complants. See under Leases
Compostella, 195
Condoma, 100
Confectioneries, 297
Confirmationes (merchants' fedelrations), 194
Confratriæ, 105

INDEX

INDEX

INDEX

INDEX

England (*continued*):
food industry of, 186
forest in, 72; clearances, 230, 317
France, ravages of, in (14th cent.), 327
gentry of, 253
horse-rearing in, 233, 317
hospitals in, 208, 262
industrial development of (15th cent.), 296
inheritance abuses in, 249
interest rates in, 166
kings of, sound administration organised by (from 11th cent.), 152; conditions under Plantagenets, 196; their policy, 283; royal support of democratic aspirations, 217
labour laws in (14th to 15th cents.), 324
labourers in (farm), 257
landholding in: collective property only among Celts, 79, 240; *bookland*, 81; private ownership, extent of, 83, 319-20; size of feudal fiefs, 128; manors, 129; *holdings*, 131; size of villeins' holdings, 141; accretions to State property, 242; copyholders, 254; freeholders (14th cent.), 321; tenant farmers (15th cent.), 323; ecclesiastical property, 244, 319
landowning class in, the, 241
livery companies of, 286
mercantile marine of, 291
merchants of the staple, 163, 283, 286; merchant gilds, 206, 286; their tyranny, 208; merchant adventurers, 283, 286
mineral products of, 294-95
monastic colonies in, 69
nobility of (13th cent.), 242
Northmen's invasion of, 115
peasantry of: rights under feudal régime, 144; charters of emancipation, 247-48; status in 14th cent., 263, 321; conditions in 15th cent., 330; peasant proprietors, 253; rural industries, 293

England (*continued*):
peasants' revolt (14th cent.), 328
population of, in 11th cent., 76; urban, in Middle Ages, 112-13; serf proportion of (11th to 13th cents.), 136; increase in (10th to 13th cents.), 237; (15th cent.), 331
prosperity of: in 13th cent., 237; in 15th cent., 308
revenue of (12th cent.), 124
serfs in, disabilities of, 138
stock-raising and sheep-farming in, 73, 74, 233, 317
Stourbridge fair, 170
sworn corporations in, 303
textile industry of, 282, 296
town administration in, type of, 199
towns in, numbers of, 191
villeinage in, 136. And see Villeinage and Villeins
vine-growing in, 236
wage-rates in (13th to 14th cents.), 259
waste lands of (11th cent.), 72, 226
weights and measures in, 154, 283
wool trade of, 163; in 15th cents., 318
wolves exterminated in, 232
yeomen of, 253
English trading abroad, 171
Engravers, 107
Epibole, 34
Epidemics, 29, 76, 146, 272, 284. See also Black death
Epitropoi, 265
Equality among townsmen, 196, 197, 202, 212, 215, 223; affirmation of natural equality, 245
Erfurt, 315; monastery, 70
Escheat, right of, 160, 170, 171
Escorts, armed, 109, 170, 171, 193, 289, 291
Esgardeurs, 213-14
Estates, great. See Domains
Esthonia, Danish settlers in, 274
Etampes, 210
Ethel, 80-81
Euric the Visigoth, 62
Evesham Abbey, 70
Exchange, treatises on, 287

INDEX

INDEX

Feudalism (*continued*):
  Byzantine approximation to, 39, 264-65
  centralised States emerging from, 152
  characteristics of, 123, 131, 151
  Church's position in, 123; its attitude to, 154-55
  concession, deed of, 125
  decline of, 242, 279, 333
  dues under, fixation of, 134, 143
  fiefs. See that heading
  fiscal disabilities of, 192
  foundation of, 126
  free landowners overthrown by, 121
  growth, tyranny and decay of, 333
  insecurity under, 150, 159, 160, 192
  investiture and Oath of Fidelity, 123, 125, 126
  knights under, 119, 127, 128
  land ownership under, by nobles, 120, 125, 133; by villeins, 134
  leases under. See Leases
  limitations of, 150-51
  lords under. See Feudal lords
  military service of, charged upon free land, 123
  monopolies of, 140, 145, 159, 198; *banvin*, 140, 198
  peasants' conditions under, 144-45; right of recapture, 147
  principle of, contemporaneously defined, 119
  protection afforded by, 143; protection to the working masses *not* secured by, 150, 159
  Russia, in, 271
  squires under, 127, 129
  tolls under, 159, 198; reduction in number of, attempted, 164
  trade hampered by, 159, 192
  urban communes' place in, 207
  vassalage, 119; vassals contrasted with tenants, 131
  villeins. See Villeinage and Villeins

Feudalism (*continued*):
  wars of, 136, 146; their savagery and frequency, 151-52; prohibited, 153; truce of God as affecting, 155; diminution in, 260
  weights and measures under, diversity of, 159
Fiefs:
  Central Europe, in, 271
  hereditary, 125, 207
  nature of, 120, 125
  peasant owners of, 134, 252
  size of, 128
  small free proprietors transformed into, 121
  Sonnenlehen, 121
  subdivision of, 241
  universality of, presumed, 125
Figs, 235
Fines (free proprietors), 87
Fines replacing death and banishment, 218
Finland, Swedish colonisation of, 274
Finnish lands, Russian colonisation of (14th to 15th cents.), 316-17
Finns, 5, 8, 268, 274
Fire brigade, 216
Fisc, 129
Fish: trade in, 162, 177; as food staple, 261
Fisheries:
  Byzantine, 35
  Carolingian period, in, 72
  deep-sea, development of, 231
  North-west European (14th cent.), 317
  pisciculture, 72, 231
  Scandinavian, 274
Fishing: among German tribes, 11; peasants' rights in, 250
Flanders:
  agriculture encouraged in, 153
  beer production of, 186
  cattle-farming in, 233
  city fraternities of, 199
  coinage of, 154, 165
  democratic revolts in (8th to 9th cents.), 101; revolution from 1275, 218; Jacquerie of 14th cent., 328
  desolation of, in 6th cent., 25-26
  dyers of, 188
  exclusive policy of, 201
  fisheries of, 231

INDEX

361

INDEX

France (*continued*):
black death in, 285
burgesses in: *lignaiges* of,
206; dwellings of, 209;
bourgeois dowries, 301
capitation men, 136
censitaires in, prosperity of, 259
Church in: lands of, 124, 319;
truce of God spread by,
155. See also sub-heading,
Monastic Orders
coinage of, 154, 165
dairy exports of, 234
democratic movement in (13th
cent.), 218-19; democracy
in decline (14th cent.), 312
economic policy of (14th to
15th cents.), 280-81
fairs of, 170
famines in, 145, 284
feudalism in, 85, 121; the
feudal maxim, 120, 126
forest preservation in, 232
fruit exported from, 235
housing in: burgesses', 209;
working class, 222; pea-
sants', 260
industries of: linen, 176, 188;
iron-mining, 184, 294; iron
manufactures, 186; arms
manufacture, 185; dyeing,
188; art industry, 189;
furniture-making, 189; glass
works, 189; leather in-
dustry, 189; luxury industries, 282; silk, 282; salt,
294; silver-mining, 294; metallurgical industry, 295;
effects of war on trade and
industry, 287, 290, 294-96
interest rates in, 166
international trade developed
by, 182-83
kings of, sound administration organised by (from
11th cent.), 152; conditions
under Capetian rule, 196;
royal support for demo-
cratic aspirations, 217;
policy of Valois kings, 280,
283
knightly class in, decline of,
242
labour laws in (14th cent.), 324
land appreciation in (11th to
14th cents.), 239; deprecia-
tion (14th to 15th cents.),
318

France (*continued*):
Levantine trade of, 111
290
lignaiges of, 206
merchants' associations in,
163, 283, 286; their political rights (12th cent.),
194
métayage in, 256
monastic orders of: as colonists, 227, 228, 230, 231;
their market gardening,
235; their civilising activities in central Europe, 267;
Scandinavia civilised by,
273
navy of, 289
nobility of, 127, 206, 242;
peasant nobles, 252
Northmen's invasion of, 115
peasants in: risings of (1095),
148; in 14th cent., 327;
charters of emancipation,
247-48, 250; rural industries,
293; general landowning
by, 320-21; status of, in
14th cent., 321; rural conditions of, in 15th cent.,
330
population of (10th to 13th
cents.), 237; urban, in 14th
cent., 315
postal and passenger services
in (14th to 15th cents.), 284,
287
prosperity of (14th cent.), 203,
237
quémans in, 307
questaux, 136
revenue of (12th cent.), 125
roads of (15th cent.), 287;
royal highways, 163-64
roturiers in, 132
serfdom in, 147, 258
sheep-farming in, 233
slavery revived in (12th to
14th cents.), 259; slave trade
in (14th cent.), 326
social spirit in (14th cent.),
263
State property in, 242-43
strikes in, 217
tenant farming in (13th
cent.), 255; in 15th cent.,
323
terra fiscalis, 129
thermal and mineral springs
of, 295

362

INDEX

INDEX

Germany (*continued*):
  iron manufactures of, 186
  Junker class in, 242
  kings of (from 11th cent.), sound administration, organised by, 152
  land reclamation in, 228-30
  landholding in: decline of the mark (village property), 79, 80; the *alod*, 81; *hörigen* (10th cent.), 90, 132; seigniorial acquisition of marks, 120; non-feudal property surviving, 81, 121; *schäffenbären, lehnbauern, sonnenlehen,* 121-22, 252; royal domains, 125; *eigen,* 126; *frönhof,* 129; tenant holders, 131; free villeinage, 132; size of villeins' holdings, 141; cessation of collective ownership, 240; accretions to State property, 242; peasant appropriation of assarts, 253; size of the *hufe,* 80, 95, 254; *Kossaten,* 324
  leather industry of, 189
  Leibeigenen, 136
  maritime efforts of, 176
  metallurgical supremacy of, 295
  middle-class incomes in (15th cent.), 301
  miners from, 269, 275
  mining activity in, 12, 184, 294, 295
  nobility of, 84; lesser, under feudalism, 127; in 13th cent., 242
  patriciate in, 206
  peasants' leases in (*erbpachten*), 253
  peasant life in, 98-99, 330; peasant status, 121-22, 144; fief-owning peasants, 121, 252; peasant revolts, 247; rural emancipation, 248; peasant appropriation of assarts, 253; size of the peasant holdings, 254, 324; rural industries, 293; risings in 15th cent., 329
  population of (10th cent.), 76; increase in (10th to 13th cents.), 237; (15th cent.), 331

Germany (*continued*):
  postal service in (13th cent.), 164-65; postal and passenger service (14th to 15th cents.), 284, 287
  Pruss populations enslaved by, 258, 268, 271
  reclamation of (8th cent.), 68
  roads in, national, 164
  rural charters in, 247-48. See also sub-heading Peasant
  salt-pits of, 12
  Scandinavian invasion of, 115
  sheep and cattle farming in, 233
  silver-mining in, 294
  Slav occupation of, 6
  sworn corporations in, 303
  thermal and mineral springs of, 295
  towns in: numbers of, 191; types of administration, 199; urban communes (14th to 15th cents.), 279
  trading methods of, 291-92
  vine-growing in, 236; wine trade (9th cent.), 75
  wastelands of, 72, 226
Gerona, 185
Ghent, 113:
  gilds in, 206
  industrial development of, 192; cloth industry, 183, 187; industrial revolution (14th cent.), 311-12
  insurrections at, 195, 218, 314
  population of, 203; in 14th cent., 315
Gildhalls, 193, 206
Gilds (see also Corporations):
  banners of, 214, 224
  burgesses', 193
  craft (*arti*), 104
  defence, for, 89
  economic tyranny of, 208
  mercantile. See Merchants' associations
  origin of, 101
  personnel and power of, 206-07
  religious type of (*confratriœ*) 105
  status of, 206
  Umiliati (of Milan), 186

INDEX

Ischia, 184
Istria, 57, 236
Italy:
> agriculture and stock-raising: prosperity in 9th cent., 76; free cultivators, 91; pasture-farming in South and Central, 233, 317; intensive methods, 234; industrial crops, 236; co-operative farming, 323
>
> arms manufacture in, 185
> art in, 107; artistic pioneers from, 269-70
> bankers of. See under Bankers
> banking system of, international, 288
> barbarian invasion of, 15, 16, 27
> black death in, 285
> Byzantine restoration of, 57; loss of the south, 264
> Byzantine trade secured by, 266
> *canons* in, 255
> capitalists from, developing foreign mines, 269
> colonisation of south by freed slaves, 33
> commons in, 319
> dairy exports of, 234
> day labourers in (*braccianti*, *pimenti*), in 13th cent., 257, 259
> democratic movement in (13th cent.), 218-19
> ducats of, 288
> ecclesiastical property in north and central, 319
> economic policy of (14th to 15th cents.), 280-81
> fairs in, 170, 287
> famines and epidemics in, 29
> fashion leader (13th cent.), 189
> feudalism in, 120; non-feudal proprietors (*bozadores*) surviving, 87, 88, 121; size of estates, 128; their minute subdivision, 241
> forest in, 73; clearances, 231, 317; preservation in the south, 232
> fruit exports from, 235
> horse-breeding in, 233, 317
> industrial activity of (15th cent.), 294; conditions, 308

Italy (*continued*):
> industries of: iron-mining, 184, 186, 294; food, 186; cloth, 186-87; dyeing, 188; linen, 188; furniture, ivory, leather, 189; luxury, 282; salt, 294; silver-mining, 294; metal, 295; silk-weaving, 296-97; inlaying, 297
>
> interest rates in, 166
> labour laws in (14th cent.), 324
> land drainage in, 229
> landholding in: extent of royal lands, 81-82; tenant farming, 131; in 13th cent., 255; in 15th cent., 323; the *rivello*, 254; land subdivision, 254-55; private estates, 319-20; general landowning, 320
> market gardening and horticulture, 235
> mercantile colonies in, 109; mercantile activity, 159, 162-63, 167-68, 171; merchant nobility, 192; merchants' political rights in 12th cent., 194; Italian merchants in Byzantium, 52; merchant republics of, see Florence, Genoa, Pisa, Venice
> money economy originating in, 165
> nobility of, 84; merchant, 192; their fate in 13th cent., 242
> peasant life in, 99; revolts, 101; emancipation, 246, 248; rural conditions in 15th cent., 330
> Po embankment, 316
> population; increase in (8th cent.), 76; in 14th cent., 237; increase in (15th cent.), 331
> postal and passenger service in (14th to 15th cents.), 164, 284, 287
> prosperity of, under Roman Empire, 4; consequent on urban activities, 203
> Saracen invasion of, 115
> serfs in (*Vassali* or *Aldions*), 136
> slavery revived in (12th to 14th cents.), 259; slave trade in 14th cent., 326

INDEX

Lard, 172, 233, 274
Las Huelgas Abbey, 243
Law: variations in fiscal law, 174; maritime law, 173
Lazar houses, 156, 262
Le Mans, 194
Lead, trade in, 176
Lead-mining, 49, 105, 269, 294
Leases (see also Rent): *à cens, à complants*, 91, 103, 132, 133, 241, 247, 249, 253, 254; restrictions in, 198; *emphyteotiques*, 247; *à cheptel* (stock leases), 256; perpetual leasehold, 91, 133; *métayage*, 256; length of tenant farmers' leases, 255
Leather, trade in, 172, 176, 177
Leather work, in Roman Empire, 4; in Byzantine Empire, 49, 111; trade in, 111, 168; saddlery, etc., 189; gilded, 189, 297
Leipzig fair, 269
Lemons, 235
Lens Abbey, 69
Leo III, Emperor, 53
Leon, 200
Leprosy, 146, 284
Lerida, 185
Les Andelys, 187
Letters of Marque, 173
Letts, 7
Levant:
    cotton exports of, 297
    feudalism in, 120
    French trade with, 111, 290
    importance of trade with, 108, 112
    maritime powers' concessions in, 174
    Scandinavian relations with, 275
Liberty, personal, rural acquisition of (11th to 14th cents.), 248, 251; attainment of freedom the cardinal achievement of the Middle Ages, 335-36
Lides, 91, 92. See also *coloni*
Liège, 113; coal - mining and metallurgy in, 295; insurrection in (12th cent.), 195; democratic risings (1253), 217; revolutionary temper at (14th cent.), 312, (15th cent.), 314; *cluppelslagers'* revolt, 328

Lighthouses, 174
Lille, British trade with, 163; fair at, 170; industries of, 183, 187, 188; population of, 203; democratic successes at, 218
Limagne, 236
Limburg, 185, 270
Limoges, 188, 297-98
Limousine March, 133, 325
Lindisfarne, 107
Linen clothes, 261
Linen manufactures, 12, 49, 106, 176, 188, 297
Lipany, battle of, 329
Literature, urban, 223
Lites, 132
Lithuania: civilising of, 267-68; rural slavery in, 271
Lithuanians, 6, 326
Livellarii, 91
Livestock, small, predominating over large, 74, 141, 232-33
Livonia, civilising of, 267-68
Livonians, 6
Loans, 52, 166; negotiated at fairs, 172. See also Credit and Interest
Local government, peasants' association with, 250-51, 334. See also Municipal government
Locks (sluice), 287
Locksmiths' work, 186, 295
Lodi, 194
Lodigiano, 229
Lods et ventes, rights of, 254
Logroño, " customs " of, 247
Loire district, 230, 236
Loire river, 283, 287
Lollards, 224
Lombards, 9, 33; spoliation by, 16, 19-21, 24; aristocratic organisations of, 18; savagery of, 23
Lombardy:
    banking companies of, 288; merchant bankers and money-lenders from, 168, 288; royal policy as to (14th to 15th cents.), 283
    black death in, 285
    Church lands in, 124
    city fraternities of, 200
    feudal power broken in 195
    free proprietors in, 122

372

INDEX

INDEX

INDEX

378

INDEX

Scotland:
- Celts enslaved in, 258
- fisheries of, developed, 317
- Northmen's invasion of, 115
- poverty of (14th cent.), 316
- rural industries of, 293; conditions in 15th cent., 330
- tribal property in, survival of, 78
- wasteland in, 72

Scots trading abroad, 171

Sculpture, 107, 223, 297; monastic instruction in, 157; French supremacy in, 189

Sea biscuits, 186

Sea charts and sea pilotage, 174

Seal-hunting, 317

Sebastades, 265

Secret associations, 101

Seebohm cited, 90

Seigniorial régime, 85 (and see Feudal lords and Feudalism)

Seine or Marne, battle of (351), 16

Selymbria, 54

Senegal, 289

Seniores, 84

Senlis, 187, 327

Sens, 195, 314

Septimania (Lower Languedoc), 68 (and see Languedoc)

Sequins (gold coins), 165

Serbia: mines of, 269; serfdom in (13th cent.), 271; rural misery in (14th cent.), 326

Serbian Empire, 269

Serbs: invasions by, 6; Byzantine culture of, 57-58, 267

Sereonœ, 103

Serfdom:
- abolition of, causes of, 245-46
- artisans' reduction to, 104
- Byzantine peasants' reduction to, 42, 265
- Central Europe, in (13th cent.), 271
- characteristics of, 44, 139
- Denmark, in (15th cent.), 330
- prevalence of, in the West, 95
- recrudescence of (14th cent.), 258, 322, 326-26, 335
- substitution of, for slavery, 117, 332
- suppression of, attempted: by the State, 153, 281; by the Church, 157
- survivals of, 197, 258

Serfs:
- agricultural, among the Germans, 10
- assimilation of, to slave class, 21
- burdens imposed on, 139-40
- capture rights over escaped, 138
- Carolingian protection of, 64
- categories of, 137
- civil rights granted to, by town communities, 197
- *coloni* merged with, 44
- development of, into artisans, 224-25
- discontent general among, 101
- domestic, 137
- hard lot of, 147-48, 258
- inheritance by, 139
- oblates, 137
- peasants synonymous with (7th to 10th cents.), 95
- preponderance of (10th to 12th cents.), 136
- price of, 147
- privileged classes of, 135, 137
- recruitment of, 136-37
- seigniorial domains, on, 86
- status of, 137-39
- value of, determined by skill, 103

Serfs of the glebe, 44, 95-97, 258

Serge, 187, 188

Servants, 10, 137; wage rates of (14th cent.), 260

Seville, 113, 170, 188, 189

Shallots, 335

Sheep-breeding, 35, 39, 74, 232; *présalé*, 233; development of (14th cent.), 317

Sheriffs, 199

Ship-building, 28, 189

Ships, trading, 111, 174, 193

Shops, 109, 162, 192, 214

Sicilies, the two:
- agriculture encouraged in, 153
- Anglo-Norman rule in, conditions under, 196
- coinage of, 154, 165
- deforestation of, 231
- ecclesiastical property in, 319
- feudalism in, 120, 125
- free properties in, 122, 129
- Jews and Moslems in, conditions of (13th cent.), 258
- kings of (from 11th cent.), sound administration organised by, 152

INDEX

INDEX

INDEX

INDEX

INDEX

Vandals, 9; invasions by (406), 15; (430-55), 16; disappearance of, 18; spoliation by, 24, 27
Varangians, 8, 53, 59
Vascongades, 231
Vassalage, 119, 120, 122
Vaudois, 224
Vavasours, 122
Veedores, 213-14
Vegetable: fuel, 185, 232, 293; manures, 234; cultivation, 235
Velvet, 297
Venetia: Byzantine restoration of, 57; slave labour in, 326
Vengeance, Church's restriction of right of, 65
Venice:
    black death in, 285
    bourse of, 287
    Byzantine trade secured by, 268
    capitalists of, 299
    coinage of, 165
    Danube trade route from, 176
    dockyard at, 174
    Doges of, 192-94
    ecclesiastical property in (15th cent.), 319
    exclusiveness of, 201
    fair at, 170
    Genoese rivalry with, 266
    house property in, value of, 300
    industrial development of, 192
    industries of: arms, 185; textile, 296; silk, 183, 188, 296-97; cloth, 186; fustian, linen, tapestry, 297; glasswork, 189, 297; leather, 189; gilded leather work, 297
    merchant bankers of, 167
    merchants from, privileged in Byzantium, 52, 109
    navy of, 174, 289
    patriciate of, 192, 205
    population of (12th to 13th cents.), 203; (14th cent.), 315
    prostitutes of, 308
    rise of, 55, 175-76
    State bank of, 288
    sworn corporations in, 303
    trade of (15th cent.), 289
Verdun, 109, 113, 312
Vernaculi, 137
Vernon, 187

Verona, 113, 186
Verrières, demesne at, 86-87
Vestments, 48
Veterinary art, 232
Vézelay, 195, 247
Viacenza, 194
Vicars (administrators) of corporations, 213-14
Vich ironworks, 185
Vici (townships): in Roman Empire, 2; refuges for small cultivators, 26; artisans living in, 104; decline of, 80, 99
Vicini, 114
Vicinia, 100
Vienna: trade route to, 176; black death in, 285; crafts in (15th cent.), 302; sworn corporations in, 303; golden age of, 315
Vienne, 113
Villach, 284
Villæ: in Roman Empire (15th cent.), 2; supersession of, by village communities, 19, 129; of Charlemagne, 64; organisation of, 85; industry on, 103; urban centres at, 112; villeins called after, 132; development of, into towns, 191
Village communities: German, 6, 10-11; barbarian policy regarding, 19; organisation of, 79; alienations by, 80; in feudal times, 129
Villard de Honnecourt, 186
Villehardouin quoted, 54, 266
Villeinage: characteristics of free, 133; survivals of, 197; nature of, 271; in Denmark (15th cent.), 330
Villeins:
    agricultural backwardness of, 140-41
    censitaires, 253
    charters of, 247
    civil rights granted to, by town communities, 197
    classes of, two, 132
    conditions of life of, 145-46
    emancipation of: causes of, 245; aspects of, 248-50
    encroachments against, 322
    food of (14th cent.), 261
    forerunners of, 3, 90
    growth of the class, 91-92

INDEX

Western Empire. See Roman Empire

Westphalia, iron-mining in, 184, 185, 296; wage-rates in (15th cent.), 308

Whales, 317

Wheat production. See Corn-growing

White Sea, 274

Wild beasts, 232, 280

William the Conqueror, 152

Wills, 81, 270

Winchester, 112

Wind power, 180, 186

Wine:
  burgesses' consumption of, 209
  Byzantine, 35, 53
  French, etc., supplementing Greek, 236
  rent levy on, 255
  Roman trade in, 12
  trade in, 162, 168, 172, 176; widespread in 9th cent., 75
  working class consumption of, 222; peasants', 262

Winfrith (Boniface), 70

Wisby, 275; ordinances of, 173

Wissenburg Monastery, 70

Woad, 76

Wolves, 72

Women:
  aristocratic Byzantine land-owners, 39
  atrocities perpetrated on, in feudal warfare, 152
  cheap labour by, men protected from, 216, 221
  Church's influence on status of, 65
  emancipation of, a Taborite tenet, 329
  harlots and prostitutes, 173, 303, 308
  inheritance rights of, 270, 275; withheld, 272
  labour federations open to, 305
  peasant, 97; adornments of, 261; status of (14th cent.), 262
  servant girls, 257-58
  wages of, 221; in 13th cent., 259

Wood, trade in, 162

Wood carvers, 223

Wood cutters, wage-rates of, 259

Wool: German, 12; Frisian, 106; trade in, 162, 163, 168, 172, 176; French and English, 233; speculation in, 300; large-scale production of, 317-18

Woollen industry: Byzantine, 49, 53; trade in woollen goods, 168, 172; subdivisions in, 182; international centres of, 183. See Cloth

Work, insistence on obligation to, 65; regulation of hours of, 209; right to, recognised, 216

Working classes (see also Artisans, Peasants, and Wage-earners):
  characteristics of (11th to 14th cents.), 223; in 14th cent., 262
  Church's attitude to, 155-57
  democratic movement, rise of, 216-17; increasing powers of, 298
  moral condition of, 223
  position of, under feudalism, 131
  protection of, not secured by feudalism, 150, 159
  servile status of (10th to 12th cents.), 136
  trade expansion as affecting, 177-78

Workshops:
  increase of, under trade expansion, 177, 181
  metal, 185
  monastic, 65
  rural, on large estates, 46
  seigniorial, male and female, 103
  town, 46-48, 104

Worms, 113, 192, 195

Worsted trade, 183

Wreck, right of, 160; abolition of, 173

Wreckage, 158

Wurzburg, 113

York, 285

Yorkist kings' landed possessions 319

Ypres:
  democratic successes at, 218, 311
  Echevins of, 321
  fair at, 170

INDEX

A CATALOG OF SELECTED
DOVER BOOKS
IN ALL FIELDS OF INTEREST

A CATALOG OF SELECTED DOVER
BOOKS IN ALL FIELDS OF INTEREST

CONCERNING THE SPIRITUAL IN ART, Wassily Kandinsky. Pioneering work by father of abstract art. Thoughts on color theory, nature of art. Analysis of earlier masters. 12 illustrations. 80pp. of text. 5⅜ x 8½. 23411-8

ANIMALS: 1,419 Copyright-Free Illustrations of Mammals, Birds, Fish, Insects, etc., Jim Harter (ed.). Clear wood engravings present, in extremely lifelike poses, over 1,000 species of animals. One of the most extensive pictorial sourcebooks of its kind. Captions. Index. 284pp. 9 x 12. 23766-4

CELTIC ART: The Methods of Construction, George Bain. Simple geometric techniques for making Celtic interlacements, spirals, Kells-type initials, animals, humans, etc. Over 500 illustrations. 160pp. 9 x 12. (Available in U.S. only.) 22923-8

AN ATLAS OF ANATOMY FOR ARTISTS, Fritz Schider. Most thorough reference work on art anatomy in the world. Hundreds of illustrations, including selections from works by Vesalius, Leonardo, Goya, Ingres, Michelangelo, others. 593 illustrations. 192pp. 7⅛ x 10¼. 20241-0

CELTIC HAND STROKE-BY-STROKE (Irish Half-Uncial from "The Book of Kells"): An Arthur Baker Calligraphy Manual, Arthur Baker. Complete guide to creating each letter of the alphabet in distinctive Celtic manner. Covers hand position, strokes, pens, inks, paper, more. Illustrated. 48pp. 8¼ x 11. 24336-2

EASY ORIGAMI, John Montroll. Charming collection of 32 projects (hat, cup, pelican, piano, swan, many more) specially designed for the novice origami hobbyist. Clearly illustrated easy-to-follow instructions insure that even beginning papercrafters will achieve successful results. 48pp. 8¼ x 11. 27298-2

THE COMPLETE BOOK OF BIRDHOUSE CONSTRUCTION FOR WOODWORKERS, Scott D. Campbell. Detailed instructions, illustrations, tables. Also data on bird habitat and instinct patterns. Bibliography. 3 tables. 63 illustrations in 15 figures. 48pp. 5¼ x 8½. 24407-5

BLOOMINGDALE'S ILLUSTRATED 1886 CATALOG: Fashions, Dry Goods and Housewares, Bloomingdale Brothers. Famed merchants' extremely rare catalog depicting about 1,700 products: clothing, housewares, firearms, dry goods, jewelry, more. Invaluable for dating, identifying vintage items. Also, copyright-free graphics for artists, designers. Co-published with Henry Ford Museum & Greenfield Village. 160pp. 8¼ x 11. 25780-0

HISTORIC COSTUME IN PICTURES, Braun & Schneider. Over 1,450 costumed figures in clearly detailed engravings–from dawn of civilization to end of 19th century. Captions. Many folk costumes. 256pp. 8⅜ x 11¾. 23150-X

STICKLEY CRAFTSMAN FURNITURE CATALOGS, Gustav Stickley and L. & J. G. Stickley. Beautiful, functional furniture in two authentic catalogs from 1910. 594 illustrations, including 277 photos, show settles, rockers, armchairs, reclining chairs, bookcases, desks, tables. 183pp. 6½ x 9¼.   23838-5

AMERICAN LOCOMOTIVES IN HISTORIC PHOTOGRAPHS: 1858 to 1949, Ron Ziel (ed.). A rare collection of 126 meticulously detailed official photographs, called "builder portraits," of American locomotives that majestically chronicle the rise of steam locomotive power in America. Introduction. Detailed captions. xi+ 129pp. 9 x 12.   27393-8

AMERICA'S LIGHTHOUSES: An Illustrated History, Francis Ross Holland, Jr. Delightfully written, profusely illustrated fact-filled survey of over 200 American lighthouses since 1716. History, anecdotes, technological advances, more. 240pp. 8 x 10¾.
                                 25576-X

TOWARDS A NEW ARCHITECTURE, Le Corbusier. Pioneering manifesto by founder of "International School." Technical and aesthetic theories, views of industry, economics, relation of form to function, "mass-production split" and much more. Profusely illustrated. 320pp. 6⅛ x 9¼. (Available in U.S. only.)   25023-7

HOW THE OTHER HALF LIVES, Jacob Riis. Famous journalistic record, exposing poverty and degradation of New York slums around 1900, by major social reformer. 100 striking and influential photographs. 233pp. 10 x 7⅞.   22012-5

FRUIT KEY AND TWIG KEY TO TREES AND SHRUBS, William M. Harlow. One of the handiest and most widely used identification aids. Fruit key covers 120 deciduous and evergreen species; twig key 160 deciduous species. Easily used. Over 300 photographs. 126pp. 5⅜ x 8½.   20511-8

COMMON BIRD SONGS, Dr. Donald J. Borror. Songs of 60 most common U.S. birds: robins, sparrows, cardinals, bluejays, finches, more—arranged in order of increasing complexity. Up to 9 variations of songs of each species.
                                 Cassette and manual 99911-4

ORCHIDS AS HOUSE PLANTS, Rebecca Tyson Northen. Grow cattleyas and many other kinds of orchids—in a window, in a case, or under artificial light. 63 illustrations. 148pp. 5⅜ x 8½.   23261-1

MONSTER MAZES, Dave Phillips. Masterful mazes at four levels of difficulty. Avoid deadly perils and evil creatures to find magical treasures. Solutions for all 32 exciting illustrated puzzles. 48pp. 8¼ x 11.   26005-4

MOZART'S DON GIOVANNI (DOVER OPERA LIBRETTO SERIES), Wolfgang Amadeus Mozart. Introduced and translated by Ellen H. Bleiler. Standard Italian libretto, with complete English translation. Convenient and thoroughly portable—an ideal companion for reading along with a recording or the performance itself. Introduction. List of characters. Plot summary. 121pp. 5¼ x 8½.   24944-1

TECHNICAL MANUAL AND DICTIONARY OF CLASSICAL BALLET, Gail Grant. Defines, explains, comments on steps, movements, poses and concepts. 15-page pictorial section. Basic book for student, viewer. 127pp. 5⅜ x 8½.   21843-0

THE CLARINET AND CLARINET PLAYING, David Pino. Lively, comprehensive work features suggestions about technique, musicianship, and musical interpretation, as well as guidelines for teaching, making your own reeds, and preparing for public performance. Includes an intriguing look at clarinet history. "A godsend," *The Clarinet,* Journal of the International Clarinet Society. Appendixes. 7 illus. 320pp. 5⅜ x 8½. 40270-3

HOLLYWOOD GLAMOR PORTRAITS, John Kobal (ed.). 145 photos from 1926-49. Harlow, Gable, Bogart, Bacall; 94 stars in all. Full background on photographers, technical aspects. 160pp. 8⅜ x 11¼. 23352-9

THE ANNOTATED CASEY AT THE BAT: A Collection of Ballads about the Mighty Casey/Third, Revised Edition, Martin Gardner (ed.). Amusing sequels and parodies of one of America's best-loved poems: Casey's Revenge, Why Casey Whiffed, Casey's Sister at the Bat, others. 256pp. 5⅜ x 8½. 28598-7

THE RAVEN AND OTHER FAVORITE POEMS, Edgar Allan Poe. Over 40 of the author's most memorable poems: "The Bells," "Ulalume," "Israfel," "To Helen," "The Conqueror Worm," "Eldorado," "Annabel Lee," many more. Alphabetic lists of titles and first lines. 64pp. 5$\frac{3}{16}$ x 8¼. 26685-0

PERSONAL MEMOIRS OF U. S. GRANT, Ulysses Simpson Grant. Intelligent, deeply moving firsthand account of Civil War campaigns, considered by many the finest military memoirs ever written. Includes letters, historic photographs, maps and more. 528pp. 6⅛ x 9¼. 28587-1

ANCIENT EGYPTIAN MATERIALS AND INDUSTRIES, A. Lucas and J. Harris. Fascinating, comprehensive, thoroughly documented text describes this ancient civilization's vast resources and the processes that incorporated them in daily life, including the use of animal products, building materials, cosmetics, perfumes and incense, fibers, glazed ware, glass and its manufacture, materials used in the mummification process, and much more. 544pp. 6⅛ x 9¼. (Available in U.S. only.) 40446-3

RUSSIAN STORIES/RUSSKIE RASSKAZY: A Dual-Language Book, edited by Gleb Struve. Twelve tales by such masters as Chekhov, Tolstoy, Dostoevsky, Pushkin, others. Excellent word-for-word English translations on facing pages, plus teaching and study aids, Russian/English vocabulary, biographical/critical introductions, more. 416pp. 5⅜ x 8½. 26244-8

PHILADELPHIA THEN AND NOW: 60 Sites Photographed in the Past and Present, Kenneth Finkel and Susan Oyama. Rare photographs of City Hall, Logan Square, Independence Hall, Betsy Ross House, other landmarks juxtaposed with contemporary views. Captures changing face of historic city. Introduction. Captions. 128pp. 8¼ x 11. 25790-8

AIA ARCHITECTURAL GUIDE TO NASSAU AND SUFFOLK COUNTIES, LONG ISLAND, The American Institute of Architects, Long Island Chapter, and the Society for the Preservation of Long Island Antiquities. Comprehensive, well-researched and generously illustrated volume brings to life over three centuries of Long Island's great architectural heritage. More than 240 photographs with authoritative, extensively detailed captions. 176pp. 8¼ x 11. 26946-9

NORTH AMERICAN INDIAN LIFE: Customs and Traditions of 23 Tribes, Elsie Clews Parsons (ed.). 27 fictionalized essays by noted anthropologists examine religion, customs, government, additional facets of life among the Winnebago, Crow, Zuni, Eskimo, other tribes. 480pp. 6⅛ x 9¼. 27377-6

FRANK LLOYD WRIGHT'S DANA HOUSE, Donald Hoffmann. Pictorial essay of residential masterpiece with over 160 interior and exterior photos, plans, elevations, sketches and studies. 128pp. 9¼ x 10¾.   29120-0

THE MALE AND FEMALE FIGURE IN MOTION: 60 Classic Photographic Sequences, Eadweard Muybridge. 60 true-action photographs of men and women walking, running, climbing, bending, turning, etc., reproduced from rare 19th-century masterpiece. vi + 121pp. 9 x 12.   24745-7

1001 QUESTIONS ANSWERED ABOUT THE SEASHORE, N. J. Berrill and Jacquelyn Berrill. Queries answered about dolphins, sea snails, sponges, starfish, fishes, shore birds, many others. Covers appearance, breeding, growth, feeding, much more. 305pp. 5¼ x 8¼.   23366-9

ATTRACTING BIRDS TO YOUR YARD, William J. Weber. Easy-to-follow guide offers advice on how to attract the greatest diversity of birds: birdhouses, feeders, water and waterers, much more. 96pp. 5³⁄₁₆ x 8¼.   28927-3

MEDICINAL AND OTHER USES OF NORTH AMERICAN PLANTS: A Historical Survey with Special Reference to the Eastern Indian Tribes, Charlotte Erichsen-Brown. Chronological historical citations document 500 years of usage of plants, trees, shrubs native to eastern Canada, northeastern U.S. Also complete identifying information. 343 illustrations. 544pp. 6½ x 9¼.   25951-X

STORYBOOK MAZES, Dave Phillips. 23 stories and mazes on two-page spreads: Wizard of Oz, Treasure Island, Robin Hood, etc. Solutions. 64pp. 8¼ x 11. 23628-5

AMERICAN NEGRO SONGS: 230 Folk Songs and Spirituals, Religious and Secular, John W. Work. This authoritative study traces the African influences of songs sung and played by black Americans at work, in church, and as entertainment. The author discusses the lyric significance of such songs as "Swing Low, Sweet Chariot," "John Henry," and others and offers the words and music for 230 songs. Bibliography. Index of Song Titles. 272pp. 6½ x 9¼.   40271-1

MOVIE-STAR PORTRAITS OF THE FORTIES, John Kobal (ed.). 163 glamor, studio photos of 106 stars of the 1940s: Rita Hayworth, Ava Gardner, Marlon Brando, Clark Gable, many more. 176pp. 8⅜ x 11¼.   23546-7

BENCHLEY LOST AND FOUND, Robert Benchley. Finest humor from early 30s, about pet peeves, child psychologists, post office and others. Mostly unavailable elsewhere. 73 illustrations by Peter Arno and others. 183pp. 5⅜ x 8½.   22410-4

YEKL and THE IMPORTED BRIDEGROOM AND OTHER STORIES OF YIDDISH NEW YORK, Abraham Cahan. Film Hester Street based on *Yekl* (1896). Novel, other stories among first about Jewish immigrants on N.Y.'s East Side. 240pp. 5⅜ x 8½.   22427-9

SELECTED POEMS, Walt Whitman. Generous sampling from *Leaves of Grass.* Twenty-four poems include "I Hear America Singing," "Song of the Open Road," "I Sing the Body Electric," "When Lilacs Last in the Dooryard Bloom'd," "O Captain! My Captain!"—all reprinted from an authoritative edition. Lists of titles and first lines. 128pp. 5³⁄₁₆ x 8¼.   26878-0

THE BEST TALES OF HOFFMANN, E. T. A. Hoffmann. 10 of Hoffmann's most important stories: "Nutcracker and the King of Mice," "The Golden Flowerpot," etc. 458pp. 5⅜ x 8½. 21793-0

FROM FETISH TO GOD IN ANCIENT EGYPT, E. A. Wallis Budge. Rich detailed survey of Egyptian conception of "God" and gods, magic, cult of animals, Osiris, more. Also, superb English translations of hymns and legends. 240 illustrations. 545pp. 5⅜ x 8½. 25803-3

FRENCH STORIES/CONTES FRANÇAIS: A Dual-Language Book, Wallace Fowlie. Ten stories by French masters, Voltaire to Camus: "Micromegas" by Voltaire; "The Atheist's Mass" by Balzac; "Minuet" by de Maupassant; "The Guest" by Camus, six more. Excellent English translations on facing pages. Also French-English vocabulary list, exercises, more. 352pp. 5⅜ x 8½. 26443-2

CHICAGO AT THE TURN OF THE CENTURY IN PHOTOGRAPHS: 122 Historic Views from the Collections of the Chicago Historical Society, Larry A. Viskochil. Rare large-format prints offer detailed views of City Hall, State Street, the Loop, Hull House, Union Station, many other landmarks, circa 1904-1913. Introduction. Captions. Maps. 144pp. 9⅜ x 12¼. 24656-6

OLD BROOKLYN IN EARLY PHOTOGRAPHS, 1865-1929, William Lee Younger. Luna Park, Gravesend race track, construction of Grand Army Plaza, moving of Hotel Brighton, etc. 157 previously unpublished photographs. 165pp. 8⅞ x 11¾. 23587-4

THE MYTHS OF THE NORTH AMERICAN INDIANS, Lewis Spence. Rich anthology of the myths and legends of the Algonquins, Iroquois, Pawnees and Sioux, prefaced by an extensive historical and ethnological commentary. 36 illustrations. 480pp. 5⅜ x 8½. 25967-6

AN ENCYCLOPEDIA OF BATTLES: Accounts of Over 1,560 Battles from 1479 B.C. to the Present, David Eggenberger. Essential details of every major battle in recorded history from the first battle of Megiddo in 1479 B.C. to Grenada in 1984. List of Battle Maps. New Appendix covering the years 1967-1984. Index. 99 illustrations. 544pp. 6½ x 9¼. 24913-1

SAILING ALONE AROUND THE WORLD, Captain Joshua Slocum. First man to sail around the world, alone, in small boat. One of great feats of seamanship told in delightful manner. 67 illustrations. 294pp. 5⅜ x 8½. 20326-3

ANARCHISM AND OTHER ESSAYS, Emma Goldman. Powerful, penetrating, prophetic essays on direct action, role of minorities, prison reform, puritan hypocrisy, violence, etc. 271pp. 5⅜ x 8½. 22484-8

MYTHS OF THE HINDUS AND BUDDHISTS, Ananda K. Coomaraswamy and Sister Nivedita. Great stories of the epics; deeds of Krishna, Shiva, taken from puranas, Vedas, folk tales; etc. 32 illustrations. 400pp. 5⅜ x 8½. 21759-0

THE TRAUMA OF BIRTH, Otto Rank. Rank's controversial thesis that anxiety neurosis is caused by profound psychological trauma which occurs at birth. 256pp. 5⅜ x 8½. 27974-X

A THEOLOGICO-POLITICAL TREATISE, Benedict Spinoza. Also contains unfinished Political Treatise. Great classic on religious liberty, theory of government on common consent. R. Elwes translation. Total of 421pp. 5⅜ x 8½. 20249-6

MY BONDAGE AND MY FREEDOM, Frederick Douglass. Born a slave, Douglass became outspoken force in antislavery movement. The best of Douglass' autobiographies. Graphic description of slave life. 464pp. 5⅜ x 8½. 22457-0

FOLLOWING THE EQUATOR: A Journey Around the World, Mark Twain. Fascinating humorous account of 1897 voyage to Hawaii, Australia, India, New Zealand, etc. Ironic, bemused reports on peoples, customs, climate, flora and fauna, politics, much more. 197 illustrations. 720pp. 5⅜ x 8½. 26113-1

THE PEOPLE CALLED SHAKERS, Edward D. Andrews. Definitive study of Shakers: origins, beliefs, practices, dances, social organization, furniture and crafts, etc. 33 illustrations. 351pp. 5⅜ x 8½. 21081-2

THE MYTHS OF GREECE AND ROME, H. A. Guerber. A classic of mythology, generously illustrated, long prized for its simple, graphic, accurate retelling of the principal myths of Greece and Rome, and for its commentary on their origins and significance. With 64 illustrations by Michelangelo, Raphael, Titian, Rubens, Canova, Bernini and others. 480pp. 5⅜ x 8½. 27584-1

PSYCHOLOGY OF MUSIC, Carl E. Seashore. Classic work discusses music as a medium from psychological viewpoint. Clear treatment of physical acoustics, auditory apparatus, sound perception, development of musical skills, nature of musical feeling, host of other topics. 88 figures. 408pp. 5⅜ x 8½. 21851-1

THE PHILOSOPHY OF HISTORY, Georg W. Hegel. Great classic of Western thought develops concept that history is not chance but rational process, the evolution of freedom. 457pp. 5⅜ x 8½. 20112-0

THE BOOK OF TEA, Kakuzo Okakura. Minor classic of the Orient: entertaining, charming explanation, interpretation of traditional Japanese culture in terms of tea ceremony. 94pp. 5⅜ x 8½. 20070-1

LIFE IN ANCIENT EGYPT, Adolf Erman. Fullest, most thorough, detailed older account with much not in more recent books, domestic life, religion, magic, medicine, commerce, much more. Many illustrations reproduce tomb paintings, carvings, hieroglyphs, etc. 597pp. 5⅜ x 8½. 22632-8

SUNDIALS, Their Theory and Construction, Albert Waugh. Far and away the best, most thorough coverage of ideas, mathematics concerned, types, construction, adjusting anywhere. Simple, nontechnical treatment allows even children to build several of these dials. Over 100 illustrations. 230pp. 5⅜ x 8½. 22947-5

THEORETICAL HYDRODYNAMICS, L. M. Milne-Thomson. Classic exposition of the mathematical theory of fluid motion, applicable to both hydrodynamics and aerodynamics. Over 600 exercises. 768pp. 6⅛ x 9¼. 68970-0

SONGS OF EXPERIENCE: Facsimile Reproduction with 26 Plates in Full Color, William Blake. 26 full-color plates from a rare 1826 edition. Includes "The Tyger," "London," "Holy Thursday," and other poems. Printed text of poems. 48pp. 5¼ x 7. 24636-1

OLD-TIME VIGNETTES IN FULL COLOR, Carol Belanger Grafton (ed.). Over 390 charming, often sentimental illustrations, selected from archives of Victorian graphics—pretty women posing, children playing, food, flowers, kittens and puppies, smiling cherubs, birds and butterflies, much more. All copyright-free. 48pp. 9¼ x 12¼. 27269-9

PERSPECTIVE FOR ARTISTS, Rex Vicat Cole. Depth, perspective of sky and sea, shadows, much more, not usually covered. 391 diagrams, 81 reproductions of drawings and paintings. 279pp. 5⅜ x 8½. 22487-2

DRAWING THE LIVING FIGURE, Joseph Sheppard. Innovative approach to artistic anatomy focuses on specifics of surface anatomy, rather than muscles and bones. Over 170 drawings of live models in front, back and side views, and in widely varying poses. Accompanying diagrams. 177 illustrations. Introduction. Index. 144pp. 8⅜ x11¼. 26723-7

GOTHIC AND OLD ENGLISH ALPHABETS: 100 Complete Fonts, Dan X. Solo. Add power, elegance to posters, signs, other graphics with 100 stunning copyright-free alphabets: Blackstone, Dolbey, Germania, 97 more–including many lower-case, numerals, punctuation marks. 104pp. 8⅛ x 11. 24695-7

HOW TO DO BEADWORK, Mary White. Fundamental book on craft from simple projects to five-bead chains and woven works. 106 illustrations. 142pp. 5⅜ x 8. 20697-1

THE BOOK OF WOOD CARVING, Charles Marshall Sayers. Finest book for beginners discusses fundamentals and offers 34 designs. "Absolutely first rate . . . well thought out and well executed."–E. J. Tangerman. 118pp. 7¾ x 10⅝. 23654-4

ILLUSTRATED CATALOG OF CIVIL WAR MILITARY GOODS: Union Army Weapons, Insignia, Uniform Accessories, and Other Equipment, Schuyler, Hartley, and Graham. Rare, profusely illustrated 1846 catalog includes Union Army uniform and dress regulations, arms and ammunition, coats, insignia, flags, swords, rifles, etc. 226 illustrations. 160pp. 9 x 12. 24939-5

WOMEN'S FASHIONS OF THE EARLY 1900s: An Unabridged Republication of "New York Fashions, 1909," National Cloak & Suit Co. Rare catalog of mail-order fashions documents women's and children's clothing styles shortly after the turn of the century. Captions offer full descriptions, prices. Invaluable resource for fashion, costume historians. Approximately 725 illustrations. 128pp. 8⅜ x 11¼. 27276-1

THE 1912 AND 1915 GUSTAV STICKLEY FURNITURE CATALOGS, Gustav Stickley. With over 200 detailed illustrations and descriptions, these two catalogs are essential reading and reference materials and identification guides for Stickley furniture. Captions cite materials, dimensions and prices. 112pp. 6½ x 9¼. 26676-1

EARLY AMERICAN LOCOMOTIVES, John H. White, Jr. Finest locomotive engravings from early 19th century: historical (1804–74), main-line (after 1870), special, foreign, etc. 147 plates. 142pp. 11⅜ x 8¼. 22772-3

THE TALL SHIPS OF TODAY IN PHOTOGRAPHS, Frank O. Braynard. Lavishly illustrated tribute to nearly 100 majestic contemporary sailing vessels: Amerigo Vespucci, Clearwater, Constitution, Eagle, Mayflower, Sea Cloud, Victory, many more. Authoritative captions provide statistics, background on each ship. 190 black-and-white photographs and illustrations. Introduction. 128pp. 8⅞ x 11¾. 27163-3

LITTLE BOOK OF EARLY AMERICAN CRAFTS AND TRADES, Peter Stockham (ed.). 1807 children's book explains crafts and trades: baker, hatter, cooper, potter, and many others. 23 copperplate illustrations. 140pp. 4⅝ x 6.   23336-7

VICTORIAN FASHIONS AND COSTUMES FROM HARPER'S BAZAR, 1867–1898, Stella Blum (ed.). Day costumes, evening wear, sports clothes, shoes, hats, other accessories in over 1,000 detailed engravings. 320pp. 9⅜ x 12¼.   22990-4

GUSTAV STICKLEY, THE CRAFTSMAN, Mary Ann Smith. Superb study surveys broad scope of Stickley's achievement, especially in architecture. Design philosophy, rise and fall of the Craftsman empire, descriptions and floor plans for many Craftsman houses, more. 86 black-and-white halftones. 31 line illustrations. Introduction 208pp. 6½ x 9¼.   27210-9

THE LONG ISLAND RAIL ROAD IN EARLY PHOTOGRAPHS, Ron Ziel. Over 220 rare photos, informative text document origin (1844) and development of rail service on Long Island. Vintage views of early trains, locomotives, stations, passengers, crews, much more. Captions. 8⅞ x 11¾.   26301-0

VOYAGE OF THE LIBERDADE, Joshua Slocum. Great 19th-century mariner's thrilling, first-hand account of the wreck of his ship off South America, the 35-foot boat he built from the wreckage, and its remarkable voyage home. 128pp. 5⅜ x 8½.
40022-0

TEN BOOKS ON ARCHITECTURE, Vitruvius. The most important book ever written on architecture. Early Roman aesthetics, technology, classical orders, site selection, all other aspects. Morgan translation. 331pp. 5⅜ x 8½.   20645-9

THE HUMAN FIGURE IN MOTION, Eadweard Muybridge. More than 4,500 stopped-action photos, in action series, showing undraped men, women, children jumping, lying down, throwing, sitting, wrestling, carrying, etc. 390pp. 7⅞ x 10⅝.
20204-6 Clothbd.

TREES OF THE EASTERN AND CENTRAL UNITED STATES AND CANADA, William M. Harlow. Best one-volume guide to 140 trees. Full descriptions, woodlore, range, etc. Over 600 illustrations. Handy size. 288pp. 4½ x 6⅜.   20395-6

SONGS OF WESTERN BIRDS, Dr. Donald J. Borror. Complete song and call repertoire of 60 western species, including flycatchers, juncoes, cactus wrens, many more–includes fully illustrated booklet.   Cassette and manual 99913-0

GROWING AND USING HERBS AND SPICES, Milo Miloradovich. Versatile handbook provides all the information needed for cultivation and use of all the herbs and spices available in North America. 4 illustrations. Index. Glossary. 236pp. 5⅜ x 8½.
25058-X

BIG BOOK OF MAZES AND LABYRINTHS, Walter Shepherd. 50 mazes and labyrinths in all–classical, solid, ripple, and more–in one great volume. Perfect inexpensive puzzler for clever youngsters. Full solutions. 112pp. 8⅛ x 11.   22951-3

PIANO TUNING, J. Cree Fischer. Clearest, best book for beginner, amateur. Simple repairs, raising dropped notes, tuning by easy method of flattened fifths. No previous skills needed. 4 illustrations. 201pp. 5⅜ x 8½.   23267-0

HINTS TO SINGERS, Lillian Nordica. Selecting the right teacher, developing confidence, overcoming stage fright, and many other important skills receive thoughtful discussion in this indispensible guide, written by a world-famous diva of four decades' experience. 96pp. 5⅜ x 8½.   40094-8

THE COMPLETE NONSENSE OF EDWARD LEAR, Edward Lear. All nonsense limericks, zany alphabets, Owl and Pussycat, songs, nonsense botany, etc., illustrated by Lear. Total of 320pp. 5⅜ x 8½. (Available in U.S. only.)   20167-8

VICTORIAN PARLOUR POETRY: An Annotated Anthology, Michael R. Turner. 117 gems by Longfellow, Tennyson, Browning, many lesser-known poets. "The Village Blacksmith," "Curfew Must Not Ring Tonight," "Only a Baby Small," dozens more, often difficult to find elsewhere. Index of poets, titles, first lines. xxiii + 325pp. 5⅜ x 8¼.   27044-0

DUBLINERS, James Joyce. Fifteen stories offer vivid, tightly focused observations of the lives of Dublin's poorer classes. At least one, "The Dead," is considered a masterpiece. Reprinted complete and unabridged from standard edition. 160pp. 5³⁄₁₆ x 8¼.   26870-5

GREAT WEIRD TALES: 14 Stories by Lovecraft, Blackwood, Machen and Others, S. T. Joshi (ed.). 14 spellbinding tales, including "The Sin Eater," by Fiona McLeod, "The Eye Above the Mantel," by Frank Belknap Long, as well as renowned works by R. H. Barlow, Lord Dunsany, Arthur Machen, W. C. Morrow and eight other masters of the genre. 256pp. 5⅜ x 8½. (Available in U.S. only.)   40436-6

THE BOOK OF THE SACRED MAGIC OF ABRAMELIN THE MAGE, translated by S. MacGregor Mathers. Medieval manuscript of ceremonial magic. Basic document in Aleister Crowley, Golden Dawn groups. 268pp. 5⅜ x 8½.   23211-5

NEW RUSSIAN-ENGLISH AND ENGLISH-RUSSIAN DICTIONARY, M. A. O'Brien. This is a remarkably handy Russian dictionary, containing a surprising amount of information, including over 70,000 entries. 366pp. 4½ x 6⅛.   20208-9

HISTORIC HOMES OF THE AMERICAN PRESIDENTS, Second, Revised Edition, Irvin Haas. A traveler's guide to American Presidential homes, most open to the public, depicting and describing homes occupied by every American President from George Washington to George Bush. With visiting hours, admission charges, travel routes. 175 photographs. Index. 160pp. 8¼ x 11.   26751-2

NEW YORK IN THE FORTIES, Andreas Feininger. 162 brilliant photographs by the well-known photographer, formerly with *Life* magazine. Commuters, shoppers, Times Square at night, much else from city at its peak. Captions by John von Hartz. 181pp. 9¼ x 10¾.   23585-8

INDIAN SIGN LANGUAGE, William Tomkins. Over 525 signs developed by Sioux and other tribes. Written instructions and diagrams. Also 290 pictographs. 111pp. 6⅛ x 9¼.   22029-X

ANATOMY: A Complete Guide for Artists, Joseph Sheppard. A master of figure drawing shows artists how to render human anatomy convincingly. Over 460 illustrations. 224pp. 8⅜ x 11¼. 27279-6

MEDIEVAL CALLIGRAPHY: Its History and Technique, Marc Drogin. Spirited history, comprehensive instruction manual covers 13 styles (ca. 4th century through 15th). Excellent photographs; directions for duplicating medieval techniques with modern tools. 224pp. 8⅜ x 11¼. 26142-5

DRIED FLOWERS: How to Prepare Them, Sarah Whitlock and Martha Rankin. Complete instructions on how to use silica gel, meal and borax, perlite aggregate, sand and borax, glycerine and water to create attractive permanent flower arrangements. 12 illustrations. 32pp. 5⅜ x 8½. 21802-3

EASY-TO-MAKE BIRD FEEDERS FOR WOODWORKERS, Scott D. Campbell. Detailed, simple-to-use guide for designing, constructing, caring for and using feeders. Text, illustrations for 12 classic and contemporary designs. 96pp. 5⅜ x 8½.
25847-5

SCOTTISH WONDER TALES FROM MYTH AND LEGEND, Donald A. Mackenzie. 16 lively tales tell of giants rumbling down mountainsides, of a magic wand that turns stone pillars into warriors, of gods and goddesses, evil hags, powerful forces and more. 240pp. 5⅜ x 8½. 29677-6

THE HISTORY OF UNDERCLOTHES, C. Willett Cunnington and Phyllis Cunnington. Fascinating, well-documented survey covering six centuries of English undergarments, enhanced with over 100 illustrations: 12th-century laced-up bodice, footed long drawers (1795), 19th-century bustles, 19th-century corsets for men, Victorian "bust improvers," much more. 272pp. 5⅜ x 8¼. 27124-2

ARTS AND CRAFTS FURNITURE: The Complete Brooks Catalog of 1912, Brooks Manufacturing Co. Photos and detailed descriptions of more than 150 now very collectible furniture designs from the Arts and Crafts movement depict davenports, settees, buffets, desks, tables, chairs, bedsteads, dressers and more, all built of solid, quarter-sawed oak. Invaluable for students and enthusiasts of antiques, Americana and the decorative arts. 80pp. 6½ x 9¼. 27471-3

WILBUR AND ORVILLE: A Biography of the Wright Brothers, Fred Howard. Definitive, crisply written study tells the full story of the brothers' lives and work. A vividly written biography, unparalleled in scope and color, that also captures the spirit of an extraordinary era. 560pp. 6⅛ x 9¼. 40297-5

THE ARTS OF THE SAILOR: Knotting, Splicing and Ropework, Hervey Garrett Smith. Indispensable shipboard reference covers tools, basic knots and useful hitches; handsewing and canvas work, more. Over 100 illustrations. Delightful reading for sea lovers. 256pp. 5⅜ x 8½. 26440-8

FRANK LLOYD WRIGHT'S FALLINGWATER: The House and Its History, Second, Revised Edition, Donald Hoffmann. A total revision—both in text and illustrations—of the standard document on Fallingwater, the boldest, most personal architectural statement of Wright's mature years, updated with valuable new material from the recently opened Frank Lloyd Wright Archives. "Fascinating"—*The New York Times.* 116 illustrations. 128pp. 9¼ x 10¾. 27430-6

PHOTOGRAPHIC SKETCHBOOK OF THE CIVIL WAR, Alexander Gardner. 100 photos taken on field during the Civil War. Famous shots of Manassas Harper's Ferry, Lincoln, Richmond, slave pens, etc. 244pp. 10⅝ x 8¼.   22731-6

FIVE ACRES AND INDEPENDENCE, Maurice G. Kains. Great back-to-the-land classic explains basics of self-sufficient farming. The one book to get. 95 illustrations. 397pp. 5⅜ x 8½.   20974-1

SONGS OF EASTERN BIRDS, Dr. Donald J. Borror. Songs and calls of 60 species most common to eastern U.S.: warblers, woodpeckers, flycatchers, thrushes, larks, many more in high-quality recording.   Cassette and manual 99912-2

A MODERN HERBAL, Margaret Grieve. Much the fullest, most exact, most useful compilation of herbal material. Gigantic alphabetical encyclopedia, from aconite to zedoary, gives botanical information, medical properties, folklore, economic uses, much else. Indispensable to serious reader. 161 illustrations. 888pp. 6½ x 9¼. 2-vol. set. (Available in U.S. only.)   Vol. I: 22798-7
Vol. II: 22799-5

HIDDEN TREASURE MAZE BOOK, Dave Phillips. Solve 34 challenging mazes accompanied by heroic tales of adventure. Evil dragons, people-eating plants, blood-thirsty giants, many more dangerous adversaries lurk at every twist and turn. 34 mazes, stories, solutions. 48pp. 8¼ x 11.   24566-7

LETTERS OF W. A. MOZART, Wolfgang A. Mozart. Remarkable letters show bawdy wit, humor, imagination, musical insights, contemporary musical world; includes some letters from Leopold Mozart. 276pp. 5⅜ x 8½.   22859-2

BASIC PRINCIPLES OF CLASSICAL BALLET, Agrippina Vaganova. Great Russian theoretician, teacher explains methods for teaching classical ballet. 118 illustrations. 175pp. 5⅜ x 8½.   22036-2

THE JUMPING FROG, Mark Twain. Revenge edition. The original story of The Celebrated Jumping Frog of Calaveras County, a hapless French translation, and Twain's hilarious "retranslation" from the French. 12 illustrations. 66pp. 5⅜ x 8½.
22686-7

BEST REMEMBERED POEMS, Martin Gardner (ed.). The 126 poems in this superb collection of 19th- and 20th-century British and American verse range from Shelley's "To a Skylark" to the impassioned "Renascence" of Edna St. Vincent Millay and to Edward Lear's whimsical "The Owl and the Pussycat." 224pp. 5⅜ x 8½.
27165-X

COMPLETE SONNETS, William Shakespeare. Over 150 exquisite poems deal with love, friendship, the tyranny of time, beauty's evanescence, death and other themes in language of remarkable power, precision and beauty. Glossary of archaic terms. 80pp. 5³⁄₁₆ x 8¼.   26686-9

THE BATTLES THAT CHANGED HISTORY, Fletcher Pratt. Eminent historian profiles 16 crucial conflicts, ancient to modern, that changed the course of civilization. 352pp. 5⅜ x 8½.   41129-X

THE WIT AND HUMOR OF OSCAR WILDE, Alvin Redman (ed.). More than 1,000 ripostes, paradoxes, wisecracks: Work is the curse of the drinking classes; I can resist everything except temptation; etc. 258pp. 5⅜ x 8½. 20602-5

SHAKESPEARE LEXICON AND QUOTATION DICTIONARY, Alexander Schmidt. Full definitions, locations, shades of meaning in every word in plays and poems. More than 50,000 exact quotations. 1,485pp. 6½ x 9¼. 2-vol. set.
Vol. 1: 22726-X
Vol. 2: 22727-8

SELECTED POEMS, Emily Dickinson. Over 100 best-known, best-loved poems by one of America's foremost poets, reprinted from authoritative early editions. No comparable edition at this price. Index of first lines. 64pp. 5³⁄₁₆ x 8¼. 26466-1

THE INSIDIOUS DR. FU-MANCHU, Sax Rohmer. The first of the popular mystery series introduces a pair of English detectives to their archnemesis, the diabolical Dr. Fu-Manchu. Flavorful atmosphere, fast-paced action, and colorful characters enliven this classic of the genre. 208pp. 5³⁄₁₆ x 8¼. 29898-1

THE MALLEUS MALEFICARUM OF KRAMER AND SPRENGER, translated by Montague Summers. Full text of most important witchhunter's "bible," used by both Catholics and Protestants. 278pp. 6⅝ x 10. 22802-9

SPANISH STORIES/CUENTOS ESPAÑOLES: A Dual-Language Book, Angel Flores (ed.). Unique format offers 13 great stories in Spanish by Cervantes, Borges, others. Faithful English translations on facing pages. 352pp. 5⅜ x 8½. 25399-6

GARDEN CITY, LONG ISLAND, IN EARLY PHOTOGRAPHS, 1869–1919, Mildred H. Smith. Handsome treasury of 118 vintage pictures, accompanied by carefully researched captions, document the Garden City Hotel fire (1899), the Vanderbilt Cup Race (1908), the first airmail flight departing from the Nassau Boulevard Aerodrome (1911), and much more. 96pp. 8⅞ x 11¾. 40669-5

OLD QUEENS, N.Y., IN EARLY PHOTOGRAPHS, Vincent F. Seyfried and William Asadorian. Over 160 rare photographs of Maspeth, Jamaica, Jackson Heights, and other areas. Vintage views of DeWitt Clinton mansion, 1939 World's Fair and more. Captions. 192pp. 8⅞ x 11. 26358-4

CAPTURED BY THE INDIANS: 15 Firsthand Accounts, 1750-1870, Frederick Drimmer. Astounding true historical accounts of grisly torture, bloody conflicts, relentless pursuits, miraculous escapes and more, by people who lived to tell the tale. 384pp. 5⅜ x 8½. 24901-8

THE WORLD'S GREAT SPEECHES (Fourth Enlarged Edition), Lewis Copeland, Lawrence W. Lamm, and Stephen J. McKenna. Nearly 300 speeches provide public speakers with a wealth of updated quotes and inspiration–from Pericles' funeral oration and William Jennings Bryan's "Cross of Gold Speech" to Malcolm X's powerful words on the Black Revolution and Earl of Spenser's tribute to his sister, Diana, Princess of Wales. 944pp. 5⅜ x 8⅜. 40903-1

THE BOOK OF THE SWORD, Sir Richard F. Burton. Great Victorian scholar/adventurer's eloquent, erudite history of the "queen of weapons"–from prehistory to early Roman Empire. Evolution and development of early swords, variations (sabre, broadsword, cutlass, scimitar, etc.), much more. 336pp. 6⅛ x 9¼. 25434-8

AUTOBIOGRAPHY: The Story of My Experiments with Truth, Mohandas K. Gandhi. Boyhood, legal studies, purification, the growth of the Satyagraha (nonviolent protest) movement. Critical, inspiring work of the man responsible for the freedom of India. 480pp. 5⅜ x 8½. (Available in U.S. only.) 24593-4

CELTIC MYTHS AND LEGENDS, T. W. Rolleston. Masterful retelling of Irish and Welsh stories and tales. Cuchulain, King Arthur, Deirdre, the Grail, many more. First paperback edition. 58 full-page illustrations. 512pp. 5⅜ x 8½. 26507-2

THE PRINCIPLES OF PSYCHOLOGY, William James. Famous long course complete, unabridged. Stream of thought, time perception, memory, experimental methods; great work decades ahead of its time. 94 figures. 1,391pp. 5⅜ x 8½. 2-vol. set.
Vol. I: 20381-6 Vol. II: 20382-4

THE WORLD AS WILL AND REPRESENTATION, Arthur Schopenhauer. Definitive English translation of Schopenhauer's life work, correcting more than 1,000 errors, omissions in earlier translations. Translated by E. F. J. Payne. Total of 1,269pp. 5⅜ x 8½. 2-vol. set. Vol. 1: 21761-2 Vol. 2: 21762-0

MAGIC AND MYSTERY IN TIBET, Madame Alexandra David-Neel. Experiences among lamas, magicians, sages, sorcerers, Bonpa wizards. A true psychic discovery. 32 illustrations. 321pp. 5⅜ x 8½. (Available in U.S. only.) 22682-4

THE EGYPTIAN BOOK OF THE DEAD, E. A. Wallis Budge. Complete reproduction of Ani's papyrus, finest ever found. Full hieroglyphic text, interlinear transliteration, word-for-word translation, smooth translation. 533pp. 6½ x 9¼. 21866-X

MATHEMATICS FOR THE NONMATHEMATICIAN, Morris Kline. Detailed, college-level treatment of mathematics in cultural and historical context, with numerous exercises. Recommended Reading Lists. Tables. Numerous figures. 641pp. 5⅜ x 8½. 24823-2

PROBABILISTIC METHODS IN THE THEORY OF STRUCTURES, Isaac Elishakoff. Well-written introduction covers the elements of the theory of probability from two or more random variables, the reliability of such multivariable structures, the theory of random function, Monte Carlo methods of treating problems incapable of exact solution, and more. Examples. 502pp. 5⅜ x 8½. 40691-1

THE RIME OF THE ANCIENT MARINER, Gustave Doré, S. T. Coleridge. Doré's finest work; 34 plates capture moods, subtleties of poem. Flawless full-size reproductions printed on facing pages with authoritative text of poem. "Beautiful. Simply beautiful."–*Publisher's Weekly*. 77pp. 9¼ x 12. 22305-1

NORTH AMERICAN INDIAN DESIGNS FOR ARTISTS AND CRAFTSPEOPLE, Eva Wilson. Over 360 authentic copyright-free designs adapted from Navajo blankets, Hopi pottery, Sioux buffalo hides, more. Geometrics, symbolic figures, plant and animal motifs, etc. 128pp. 8⅜ x 11. (Not for sale in the United Kingdom.) 25341-4

SCULPTURE: Principles and Practice, Louis Slobodkin. Step-by-step approach to clay, plaster, metals, stone; classical and modern. 253 drawings, photos. 255pp. 8⅛ x 11. 22960-2

THE INFLUENCE OF SEA POWER UPON HISTORY, 1660–1783, A. T. Mahan. Influential classic of naval history and tactics still used as text in war colleges. First paperback edition. 4 maps. 24 battle plans. 640pp. 5⅜ x 8½. 25509-3

CATALOG OF DOVER BOOKS

THE STORY OF THE TITANIC AS TOLD BY ITS SURVIVORS, Jack Winocour (ed.). What it was really like. Panic, despair, shocking inefficiency, and a little heroism. More thrilling than any fictional account. 26 illustrations. 320pp. 5⅜ x 8½. 20610-6

FAIRY AND FOLK TALES OF THE IRISH PEASANTRY, William Butler Yeats (ed.). Treasury of 64 tales from the twilight world of Celtic myth and legend: "The Soul Cages," "The Kildare Pooka," "King O'Toole and his Goose," many more. Introduction and Notes by W. B. Yeats. 352pp. 5⅜ x 8½. 26941-8

BUDDHIST MAHAYANA TEXTS, E. B. Cowell and others (eds.). Superb, accurate translations of basic documents in Mahayana Buddhism, highly important in history of religions. The Buddha-karita of Asvaghosha, Larger Sukhavativyuha, more. 448pp. 5⅜ x 8½. 25552-2

ONE TWO THREE . . . INFINITY: Facts and Speculations of Science, George Gamow. Great physicist's fascinating, readable overview of contemporary science: number theory, relativity, fourth dimension, entropy, genes, atomic structure, much more. 128 illustrations. Index. 352pp. 5⅜ x 8½. 25664-2

EXPERIMENTATION AND MEASUREMENT, W. J. Youden. Introductory manual explains laws of measurement in simple terms and offers tips for achieving accuracy and minimizing errors. Mathematics of measurement, use of instruments, experimenting with machines. 1994 edition. Foreword. Preface. Introduction. Epilogue. Selected Readings. Glossary. Index. Tables and figures. 128pp. 5⅜ x 8½. 40451-X

DALÍ ON MODERN ART: The Cuckolds of Antiquated Modern Art, Salvador Dalí. Influential painter skewers modern art and its practitioners. Outrageous evaluations of Picasso, Cézanne, Turner, more. 15 renderings of paintings discussed. 44 calligraphic decorations by Dalí. 96pp. 5⅜ x 8½. (Available in U.S. only.) 29220-7

ANTIQUE PLAYING CARDS: A Pictorial History, Henry René D'Allemagne. Over 900 elaborate, decorative images from rare playing cards (14th–20th centuries): Bacchus, death, dancing dogs, hunting scenes, royal coats of arms, players cheating, much more. 96pp. 9¼ x 12¼. 29265-7

MAKING FURNITURE MASTERPIECES: 30 Projects with Measured Drawings, Franklin H. Gottshall. Step-by-step instructions, illustrations for constructing handsome, useful pieces, among them a Sheraton desk, Chippendale chair, Spanish desk, Queen Anne table and a William and Mary dressing mirror. 224pp. 8⅛ x 11¼. 29338-6

THE FOSSIL BOOK: A Record of Prehistoric Life, Patricia V. Rich et al. Profusely illustrated definitive guide covers everything from single-celled organisms and dinosaurs to birds and mammals and the interplay between climate and man. Over 1,500 illustrations. 760pp. 7½ x 10⅛. 29371-8

Paperbound unless otherwise indicated. Available at your book dealer, online at **www.doverpublications.com**, or by writing to Dept. GI, Dover Publications, Inc., 31 East 2nd Street, Mineola, NY 11501. For current price information or for free catalogues (please indicate field of interest), write to Dover Publications or log on to **www.doverpublications.com** and see every Dover book in print. Dover publishes more than 500 books each year on science, elementary and advanced mathematics, biology, music, art, literary history, social sciences, and other areas.